Making Transcendents

Making Transcendents

Ascetics and Social Memory
in Early Medieval China

Robert Ford Campany

University of Hawai'i Press
Honolulu

LIBRARY OF CONGRESS CATALOGING-IN-PUBLICATION DATA
Campany, Robert Ford.
   Making transcendents : ascetics and social memory in
early medieval China / Robert Ford Campany.
      p. cm.
   Includes bibliographical references and index.
   ISBN 978-0-8248-3333-6 (hard cover : alk. paper)
   1. Asceticism—Taoism—History—To 1500.
2. Taoism—Social aspects—China—History—To 1500. I. Title.
II. Title: Ascetics and social memory in early medieval China.
   BL1923.C34 2009
   299'.51461—dc22
                        2008043542

University of Hawai'i Press books are printed on acid-free
paper and meet the guidelines for permanence and durability
of the Council on Library Resources.

Designed by University of Hawai'i Press production staff
Printed by the Maple-Vail Book Manufacturing Group

To my brother Chris

We were unable to reach the islands, but we could see them in the distance!
未能至，望見之焉
   —Sima Tan 司馬談 and Sima Qian 司馬遷, *Shi ji* 史記 (*Records of the Historian*)

Eternity is in love with the productions of time.
   —Blake, *The Marriage of Heaven and Hell*

Contents

Acknowledgments

RESEARCH AND WRITING are usually imagined to be entirely solitary endeavors, but fortunately they are not. My thanks to those colleagues and friends who took time from their own busy writing schedules to read and comment on this book in manuscript: Terry Kleeman, Lisa Bitel, and John R. McRae, as well as an anonymous reviewer for the University of Hawai'i Press. Thanks also to others who commented on particular parts of the work: Steve Bokenkamp, Jan Nattier, Sarah Schneewind, John Kieschnick, John Lagerwey, Victor Mair, and several colleagues in the excellent Department of Religious Studies at Indiana University (particularly Richard Miller, David Haberman, David Brakke, Nancy Levene, and Shaul Magid during a faculty colloquium). Lynn Dodd Swartz provided last-minute technical help with illustrations. The kindness of Sylvie Hureau made it possible to complete the final revisions in a very inspiring and stimulating environment. Many other colleagues, friends, and students too numerous to thank individually have made this book better in a thousand ways. The work of a large number of other scholars has made mine possible.

I wish also to thank the institutions and bodies before which I was fortunate to have the opportunity to present my thinking as it emerged. These include the École Pratique des Hautes Études in Paris (a major conference organized by John Lagerwey, as well as an invitation to lecture); Trinity College, Cambridge University (a memorable colloquium on religion and food organized by Roel Sterckx); the National University of Singapore (a conference organized by Alan Chan and Y. K. Lo); the Harvard-Yenching Institute, the Fairbank Center, and the Department of East Asian Languages and Civilizations of Harvard University (several gatherings organized by my friends Michael Puett and Tian Xiaofei); Boston University; the University of Southern California; the University of Chicago (a symposium on Daoism organized by Donald Harper); Columbia University (a session of the Early Medieval China Workshop hosted by Wendy Swartz); Swarthmore College; the University of California at Los Angeles; the University of Illinois; the American

Academy of Religion; and the Association for Asian Studies. Some of these events were funded by the Chiang Ching-kuo Foundation, the American Council of Learned Societies, the University of Chicago Press, E. J. Brill, and other entities. It is thanks to the support of institutions like these that scholarly work in the humanities remains possible.

A sabbatical leave at the University of Southern California enabled me to complete the manuscript. I am especially grateful to the deans and faculty of the College of Letters, Arts & Sciences at USC for providing a supportive research environment for faculty, and to Don Miller and the School of Religion for a publication subvention.

Executive Editor Patricia Crosby, Managing Editor Ann Ludeman, and the staff at the University of Hawai'i Press were simply lovely to work with. They, along with Margaret Black, superb and good-humored copyeditor, made me feel as if I were working with a publishing dream team. Every author should be so fortunate.

Earlier versions of several portions of this book have appeared or will appear in print elsewhere as articles or chapters, and I thank the respective publishers for permission to reprint those materials here in their new forms: Koninklijke Brill N.V. and Palgrave Macmillan (Chapter 3), the University of Chicago Press (Chapter 4), the State University of New York Press (Chapter 5), and Koninklijke Brill N.V. (Chapter 6).

My deepest gratitude goes to Lee Ann Sherry, whose encouragement and humor sustained me during the writing; to Linda Campany, who helped more than she realizes; and to Chris Campany, a treasure among human beings. This book is dedicated to him.

Introduction

IN CHINA, BEFORE THERE was any such thing as a Daoist[1] priest or Daoist scripture, before Buddhist scriptures and images were brought in along the Silk Road or the coast, before there were monasteries where religious practitioners from either of these traditions gathered, there existed an only loosely cohesive tradition, a body of ideas and practices that I will call the quest for transcendence. Its main elements were already in place by the late third century B.C.E., well established by the turn of the first millennium, and increasingly well documented in sources dating from the second, third, and early fourth centuries C.E. Men and women who, by means of esoteric biospiritual practices, were deemed to have succeeded in this quest became known as *xian* 仙, "immortals," "transcendents," or perhaps "ascendants":[2] extraordinarily long-lived if not deathless beings to whom godlike powers and celestial status were attributed and memory of whom was preserved in oral and written narrative and at cultic sites. As yet this loose body of traditions had no fixed name, though in later texts it came to be referred to as *xiandao* 仙道, or "the way of transcendence," and its practices as *xianshu* 仙術, or "arts of transcendence."

I have long marveled that in a civilization noted for its veneration of ancestors and the centrality of the patrilineal family, a tradition was created consisting of the pursuit of individual, bodily deathlessness and godlike transcendence. It may be that every civilization confronts this choice between collective and individual immortality. In an epic preserved in Akkadian from ancient Mesopotamia, the hero Gilgamesh quests for a plant that will convey immortality; in this he fails, but by doing noble deeds and leaving a record of them inscribed on the wall of his city, Uruk, he attains instead the cultural sort of immortality whose medium is social memory.[3] He

---

1. Some nonspecialist readers may be familiar with an older, alternative spelling of this term: "Taoist." Similarly, the term *xian* has sometimes been rendered in roman letters as *hsien*.
2. I further discuss this term and various candidate translations near the end of Chapter 1.
3. See Kovacs, *The Epic of Gilgamesh.*

can be said to have succeeded admirably considering that, although his civilization long ago turned to dust, we still read and talk about his story today. From among the Bara people of Madagascar was recently summarized the following legend of the origin of death: "God gave the first man and woman a choice between two kinds of death. They could die like the moon, being reborn over and over. Or they could die like the tree, which puts forth new seeds and, although dying itself, lives on through its progeny. It was a difficult decision, but the first man and woman chose to have children even at the cost of their own lives. And which of us, asks the storyteller, would not make the same choice today?"[4] The ancestral Bara too, while aware of the other alternative, opted for the collective sort of immortality.

In late classical and early medieval China, both paths toward immortality were widely held to be possible. The collective one, centered on the ritual care, feeding, and commemoration of ancestors, was better known and more widely practiced (then and now), the individual one less so.[5] But I hope to show how deeply it is true that the latter sort of immortality, despite its apparently individual nature, was in fact a social affair: that there, too, community and collective memory proved decisive.

Literary and social historian Stephen Greenblatt once observed, "I am committed to the project of making strange what has become familiar, of demonstrating that what seems an untroubling and untroubled part of ourselves (for example, Shakespeare) is actually part of something else, something different."[6] In the book you now hold, I seek to do just the opposite for *xian* in early medieval China. They have seemed so utterly strange, even when we know a good deal about the

---

4. Metcalf and Huntington, *Celebrations of Death*, 130.

5. Lothar von Falkenhausen ("Sources of Taoism") has tried to sketch the path that may have led from the one notion to the other in early China, a path he links to the origins of Daoism. For members of the Western Zhou nobility, immortality was a non-issue, "for the departed ancestor was kept alive, albeit in a different form of being, through the continuing worship by an endless line of latter-day descendants" (9). These practices had been handed down from the preceding Shang society. Late in the Shang, however, the number of ancestors had become overwhelming, their cults unmanageable. A similar proliferation, he argues, occurred in the middle Western Zhou, so lineages were divided, and the sacrificial system was rationalized so that all ancestors save founders of lineages were dropped from the schedule after five generations. "Those concerned with being kept alive *post mortem* could thus no longer rely on their descendants in more remote generations" (9). This, von Falkenhausen says, could explain the Eastern Zhou changes in burial practices and afterlife notions, "resulting in the creation of a radically separate new world *outre-tombe*, combined with a more abstract, less kin-centered notion of immortality" (9). He goes on to try to link some of the kinds of objects found in tombs—maps, cosmic diagrams, game boards—with a very abstract notion of immortality (one considerably more abstract than that imaged in the early medieval sources on which I will focus below). The argument is suggestive but speculative and will not figure in the present study.

6. Greenblatt, *Learning to Curse*, 11.

methods they practiced and the theories behind these. This strangeness, I will argue, is not due solely to their cultural and temporal distance from us; it is also an effect practitioners themselves cultivated, helped by some who wrote about them and preserved their memory. Without wishing to reduce *xian* to something pedestrian, I have set out here, if only for a little time, to bring them down to earth. If the strangeness of *xian* was essential to their mystique, I would at least like to understand how the mystique was created and expressed—how it was made, and by whom. I aim neither to debunk nor to affirm their shocking claims to have escaped death, living hundreds of years. Instead, I hope to illuminate the social settings that made such claims possible, an illumination that will have the effect of rendering the claims a little less strange. I aim, not to dissolve the magic surrounding *xian*, but only to point out its social basis; "it is because society becomes activated that magic works."[7]

Pursuing this goal has not meant adducing much new evidence. Almost all of the requisite evidence was ready to hand. What was needed was to introduce certain ways of reading it. Some explicit discussion of theories, methods, and models has therefore been unavoidable. I hope that scholars of early medieval China may feel that they have profited from this discussion and will agree that these models help us to see the Chinese texts in new ways. In addition, I hope that the wider study of religion and culture, which sometimes relegates sinological scholarship to the hyperspecialized margins, may finally begin to admit the premodern China case to its dossier.[8] Both the broader study of religion and the more specialized study of premodern China stand only to gain thereby.

For readers unfamiliar with the quest for transcendence, the following few paragraphs sketch its most basic ideas and types of practices up to around 350 C.E. Those wishing more detail may consult Part One of my *To Live as Long as Heaven and Earth*,[9] which offers an extended synthetic account of the methods practiced by the early fourth century of the common era and of their basic assumptions and cosmological backgrounds. Part Two of this work glosses the many mentions of specific techniques found in Ge Hong's 葛洪 (283–343 C.E.) early-fourth-century

---

7. Mauss, *A General Theory of Magic*, 133.

8. It is instructive to pick up a recent attempt to construct a cross-cultural model of one major religious topos from numerous case studies drawn from around the world—such a volume as *Asceticism* (ed. Wimbush and Valantasis): out of 42 essays and 638 pages, not a single essay takes any Chinese phenomenon as its primary subject (although the fine essay by Jason BeDuhn on Manichaeism takes account of Chinese sources); "China," "Chinese," and so forth, do not appear in the index.

9. Hereafter referred to in the notes as *TL*. The first 128 pages are devoted to an exposition of the biospiritual practices that were held to lead to transcendence and the physiological, cosmological, and theological notions associated with them.

hagiographic collection devoted to figures he deemed successful *xian*, *Shenxian zhuan* 神仙傳 or *Traditions of Divine Transcendents*.[10]

Transcendence was a deathless state, but it was also (normally) a celestial status that entailed supernormal powers. Practitioners engaged in gradual ascetic disciplines that were designed and claimed to thwart death in two parallel ways: by purifying and divinizing their biospiritual organisms so that mortal elements were removed, and by extricating their social identities from a celestial system of sin-reportage and enforcement of lifespan limits that had long been part of the imagined Chinese cosmos.

In traditional China there was little matter/spirit dualism: all things, save perhaps the Dao (primordial source of all things, though in most accounts not itself a thing among things), from high celestial beings to lowly creatures and inanimate objects, from subtle spirits to rocks and dirt, were made of *qi* 氣, which came in finer or grosser forms but could be refined into more potent *jing* 精 or "essence." One way or another, much of what *xian*-arts practitioners did amounted to gathering and refining *qi* and *jing*. And much of this work involved some sort of ingestion—a physical taking in of *qi* or *jing* in any of their numerous forms, such as herbs and minerals (taken singly or, more often, in compounds), alchemical products (the result of long, multistaged processes of refinement), the sexual fluids or energies of one's partner, breath itself, or distant essences that were ingested via visualization exercises (one imagined an herb or alchemical product associated with a certain direction of the cosmos, for example, and then imagined oneself swallowing it). The major classes of disciplines thus included dietary restrictions, the fashioning and ingestion of herbal or mineral compounds, the making and taking of elixirs (usually featuring metallic ores but incorporating many other materials), regimes of sexual practices, and the control of breathing, including the distribution of *qi* throughout the body. In addition, the body was often imagined as microcosmically recapitulating the structures and processes of the universe writ large, or of the polity, or both. Underlying all of these diverse types of practice, then, was the basic idiom of *qi*; each practice had as its ultimate rationale some sort of manipulation of *qi* in the biospiritual organism.

The other major idiom of *xian* arts was bureaucratic. From early times it had been widely understood that the gods of the heavens were organized in a hierarchy of offices, each with its functions and title; that one of this bureaucracy's many

---

10. Shortly before my study of these practices went to press, and since its publication, other important studies have appeared, among them Li Ling, *Zhongguo fangshu kao* and *Zhongguo fangshu xukao*; and Pregadio, *Great Clarity*. The recent French translation of some chapters of Ge Hong's *Baopuzi neipian* completely supersedes the English translation of that work by James Ware (at least for readers of French): see Che, *La voie des divins immortels*.

tasks was to keep track of human lifespans and enforce their limits (and it typically did so by registering people by name and place of residence, much as did the central government); and that representatives of this bureaucracy dwelled within, or periodically visited and inspected, the biospiritual organisms of individual persons—the somatic equivalent of the god of the local community—and reported the individual's sins and merits to the celestial offices, where they were recorded in ledgers. Some *xian* arts, then, worked in this idiom to address or manipulate the ledger system so that the practitioner might live past his officially designated and enforced lifespan. Many arts also blended the *qi*-based and bureaucratic idioms.

These arts were prescribed in texts—most of them esoteric texts transmitted in solemn ceremonies featuring the recipient's oath of secrecy, and most claiming to have been divinely revealed—that were typically passed from master to disciple. The methods of transcendence, that is, were not experimental in nature, at least in terms of how they were presented to readers: they were encountered as transmissions within sacred traditions of teaching, transmissions structured by ritual that restricted access to them. Some of these early texts have survived and will be referred to from time to time, along with the more properly hagiographic, historiographic, and polemical texts that are the main source for this study.

Properly practiced, these activities were thought to produce *xian*, figures with paranormal powers who had escaped death and lived for hundreds of years, often (but not always) taking a post in the celestial bureaucracy, and about whom, in many cases, stories circulated and were preserved. This book examines the social matrices in which such figures operated and were recognized.

Chapter 1 is methodological; it takes up difficult questions about how to read the sorts of evidence that survive concerning the quest for transcendence and explains and defends the approaches taken in this book. The rest of the book offers an account of the *roles* of the transcendent and transcendence-seeker (in Chapters 2 and 3) and an account not only of how individuals filled those roles but also of how others deemed or argued that they did so (Chapters 4 through 8). Chapter 2, "The Transcendent's Cultural Repertoire," summarizes the repertoire of features that constituted the role of *xian* and of adepts seeking to become *xian*. I argue that each of these features was contrastive in nature: in addition to its intrinsic rationale, each feature also had the extrinsic function of likening or contrasting the role of transcendence-seeker to other roles in Chinese culture. This likening and contrasting were crucial to establishing what a *xian*, and a person seeking this status, was or could be. Chapter 3, "Deeper Repertoire Analysis: 'Avoiding Grains,'" presents a more detailed analysis of cultural repertoires and the likening and contrastive functions of the particular items they comprise. I focus here on one particular, indeed crucial, aspect of the discipline—the avoidance of "grains," by which I mean the avoidance of ordinary, culturally mainstream foods in general, and specifically of foodstuffs offered to gods and ancestors in sacrifice. I trace some of the ideological and mythical background of the practice in early texts and demonstrate that, by this single, powerful gesture, adepts were distinguishing themselves as a class of figures and arguing the superiority of their kind over all others, even ancestors and gods.

I then consider how individuals came to take on the role of transcendence-seeker, whether by their own agency, by that of others, or often both. Chapter 4, "Secret Arts, Manifest Wonders," charts the basic dialectic in the self-presentations of adepts: they and their scriptures constantly insisted on the secrecy of their methods, on their inaccessibility to others; yet they constantly insisted on these matters before audiences, displaying their powers and thus flaunting their possession of secrets. This tension between secrecy and display was essential to the public persona of the transcendence-seeker. Chapter 5, "Verbal Self-Presentation and Audience Response," examines the sort of narratives attributed to adepts about themselves. It also touches on how the members of their audience received such narratives. Chapter 6, "Adepts and Their Communities," portrays the array of social relations evidenced in texts between transcendence-arts practitioners and other people, many of whom were their clients in service-providing relationships. Chapter 7, "Adepts, Their Families, and the Imperium," looks at the relations of adepts with their families on the one hand and with rulers and officials on the other. Chapter 8, "Hagiographic Persuasions," discusses hagiographies as attempts to persuade readers as to the identities and reputations of past individuals. The survival in some cases of multiple versions of a life allows us to see how the makers of hagiographies reprised and recast earlier figures, shaping new reputations for them and co-opting them—sometimes quite surprisingly—into the ranks of *xian*.

THIS STUDY moves the content of practitioners' ascetic disciplines off center stage. It brackets questions about the real motivations—and, for that matter, the real existence—of this or that individual said to have become a *xian*. Instead, it describes the role of transcendence-seeker as one among other roles, understanding what transcendence was by, in part, noting what it was not. It understands the ideal of transcendence and the status of successful transcendents as socially constituted, and it attempts to chart the social, narrative, and textual processes by which these remarkable results—the making of transcendence and of individual transcendents—were achieved. The texts we will examine here were integral to those creative processes.

CHAPTER 1

Bringing Transcendents Down to Earth

CONSIDER THE FOLLOWING passage from Ge Hong's *Traditions of Divine Transcendents:*

> Ling Shouguang 靈壽光 ... at the age of over seventy obtained a method for [making] "efflorescence of vermilion" pills. These he synthesized and ingested.... By the first year of the [Later] Han *jian'an* period [196 C.E.] he was already two hundred and twenty years old. Later, without having shown any signs of illness, he died at the home of Hu Gang 胡岡 in Jiangling. Over a hundred days after his funeral and burial, someone saw Ling [alive] in Xiaohuang. This person sent a letter to Hu Gang, who, upon receiving the letter, dug up the coffin and looked inside. It was empty except for an old shoe.[1]

Even in such a short narrative as this, there is much that may strike us as curious. The name of the alchemical product ingested by the adept, in this and other variants, provides a thread faintly traceable through some texts on transcendence arts.[2] The strange business of the empty coffin and the old shoe points to an esoteric technique, known as "escape by means of a simulated corpse" or *shijie* 尸解, by which the adept was supposed to elude the spirits who enforce lifespan limits and thus live past his destined time of death.[3] These are the elements on which most previous analyses would have focused. But consider the otherwise unknown Hu Gang[4] and the unnamed letter-writer. Their roles in the story are by no means

---

1. See *TL*, 232–233.

2. See ibid., 233.

3. See ibid., 52–60. We will see this method alluded to repeatedly.

4. The figure mentioned in the hagiography may be the Hu Gang 剛 briefly mentioned in *Hou Han shu* 44:1504; see also Loewe, *A Biographical Dictionary of the Qin, Former Han and Xin Periods*, 160. The time periods mentioned in the two accounts match nicely.

marginal. The letter-writer has to have recognized the adept Ling in the distant locale of Xiaohuang and to have considered his sighting noteworthy enough to warrant a letter to Hu Gang; he also knows that it is Hu Gang to whom he should report the sighting. It is Hu Gang who, receiving this letter, exhumes the coffin and thus confirms that Ling was never buried in it. Quite probably, Hu had furnished the coffin and underwritten the funeral in the first place after Ling died at his home. Nothing suggests that Hu Gang was a relative of Ling's, nor a practicing disciple, yet his actions and those of his correspondent are instrumental to the story and to the recognition that Ling had in fact become a transcendent. What had Ling been doing at Hu's home? How did it come to pass that Hu, who was neither Ling's disciple nor his relative, was the one to whom the letter was delivered and who exhumed Ling's corpse-free coffin? Why did the letter-writer recognize Ling at such a distant place, and how did he know whom to contact? These questions, sparked by elements of the story that go beyond the adept himself and his methods, point to a certain social setting for the adept's practice and a social process by which his achievement of *xian*-hood would have come to be recognized.

Recent research partially explains the workings and rationales of the esoteric methods that claimed to render adepts into transcendents.[5] Clearly much more research is needed into these techniques of self-transformation and on the scriptures on which our understanding of them must largely depend, and such research is ongoing in the international scholarly community.[6] But the more I have studied the quest for transcendence, the more it has become clear that to explicate it primarily in the terms presented by and to initiates in their scriptures is to leave a great deal unexplained. To begin with, there is scarcely a story of a seeker of transcendence that does not involve other sorts of people, and these people are not marginal but central: how are we to understand this? Accounting for how and why adepts valued the ascetic practices and goals of adepts is one thing; quite another is explaining how and why they were valued by ordinary people of many kinds,

---

5. Parts 1 and 2 of *TL* provide a synthetic overview and commentary on many specific techniques, texts, and terminologies. Other recent studies include Li Ling, *Zhongguo fangshu kao* and *Zhongguo fangshu xukao*; and Pregadio, *Great Clarity*. There is also a recent French translation of some chapters of Ge Hong's *Baopuzi neipian*: see Che, *La voie des divins immortels*.

6. It should be emphasized that I am not arguing that these techniques are unimportant subjects for research; they are important for a number of reasons, not least of which is that their basic character was itself part of the *imaginaire* of transcendence. Everyone who knew anything about *xian* knew, for example, that they were associated with exotic herbs or mushrooms of deathlessness, that they prepared elixirs for the same purpose, and so forth; this much is depicted repeatedly in scenes of *xian* on the walls of tombs, on gate towers and decorative objects. However, in this study, I am attending to other aspects of the quest for transcendence—aspects that have been less well understood.

and this explanation is much less obvious since the practices of transcendence-seekers could, almost by definition, be an option only for few. It is not a question of motivations, which vary by person, but of how and why these practitioners were accorded status by others who did not themselves pursue their ascetic disciplines. Not only did others not pursue them, they *could not*, at least in theory. The shapers of the tradition of *xian*-seeking postulated transcendence as a goal beyond the here-and-now, and, as we will see, they also located access to it in secret methods over which they claimed exclusive control. Antagonism with other sorts of power-wielders and other roles in society—indeed, with all who had not been vouchsafed access to the methods—was therefore built into the very nature of the quest for *xian*-hood. How, then, were *xian* and aspirants to *xian*-hood made to seem relevant and necessary to the many?[7] Continuing to unpack the finer points of adepts' meditative, biospiritual, and ritual procedures and the cosmological, theological, and anthropological assumptions that underlay them is a worthy task for scholarship, but it will not bring us any closer to understanding the nature of the ideal of *xian* and the social role of the *xian*-seeker, for these were the ideological project for a large swath of Chinese culture, not just for the relatively few persons who strove to become *xian* themselves.

I set out, then, to answer the question: What were *xian* and *xian*-in-training to others? I quickly found that this question cannot be addressed without also reversing it to ask: What were those others to the adept? The answers constitute an untold and, as it turns out, surprising story in the history of religion in China.

It is surprising because, for a century now, standard scholarly practice has been to portray *xian* and those who sought to transform themselves into *xian* as socially distant figures, isolated on mountaintops or residing in the heavens.[8] One need not go far to seek possible bases for this scholarly stereotype. The earliest written sources that mention these figures seem, at first blush, to portray them precisely thus. The early poetic narratives, so dear to historians of literature, depict the adept as a solitary, sometimes even bodiless ego journeying through space and eventually merging with the primordium.[9] The prototype of all these works, the *Songs of Chu* (*Chuci* 楚辭) poem "Far Roaming" ("Yuanyou" 遠遊), is in particular "a kind of *xian*-cult credo."[10] Perhaps dating to as early as the third century B.C.E.,[11] the poem

---

7. I am indebted here to Steven Collins, *Nirvana and Other Buddhist Felicities,* 57–58.

8. For a brief review of the literature in documentation of this point, see the opening of Chapter 6.

9. For a recent study, see Huntington, "Crossing Boundaries."

10. Harper, *Early Chinese Medical Literature,* 115 n.1.

11. The dating of this poem is vexed and uncertain; see Hawkes, "Ch'u tz'u," and Kroll's introduction to his translation in "An Early Poem of Mystical Excursion." I return to it in Chapter 3.

uses carefully crafted, literarily fashioned language[12] to portray just such a cosmic flight in the first person: the only beings its protagonist encounters are celestial gods and transcendents. Invariably visual scenes from mirrors, tomb walls, recovered manuscripts, and other burial goods likewise depict *xian* as scarcely human creatures, sometimes feathered and with enlarged ears, wearing strange headgear, visiting celestial courts or the throne of the Queen Mother the West atop distant Mount Kunlun, flying through space, or riding mythical beasts through the clouds.[13] These poems and scenes portray the imagined end-state of *xian* and show a highly cosmicized, lyrical (rather than theoretical or methodical) version of how a person might reach it, but they say little about the place of practitioners in a recognizably human world, a world that figures in these genres, if at all, only as an impediment. And surviving prescriptions for the arts of transcendence, particularly those for fashioning alchemical elixirs, often enjoin the adept to withdraw from profane contacts into ritual and biospiritual purity, sometimes achieved in a specially constructed chamber,[14] sometimes on a mountain. The stereotype thus has its sources in certain indigenous representations of *xian* and is not merely a figment of modern scholarship.

But I will show that other sources allow us to glimpse, as if from the corner of the eye, the communal settings in which adepts moved, the public responses that constituted their reputations, and the salient cultural values and religious institutions to which they presented alternatives, and thus to bring them back to earth. I here offer a portrayal not simply of transcendents and seekers of *xian*-hood but also of the larger religious and social domains in which they were among the premier, but certainly not the only, participants. Indeed I argue that we cannot understand these

---

12. If any texts can be said to be maximally "fictive" representations of *xian*, it is songs and poems such as these, not the hagiographies. For more on "fictiveness," see below.

13. See, for example, Wu Hung, *The Wu Liang Shrine*, 108–141; Little and Eichman, eds., *Taoism and the Arts of China*, 149 (unfortunately almost all of this work's discussions of images of "immortals" focus on much later materials); Finsterbusch, *Verzeichnis und Motivindex der Han-Darstellungen*, figs. 104, 131, 148, 173, 296, 298, 325, 326, 330, 330b, 388, 392, 394, 396, 398, 429, 436, 437, 528, 563, 694a, 709, 940, 941 (all in v. 2); Juliano, *Teng-hsien*, fig. 20; Lim et al., *Stories from China's Past*, 176 (fig. 23), 178 (fig. 70a); *Nanyang Handai huaxiang zhuan*, plates 159, 161, 171, 179–185; Bulling, *The Decorations of Mirrors of the Han Dynasty*, 98–99, plates 67, 68, 78a; *Mixian Dahuting Han mu*, figs. 22, 121, 125, 159, 187, 214, and plates 20 and 21; *Sichuan Handai shique*, figs. 34, 106, 165, 166, 183, 219, 230–232; Sofukawa, "Kandai gazōseki ni okeru shōsenzu no keifu" and "Konron-san to shōsenzu"; etc. These examples comprise many areas and centuries. Much more research is needed on early visual representations of *xian* and of the relationships between textual and visual images of transcendents in late Warring States, Han, Wei, and Jin times. The most recent study of visual *xian* imagery of which I am aware is Hayashi, "Chūgoku kodai no sennin no zuzō ni tsuite."

14. On these, see Yoshikawa, "Seishitsu kō."

FIGURE 1. Top register of pictorial slab from Songshan in Jiaxiang, Shandong province, second century C.E. The Queen Mother of the West in her court, attended by winged transcendents bearing stalks of longevity-inducing herbs. *Source:* Wu Hung, *The Wu Liang Shrine,* fig. 48 (detail).

FIGURE 2. Brick from Nanyang, Henan province, late Western Han or Eastern Han. The Queen Mother of the West attended by transcendent (upper right). *Source: Nanyang Handai huaxiang zhuan,* fig. 161.

figures without seeing them in these social settings. Proceeding in this way means no longer privileging insiders' viewpoints but rather seeing the entire matrix of phenomena denoted by the phrase "the quest for transcendence" as comprising not just the secret methods of a few but also wide networks of practices, understandings, and social relations. These networks were a domain of action in which many took part: some as virtuoso practitioners, some as disciples, some as lay patrons, and a great many as fascinated, intrigued, or skeptical members of audiences across most regions of China.[15]

Our current state of understanding to some extent resembles the one in the study of early Indian Buddhism recently remarked by Gregory Schopen:

> The life of a monk [that the *vinaya* texts] envision or take for granted has little in common with the image of the Buddhist monk that is commonly found in our textbooks, or even in many of our scholarly sources. That image . . . presents the Buddhist monk as a lone ascetic who has renounced all social ties and property to wander or live in the forest, preoccupied with meditation and the heroic quest for *nirvāṇa* or enlightenment. But Buddhist monastic literature is more gritty. . . . The monk it knows is caught in a web of social and ritual obligations, is fully and elaborately housed and permanently settled, preoccupied not with *nirvāṇa* but with bowls and robes, bathrooms and door bolts, and proper behavior in public.[16]

Regarding the quest for transcendence in China prior to 350 C.E.[17] we possess no monastic literature (and there were as yet no monasteries), but we do have other texts which, if read carefully, are equally revealing of adepts' places in social life.

---

15. In some ways, then, I am moving in a direction opposite to that of Peter Brown in his recent reappraisal of his seminal 1971 article on the holy man in late antiquity ("The Rise and Function of the Holy Man in Late Antiquity, 1971–1997"). Brown writes there: "To be effective, I believed [in 1971] that the holy man had to be starkly different from everyone else. . . . His asceticism had less to do with a notion of the relation of body and spirit within himself as it did to separating himself out, through a melodramatically afflicted body, from his fellows. . . . To go to the desert was simply for me, at that time, to translocate: it was to step into a special niche, as an outsider, crisply defined by contrast to other niches. . . . It was not to transform oneself" (368–370). Brown can be read here as saying that he earlier had essentially bracketed the contents of the ascetic's self-discipline and focused instead on his social function, or, to be more precise, the way in which his power derived from his self-imposed social position as outsider (yet an outsider who was, as Brown showed, involved in many ways with others in society). In the history of Chinese religion, by contrast, we have had studies of the disciplines involved in becoming *xian*, but almost no attention has been paid to the social roles and positionings of the practitioners of those disciplines.

16. Schopen, *Buddhist Monks and Business Matters*, 91.

17. I stop at around this date for reasons explained later in this chapter.

Chief among these are the two earliest hagiographical collections that have survived. *Traditions of Exemplary Transcendents* (*Liexian zhuan* 列仙傳), traditionally attributed to the Western Han courtier Liu Xiang 劉向 (79–78 B.C.E.), but now thought by most scholars to have been written sometime during the Eastern Han (25–220 C.E.), comprises seventy tersely worded hagiographies in its extant version.[18] *Traditions of Divine Transcendents* (*Shenxian zhuan* 神仙傳) by the Jin-era official Ge Hong 葛洪 (283–343 C.E.) comprises over one hundred hagiographies, parts of which are attributable to Ge Hong (or at least to his lifetime) with varying degrees of confidence but much of which represents early-fourth-century material.[19] In addition to these works, certain passages in Ge Hong's polemical essays in *The Master Who Embraces Simplicity: Inner Chapters* (*Baopuzi neipian* 抱朴子內篇),[20] which, like his hagiographic collection, were completed by 317, will prove useful, as will passages from other essayists, particularly Wang Chong 王充 (27–ca. 100 C.E.) in his *Arguments Weighed* (*Lunheng* 論衡) and Cao Zhi 曹植 (192–232 C.E.) in his *Resolving Doubts* (*Shiyi lun* 釋疑論) and *Disputations on the Dao* (*Biandao lun* 辯道論). Passages in the annals and biographical sections of the histories of the period, from the *Shi ji* 史記 forward in time to Chen Shou's 陳壽 (233–297) *Record of the Three Kingdoms* (*Sanguo zhi* 三國志, with its 429 commentary by Pei Songzhi 裴松之) and Fan Ye's (398–446) 范曄 *History of the Latter Han* (*Hou Han shu* 後漢書),[21] also provide accounts of adepts' activities. Sections of the *Annotated Classic on Waterways* (*Shuijing zhu* 水經注) by Li Daoyuan 酈道元 (d. 527) will prove useful for their accounts of cultic sites associated with *xian*. Early texts of the "accounts of anomalies" (*zhiguai* 志怪) genre preserve narratives of adepts' abilities and exploits that are largely comparable to those found in the hagiographic collections.[22] Scriptures now preserved in the Daoist canon,

---

18. The attribution to Liu Xiang is, to my mind, not wholly incredible, but the text we have today contains later accretions and has also dropped some passages. We know that a text by this title existed by the beginning of the second century C.E., because it is cited in historical commentaries dating from that time. The best discussion of authorship and dating is still the one found in Kaltenmark, *Le Lie-sien tchouan*, 1–8.

19. I have commented extensively on the dates of attestation of each passage in the extant text in *TL*, especially in Part 3 of that work, 373–552.

20. Unfortunately I learned of a new, partial French translation of this work (Che, *La voie des divins immortels*, comprising chaps. 1–3, 5, 7–10, 12, and 20) only after completing this book.

21. The monographic sections of this work were the product of another author, Sima Biao 司馬彪 (240–306), and were added to the *Hou Han shu* in 1022, but the biographical compilations, including those grouped under the heading "Fangshu liezhuan," are Fan's. See Twitchett, *The Writing of Official History under the T'ang*, 86–87.

22. In some cases they seem to have been a source for hagiographers; in other cases they are clearly extracting material from hagiographies. On the early texts of this genre and on how the genre was constituted among its others in early medieval China, see Campany, *Strange Writing*, hereafter abbreviated as *SW*.

though primarily intended for insiders, will also be an important source for this
inquiry. Finally, we possess a very small number of stone inscriptions (or records
of inscriptions now lost) narrating the careers of *xian* or alluding to them. When
the relevant texts and passages of these various genres are read side by side in their
entirety, a picture begins to form of adepts' social roles and of the social processes
by which their reputations and identities were fashioned. But the question of
how we ought to read such sources as evidence for reconstructing the social lives
of adepts is complex and must be considered before we proceed. Most of the
following discussion applies to the study of past holy persons in any society, not
simply to the study of *xian*.

Interpreting Hagiographic Sources

Anyone wishing to read narratives about religious figures for information about
their lives, practices, and social worlds—particularly figures from the distant past,
about whom there is often no other information—immediately faces the question of how those narratives related to life. At one extreme is the view—which
no serious scholar would now hold, at least in the abstract—that narratives of past
events and activities can simply be taken at face value as accurate portrayals of what
occurred. Perhaps the author got this or that fact wrong, but in principle there is
no hermeneutical problem in a straightforward reading of hagiographies as objective, accurate reports of events. We have learned too much about the "formed"
elements of narrative to take this view seriously any longer.[23] In the middle is a
hermeneutic style most notably associated with the Bollandist project interpreting
saints' lives and the work of Hippolyte Delehaye, but now much more widespread,
that assumes hagiographies are, at their core, factual reports of holy persons' lives
with an added layer of the miraculous; strip away the marvelous, fantastic elements,
and what you have left is the facts.[24] This interpretive mode, too, has been well
and largely abandoned, and I do not propose to revive it here, in part because the
marvelous elements it expunges are precisely part of what I seek to understand. At
the other extreme is a view that sees a total disjunction between life as it is lived
and post-facto attempts to gather life's messiness up into coherent narratives. In the
words of Hayden White, who, along with Louis Mink, has been a major proponent
of this view, "I . . . suggest that [the] value attached to narrativity in the representation of real events arises out of a desire to have real events display the coherence,

---

23. Compare Castelli, *Martyrdom and Memory*, 26, who takes as a starting point the rhetorical
nature of early Christian texts and rejects "approaches that presume their documentary status."
24. See Delehaye, *The Legends of the Saints.*

integrity, fullness, and closure of an image of life that is and can only be imaginary."[25] Here, past narratives are seen as so full of literary devices, so structured by ways of framing, shaping, highlighting, or backgrounding in the presentation of life (and life itself is understood to be devoid of such tropes), that all such narratives can really tell us about are themselves and perhaps their authors' intentions. This view valuably instructs us that narrative does not simply recapitulate past events blow-for-blow in any straightforward, uncomplicated way, but in its extreme form it rules out the use of past narratives as data for studying religious life, since it places lives and narrative texts on opposite sides of a gulf.

This position seems at its strongest when it comes to hagiography, a genre of writing about the past whose very name has, for some writers, conjured up something so entirely "made up," "fictive," or idealized that it lacks any relation to extra-literary reality.[26] In the case of China, matters are only exacerbated by the tendency of many scholars to portray the genre of anomaly accounts or *zhiguai* (a genre very close to that of hagiography in early medieval times) as the birthplace of fiction.[27] A sharp divide between literature and life is convenient for those who want to study literature formalistically and bracket its social and religious significances. But it is falsifying if we want to understand literature's role in the fashioning of religious worlds, roles, and selves and if we want to consider the possibility that literature is itself produced by such fashionings—falsifying because it dissolves any connection between texts and their worlds.[28]

Ironically, the way out of this methodological false dilemma and the dead end presented in the second extreme lies in recognizing the rhetorical nature of hagiographic and other narratives from and about the past, which means resituating

---

25. White, "The Value of Narrativity in the Representation of Reality," 23. Elsewhere White writes, "No one and nothing *lives* a story" (*Tropics of Discourse*, 111). See also Mink, "History and Fiction as Modes of Comprehension," "Narrative Form as a Cognitive Instrument," and *Historical Understanding*. On the epistemological aspects and philosophical contexts of White's and similar theories, see Polkinghorne, *Narrative Knowing and the Human Sciences*, 37–69. I find White's historiographic and narratological studies quite informative, but am here disagreeing with the extent to which he sees narration of the past and everyday, lived experience as different in kind. I have benefited from an exchange with David Schaberg on this topic.

26. In this vein, writing twenty years ago of a recently published biography of Thomas More, the distinguished historian G. R. Elton observed: "It takes some courage to venture beyond the hagiographical fiction and write about More as the man he really was"; cited in Heffernan, *Sacred Biography*, 64.

27. In *SW* I discuss this view of the genre in scholarship and offer an alternative.

28. Compare Greenblatt, *Renaissance Self-Fashioning*, 3: "We wall off literary symbolism from the symbolic structures operative elsewhere, as if art alone were a human creation, as if humans themselves were not ... cultural artifacts."

them in their life-settings. Each hagiographic narrative is an artifact of an attempt to persuade an audience. Reading such narratives for information about the past depends on understanding what this means and entails.

We may begin by recalling that, in general, stories are made and exchanged by people. Old texts as they have come down to us may appear to be isolated artifacts floating free of any context, but they did not begin that way. Barbara Herrnstein Smith reminds us that narrative is a quintessentially social transaction, calling attention to aspects missed when it is taken as "a kind of text or structure or any other form of detached and decontextualized entity." Those aspects include the following: (1) Every version, instance, or telling of a story, whether oral or written, is a performance undertaken by certain narrators for some audience, not a "structure" somehow existing independently of particular contexts. (2) "Every telling [including every distinct 'version' of a supposedly most basic 'original'—indeed she doubts that there is any most basic, contextless version of any given plot] is produced and experienced under certain social conditions and constraints." (3) Every telling "always involves [at least] two parties, an audience as well as a narrator." (4) "As in any social transaction, each party must be individually motivated to participate. . . . Each party must have some *interest* in telling or listening to that narrative."[29] Regarding the last two points, one thinks of the recent work by Elinor Ochs and Lisa Capps on what they term "living narrative," the role of everyday storytelling in negotiating lives, relationships, and self-understandings. They show, first, that telling stories is nothing less than essential to living and, second, that *conversational* narrative—the most primary level of narrative in which human beings engage—is intensely interactive, a social activity: to put it the other way round, social life is fundamentally conducted via the exchange and the co-fashioning of stories. Noting that Mikhail Bakhtin considered even readers to be authors,[30] Ochs and Capps point out that, in everyday narrative, interlocutors are much more actively involved in shaping narrative than Bakhtin's readers of finished texts can ever be. At this ground level, narratives often are open-ended, uncertain, unfinished affairs; prevailing narratives and their counter-narratives spring up together.[31] The hagiographic narratives that have come down to us from ancient and medieval societies thus stand at the end of very long chains of transmission ultimately rooted in informal, interactive oral dis-

---

29. All of these juxtaposed quotations are from Barbara Herrnstein Smith, "Narrative Versions, Narrative Theories," 232–233; emphasis in the original. See also her *On the Margins of Discourse*, 79–107.

30. Compare also Bruner, *Actual Minds, Possible Worlds*, 24–25; and Iser, *The Act of Reading*.

31. Ochs and Capps, *Living Narrative*. Their work builds on earlier studies such as those collected in Atkinson and Heritage, eds., *Structures of Social Action*.

course in small communities of people, even if those oral sources are almost always destined to remain invisible to us.

To grasp this is to reject one thing that scholars mean when they call hagiographic narratives, from early medieval China for example, "fictive." This label conjures up an image of the author sitting in his studio and imaginatively creating tales ex nihilo in the manner of a medieval Stephen King, a fertile mind his only source; he is not *reporting* anything but is rather *making it up.* For the most part, this is an anachronistic projection of a quite recent mode of authorship onto early medieval times and rests on a profound misunderstanding of hagiography's relation to its contemporary audience and its social, cultural, and religious world.[32] To put a complex point briefly, an early medieval Chinese hagiographer such as Ge Hong to a large extent *collected and transmitted* narrative material that was already circulating among contemporaries, widely in some cases, narrowly in others, or else material that had been handed down in earlier texts. What such figures wrote were transmissions or traditions, the nominal senses, after all, of *zhuan* 傳, a frequent generic suffix (along with *ji* 記 "records") to the titles of their works.[33] To be sure, these authors, as well as the authors of the texts they relied on, often reshaped stories to fit their own particular persuasions and predilections; in a few cases we can even demonstrate that they did so, and how. But, fundamentally, authors did not make up these narratives in a vacuum and spring them on an audience that was unprepared for them and would have perceived them as completely new; rather, they collected them from various sources, reworked and recontextualized them, and put them into renewed, often broader circulation.[34]

Another rejoinder to the almost total divide between narrative and life argued by Hayden White, Louis Mink, and others is this: People in the course of living their lives are already living in, through, and by means of narrative schemes. Narration is

---

32. The exceptions that prove the rule in pre-350 C.E. China are the *Zhuangzi* and *Liezi*, in which very clearly made-up stories—full of linguistic indicators of their self-consciously fictive status—are deployed to make instructive points about life and the world.

33. This is why I translate that suffix as "traditions" rather than the commoner "biographies," which is not the literal meaning of the term. Implicit in my translation is the claim that something analogous to what we term collective memory was a concept indigenous to early medieval Chinese culture (compare Castelli, *Martyrdom and Memory*, 24). For discussions of the senses and usages of *zhuan*, see Ryckmans, "A New Interpretation of the Term *Lieh-chuan* as Used in the *Shih-chi*"; Durrant, *The Cloudy Mirror*, xx; and Lewis, *Writing and Authority in Early China*, 300–301.

34. Peter Brown, in his still-seminal article "The Rise and Function of the Holy Man," similarly insisted on seeing stories of holy persons in social contexts rather than as "bizarre fragments of folk-lore" (89); they were, he said, "a product of the society around the holy man" (81). I follow his lead here.

therefore not merely imposed on a purely narrative-free raw material of life, but is already intrinsic to life as lived. As Jerome Bruner puts it, "Just as our experience of the natural world tends to imitate the categories of familiar science, so our experience of human affairs comes to take the form of the narratives we use in telling about them."[35] Or, in the words of David Carr, "Narrative is not merely a possibly successful way of describing events; its structure inheres in the events themselves. Far from being a formal distortion of the events it relates, a narrative account is an extension of one of their primary features."[36] Cheryl Mattingly, in her instructive study of the role of narration in the clinical experience of physical therapy patients and their therapists, agrees:

> Narratives are not just about experiences. Experiences are, in a sense, about narratives. That is, narratives are not primarily after-the-fact imitations of the experiences they recount. Rather, the intimate connection between story and experience results from the structure of action itself. Many kinds of social actions (including many therapeutic actions) are organized and shaped by actors so that they take on narrative form. Thus narrative and experience are bound in a homologous relationship, not merely a referential one.[37]

Promising in this analysis is not simply the general notion that experience is narrative in nature but more specifically the recognition that: (1) we are dealing with life processes (in Mattingly's case, therapeutic ones) and their real effects on people; (2) these processes are inherently interpersonal; (3) narrative is central to them, not incidental, in that patients' healing depends in part on their successful shaping of coherent self-narratives; (4) the narratives that figure in these processes are interpersonally shaped; and, for all these reasons, (5) narratives about life processes such as healing are not mimetic of those processes but already belong to them, in that the shaping of narrative is of a piece with the shaping of experience and affects outcomes; "narrative imitates experience because experience already has in it the seeds of narrative."[38] This is not to say that people live their lives with all the orga-

---

35. Bruner, "The Narrative Construction of Reality," 5.

36. "Narrative and the Real World," 1. Carr develops the argument at greater length in his book, *Time, Narrative, and History*. A similar case is made in William Cronon, "A Place for Stories."

37. Mattingly, *Healing Dramas and Clinical Plots*, 19. For other critiques of White's position on the relation of narrative to life, see Carr, *Time, Narrative, and History*; Carr, "Narrative and the Real World"; and Cornell, *Realm of the Saint*, 156–157.

38. Mattingly, *Healing Dramas and Clinical Plots*, 46. Jerome Bruner even goes so far as to write that "There seems indeed to be some sense in which narrative, rather than referring to 'reality,' may in fact create or constitute it" ("The Narrative Construction of Reality," 13), though,

nized, coherent narrative finality of a novel or a history, only that narrative, however fragmented and disjointed, figures in life as we live it.

Some who have argued in these ways have gone so far as to deny that there are any such things as "experience" or "events" without narrative always already present in them. Thus Richard Bauman writes: "Events are not the external raw materials out of which narratives are constructed, but rather the reverse: Events are abstractions from narrative. It is the structures of signification in narrative that give coherence to events in our understanding."[39] Even more radically, F. Wyatt claims: "The past cannot be said to be. Instead we should say rather the past is made whenever it is reconstructed."[40] Without weighing in on the ontological status of the past, my point is that there is no profound gap for the modern interpreter to overcome between hagiographic or historical narrative on the one hand, and the religious and social life settings in which those narratives were formed on the other. Stories are already part and parcel of religious life as it is lived. Stories were an essential medium in which the notion and imagery of *xian*, the cosmic and somatic contexts of transcendence arts, and the reputations of particular transcendents were all constructed and contested. There is nothing that compels us to assume that the *sorts* of stories of transcendents that have reached us are of a radically different *kind* than those told during the lives of the adepts, or that it cannot have been the case that such stories both informed and emerged from their and others' lives. The burden of proof lies with those who would insist otherwise. Literature and social life are not unrelated things.[41]

Saying this is vastly different, of course, from saying that the achievements reported of a particular adept must actually have been as reported. In this book I am emphatically not interested in questing for the historical Li Babai 李八百, to choose one adept at random, trying to ascertain whether he really did live eight hundred years or perform the other feats attributed to him in *Traditions of Divine*

---

unlike Bruner, I would want to point to the presence of extra-narrative realities, as well as the co-presence of counter-narratives, as strong limiters of this constitutive power of any particular narrative. Of some relevance here is the additional notion of narrative thought (as distinguished from paradigmatic thought) in Bruner, *Actual Minds, Possible Worlds*; Carrithers, *Why Humans Have Cultures*, 76–91, 166–167; and Bohannan, *How Culture Works*, 77–79. Compare also the statement by Peter Brown that "the very act of thought contains a strong narrative element" ("Enjoying the Saints in Late Antiquity," 19) and that by L. Hudson: "Asleep and awake it is just the same: we are telling ourselves stories all the time" (quoted in Carrithers, *The Forest Monks of Sri Lanka*, 86; and in P. Brown, "Enjoying the Saints in Late Antiquity," 19 n.69).

39. Bauman, *Story, Performance, and Event*, 5. This is similar to the view of narrative in life and in history articulated by Paul Ricoeur and summarized (apparently not with assent) by Hayden White in *The Content of the Form*, 172–181.

40. "The Narrative in Psychoanalysis," 196.

41. See Greenblatt, *Renaissance Self-Fashioning*, 3; and his *Learning to Curse*, 213, 118–119.

Transcendents, or even whether he really did hail from the Shu region. Generations of hagiography scholars have devoted themselves to sorting the miraculous
from the realistic elements of narratives about holy persons, simply rejecting the
former as mere fancy and retaining the other as purified history. Such will not be
my method. Even if I were interested in the quest for the historical Li Babai, for
example, I know of no sources that would allow us to pursue it successfully. Even
if a local stone inscription about him were to be unearthed in one of the countless
archeological digs being carried out in China today, that inscription, valuable as it
would be, would tell us things that a *particular* group of parties at a *particular* place
and time (and herein would lie its value[42]) publicly and durably maintained to be
the case about him, and that is all: even the stone-inscribed Li Babai is not the
"real," the "original" Li Babai; inscriptions are not "raw" but "cooked" like other
sources.[43] What is useful about all these old narratives, whether they come to us
inscribed on unearthed stones or transmitted in received texts, is that they attest to
what some *groups* of people in early medieval China—and not merely the individuals who gathered these stories into their hagiographic collection—believed to be
the case about one such as Li Babai or, at least, what they wanted others to know
and believe about him.

On this point I join the company of a number of recent students of hagiographies and other narratives from classical and medieval Europe and elsewhere,
who have turned away from attempts to recover the "real" figures behind stories
and turned instead toward reading stories as ways of recovering the "collective
mentality,"[44] collective memory, or communally shaped traditions in which the figures were invested with special status.[45] As Donald Weinstein and Rudolph Bell

---

42. That is to say, inscriptional and other archeologically recovered materials, since they have
not been subject to the shifting interests of later transmitters and since they often attest to decidedly local, site-specific practices, are valuable for those reasons, because they attest to a collective
perception at a securely isolable place and time, but not because they offer unmediated access to
historical "real events."

43. The same could even be said of a hypothetical first-person account attributed to one
such as Li Babai and recovered archeologically.

44. A term that, along with "collective representations," dates back to Marcel Mauss and
Émile Durkheim and is used by many recent students of hagiography, including Heffernan, *Sacred
Biography,* 59; and Weinstein and Bell in the passage quoted a few lines below.

45. In the inimitable phrasing of John McRae: "*It's not true, and therefore it's more important.*
The contents of Zen texts should not be evaluated using a simpleminded criterion of journalis-
tic accuracy, that is, 'Did it really happen?' For any event or saying to have occurred would be a
trivial reality involving a mere handful of people at one imagined point in time, which would be
overwhelmed by the thousands of people over the centuries who were involved in the creation of
Zen legends" (*Seeing Through Zen,* xix, emphasis in original). I would add that it need not only be
later generations who were involved in the creation of legends; the "mere handful" of people at

put it in their influential *Saints and Society: The Two Worlds of Western Christendom, 1000–1700:*

> More often than not, even before [the hagiographer] had begun to write the story of his saint, fact was already being transmuted into legend; the holy life was being recreated by the imagination and the needs of the faithful.

(Here I must interject that this way of putting things still presupposes a gap between "fact" and "legend," "life" and "imagination," and that hagiography necessarily represents a departure from life. It does, surely, to the extent that the preserved vita that has come down to us represents only one of a theoretically infinite number of possible ways of telling the story of the holy person's life, highlighting certain facets while obscuring others. But this much is true of any story of anything. The holy person's life did not need to be "transmuted" into story, because it was already suffused with story; the narrative processes that went on after a holy person's death or departure were only continuations of processes that were under way while he was present in the community and himself actively involved, alongside many others, in shaping and disseminating stories about his life.) Weinstein and Bell continue:

> The hagiographer's main contribution was to shape the received material according to the current, partly implicit, pressures of the saint-making process, including the tastes of his bishop, the interests of his house or order, political interests, and, not least, the expectations of local devotees, both clerical and lay. In short, as Delehaye pointed out, the hagiographer was not a biographer, at least in the modern sense. He was an agent of a mythmaking mechanism that served a variety of publics.... We try to turn this to our advantage by setting our sights on the collective mentality rather than on the uncertain empirical record. Our "facts," then, are perceptions.[46]

Or, as Elizabeth A. Castelli has written in her study of the collective memory of martyrdom in early Christianity: "This book is not a history of early Christian martyrdom but an exploration of the culture-making aspects of its representations.... The notion of collective memory allows one to move past often irresolvable questions of 'what really happened' to questions of how particular ways of construing the past

---

the beginning of the process—whoever they might have been, and whether or not we can know much about them—were involved too (though by this phrasing I do not mean to imply that those who lived close in time to the figures in question, and those who came much later, are necessarily connected by any sort of unbroken "stream" of oral or written tradition—they may or may not have been in any particular case, and we have no grounds for assuming a priori that they were).

46. Weinstein and Bell, *Saints and Society*, 12–13.

enable later communities to constitute and sustain themselves."[47] It is this turn to the collective mentality and memory preserved in stories that I will follow.

This turn becomes possible because the hagiographer, even when he or she does not collect already circulating stories but writes stories himself, does so for an audience, under the pressure of their expectations, assumptions, and interests. The hagiographer is not free to invent his subjects from whole cloth but is writing about known figures; he may not assert just anything about his subjects, or take whatever liberties or wield whatever narrative devices he might choose: he is constrained to some extent by what his audience will recognize and approve. To invoke once again Barbara Herrnstein Smith's way of putting things, every telling of a story "always involves two parties, an audience as well as a narrator. . . . As in any social transaction, each party must be individually motivated to participate. . . . Each party must have some *interest* in telling or listening to that narrative."[48] The role of the audience, then, is crucial to the hagiographic process and to the making of holy persons' reputations (more on this below). Theirs is an active, not a merely passive role in a social process that is no less real, and no less generative of the texts that have eventually made their way down to us through the accidents of transmission, for being mostly hidden from our view.[49]

---

47. *Martyrdom and Memory*, 4–5 (I have juxtaposed two sentences that in Castelli's text are separated by a page of intervening prose). Compare 29.

48. Barbara Herrnstein Smith, "Narrative Versions, Narrative Theories," 232–233. Or, if we think of a hagiographic text as a sort of art work, then Stephen Greenblatt's comments are apt: "Artistic expression is never perfectly self-contained and abstract, nor can it be derived satisfactorily from the subjective consciousness of an isolated creator. Collective actions, ritual gestures, paradigms of relationship, and shared images of authority penetrate the work of art and shape it from within" (*Learning to Curse*, 118; compare 213). Greenblatt goes on to observe that the work of art, in its turn, "contributes to the formation, realignment, and transmission of social practices," a point to which I return at various moments below.

49. For similar attention to the role of communities and their standards in the shaping of texts, and the importance of these texts in turn in the making of selves, see Shaw, "*Askesis* and the Appearance of Holiness"; and for a sensitive study of the management of reputations by and among holy persons, see Gleason, "Visiting and News." Scholars are beginning to attend seriously to the active and indispensable nature of participants' roles in religious rituals and activities, seeing them not simply as passive, inert onlookers but as shaping proceedings in important ways. For some initial forays in this area of research, see Hanks, "Exorcism and the Description of Participant Roles," and Edith Turner, *Experiencing Ritual*. The groundwork for this realization was laid a hundred years ago by Marcel Mauss toward the end of his treatise on magic; we find there the seeds (but only that) of a full theory of audience participation. For Mauss, the phenomena that must be studied are social, collective phenomena, and magical rites are held to be efficacious because of social traditions, not principles of rationality calculated by individuals. Magic's effectiveness is a matter of the suggestive, social milieu in which the magician operates. See Mauss, *A General Theory of Magic*, 132–140.

But what about the more writerly, narratologically sophisticated aspects of stories of holy persons? Must they not have been added by learned authors, far removing the products from what the saints' stories looked like on the ground? Here I would point to Natalie Davis' study of remission narratives in sixteenth-century France, provocatively titled *Fiction in the Archives*. Noting that historians are (or once were) trained "to peel away the fictive elements in our documents so we could get at the real facts," Davis decides instead "to let the 'fictional' aspect of these documents be the center of analysis," explaining that "fiction" etymologically has to do not with the "feigned elements" of stories but with "their forming, shaping, and molding elements: the crafting of a narrative."[50] In doing so, Davis attends to three things: (1) "the means and settings for producing the stories," in which she shows that remission narratives were *collaborative* productions involving at least two parties, the supplicant himself and the recording secretary, not to mention the reception by the audience and the silent pressure of the audience's anticipated reception on how the story is told;[51] (2) "the interests held by both narrator and audience in the story-telling event"; and (3) (contra Herrnstein Smith) "'structures' existing prior to that event in the minds and lives of the ... participants: possible story lines determined by [any relevant] constraints ... and approaches to narrative learned in past listening to and telling of stories or derived from other cultural constructions."[52] Against the familiar notion that simple people speak straightforwardly and only clever, literary types embellish stories with rhetorical structures and flourishes, Davis retorts: "The remission tales show that the 'stuff of invention' was widely distributed throughout society" and not the exclusive preserve of learned scribes.[53] The "fiction" Davis finds in the archives results from a collaborative exchange between several parties, including the petitioner himself, the one personally involved in the events narrated,

---

50. Natalie Davis, *Fiction in the Archives*, 2–3; compare Burke, *History and Social Theory*, 126–129. For a parallel move from treating "fictiveness" as "imagined" or "made up" to regarding it as "shaping" or "molding," see Nienhauser, "The Origins of Chinese Fiction," 193 and passim. Both authors refer to the Latin root of "fiction," *fingere*, to fashion or form. Compare Ebersole, *Captured by Texts*, 99–101, on the impossibility of neatly distinguishing "fictional" from "historical" captivity narratives.

51. On the collaborative production of the narratives, see esp. *Fiction in the Archives*, 15–25. For more on the role of the audience and its expected reception in the shaping of stories, see also Barbara Herrnstein Smith, "Narrative Versions, Narrative Theories," 234; and Crapanzano, "'Self'-Centering Narratives," 107. On the audience's capacity, once texts are set into circulation, to receive and creatively "misread" works in ways unintended by their authors, see Wallace Martin, *Recent Theories of Narrative*, 175ff.

52. *Fiction in the Archives*, 4. Parallel to what Davis distinguishes as "stories" (narratives that get told and recorded) and "structures" (mental and cultural stocks of possible story lines and action patterns) is Dan Sperber's distinction between "narratives" and "stories"; see *Explaining Culture*, 28.

53. *Fiction in the Archives*, 111, responding to a famous passage in Montaigne that wonderfully captures this commonly held but erroneous notion; I discuss that passage in the Epilogue.

and was not simply or solely added by secretaries reporting the proceedings.[54] In short: recognizing the rhetoricity of texts does not require us to divorce them utterly from the social worlds that produced and consumed them, since rhetoricity is part of life as lived just as much as it is part of texts.

Two common assumptions about hagiographic narratives further color our view of how they related to the life worlds that produced them. One is that hagiography's essential function is didactic, that it exists to present models for readers to emulate, and hence that in its very existence it argues the imitability of holy persons.[55] Peter Brown, while he has given us a fine study of how early medieval Christian saints functioned as exemplars,[56] has, in a more recent article, questioned the common assumption that early Christian saints were always and everywhere to be imitated; such, he grants, was perhaps the exception, but he calls attention to the rule, which was that saints were basically *enjoyed*, their attainments celebrated in festivals by people who neither aspired to emulate them nor were expected to.

> It was precisely by keeping the saints *in*imitable . . . that the Christians of late antiquity and the early Middle Ages kept the saints sacred. For, in keeping the saints sacred, they felt able to bring them back into worldly affairs, as invulnerable presences, capable of reaching into the deepest, most potentially polluted and polluting levels of daily life. To build a frail bridge of imitation between oneself and such persons was the exact opposite of what one wanted from them. It did far more than destroy the fun of the festivals. It brought the saints down to the level of their imitators, and, in so doing, it undermined the fundamental antithesis between the sacred and the profane. For if sacred figures such as the saints were no longer seen as utterly, inimitably different from the profane,

---

54. See in particular *Fiction in the Archives*, 22–25. Raymond Van Dam has recently made the same move in his study of late antique miracle stories from Gaul: see *Saints and Their Miracles in Late Antique Gaul*, 86. I am here disagreeing, then, with recent statements by Elizabeth A. Clark ("Holy Women, Holy Words," 415–422), though I grant that the gender differential in the cases she discusses (male hagiographers writing about holy women) does make the issue much more complex. On the other hand, I agree with the formulations in Castelli, *Martyrdom and Memory*, 28 (although she presents these as tallying with Clark's views). In short: recognizing the rhetoricity of texts does not (*pace* Clark) require us to divorce them utterly from the social world that produced them, since rhetoricity is part of life as lived just as much as it is part of texts.

55. This view is widespread; for examples, see Noble and Head, *Soldiers of Christ*, xvii–xviii; and Hawley, "Introduction," in Hawley, ed., *Saints and Virtues*, xiii–xvi, though to Hawley's credit he does complicate the point by noting that not all saints everywhere were deemed imitable by others, as do Kieckhefer and Bond in their preface to *Sainthood*, viii.

56. Peter Brown, "The Saint as Exemplar in Late Antiquity."

then the very life-force of the profane world, which depended on intermittent contact with the sacred, would wither away.[57]

At the very least, then, the matter is complex, and in studying any body of hagiography we must be alert to both possibilities: that its subjects were seen as essentially "like-us" and hence meant to be emulated (or that stories about them were received by audiences as calls to emulation, regardless of the hagiographer's intentions) and that they were seen as essentially "not-like-us" and were being declared inimitable, presented to be celebrated and admired.[58] For now I will simply note that each of these possibilities presumes or enacts a distinct mode of relationship between hagiography's audience and its subjects.[59]

The second assumption regarding hagiographies, found especially among sinologists, is related to the first and concerns the entertainment value of these narratives. Modern scholars who have difficulty imagining a religious and cultural world in which such fantastic stories were enthusiastically circulated must invent an authorial purpose for their supposedly solitary, fictive-in-the-recent-sense fabrication. Entertainment, coupled perhaps with a dash of merely moral didacticism, is the alternative purpose they suggest, again by silent analogy with modern genres. In the case of China, one facilitator of such readings is a persistent failure on the part of some modern academics to take the quest for transcendence seriously *as religious*. Peter Brown, by contrast, while arguing that saints through their stories were "enjoyed" by Late Antique populations, also urged that "we must . . . make an effort of the imagination to recover something of the full *religious* weight of the expectations of those who . . . enjoyed the saints without necessarily feeling obliged to imitate them." The activities that attended martyrs' festivals, of which Augustine spoke frankly,[60] "disorderly though they were, . . . were only the outermost shock waves,

---

57. Peter Brown, "Enjoying the Saints in Late Antiquity," 16–17.

58. This is among the most basic of religious, indeed cognitive (and political), taxonomies; see Jonathan Smith, "What a Difference a Difference Makes." But emulation does not have to be an all-or-nothing proposition either, as Sarah Schneewind has helpfully pointed out to me.

59. On the exemplarity side, the point has been nicely phrased by Gelber ("A Theater of Virtue: The Exemplary World of St. Francis of Assisi," 15–16): "To be exemplary is to be exemplary to others; it is to perform for an audience expected to interact with the exemplary person in what may be a great variety of ways."

60. "When I went to the vigils as a student in this city [Carthage], I spent the night rubbing up beside women, along with other boys anxious to make an impression on them and, who knows, should the opportunity present itself, to 'make it' with them" (quoted in Peter Brown, "Enjoying the Saints in Late Antiquity," 6). The passage is found in a collection of Augustine's sermons newly discovered at Mainz by François Dolbeau.

on the fringes of the martyr's festival, that registered the detonation, in its midst, of a
heavy charge of religious feeling, associated with a particular notion of the sacred."[61]
Likewise, to be sure, stories of adepts' strange doings and transcendents' sumptuous
celestial surroundings were no doubt vastly entertaining to early medieval Chinese
audiences, and indeed I will adduce evidence of this; but that such stories entertained is not at all incompatible with their having arisen in a religious milieu in
which some people, at least, took their claims seriously, it being quite possible to
believe stories literally and be entertained by them at the same time. But where the
modern assertion of entertainment value as the primary purpose of the stories fails
is in its assumption that entertainment was all such stories could provide their readers and also in its tacit assumption of how that entertainment was delivered.[62] Again
too simply, we might say that modern "supernatural fiction" pleases some readers
because, although in daily life they fundamentally disbelieve the story's fantastic
elements, for the duration of the reading they suspend disbelief and enjoy contemplating the world *as if* an alternate reality were at play than the one they normally
presume.[63] It is precisely this deep disjunction between the world described in the
text and the contemporary sociocultural-religious world that was—to our eyes—
striking by its absence in early medieval China. This is not to say that everyone in
early medieval China believed claims about *xian*. But for us (or some of us) tales of
transcendence may be fantastic (and enjoyable) in part because we can scarcely even
imagine anyone actually carrying out the disciplines the tales describe or claiming
the things that adepts in the tales claim about themselves, whereas for the early
medieval audience the tales were *not* fantastic in this way, because that audience
lived among people who really did and claimed such things. The tales must have
been enjoyable, then, in a markedly less detached way.[64] As Brown suggests, we must

---

61. "Enjoying the Saints in Late Antiquity," 6.

62. Compare Greenblatt, *Learning to Curse*, 13: "We can . . . argue that the transhistorical
stability or continuity of literary pleasure is an illusion; we can suggest that there is little reason
to believe that the pleasure generated by *The Tempest*, say, was the same for the Jacobean audience
as it is for ourselves." The ensuing two pages, too long to quote here, are highly instructive, and
directly relevant to this discussion.

63. For a literary analysis of this mechanism, see Todorov, *The Fantastic*.

64. For further discussion of the history of "fiction" and the hermeneutical issues involved
in reading hagiographies and marvel tales evidentially, see Dudbridge, *Religious Experience and
Lay Society in T'ang China*, esp. 16–17 ("a literature of record, not of fantasy or creative fiction"),
though I also feel that Dudbridge goes a bit far in taking some stories as literal accounts of events
and then trying to overlay on them a modern medical or "scientific" template. Prominent examples of attempts to read early medieval narratives of transcendents and marvels as protofictional
in the modern sense include Lu Xun's magisterial *Zhongguo xiaoshuo shilue*; DeWoskin, "The Six
Dynasties *Chih-kuai* and the Birth of Fiction"; and Kao, *Classical Chinese Tales of the Supernatural
and the Fantastic*, 1–51.

make a considerable effort of imagination to recover a sense of what such a society was like.

To return to the question posed at the opening of this section, how can we legitimately read hagiographic and other narratives of *xian* as evidence of what the early medieval social and religious world of China was like? Several things are now, I hope, clear. First, the sources that have survived, even inscriptions recovered from local sites, do not permit anything like a "quest for the historical X," where X is any of the individuals named in the texts. The surviving stories do not allow us to go behind or beneath them and recover "what really happened" in this or that particular case. What they do allow us to grasp is what someone was trying to persuade someone else of, what they were holding up to an audience as worthy of admiration and wonder and perhaps also emulation (or perhaps not). They bear witness to, because they participated in, the social processes by which the notion of *xian* and the reputations of particular practitioners as having achieved the status of *xian* were made—not, I think, "born," as in the title of Jacques Le Goff's masterly study *La naissance du Purgatoire*,[65] but actively fashioned by many people over many generations. They are, in short, artifacts of collective memory. It is these purposive social processes of the construction of collective memory that this book is, in part, about.

Second, given the pressure of audience expectations on hagiographic authors and collectors, we may justifiably read these texts as evidence of practices and understandings that were broadly shared in their authors' time. Even if not everyone would have believed or approved of their contents and claims (and we know that some did not), they would nevertheless have recognized the types of figures, practices, and scenarios found there. Since the narratives were attempts to persuade an audience, and since that audience would have needed to be familiar with the scenes, the settings, the patterns of relationship and action described in the stories in order for the portrayals to have been convincing, we can assume that, in these respects, our texts give a relatively accurate portrayal of how things were.[66] In this sense, and only in this sense, can we use hagiographic narratives to try to recover

---

65. Le Goff's *The Birth of Purgatory* has been an inspiration in several respects, not least of which is that it is one of the best portraits we have of the ongoing *social construction over time by many agents*—often by means of colorful narrative—of an extremely large and important component of a religious *imaginaire*. But this is why the process he depicts should not be imagined as a "birth" but as a *making* by dint of many parties' labors, both seen and unseen. Purgatory did not gestate as if in a womb only to emerge fully formed, but was constructed by many agents, most of whom will be forever unknown to us though the fruits of their labors survive in text and image.

66. Jan Nattier has given us an excellent enunciation of this hermeneutical strategy, which she terms "the principle of irrelevance" (so named because passages in question make "incidental mention . . . of items unrelated to the author's primary agenda"), in *A Few Good Men*, 66–67.

"what really happened"—not, perhaps, in particular cases, but in particular *types* of situations. Naturally, claims made about this or that individual would likely have been contested and controversial, supported by some but denied by others, and indeed I will present evidence that this was so. But the essential point is that the *sorts of contexts and circumstances* in which individuals were depicted as having done what they were claimed to have done would have been familiar to readers. Through the texts, then, we catch incidental glimpses not of the historicity of this or that figure but of the environments in which these *types* of figures moved, the sorts of relationships in which they engaged, the sorts of abilities and activities commonly attributed to them, and the sorts of people who did the attributing. Given enough examples, a composite portrait of this social role and environment becomes possible.

Finally, one way to adjust our portrait to account for possible distortions introduced by the shapers of stories about past holy persons is to compare diverse sources on the same subject. By juxtaposing texts with different persuasive agendas and viewpoints—some sympathetic, some hostile—as they report the same sorts of scenes, settings, patterns of relationship and action (or even, in a few cases, the same "event" or figure), a sort of evidential triangulation becomes possible. When texts with opposite agendas repeatedly report exactly the same *patterns* of activity—as we will find that they do in the case of practitioners of *xian* arts in early medieval China—we can be confident that those patterns were a feature of religious and social life and not simply the wishful construct of hagiographers or the denigrating fictions of debunkers.[67]

The Making of Transcendents

This is a book about the making of *xian*. To say this is to point at once toward three possible, seemingly distinct lines of inquiry. Studying the making of *xian* might involve studying the ascetic disciplines, imbricated as they were with certain cosmological and physiological assumptions, by which practitioners gradually and arduously made themselves into *xian*. Alternatively, it might involve studying the textual and ideological processes by which *xian*-hood was constituted over time as a role or ideal distinct from others in Chinese society, identifying the likely sources for this process of creation and considering the arguments by which it was justified and the imagery in which it was presented. Or, thirdly, it might involve studying

---

67. This reading strategy is deployed to good effect by Matthew Dickie in his magisterial recent study *Magic and Magicians in the Greco-Roman World*, 11–12 and passim. It is also articulated as "the principle of corroborating evidence" by Nattier in *A Few Good Men*, 68–69.

how particular individuals were made into *xian* by communities through processes
of social reception and collective memory. A complete study of the making of *xian*
would treat all three of these aspects. This book attends to all three, but with some
strong qualifications: (1) Since I have elsewhere dealt with many of the details
and cosmological underpinnings of practitioners' ascetic disciplines, I mostly bypass
them here and refer readers to my earlier account and other studies, both those
cited there and those published since.[68] (2) A treatment of the processes by which
xian-hood was culturally constructed as an ideal would require a separate book,
one based mostly on sources earlier than those treated here. I do mention some
elements of these processes, but this largely remains an area for future research.[69] (3)
In this book I attend primarily to the third sense, namely, the social processes by
which individuals were deemed to have achieved the status of *xian*. Even on this
aspect, however, much more remains to be done.

For now, however, I must point out that all three aspects are inextricably inter-
twined; we may disentangle them for purposes of analysis, but as a matter of social
practice they were aspects of one very complex whole. Let me mention some of the
ways in which this is so. As Gavin Flood has recently argued, practitioners of ascetic
disciplines "have all been part of tradition and linguistic community that legitimated
their practice. All have performed the memory of tradition. . . . The ascetic self shapes
the narrative of her life to the narrative of tradition. . . . The ascetic self is formed by
tradition and internalizes tradition and its goals."[70] We cannot understand the practitioner's ascetic disciplines, then, without seeing their intensely social character, even
(perhaps especially) when they call for the practitioner to isolate himself from others.
For one thing, those disciplines were produced and legitimated by social traditions
stretching back in time; in practicing them the ascetic appropriates that collective
lineage and inscribes its goals onto himself; as Flood puts it, "this appropriation of
tradition is a form of remembrance, the memory of tradition performed through the
body."[71] For another, ascetic disciplines are *performed* by practitioners, which is to say
that they are always carried out in the public domain, even when done in physical
isolation; it is not only that their rejections, reversals, and transformations are "enacted
within a community and tradition,"[72] but also that the doing of them implies an audience of others before whom, and a cast of others in distinction to whom, they are

---

68. *TL*, 1–128.

69. Headway has been made recently in Boyd, "Transcendents in Transition," but I remain
unaware of any exhaustive treatment of this important topic; such a treatment would attend fully
to archeological as well as received textual evidence.

70. Gavin Flood, *The Ascetic Self,* 1–3, juxtaposing several discontinuous sentences.

71. Ibid., 6.

72. Ibid., 7.

done, again even when done in the apparent isolation of a cell or forest.[73] To give a simple example: Shunning ordinary foods becomes a powerful act only when there is a surrounding community for whom those foods are deemed ordinary, and it gains power when important cultural and religious functions are attached to those foods and to the giving and sharing of them. We cannot understand the ascetic adept's performance without taking into account his audience's reaction to it; we must consider not only his own practice but others' responses to him as well. Finally, we cannot understand the creation of the ideal of *xian*-hood apart from the practitioners who performed the disciplines seen as enabling people to reach it and apart from the narratives and collective memories of their deeds, for the simple reason that those performances, narratives, and collective memories were the primary means (though not the only ones) by which the ideal itself was shaped and sustained.

A number of scholars, reacting against earlier attempts to isolate intrinsic properties that saints or holy persons in one or more religions must by definition possess,[74] have arrived at the position that, in Pierre Delooz's words, "to be a saint is to be a saint for others," or, as Ernest Gellner put it, "a person is a [saint] by virtue of being held to be one."[75] Their insight consists in realizing that sainthood is a social and religious role, a collectively shaped category, and that, however the role is defined in a particular culture and era, for an individual to take it on or belong to the category, he or she must be deemed by others as doing so.[76] "Sainthood" or the status of holy person is strictly an artifact of social reception and social memory. To say that a figure was a holy person is to say something about how others in a certain society perceived and remembered that person. A person may act in a certain fashion, may "present him or herself" by word and gesture in certain ways, but whether this self-presentation is taken up and ratified by other parties does not depend on the one presenting: other people's reception of the performance is the deciding factor, so much so that individuals who during their lives had no intention of fulfilling the role of saint are sometimes pressed into such service by the force of others' perceptions of them, while others who strove for recognition fail to win it.[77] On the

---

73. Mauss already pointed this out a century ago (*A General Theory of Magic*, 134).

74. For example, several essays collected in Kieckhefer and Bond, eds., *Sainthood*, exhibit this long-standing tendency.

75. Pierre Delooz, *Sociologie et canonisations*, 7; Gellner, "Political and Religious Organization of the Berbers of the Central High Atlas," 60. A more developed statement of the point by Delooz is quoted in Weinstein and Bell, *Saints and Society*, 9.

76. Or, to put things once again in terms of a communication model, an individual's performance of the social role of holy person, however it is locally defined, is the message sent; its meaning, however, will be determined by those who receive and evaluate it.

77. This is true of most social roles, of course; my point is that *xian*-hood has not been adequately seen *as* a social role.

other hand, as other recent students of hagiography, such as Vincent Cornell, have pointed out, the audience does not confront a single holy person's performance without precedent, standards, or resources; it measures that person against whatever contemporary repertoires, codes, or expectations pertain to the role for which the individual is, to borrow the language of dramaturgy, auditioning.[78] Not just anyone was likely to be deemed a saint or a transcendent, whatever achievements or status they might claim; there were standards—difficult standards—by which they were judged. We thus find other scholars recently returning to an emphasis on the limning of these specific, nonarbitrary repertoires and standards.[79] Attention to both aspects is surely needed, but we do well to recall that, whatever normative standards scholars may reconstruct as governing the roles of holy persons in a society, it remains the case that the individuals who fill those categories do so because of how they were received by audiences—audiences whose responses may or may not have conformed to scholars' expectations.[80] The fundamental insight of Delooz, Gellner, and others into the constitutive role of the social reception of would-be holy persons stands intact. In this as in several other respects, then, becoming a *xian* was an inescapably interpersonal and interactive process, even if practicing the arts of *xian*-hood sometimes required physical isolation: to become a *xian* was to be recognized as one by some community of other persons.

This perspective on what it means to be a *xian* (or any other type of holy person in any society) is central to this book. The move consists of seeing the *xian*-hood of this or that individual as a socially constructed, socially enacted attribution rather than as an intrinsic, self-sustained property. It relocates the main agency that is in fact responsible for bringing it about that one individual is recognized in some context as a *xian* while another is not: it finds that agency in the others who respond to practitioners rather than in the practitioners themselves. It is not, of course, that practitioners lack agency of their own. A practitioner may lay claim to this status and may take on the disciplines often attributed to successful *xian;* he or she may act in ways that create and sustain his reputation. But his success in achieving the status of *xian* depends radically on others' *responses* to his claim and to his ascetic performance. He may also deny or shun this status but come to be invested with it anyway. In general, then, ascetics undergo certain disciplines and represent themselves to others in certain ways, and these disciplines and self-representations are part of the *imaginaires* of their religious and social worlds. But, though they may

---

78. For incisive phrasing of the point, see Cornell, *Realm of the Saint*, 63, 94.

79. Representative works include Cornell, *Realm of the Saint;* and Weinstein and Bell, *Saints and Society.*

80. Or, in other words, how they were received by what Janet Staiger terms "perverse spectators"; see Staiger, *Perverse Spectators.*

have a hand in the processes leading to their recognition as *xian* or saints or arhats or *marabouts,* that recognition finally is not their own doing. It is the doing of others through countless acts of reputation-maintenance and the ongoing construction of collective memory. There are no self-created *xian* or saints.

This move in understanding how individuals become holy persons has a parallel in the attention paid since the 1980s by many students of literature, film, and other cultural media to how literary or film productions are *received* by readers and audiences and how that reception, not the productions considered formalistically and in isolation, is the primary locus of "meaning." This turn to reception responds to several earlier intellectual currents, among them Karl Marx's recognition that "consumption is not only the concluding act through which the product becomes a product, but also the one through which the producer becomes a producer."[81] On this view, most basically "'Meaning,'" in Janet Staiger's summary, "is not 'in' the text, put there by the agency of authorship, but originates in the event of reading: 'reading is not the discovery of meaning but the creation of it.'"[82] Staiger, however, offers a complex (and materialist) revision of reception theory on the grounds that its account of readers' receptions "seems . . . dangerously ahistorical, as though readers were tabula rasa [sic], without knowledge of the physical production of a text (or representations of the physical production of the text)" or uninfluenced by the common interpretive strategy according to which a book (for example) "means" what its author meant it to mean. While I do not here follow Staiger's materialist turn, I do follow her historical interest in recovering and understanding the reading strategies of previous reader-receivers and the social, ideational, and even material contexts in which they operated. Such a project involves studying the social processes by which a production was "read" in a certain fashion by certain agents as well, of course, as the outcome of such processes. It also involves studying their uptake and evaluation—their reception—by others: one agent's reading may be judged by another as a misreading; in such cases we must ask, "What counts as a misreading? What situations, methods, procedures, or interpretations are judged by whom to be erroneous? Within that historical context, . . . why is a meaning or significance deemed less 'true' than another?"[83]

---

81. Quoted in Staiger, *Interpreting Films,* 3. The first two chapters of Staiger's book are the best introduction I have found to the value, history, and intellectual pedigree of reception studies, a pedigree that Staiger traces through such figures as I. A. Richards, Roland Barthes, Robert Darnton, Jacques Derrida, Stanley Fish, and Michael Baxandall, among others. An important recent collection of essays from which I have also profited is Machor and Goldstein, *Reception Study.* A seminal application of this way of thinking to religious productions is Richard Davis' *Lives of Indian Images.*

82. Staiger, *Interpreting Films,* 22; the last clause is quoted from Steven Mailloux.

83. Ibid., 32.

But when we carry reception study from the realm of books, films, and art objects to that of religious virtuosi, modifications are required. On the one hand there is the fact that, during his or her own lifetime, the person in question is (or may be) involved, along with others, in the co-fashioning of his reputation: the individual does not wield complete control of the processes of reputation-fashioning, but neither is he or she simply a mute object to which others respond as they will; there is, in other words, a dynamic relationship between the potential holy person and others, a relationship that plays a part in launching the historical process in which the person's reputation will be formed and remembered. And his reputation, his image in the eyes of others—the equivalent of a "reading" in literary reception studies—is not a thing but an ongoing event, which is why I view a materialist approach as inadequate to my subject. On the other hand there is the fact that, after his or her departure from active participation in community life (into death, transcendence, celestial afterlife, extinction, or whatever next destination figures in the relevant cultural and religious *imaginaire*), the holy person is no longer involved in the processes by which his memory is shaped and transmitted, and thenceforth it is *only* the artifacts of collective memory of that individual that are available for others to respond to.[84] In other words, the reception of holy persons is in two crucial respects unlike that of texts, films, and works of art: during his lifetime, the holy person, unlike a text, *acts* as one agent among many (sometimes a key agent, sometimes not) in the interactions that shape his reception and determine the "meanings" of his actions, while after his lifetime the holy person, unlike a text or other artifact, is no longer still available in the world in the way that he or she once was or still active in negotiating his reputation.[85] In some senses at least, and speaking figuratively, the

---

84. This statement needs to be made more complex in cases where writings by the individual in question (or writings attributed to said individual) survive. Even in manuscript cultures, however, such writings are usually heavily mediated by others who stand between contemporary receivers and the authors of the texts.

85. Again this needs to be made more complex in certain cases: (1) relics (sometimes including texts or images) are sites of a holy person's "living presence," yes, but even in traditions that maintain this, the holy person is *not present in the same ways* as during his lifetime; (2) claims that holy persons continually or periodically reappear in communities, sometimes to correct misapprehensions, or that they continue to dictate newly revealed speech through mechanisms such as "spirit-writing" (a prevalent technique throughout many centuries in China and still today [see, among other studies, Jordan and Overmyer, *The Flying Phoenix*]—although I do not yet know of a case in which a transcendent is represented as having "spoken" through spirit-writing in the early medieval period): here I am at least provisionally taking the stand that such claims may themselves be seen as part of the history of a holy person's reception by and in a community of others, rather than instances of the holy person's own agency; such agency itself is among the marvelous feats communities attribute to their holy persons. To these communities, the claim that the holy person himself is the agent is obviously paramount. I wish here neither to accept this claim at face value nor to dismiss it.

holy person before his departure is more actively involved in shaping his reception than a text could be in shaping its reception, but after his departure he is less so, since texts, films, and images often survive their makers to be received anew by successive generations of audiences, while holy persons survive only by virtue of the ongoing work of memory and cross-generational transmission that summon them into a sort of ongoing presence long after they are otherwise gone.

Concepts, Terms, and Caveats

In addition to the concepts already discussed, several additional terms need explanation and some pitfalls should be noted and avoided.

At several points I have used the dramaturgical language of "performance," "role," "auditioning," "audience," and "reception." In doing so I do not mean to suggest that practitioners of *xian* arts were, as we say, *merely* "putting on a performance" for their public. In fact, in what follows I resolutely ignore the question of whether this or that agent was sincere or merely "faking it," except to note what is revealed when contemporaries debated such questions; not only is this not a helpful or interesting question for scholarship (however important it may be in the communities scholars study),[86] it is also one that cannot be answered from available evidence. Rather, in using dramaturgical language I mean to suggest the public, interpersonal nature of ascetics' lives, the performed-for-an-audience aspect of their disciplines and patterns of action, their strategies for managing the impressions they made on others, and the decisive importance for the forging of their reputations of how others received them. "Most ascetic behaviors, codes of conduct, instruments of formation, and technologies have the aspect of performance, of displaying or acting,"[87] whether or not they happen to be carried out in the physical presence of other people. In invoking this language I once again draw on a venerable tradition in literary criticism, history, and cultural studies. Peter Brown, in his groundbreaking 1971 study of the holy man in the Late Antique Mediterranean world, spoke of the *role* of holy person, a role defined by certain sets of expectations on the part of the public, and he characterized the exorcisms such persons performed as a sort of operetta.[88] Kenneth Burke pointed to the

---

86. As recognized long ago by Erving Goffman, *The Presentation of Self in Everyday Life*, 70ff. The questioning of the motives of those deemed to be practicing "magical" arts is an old trope in religious discourse; see Styers, *Making Magic*, 180–183. We will have occasion to see this old trope at work in some recent scholars' writings about practitioners in China.

87. Valantasis, "Constructions of Power in Asceticism," 798.

88. "Possession and its working through is a way in which a small community can both admit and control disruptive experiences by playing them out" ("The Rise and Function of the Holy Man," 88); see also 89, 93.

fundamentally rhetorical character of human action and developed the notion of the "dramatism" of human behavior; for Burke, actions are "strategies developed to cope with situations involving a performer and an audience."[89] Beginning in the late 1950s, Erving Goffman, in a sensitive and innovative series of sociological studies, "consider[ed]," as he put it, "the way in which the individual in ordinary . . . situations presents himself and his activity to others, the ways in which he guides and controls the impression they form of him, and the kinds of things he may and may not do while sustaining his performance before them."[90] Goffman portrays a "performed self" that is

> some kind of image, usually creditable, which the individual on stage and in character effectively attempts to induce others to hold in regard to him. While this image is entertained *concerning* the individual, so that a self is imputed to him, this self itself does not derive from its possessor, but from the whole scene of his action, being generated by that attribute of local events which renders them interpretable by witnesses. A correctly staged and performed scene leads the audience to impute a self to a performed character, but this imputation— this self—is a *product* of a scene that comes off, and is not a *cause* of it. The self, then, as a performed character, is not an organic thing that has a specific location. . . . It is a dramatic effect arising diffusely from a scene that is presented, and the characteristic issue, the crucial concern, is whether it will be credited or discredited.[91]

Similarly, Victor Turner developed the analysis of what he termed "social drama" as a way to understand key situations in societies. "These situations—arguments, combats, rites of passage—are inherently dramatic because participants not only do things, they try *to show others what they are doing or have done*; actions take on a 'performed-for-an-audience' aspect."[92] Stephen Greenblatt analyzed "Renaissance self-fashioning" in action and in texts, showing in the process that the word "fashion," used as something one could do to oneself, first came to be employed in Elizabethan times.[93] Finally, the attention paid by Judith Butler and others to the "performative"

---

89. The phrase is that of Gusfield, "The Bridge Over Separated Lands," 30.

90. Goffman, *The Presentation of Self in Everyday Life*, xi.

91. Ibid., 252–253. I have also benefited from Goffman's *Interaction Ritual*; and his *Frame Analysis*, as well as Randall Collins, *Interaction Ritual Chains*, a work in Goffman's tradition.

92. Victor Turner, *On the Edge of the Bush*, 179; he is here quoting another author's characterization of his work. Compare Victor Turner, *The Drums of Affliction*, 273–275, for a clearer and more extended treatment of "dramatic" aspects of ritual; and his "Social Dramas and Stories about Them" and *From Ritual to Theatre*, 61–123.

93. Greenblatt, *Renaissance Self-Fashioning*, 3, emphasis added.

nature of social roles—by which Butler means, drawing on J. L. Austin, John Searle, and postmodern rewritings of their ideas, the way in which roles are constituted by acts of discourse that have the power to produce what they name—valuably highlights the extent to which features of societies and identities of persons are not fixed or given but are continually created through speech, gestures, and other social signs, signs that do not simply represent states of affairs but also bring them about. I would add, however, that the changes achieved performatively that Butler and others note do not depend solely on the one sending the signs but must also elicit certain responses; otherwise there is no achievement. Performativity is necessarily interactive; performance implies audience; successful performance implies a certain response by that audience.[94]

By invoking the language of role and performance, I mean to suggest that the status accorded an ascetic practitioner or a holy person is at least as much a function of how he or she is perceived and received by others as it is a function of his intrinsic attributes; that he assumes a definite role, a role defined by a repertoire of behavioral patterns anyone in that role is expected, by the surrounding public, to demonstrate; and that many of the ascetic's activities—like the activities associated with any other social role—can be fruitfully understood as directed toward this audience of others. To understand the traits and behaviors that constituted the role, the social processes by which those playing the role interacted with their audience, and their audience's response, is to understand—in the case at hand here—the making of transcendents. That is a primary goal of this book.

By *imaginaire,* a French word that cannot be translated satisfactorily without implying falsity, I mean simply a "nonmaterial, imaginative world constituted by texts, especially works of art and literature" as well as oral performances (though of course oral performances in past times are only accessible to us by inference from surviving texts). "Such worlds are by definition not the same as the material world, but insofar as the material world is thought and experienced in part through them, they are not imaginary in the sense of being false, entirely made-up." I take the quoted phrases from Steven Collins,[95] who has given us a helpful discussion of the concept and one of the best recent deployments of it. The early medieval *imaginaire* of transcendence, then, consisted of the cosmologies and ideologies underlying the practices of seekers of transcendence, the hoped-for goals of those practices, and—my primary area of focus in this study—the body of stories told of those deemed to have achieved *xian*-hood. It also included the origins of the scriptures,

---

94. For an exhaustive discussion of performance and its many aspects, see Schechner, *Performance Theory*; and for a review of the literature, see Sullivan, "Sound and Senses."

95. *Nirvana and Other Buddhist Felicities,* 73.

techniques, and lineages held sacred by practitioners. The making and circulating of written texts was a key way in which this *imaginaire* was created and sustained. Narrative texts of several kinds were an essential vehicle for the construction of the *imaginaire* of transcendence. Nonpractitioners were involved, alongside practitioners, in the narrative and other ongoing activities by which the *imaginaire* was continually constructed.

Asceticism is a notoriously fluid concept, one that in this study does relatively little work.[96] For present purposes, I understand ascetics to be people who, following the norms of a tradition or master, renounce certain key elements, behaviors, and roles in their environing culture in order to undergo a transformation and become a new self that transcends the old one while it also transcends elements of the culture. "The ascetic self," like any other self if we follow Goffman, "is performed," Gavin Flood reminds us.[97] "The ascetic self takes on the presuppositions of a particular community, imbibes the ideology of a community's . . . traditions, and conforms his or her body to the practices determined by it. . . . Ascetic traditions are forms of collective memory enacted in the body through praxis and enacted in language through discourse."[98] One of my goals in this study is to go beyond this characterization of Flood's, however, by showing that practitioners of transcendence arts performed their ascetic selves *before, and in self-conscious contrast to, many others* who surrounded them, sought them out, and took keen interest in their doings (performance implies audience); that, despite their stereotype as solitary and isolated, they were in fact public figures who functioned in society as holy persons and who did so largely by virtue of their insistence on their difference from others, their renunciation of some kinds of power creating a more extraordinary kind. As Richard Valantasis has argued, "Asceticism begins to operate when an alternative to the social and religious givens is developed. . . . The ascetic develops a subjectivity alternative to the prescribed cultural subjectivity. . . . The ascetic develops an alternative set of social relationships usually defined in conflict to the dominant social arrangements."[99] To attend to these dissociative and extrinsic functions of ascetics' performances is not to ignore their substantive contents and intrinsic rationales, but it is to insist that in fully understanding them we do well to restore them to their social and cultural matrices. Like any other sort of social actors, ascetics do not live in a

---

96. A perusal of the recent collection edited by Wimbush and Valantasis *(Asceticism)* is enough to show the polythetic, or perhaps simply vague, nature of the category.

97. Flood, *The Ascetic Self*, 2.

98. Ibid., 8–9.

99. "Constructions of Power in Asceticism," 795.

cultural vacuum. Even when they insist on the not-here-or-now nature of their goals, they are doing so to an audience of others who may not share their goals or their ways of reaching them.

I have already said something about the social contexts and uses of narratives. Let me here say a word about what I mean by "narrative" itself. I mean any act or artifact of discourse that speaks of events arranged in some sort of temporal sequence, commonly known as a plot. While I recognize the many complexities and problems inherent in defining and interpreting narrative in general,[100] I will not entertain them here except to remind the reader that every telling of a story is a retelling for some audience. There are thus no stories without social context, though we may choose to study them as if they lacked a context, and there are, strictly speaking, no "original versions" later misnarrated—every retelling has its own contextual integrity.

Elsewhere I have suggested that we think of religious traditions not as container-like bounded entities but as *repertoires* of cultural resources used by people as they negotiate their lives.[101] The notion of cultural repertoires is a structuring motif throughout this book.

Collective memory (or social memory) is another key structuring concept of this book. Its history in scholarly discourse, which I will not rehearse here, begins with Maurice Halbwachs, a student of Henri Bergson and Émile Durkheim. Use of the concept assumes, first, that memories of the past—those maintained by social groups as well as by individuals—are intersubjective, social constructions, and second, that social memory "is not a passive receptacle, but instead a process of active restructuring, in which elements may be retained, reordered, or suppressed."[102] By actively negotiating accounts of the past, communities represent themselves and make claims in the present, often with an eye toward the future. Groups may construct "counter-memories" that go explicitly against whatever is their society's regnant narrative of the past, or against other groups' narratives.[103] Important things to investigate include: (1) the social and cultural processes by which memories are constructed and transmitted; (2) the ideological and political interests served; (3) how memories are received, responded to, and reworked in the broader culture and at specific sites; (4) the co-presence of alternative, competing narratives, attesting

---

100. See in particular Ricoeur, *Time and Narrative;* Wallace Martin, *Recent Theories of Narrative;* Mitchell, *On Narrative;* Chatman, *Story and Discourse;* and Mattingly, *Healing Dramas and Clinical Plots,* 1–47, 84–86.

101. Campany, "On the Very Idea of Religions."

102. Fentress and Wickham, *Social Memory,* 40.

103. See Castelli, *Martyrdom and Memory,* 22.

to contestation over the past.[104] The main advantage of the concept of collective memory is that it redirects our attention away from the attempt to recover "what really happened" and toward socially shaped accounts of what happened, the work that such accounts did in culture, and the ways in which they came to be shaped, transmitted, and received.

Now a word on nomenclature for the religious virtuosi who will populate these pages. By 300 C.E., at least, *xian* 仙 (or 僊), like "saint" or "champion," had become a term marking accomplishment; in texts of that era it designates a (more or less) final status attributed to an individual.[105] In early medieval[106] China there was no word for those who were on their way toward being deemed *xian,* just as in medieval Europe there was no single, separate term for future saints. It would be a mistake, however, to think that just because there was no word for such persons there must also have been no conceptual category for them.[107] When referring to those persons who would later come to have the status of *xian*-hood attributed to them, I have variously used the terms "adept" (preferable for its brevity), "practitioner," and "transcendence-seeker" (least preferable for being cumbersome); wherever they are used below, they mean anyone to whom the practice of the arts of transcendence was attributed, including cases when the individual in question claimed this status for himself. As for the term *xian* itself, there is simply no completely satisfying translation. I have preferred "transcendent" to the older and more familiar "immortal" for a number of reasons, the chief among them being that the graphs read as *xian* (whether 仙 or the older 僊) do not *mean* "immortal" but rather

---

104. This agenda is largely based on Confino, "Collective Memory and Cultural History"; compare Castelli, *Martyrdom and Memory,* 23–24. Other works I have found helpful on the topic, aside from those cited above, include Halbwachs, *On Collective Memory*; Connerton, *How Societies Remember*; Wertsch, *Voices of Collective Remembering*; and Olick and Robbins, "Social Memory Studies."

105. On the other hand, in Celestial Master and Shangqing Daoist circles this achievement was somewhat downgraded and relativized in ways that lie outside the scope of this study. And in its earliest usage *xian* may have meant not an achieved status but a different kind of being.

106. Another issue of nomenclature turns on what to call the periods of Chinese history within which this study falls. There is simply no adequate, agreed-upon designation. I sometimes use "late classical" loosely to designate the period up through the fall of the Han, and "early medieval" to name the ensuing period.

107. One related term is *fangshi* 方士 or "masters of esoterica," but this term covers a much broader range of practitioners and a much wider spectrum of arts, not all of which were related to the goal of transcendence. On *fangshi* see Li Ling, *Zhongguo fangshu kao* and *Zhongguo fangshu xukao*; Ngo, *Divination, magie et politique dans la Chine ancienne*; DeWoskin, *Doctors, Diviners, and Magicians of Ancient China* and "A Source Guide to the Lives and Techniques of Han and Six Dynasties *Fang-shih*"; and Harper, *Early Chinese Medical Literature,* 3–183.

suggest ascension, movement upward in space or, metaphorically, in station,[108] and that *xian* are not necessarily or strictly credited with immortality proper, though one essential and defining trait is that they live an extraordinarily long time. "Transcendent" has the benefit of suggesting upward movement, but to German speakers it has a Kantian ring that is utterly out of place. "Ascendant" would be the most literal and philologically accurate translation, and perhaps this usage will catch on in time. From this point forward in this work I use all of these renditions except "immortal," and often I leave *xian* untranslated.

I would now like to issue a few caveats on roads not taken here, pitfalls I prefer to avoid, and possible misunderstandings. The first and simplest is that my analysis confines itself to a specific historical period, effectively beginning around 220 B.C.E. and ending with or shortly after the death (or reputed transcendence) of Ge Hong in 343 C.E. What is said here of practitioners of *xian* arts and their clients may not apply to later periods. The Shangqing revelations beginning in 364, and the subsequent rise of Daoist monasteries, relativized the cosmological position of transcendents and changed the nature of many hagiographies.[109] Hagiographies were often thenceforth obtained by divine revelation, and what remaining pre-Tang, post-Yang Xi hagiographies we do have   notably the *Daoxue zhuan* 道學傳—bear the unmistakable marks of the new monastic environment. Not only did notions of *xian*-hood and the relative stature of *xian* in the successive cosmologies and theologies of rival movements—beginning already with the Shangqing revelations of 364–370—vary over time and by group, but we cannot assume, absent further research, that the patterns of social relation and action uncovered here persisted past the mid-fourth century. Furthermore, I am not here attempting anything like a history of *xian* lore, even during the period I focus on, but am rather concerned to highlight certain selected features of the topic that have been overlooked. So, while

---

108. An early source glosses 仙 as *qian* 遷 "to move (usually upward)"; this is the *Shi ming* 釋名, written ca. 200 C.E. by Liu Xi (see Roy Miller, "Shih ming") and cited in *DKW* 1:602a: 仙, 遷 也, 遷 入山也, "*Xian* is 'to move up,' to move up and enter the mountains." Edward Schafer had the following to say about the term *xian*: it "is a member of the word family which connotes such things as light-stepping, walking on air, going about in the clouds, carefree and buoyant. In mythology it was used of a class of beings also known as 'plumed persons' (*yuren*), represented pictorially in Han times with feathered arms. . . . In Daoism the condition of a *xian* is somewhat more etherealized, suggesting, beyond merely the magic power of flight, escape from passions, attachments, filth and illusions of the mortal condition. . . . They are not 'immortal' however, and must constantly renew their vital powers" (*Mirages on the Sea of Time*, 21). This is all well taken, except that Schafer tended to view *xian* through the lens of Shangqing texts and imagery; *xian* before Shangqing are not quite the same as *xian* portrayed in the Shangqing corpus.

109. See Robinet, *La revelation du Shangqing dans l'histoire du taoïsme*; Strickmann, "The Mao Shan Revelations"; and Bokenkamp, *Early Daoist Scriptures*.

images of transcendents have remained a fixture in Chinese art and literature ever since the early Han, and records of persons deemed to have eluded death extend well into late imperial times,[110] my composite portrait of such seekers will leave off at about the year 350 C.E. It is largely synchronic, since the evidence does not allow for an adequate grasp of changes over time.

This caveat relates closely to a second. The matters discussed here have usually been identified by modern scholars as "Daoist" and thus lumped together with many other phenomena into a single, reified religion that develops organically over time. This general tendency in scholarship on religion is one that I have lamented elsewhere.[111] My reasons, briefly, are four. (1) I do not believe that lumping the multiple phenomena surrounding the quest for transcendence into a singular "Daoism" helps us understand those phenomena any better: it often serves other, quite distinct agendas.[112] (2) It is true that texts in the Celestial Master, Shangqing, and Lingbao corpuses co-opt some earlier *xian* figures and many methods of transcendence (just as texts in the *xian* tradition co-opt earlier figures and phenomena), but that does not oblige us to follow suit, and the co-optation does not justify a language of tradition holism in this case any more than we would be justified in calling "Buddhism" "Daoist" because Lingbao texts freely appropriate elements from Buddhist scriptures. (3) "Daoism" has often been portrayed as a religion that takes long life and immortality as its goal. This is both an incomplete portrayal of what it meant to be a *xian* (it was, as we will see, much more than just living long or "not dying") and an inaccurate portrayal of other phenomena conventionally labeled "Daoism." (4) It is true that some early medieval authors, including Wang Chong and Ge Hong, clearly associate *xian* practices and traditions with the term *dao* 道 (and not just in its generic sense of any "way" or "path"). That association, however, is not based on the sort of holistic usage of "Daoism" some modern scholars are prone

---

110. Even today one can reportedly find a few hermit practitioners on Chinese mountains who understand themselves to be on a quest for immortality. See Porter, *Road to Heaven*.

111. Campany, "On the Very Idea of Religions." See also Jonathan Smith, *Drudgery Divine*, 117–118 and passim.

112. I thus concur with Donald Harper: "Efforts to understand the development of ideas concerning macrobiotic hygiene and the *xian* cult are not well served by a too easy use of the label Daoist" (*Early Chinese Medical Literature*, 114 n.1). Harper has given us a very careful, exacting, chronologically sensitive sorting of views and attitudes toward self-cultivation and macrobiotic practice in the late Warring States and Han periods (*Early Chinese Medical Literature*, 112–118; compare also Harper, "Warring States Natural Philosophy and Occult Thought," and "Warring States, Qin, and Han Manuscripts Related to Natural Philosophy and the Occult"). In the wake of such a sensitive analysis, lumping all these phenomena together under an essentialized "Daoism" seems violent, and at least should be justified by an equally careful and sustained argument.

to, and Ge Hong at several points savagely criticizes both the *Daode jing* and the *Zhuangzi* and ridicules those in his day who cited them to justify their fashionable libertinism.[113]

A common tendency in writing about all manner of religious phenomena, in China and elsewhere, is the resort to what Peter Brown has termed a "two-tiered model" of religion—a model with a pedigree stretching back to David Hume and much earlier—in which, to quote Brown, "the views of the potentially enlightened few are thought of as being subject to continuous upward pressure from habitual ways of thinking current among 'the vulgar.' . . . 'Popular religion' is presented as in some ways a diminution, a misconception or a contamination of '*un*popular religion.' Whether it is presented, bluntly, as 'popular superstition' or categorized as 'lower forms of belief,' it is assumed that 'popular religion' exhibits modes of thinking and worshiping that are best intelligible in terms of a failure to be something else"[114] and that are, furthermore, assumed to be the same at all times and places. There is, then, a triple assumption in the model. First, there is the social location of "popular" religion—it is located in the lower classes; the "popular" indicates "of the (lower) people," not "socially very widespread."[115] Second, there is an assumption about the *sort* of religion that one is likely to find there—it is "vulgar," whatever this may mean for one or another author, but whatever it means, it is not pretty.[116] And finally there is an assumption that it is unchanging and universal. This model has long ago been injected into the modern scholarly discourse on the quest for

---

113. *NP* 8:151 is one such passage. For further discussion, see Campany, "Two Religious Thinkers of the Early Eastern Jin."

114. *The Cult of the Saints*, 17, 19. The model dates to ancient times, in fact; see Dale Martin, *Inventing Superstition.*

115. There is, however, some confusion on this point in works wielding the language of "popular religion," including Poo, *In Search of Personal Welfare.*

116. Sir James George Frazer, to cite one of many authors who could be mentioned here, had little doubt: "When we survey the existing races of mankind . . . we observe that they are distinguished one from the other by a great variety of religions. . . . Yet when we have penetrated through these differences, which affect mainly the intelligent and thoughtful part of the community, we shall find underlying them all a solid stratum of intellectual agreement among the dull, the weak, the ignorant, and the superstitious, who constitute, unfortunately, the vast majority of mankind. One of the great achievements of the nineteenth century was to run shafts down into this low mental stratum in many parts of the world, and thus to discover its substantial identity everywhere. It is beneath our feet—and not very far beneath them—here in Europe at the present day. . . ." (*The Golden Bough,* 64). Those who employ the notion of "popular religion" often either unconsciously *assume* that it will be a certain *type* of religion or else explicitly attempt to demonstrate this as a necessary correlation. See, for instance, the recent reassessment of Max Weber's use of this term in Berlinerblau, "Max Weber's Useful Ambiguities and the Problem of Defining 'Popular Religion,'" esp. 611.

transcendence, with the "literati" supposedly rejecting the possibility of *xian*-hood at first, so long as it retained "deep roots in popular thought."[117] Not only does a small mountain of empirical evidence now disprove the elite's supposed disinterest in *xian,* even in early times, but the tacit model of religiosity at work here makes empirical evidence seem beside the point.

I will present evidence to show that there was keen interest in *xian* at all levels of society, and perhaps most of all among the official classes, concerning whom we also happen to have the most evidence (as is usually the case for ancient societies). Many surviving stories of successful *xian* mention someone from the official classes as among their clientele; some of our earliest narratives of *xian*-seekers show them at court discoursing with interested rulers; the Queen Mother of the West (Xi Wangmu 西王母), divine bestower of elixirs and methods of transcendence from her western palace atop Mount Kunlun, found a place in the Han imperial pantheon and cultic system before the reforms of 31 B.C.E. On the other hand, a mass movement centered on the worship and invocation of the Queen Mother— a movement that, judging from the clearly disdainful outsiders' depictions preserved in three places in the *History of the Han,* must have mobilized large numbers of people from all social levels—is recorded as having occurred in 3 B.C.E. That work related that the Queen Mother had promised deathlessness to any among the "hundred surnames" who wore her talisman.[118] The sources used here were all of them written by literate men for literate audiences; even visual images of transcendents tend to be found in the tombs of official-class persons.[119] The social scope of the phenomena I will describe was very broad, stretching to most regions of China, but how deep these phenomena were—whether large masses of illiterate or only marginally literate persons actively participated—remains an open question, since the representations on which we might decide it emanate from official-class writers. At most we can say two things with confidence: many official-class people were keenly interested in the methods and practitioners of transcendence, but any ascription of the quest for and interest in transcendence to

---

117. Yu Ying-shih, "Life and Immortality in the Mind of Han China," 109–110. Yu later softens this dichotomous statement (114).

118. *Han shu* 11:342, 26:1312, and 27C:1476; for discussion and translation of these passages (each of these translations has its problems), see Loewe, *Ways to Paradise,* 98–100; Wu, *The Wu Liang Shrine,* 128–129 and 359 n.48; and Cahill, *Transcendence and Divine Passion,* 21–22. Cahill translates only one passage but gives the best discussion of the rhetoricity of all three passages—that is, what else this phenomenon was juxtaposed with, and how it was interpreted, at the three points in question in the *Han shu.*

119. Since, however, the less sturdily constructed tombs of nonelite families are not recoverable archeologically, this statement is less significant than it may seem.

primarily "elite" or "popular" segments of the populace finds little support in the evidence.[120]

Another—and closely related—common tendency in writing about religion is to characterize religious goals, aspirations, or pursuits as "otherworldly," in contrast to the "worldliness" of everyday life and ordinary concerns. Here again there lies an implicit model, once more of ancient pedigree, specifying that whatever is religious must fix its sights on noble, celestial matters "not of this world," and that to direct religious labor or attention to such "base" concerns as health, longevity, love, or success in a competitive society is either to practice a debased form of religion or else to slip over into a lesser category of activity altogether, that of "magic."[121] This model, too, has been injected into the scholarly discourse on the quest for transcendence.[122] It is simply too blunt a tool to be of any analytical use, and its implicit valorization of one kind of religious aspiration and denigration of another—a tendency partly rooted in the sixteenth-century Reformation polemic in Europe—is sufficient grounds for setting it aside. Almost all religious activities portray (or at least imply and invoke) an ideal beyond the here-and-now while they simultaneously operate squarely in this world among the people who make, use, and perform them. This is a remarkable human phenomenon, but it is not one that the "this-worldly/other-worldly" dichotomy helps us understand.

---

120. Compare the finding of William Christian, Jr., concerning religion in sixteenth-century Spain: "I do not think devotion per se was a matter of wealth or social class" (*Local Religion in Sixteenth-Century Spain*, 147).

121. The tendency, in fact, to *define* "religion" (that is, "proper" religion) in contrast to its "worldly" other, "magic" or "superstition," is also ancient, and has been a fixture of modern writing on religion; see most recently Styers, *Making Magic*; and Dale Martin, *Inventing Superstition*.

122. Yu Ying-shih's important article, "Life and Immortality in the Mind of Han China," is structured around a worldly/otherworldly distinction that simply does not fit the evidence. Yu sees the quest for immortality as having started out as being "otherworldly" (in the sense that practitioners performed ascetic regimens in mountains, and in the sense that the goal was celestial ascension) and as having become increasingly "worldly" due in part to the interest of emperors in it, and in part to the increasing value placed on filiality and family in the Han. (He makes no mention whatever of "worldliness" in the sense of engagement with others in society.) More recently, Kohn presents *fangshi* and their quest as "otherworldly" and the realm of transcendents as "outside and beyond the known world" (*Early Chinese Mysticism*, 85).

CHAPTER 2

The Transcendent's Cultural Repertoire

AT THE MOST basic level, how ought we to think about the ways in which individuals relate to their cultures, traditions, or religions? In the study of religion, a Western discipline devoted to a concept rooted in the histories of Western societies, the relation between individuals and religions is most often framed in two ways, cognitive and social: a person (ideally at least) "believes in" (the cognitive aspect) the core claims of the religion to which he "belongs" (the social aspect).[1] This model of religious participation, usually taken for granted as universally applicable, works well in—because it arose in—contexts where religions are highly institutionalized, sharply distinguished from one another institutionally, and insist on exclusive affiliation, and where the ritualized, public affirmation of lists of beliefs is a key marker of religious identity. As it happens, none of these core features describes the social or religious contexts of the quest for transcendence in late classical and early medieval China.[2] A model that is less fixated on the inner cognitive states of individuals and less committed to viewing religions as container-like entities in which individuals (and texts, practices, ideas, and so forth) must "belong" would fit the medieval Chinese context, and surely many others, much better.

---

1. Religions are further often metaphorically imagined as *containers* (of affiliated people, ideas, texts, etc.), and so the default assumption is that an individual "belongs to" one or another of them exclusively. For further discussion, see Campany, "On the Very Idea of Religions."

2. With the possible exception of the earliest stages of the Celestial Master religion, with its spatially and liturgically organized communities, its lists of precepts, and its insistence that its members follow its guidelines exclusively and shun religious practices from which the organization's leaders sought to distance their movement. This movement's shapers appropriated elements of the quest for transcendence, but it was a fundamentally different *kind* of phenomenon, doctrinally, ritually, and socially.

I want to begin by imagining adepts seeking transcendence as assuming a certain particular religious, cultural, and social *role*, and by imagining the ultimate goal of adepts—*xian*-hood—as itself a sort of religious role or type. Since the transition from transcendence-seeker to transcendent was, in most respects, gradual, with many features of the one role shared by the other, I will, for the most part, treat them as a single type for purposes of analysis. To sketch out the role requires inferring from surviving evidence the practices and claimed abilities, the gestures and habits, and the patterns of narrative representation that constituted *xian* and aspirants to this status as a socioreligious type. By reference to what identifying traits did people recognize that they were dealing with a transcendence-seeker (or transcendent) as opposed to some other type of figure? In other words, what did people expect *xian* and aspirants to *xian*-hood to be like? As I will show, the list of expected traits extends far beyond the one we tend to regard as definitive: extraordinary longevity or deathlessness. Long life, while a necessary condition for qualifying as a successful transcendent, was only one (albeit key) part of a much larger array of features.

Two main concepts structure this analysis. The first is the notion that cultures (and, we might add, religions), when viewed from the aspect of how individuals relate to them, function as *repertoires* of resources, and that a socioreligious role, for example, may therefore be helpfully imagined as a repertoire of features. The second structuring concept is the *contrastive nature* of this repertoire.

Ann Swidler has recently shown in considerable empirical detail that people relate to their culture as if it were a toolkit or a repertoire of resources. They use items from it selectively as they make decisions and justify choices.[3] What is comprised in any given repertoire? How and in what circumstances is any given piece of it performed, on what occasions and by what agents?[4] Swidler finds that cultural repertoires are organized around certain concrete "scenes or situations of action,"[5] often narrative in nature, and that people avail themselves of multiple scenes as they negotiate their lives, even when these scenes carry contradictory implications, because each scene is especially good for talking about one particular aspect of things, and no one scene suffices for all aspects of life. Cultural repertoires are not accessible to everyone in the same degree, and people use different amounts of culture even when they have equal access to it; people use culture more in situations

---

3. *Talk of Love.* The toolkit metaphor for culture was developed by Jerome Bruner (see *Actual Minds, Possible Worlds* and "The Narrative Construction of Reality"), but Swidler richly fleshes out how this metaphor reflects people's actual behavior.

4. These ideas are introduced in Swidler, *Talk of Love,* 24 ff.

5. Ibid., 34.

of flux or novelty, when their lives are uncertain.[6] A repertoire may contain different, contradictory models of certain aspects of life because these models answer
different sets of questions; people resort to these models in their discourse about
meanings and values even when they reject certain implications of each model as
implausible, because each describes something about the real constraints of life and
institutions, or rather (more correctly) about the lines of action individuals pursue
in the context of those constraints and institutions.[7] All of this runs contrary to the
Geertzian emphasis on culture as an all-encompassing ethos and on religions as
"cultural systems"; Swidler shows us agents using culture's repertoire in complex,
changing ways on different occasions, even invoking contradictory repertoire elements in mid-discourse.[8] It also runs counter to the tendency to think of religions
as totally enveloping "conceptual systems" (Émile Durkheim), "systems of symbols" (Clifford Geertz), or "theoretical schemes" (Robin Horton), outside of which
"members" of these purported entities cannot think.[9]

We can helpfully think of the various elements of the quest for transcendence
and the role of the transcendent as constituting a repertoire of resources available
for use in early medieval China. We can also picture the entirety of early medieval
Chinese culture as a macro-repertoire of resources and roles, of which the lore
and role of *xian*-hood was one. The transcendent's repertoire was not the resource
of practitioners alone. Members of the practitioners' public—their audiences of
other practitioners, semipractitioners, and nonpractitioners—responded to them in
terms of the same repertoire, judging them against its standards and expectations
and finding their own roles to play in relation to practitioners. The repertoire was
thus a kind of public space, an array of commonly available images, patterns, and
expectations.

Most elements of that repertoire simultaneously functioned in two basic ways.
The choice of a practice or behavioral norm—especially when prescribed by a
scripture, sanctioned by a tradition, or regularly attributed to a type of holy person,
and not simply the circumstantial preference of an individual—may perform two
basic kinds of function. Functions that I will call *intrinsic* concern rationales for
practices or norms that explicitly explain and justify the practices in terms of their
benefits, properties, and functions or in terms of their authoritative origins (such as

---

6. See especially ibid., pp. 52 ff. and 99 ff.

7. See especially ibid., pp. 132–133.

8. See especially ibid., p. 79. Compare the post-Geertzian formulations of Hymes, *Way and
Byway,* 5–12. Hymes, too, adopts the metaphor of repertoire.

9. A tendency helpfully analyzed and criticized by Godlove, "In What Sense are Religions
Conceptual Frameworks?"

having been divinely revealed). Often such explanation directly links the practice or norm to a larger theory, set of beliefs, cosmology, or cosmogony; but even if the explanation is as simple as "We do X because X makes us live long," without the addition of "and it does so for reason Y," we have to deal with an intrinsic purpose or function of X. *Extrinsic* meanings or functions pertain when practices or norms have the effect (whether by intention or not) of associating practitioners with certain values in a culture and dissociating them from others. Here, regimes of practices are a way of making statements about a wide range of other matters (and often other groups of practitioners), whatever intrinsic benefits might be claimed for them. If A is important in a culture in certain specific ways, and a group makes a point of shunning A, something is being said by the group to the culture, something that may have little to do with the intrinsic properties attributed to A; the shunning of A may be, instead (or additionally), a way of saying something else, perhaps much larger in scope. Extrinsic meanings are inherently associative or contrastive, even if only implicitly so: "We do X, which is not Y, which those others do" (contrastive) or "We do X, which is what beings of class Z, too, do" (associative). While intrinsic meanings are rarely socially neutral, they may or may not claim a hierarchy of practitioners; extrinsic ones almost always do: "We who do X are thereby hierarchically superior in some respect to those who do Y."[10]

The notion that extrinsic meanings are distinct from intrinsic ones and are worth attending to springs from several sources. One is the so-called new historicism, which works to situate texts in dense connection to their surrounding social, intellectual, religious, and textual worlds rather than viewing them as self-enclosed, spontaneous, contextless products of individual genius.[11] Another is the work of Bruce Lincoln on myths as ideology in narrative form, as well as the work of certain scholars (such as Barbara Herrnstein Smith and Natalie Zemon Davis)

---

10. Extrinsic functions, when successfully impacting an audience, may be viewed as a type of perlocutionary force; see Austin, *How to Do Things with Words;* and Searle, *Speech Acts.* Another analogue of what I am envisioning in an account of meanings that includes externalist ones is what Gilbert Ryle meant by "thick description," a notion famously appropriated by Clifford Geertz (Ryle, "'Thinking and Reflecting'" and "'The Thinking of Thoughts'"; Geertz, *The Interpretation of Cultures,* chap. 1; see also Gallagher and Greenblatt, *Practicing New Historicism,* 20–31): an account of the context, setting, circumstances, intentions, expectations, purposes, and rules—the surprisingly rich array of factors lying around and beyond actions and statements themselves—that give actions and statements their meaning. Yet another is Foucault's notion of discourse; what I am attempting here, to use his terms, is an archeology of certain statements from the "archive" of China in the period ca. 320 B.C.E.–320 C.E. regarding the behaviors, traits, and capacities of "transcendents," treating each of them as a "discursive formation" deployed within a *common discourse;* see in particular Foucault, *The Archaeology of Knowledge,* 116–117, 126–131, and 138–140.

11. See, for example, Gallagher and Greenblatt, *Practicing New Historicism,* 1–19.

who read narratives as social transactions among interested parties rather than as contextless structures.[12] Yet from structuralism itself I also draw the fundamental insight that the meanings of signs are not intrinsic but are functions of their places in structures of relations to others. Also helpful are some recent attempts to rethink the Geertzian model of culture;[13] particularly useful among these has been Swidler's picture of cultures as messily coexisting repertoires.[14] And a source of inspiration specific to the study of China is the work of Michael Puett.[15] Puett's key insight is that intellectual choices made in a text take on new significance when viewed, not in isolation or according to the internal dynamics of one or another tradition, but as alternatives to contemporary competing ideas; they are not simply assertions made in a vacuum, or reports of positions arrived at haphazardly, neutrally, or solely as the result of discussions internal to the author's own group, but rather are arguments against opposed positions. If we know, for example, that adepts often repaired to mountains, what would this pattern of behavior have meant in the culture at the time? In addition to whatever intrinsic reasons for mountain-dwelling may have been supplied in scriptures and other texts—that mountains were the abodes of some who had already achieved *xian*-hood, that sacred herbs and minerals were to be found there, that mountains harbored portals to divine realms, that retreating there enabled the solitude necessary for esoteric practices—what extrinsic functions may also have been in play? What were mountains and their inhabitants associated with or contrasted to? These are the sorts of questions I will explore.

The view of cultures, societies, and religious traditions on which I am building this analysis sees them as the contestational fields[16] upon which agents assert claims and attempt to persuade others to their points of view. Ideas, traditions, and bundles of practices and disciplines are not imagined as "evolving" or "chang[ing] glacially over time as the result of impersonal processes"[17] or solely according to their own internal, neutral logic. Nor are they understood as simply belonging to large, collective things like "mythology," "popular religion," or "Daoism" that develop, Hegelian-style, as if they had some sort of life of their own and essentially invent

---

12. Lincoln, *Theorizing Myth;* Barbara Herrnstein Smith, "Narrative Versions, Narrative Theories"; Natalie Davis, *Fiction in the Archives.*

13. See, for example, Ortner, "Thick Resistance."

14. Swidler, *Talk of Love;* compare Bruner, "The Narrative Construction of Reality," 2–3.

15. "Nature and Artifice"; "Sages, Ministers, and Rebels"; *The Ambivalence of Creation; To Become a God.*

16. Foucault, *The Archaeology of Knowledge,* 126; Bourdieu, *Language and Symbolic Power,* 14–17.

17. Lincoln, *Theorizing Myth,* 18.

themselves.[18] Instead they are seen as things made by particular historical agents (even if those agents' identities are now lost to us), claims advanced against alternative positions and with significant stakes involved; they are "the sites of pointed and highly consequential semantic skirmishes fought between rival regimes of truth" and of prestige.[19] A self-cultivational discipline is, among other things, a tactical deployment of taxonomies, and the contrast it sets up between higher and lower practices is "not an idle play of categories but a social and political intervention."[20]

If to seek transcendence was to inhabit a role, each of the many features in the repertoire by which that role was defined had both intrinsic rationales and extrinsic functions, and the latter were at least as critical as the former. This role, like any other, was defined by association, contrast, and opposition to others. A complete picture of what it meant to be (or aspire to be) a *xian* emerges, therefore, only when we consider the full range of other types of figures that transcendents *were not* as well as those that they *resembled in certain respects,* each of these other types having its own always-in-formation repertoire of features, discoverable in the same genres of evidence. Transcendence and the quest for it, in other words, were differentiated from other goals, and were positioned vis-à-vis other roles, by virtue of a series of oppositions and associations, and this accounts for a lot of how they were what they were. Again we may frame things as a question: When transcendents or transcendents-to-be acted (or were represented as acting) in fashion X or as having property Y, who or what were they behaving (or being) like, unlike, or superior to, and what difference did these likenesses or differences make to them and others? To understand the pursuit of transcendence, it is not enough to consider the intrinsic justifications for adepts' austerities; we must also have some grasp of what transcendence was an alternative to.[21]

---

18. See Campany, "On the Very Idea of Religions." Even Hegel, however, with his notion of dialectic, recognized the interlocutive nature of historical action and change in a way that those who would conjure such entities fail to do. Foucault's "discourse" is admittedly impersonal and raises questions of agency, but at least it is historically specific. To use his terms, one axiom of this discussion is that the much-vaunted "traditions" of late classical and early medieval China, the "Daoism" and "Confucianism" and "popular religion" of the textbooks, can be seen not as distinct discourses but as participating in larger common discourses; thus, texts often reckoned (problematically, in my view) as "belonging to" one or another of these "isms" can be seen also (or instead) as operating strategically, intertextually, and interpractically (to coin an awkward parallel term) within the same discourse, and when we view them thus we discover unexpected dimensions of their power and meaning.

19. Lincoln, *Theorizing Myth,* 18.

20. Ibid., 118.

21. My suggestion is not, of course, that the specific elements of the repertoire of the transcendent-to-be had no intrinsic meanings or functions, but that adepts' practices, achievements, and the traits attributed to and claimed by them also had extrinsic meanings or functions. Whether

The following schema of features lists the practices, properties, and abilities with which adepts in quest of transcendence were credited in late classical and early medieval lore; it summarizes a large body of collective representations. Of course, some authors are on record during this period as denying that adepts possessed these abilities, so this list hardly represents a society-wide consensus; however, even writers who were skeptical of certain adepts' claims to long life did grant that they might possess some other of the mantic abilities listed below, and, more importantly, they would have agreed that these traits were the ones commonly attributed to adepts even though they disagreed that one or another particular adept deserved this attribution.[22] I arrived at this list by sifting through the several hundred relevant, discrete, extant narratives—found in histories, hagiographies, biographies, accounts of anomalies, essays, and inscriptions—as well as visual representations, noting recurrent patterns of representation, and organizing these patterns into a few simple groups.[23] No part of the repertoire is detectable as such merely from one or a handful of instances; a whole body of lore must be surveyed in order for the repertoire's lineaments to emerge clearly. The recurrence of patterns is an index of the importance of particular features in the collective lore concerning transcendents; features unique to one or two figures are, for present purposes, insignificant—except insofar as they indicate attempts by writers to differentiate a particular figure from the larger mass of adepts.

This separation of a particular figure from others of the group is a phenomenon I call secondary differentiation. Once a repertoire is established, we often find adepts presented as exceptional vis-à-vis other adepts by virtue of violating norms and thus (often) acting more like ordinary people in society (for example, transcendence-quest adepts who "consume grains" and drink heavily or who dwell in ordinary society with their families). When seekers of transcendence become known for avoiding grains, one way of differentiating a particular adept or *xian* is to attribute to him the consumption of grains. In a field of religious aspiration such as this one, with many possible routes toward the goal, there were ample opportunities for such secondary differentiation of holy persons.

It is not the case that every adept treated in this study has all or even many of the features in the repertoire. But each has enough of them to be recognizable,

---

intended or not, this repertoire and role were implicitly contrasted or associated with others. Almost every element of the repertoire has an inward- and an outward-facing function and meaning, though they are sometimes hard to discern, either because we lack a surviving (inward) rationale for them or because the record does not allow us to spot the specific (outward) "other" with whom the element contrasts.

22. Or even that *any* individuals deserved it. Even those who argued that *xian*-hood was impossible agreed that these traits were the ones attributed to *xian*.

23. What I prepared is actually a rough motif-index.

albeit there are some borderline instances. We may imagine two rings of features: the inner ring consists of the very small number of features necessary for an adept to be deemed a transcendent, whatever his or her other properties. Initially we may consider this inner ring as having two requisite features: (1) the adept lives an extraordinarily long time, and (2) he or she does so by virtue of some ascetic technique, not because of an unusually long pre-allotted lifespan (or *ming* 命).[24] The outer ring consists of a great many ancillary features, many of which do not seem at all necessary to achieve long life but are by-products of ascetic disciplines. Many of them, though they have little or no discernible intrinsic function, associate or contrast transcendents with other sorts of beings.[25] This is not to deny that some adepts deemed *xian* were also appropriated, co-opted, and reclassified by authors (and others) with other agendas, for whom the adept's longevity or possession of longevity-enhancing arts was not a factor: figures deemed transcendents in some texts, for example, were elsewhere ranked among noted recluses, or as wonder-working masters of esoterica whose longevity was not featured. Nor were some of this repertoire's features attributed *only* to transcendence-seeking adepts.

It is usually impossible to detect in surviving historical sources the absolute points of origin of cultural and religious repertoires, since by the time there is any substantial record, they are already established to some degree. Once created, repertoires are always in the process of being changed, but they would not be repertoires if they were not somewhat stable, which is in part to say, collectively shared. In order for the behaviors and traits of a religious adept to be recognizable as those of a particular *type* of adept—as those of a person inhabiting a particular, known role—the behaviors and traits had to have already become standardized to some degree; otherwise they would constitute not a clearly recognizable signal but merely random noise.[26] On the one hand, then, adepts in quest of transcendence, like other types of ideological and religious achievers in late classical and early medieval China (the recluse, the master of esoterica or *fangshi,* the eminent monk), were credited with many sorts of feats and behaviors that were extraordinary from an implied everyday perspective. On the other hand, to read the texts is to see that their extraordinariness was quickly channeled into a limited set of patterns: adepts

---

24. Only very rarely do we find the exception that proves this rule; in Ge Hong's writings, for example, the figure of Shen Xi represents the possibility of a lesser sort of *xian*-hood by divine gift in recognition of merit (see *TL,* 255–258).

25. This outer ring of features constitutes a classic case of Wittgenstein's notion of family resemblance: there is no one feature among them that all adepts share, but each adept exhibits enough of them to be recognized as a transcendence-quest adept and not some other type.

26. Marshall Sahlins' comment on "interchanges between the collective and the personal" is apposite here: "Not just any old story will do. It has to be a good story, structurally speaking" (*Apologies to Thucydides,* 172).

were strange with respect to ordinary nonpractitioners, but they were all strange in more or less the same ways. We have to deal with the creation of a set of features or traits that, initially shocking or surprising—thus separating the role from the ordinary run of human beings—came to form the expected set of tropes and traits by which adepts will be recognized as such. Eventually there was established a repertoire of behaviors and properties that was always in formation and always subject to change. The familiarity and typicality of these patterns of action and narrative, rather than making for bad literature, were elements of their effectiveness in cultural and religious claim-staking and role-defining.[27]

The Transcendent's Repertoire

ESOTERIC PRACTICES

Transcendence-seekers were known, above all, for practicing certain classes of ascetic methods, most of which shared two basic features: they were claimed to lengthen lifespan, and their details were not widely known since they were (allegedly at least) transmitted secretly from master to disciple. Common types of practice included dietary restrictions (most notably "avoiding grains") and the supplementation of the culturally ordinary diet with herbal or mineral substances not normally considered food; the intake, refinement, and circulation of *qi* 氣 in the body through breathing exercises; meditation and visualization; sexual disciplines; elaborate alchemical procedures; and various practices in the bureaucratic idiom, including the use of talismans (*fu* 符) to communicate with spirits and a type of administrative ruse known as "escape by means of a simulated corpse" (*shijie* 尸解). Insofar as the details of these practices were secret, endowed (at least for many) with considerable mystique and prestige and supposed to bestow impressive new powers and status on their wielders, anyone credited with their use was rendered

Superior to: ordinary persons

On the other hand, possession of esoteric arts of many kinds, including arts of longevity, was a property that overlapped with the repertoire of the masters of esoterica *(fangshi)* more generally, so the attribution of such arts also placed transcendence-seekers

On a par with: masters of esoterica

THE PRACTITIONER'S ASCETICALLY ENHANCED BODY

As a result of their self-cultivational regimens, adepts are repeatedly represented as being able to demonstrate the following physical capacities, among others:

---

27. On the functions of stereotypes in narratives, see Ebersole, *Captured by Texts,* 11–12, 100–101.

Achieve temporary invisibility, self-concealment
Penetrate surfaces and walls
Remain underwater for long periods
Radiate or emit light
Transform into other shapes
Remain impervious to extreme heat and cold
Easily resist physical attack

Some of these features have intrinsic rationales and functions. We know of talismans, for example, that worked to summon spirit-troops to guard adepts from attack. Techniques of "fetal breathing" 胎息, wherein the adept sealed off body passages and recirculated *qi* within himself rather than breathing normally, may be cited to explain the capacity for remaining underwater. The ability to pass through surfaces may be rooted in an early ideology of bodilessness, found in certain strands of texts, wherein the physical form wastes away and the adept becomes an increasingly spirit-like being. This notion was by no means shared among all texts advocating methods of transcendence.[28]

Extrinsically, these traits obviously separate adepts from ordinary persons who do not practice esoteric regimens. To put it less neutrally: these traits mark adepts as superior to ordinary persons. Less obviously to us, perhaps, these capacities, especially the abilities to become invisible, change shapes, and pass through surfaces, marked them as similar to a variety of potent, feared spirit-beings—gods, ghosts, and demons—on whom there is a large body of lore documenting these same abilities.[29]

We may summarize these associations and contrasts by saying that these traits mark transcendence-quest adepts as:

Superior to: ordinary persons
On a par with: gods, ghosts, demons

The most salient mark of transcendents, of course, was extreme longevity, combined with a disjunction between actual and apparent age:

Extreme longevity (hundreds, sometimes thousands of years)
Youthful appearance despite advanced age
Reversion from aged to youthful appearance

These properties, too, were not unique to transcendents; gods, nature spirits (such as the spirits of long-lived trees or animals), and demons are similarly represented.

---

28. For examples, see Campany, "The Meanings of Cuisines of Transcendence," and Puett, *To Become a God*, 201–224.

29. Many examples can be found in *SW*, 205–394. These features once again emerge most clearly when one sifts through a large body of narratives concerning such beings and compiles a motif-index—as I have done in the case of pre-Tang *zhiguai* literature.

On a par with: gods, spirits, demons
Superior to: ordinary persons
Not only in texts but also in visual scenes on the walls of excavated tombs, we find transcendents repeatedly represented with avian features. In narratives they are sometimes said to transform into birds or described as possessing bird-like features such as feathers and wings and the ability to fly; in visual scenes they are shown with wings or as hybrid beings with birds' bodies and human heads.

Body winged or feathered; transformation into bird forms (and the reverse)
This aspect of the lore of transcendents associated them with one specific class of animal, a class uniquely possessing the capacity for flight and thus metaphorically associated with access to the heavens and dissociated them from the ordinary run of humanity, whose fate was to descend into the earth at death and become subject to the underworld bureaus:

On a par with: birds
Superior to: ordinary persons
A recurrent story-type portrays some practitioners of transcendence arts as having the capacity to see and hear events as they transpire hundreds of miles away. In this they resemble the "sages" (*shengren* 聖人) of certain early texts, who were claimed to possess hyperacute senses as a mark of sagehood, as well as spirit-beings whose sensory capacities were not limited by spatial proximity.[30] Such stories, however, invariably portray transcendence-art practitioners as not simply aware of distant events but also able to change their outcomes from a distance, whether by dispatching unseen spirit-agents or by other means. Such practitioners were thus implicitly being claimed to be similar to sages but also superior to them:

On a par with: gods, ghosts
Superior to: sages and ordinary persons
Finally, transcendents' bodies were occasionally asserted to possess two unusual and identifying characteristics, signs by which an otherwise apparently ordinary person might be discerned to be, in fact, a transcendent walking the earth:

Square pupils
Unlike any other class of being
Body casts no shadow
On a par with ghosts and spirits
Superior to ordinary persons
And they were only very occasionally (but more than once) said to exhibit one other unusual cluster of features:

Gender transformation or extreme gender ambiguity
(On a par with demons and spirits; unlike ordinary persons)

---

30. See Csikszentmihalyi, *Material Virtue*, 161–200.

It is needless to elaborate here how indeterminacy of gender would have enabled an adept to cut across or exempt him- or herself from various hierarchies and complexes of customs fundamental to society at the time.

MASTERY OF SPACE, TIME, AND ELEMENTS

Other abilities credited to adepts involve control or transcendence of the elements and of the spatiotemporal limits to which ordinary mortals are subject:

Flying, levitation

Marvelously fast locomotion over great distances (including ability to enable others to do this)

Simultaneous multilocality ("body division")

Miniaturization (of self, objects, and terrain)

Arts of "illusion" and ability to transform things across taxonomic boundaries

Control of fire, rain, water currents, thunder, other weather phenomena

Ability to obtain fresh foods out of season

Prognostication

Resurrection (of others)

Most of these abilities are ancillary if not irrelevant to the quest for transcendence, but they are ubiquitous in narratives of adepts and make for colorful episodes. Although incidental to the adept's own pursuit of longevity, they served another function vital to his recognition as an adept by others: they enabled him to display his hard-won powers to audiences and, at times, to employ those powers on behalf of others.

Flying, marvelous locomotion, transformation of objects, prognostication, and resurrection were powers also commonly attributed to gods and demons. Prognostication was an ability often credited to "sages" such as Confucius.[31] We have, then, the following sets of associations and dissociations:

---

31. One unusual property that we see attributed to certain high gods and sages but that is *not* attributed to transcendents is appearance (in some cases followed by reappearance) in grand cycles of cosmic time. Mencius and other early writers claimed that sages appeared in the world according to a cosmic schedule; by the Eastern Han, Laozi was widely seen as a cosmic deity who periodically appeared in human history under different identities and names to correct humanity's course. For Ge Hong in the early fourth century C.E., at least, transcendents were to be understood as sharply differentiated from such beings. They might vanish and reappear to certain individuals or in certain areas, but they had a single lifetime rather than actually dying and then being reborn as other persons; they might appear to die but their death was only a staged event, and they were not subsequently reborn in different form, though they might take different names. One of Ge Hong's reasons for taking such care to make this point clear was his opposition to any view of transcendents that saw them as born, not made, and hence as so elevated in their cosmic station that transcendence became an impossible goal (see in particular his hagiography of Laozi, *TL,* 194–211).

On a par with: gods, demons, sages
Superior to: ordinary persons

EATING

Other than deathlessness, no bundle of practices and features is as characteristic of
the quest for transcendence as those regarding eating. Adepts were reputed to shun
the staples of the mainstream diet and subsist on alternate foodstuffs. Whatever the
specific practices used or claimed—and there were almost as many variations on
this theme as there were practitioners—this dedication to an alternate cuisine was
a hallmark of seekers of transcendence from the very earliest textual and visual
sources, including representations on tomb walls of transcendents holding stalks of
strange plants. The most ubiquitous practice of all was "avoiding grains"—a synecdoche for the avoidance of mainstream agricultural foods in general—and substi-
tuting various alternate substances and practices, along with a general lessening in
the quantity of substances ingested. There were no corpulent transcendents: texts
and images consistently show transcendents as slender, waif-like beings, and some
texts explicitly link transcendence with lightness of weight and deride excess flesh
as an impediment to celestial ascension. Some methods for appetite suppression are
discussed in scriptures and manuals, as are, of course, many dozens of distinct recipes
for elixirs or herbal preparations claimed to enhance the adept's biospiritual organism and prepare him or her for, or lead them into, transcendence.

We have, then, the following prominent features in the transcendent's repertoire:

"Avoidance of grains" (that is, avoidance of mainstream dietary staples)
Avoidance of meat and alcohol
Ingestion of medicinal herbs, fungi, minerals, rare substances, elixirs, "dew," and so forth
   as substitute diet
Subsistence on recycled saliva and qi
Lack of hunger or thirst (as effect of regimen)

In Chapter 3 I analyze in detail the many extrinsic functions of this set of features.

DWELLING

Practitioners of transcendence arts were enjoined in scriptures to avoid excessive
contact with ordinary persons, to retire from village life and from agricultural communities, and to dwell in solitude in the mountains. They are repeatedly portrayed in
stories as leaving home permanently or periodically to live in mountains (or in other
places sharing the properties of *elevation* and *isolation*) or as wandering from place to
place without fixed abode.[32] We thus find these features evidenced in the repertoire:

---

32. Although, as we will see in Chapters 6 and 7, the texts reveal a spectrum of possibilities
in practice, and adepts are by no means universally portrayed as socially isolated.

FIGURE 3. Brick from Nanyang, Henan province, late Western Han or Eastern Han. Winged transcendent bearing longevity-inducing herb, astride a tiger. *Source: Nanyang Handai huaxiang zhuan*, fig. 182.

FIGURE 4. Brick from Nanyang, Henan province, late Western Han or Eastern Han. Winged transcendents carrying stalks of longevity-inducing herbs. *Source: Nanyang Handai huaxiang zhuan*, fig. 171.

Dwells alone; "cuts off traces"
Dwells on a mountain
Dwells in a cave
Dwells in a tower
Dwells in a miniature space (for example, a gourd)
Wanders constantly; itinerant life; no fixed abode

There were, to be sure, intrinsic reasons for some of these features. The practice of secret arts demanded some degree of spatial and social removal from curious outsiders, and a breach of this boundary is said in some alchemical scriptures to introduce impurity that offends the gods attending the process. The very nature of many of the arts of transcendence—the avoidance of ordinary food, the careful control of sexual activity, the need to serve one's master, the requirement of secrecy—precluded many routines of normal life. And methods of "escape by means of a corpse substitute" required adepts to leave their homes and flee to the mountains so as to avoid detection by the death-register-keeping spirits who otherwise would come to summon them to the underworld.

But these same features functioned extrinsically in several ways. For several centuries the rise of settled agricultural communities had been seen as a key step in the progress of civilization, and increasingly formidable systems of bureaucratic census-taking and record-keeping had allowed states new degrees of control over their populations. People were kept track of by their names and ancestral places of residence. To withdraw from settled communities and stay on the move was, in an important way, both to renounce what passed for the civilization of the cultural center, returning to what was centrally portrayed as the barbaric periphery of nomadic tribal ways, and to slip outside the bonds of bureaucratic registration. Mountains were associated with recluses, with unregistered refugees and criminals, with lawless mountain gods and spirits, with wild animals, and with the rare herbs and minerals sought by adepts. To dissociate oneself from any fixed dwelling place was to resemble, in this respect, those higher deities—gods of heaven and earth, celestial beings of higher ranks—who were *translocal* in contrast to the lesser but more accessible spirits of particular places. In their habits of dwelling, then, adepts avoided bureaucracies both human and divine and established themselves as:

Unlike: ordinary citizens of states
On a par with: non-Chinese peoples, pre-civilizational ancients, recluses, refugees,
    mountain gods, spirits of the wild, alocal deities

The notion that adepts must leave home as a prerequisite of success in esoteric pursuits also set up another dissociation, one identified by opponents of the quest for transcendence as particularly troubling:

Superior to: members of families

Proponents of the goal of transcendence felt compelled to defend it against the charge that adepts were unfilial. This sticking point doubtless explains the well-developed secondary differentiation we find with regard to this bundle of repertoire features: some adepts are portrayed as completing their methods while at home; taking their families with them into the mountains and, at the end of their careers, into the heavens; transmitting secret methods of transcendence within their own families rather than to non-kin disciples; or alternating between home and the mountains, periodically returning home then leaving again. This secondary differentiation suggests a degree of accommodation on the part of practitioners to the cultural centrality of the family and the cult of ancestors.

MASTERY OF NONHUMAN OTHERS

Adepts are often shown consorting with, controlling, defeating in combat, or enlisting the aid of four classes of beings mostly feared by ordinary people: wild animals, the human dead, demons and spirits, and the gods of particular localities. Recurrent patterns in textual and visual representation allow us to identify the following features in the adept's repertoire:

> *Is impervious to attack by animals*
>
> *Commands and controls wild animals; uses them to deliver objects; understands their speech*
>
> *Controls the movements, and can affect the fate, of ghosts (that is, the ordinary human dead)*
>
> *Exterminates extortionist god or demon posing as god, eradicates cult*
>
> *Rectifies incorrect behavior of local god*
>
> *Declines to make requisite offerings when passing by temple, with no ill effect*
>
> *Perseveres when "tested" by mountain spirits; withstands attacks by demons*
>
> *Receives the respects of local gods and spirits when passing through*
>
> *Is conversant with gods and spirits of the unseen realm*
>
> *Deploys spirits who follow commands; is aided by spirits who guard and provide sustenance*
>
> *Exorcises demons or ghosts (usually as a means of healing the sick)*

There were, of course, intrinsic rationales for some of these traits. Demonic attack or possession, for example, was seen as one of the major causes of disease, and healing required methods for spirits' expulsion. Mantic modes of self-protection from mountain predators, both animal and spiritual, were seen as key accoutrements of the practitioner's toolkit. But extrinsic functions predominate here: in being endowed with these traits, transcendents and adepts were being declared:

Superior to: wild animals, the dead, demons, spirits, local gods

*On a par with or superior to: shamans or spirit-mediums (*wu 巫*)*[33]

The latter feature is highlighted in narratives in which a transcendence-quest adept encounters a shaman or spirit medium attached to a local temple and defeats him or her in a contest of mantic arts.

From the viewpoint of ordinary people—and viewpoint is crucial here—adepts, to the extent that they controlled and employed such beings as gods and spirits, came to be associated with them. They were deemed, that is, as *like* them in power, and yet in these stories they were also argued to be *superior* to them by virtue of their ability to control them. Spirits, ghosts, and local gods were beings normally venerated or feared (or both) by the populace; in these features of the repertoire, adepts were argued to be superior to them in power. Adepts are repeatedly portrayed as uniquely having the prerogative to command spirits and gods and to ignore their demands for sacrifice—demands that pressed ominously upon local communities of farmers and merchants but that the adept could afford to dismiss as the overweening impudence of lesser beings.[34]

FREEDOM FROM SOCIAL CONVENTION AND CONSTRAINT

Although adepts interacted with many other parties, they are also repeatedly depicted as ignoring custom; flaunting mores; shunning their default obligations as family members, community residents, and imperial subjects; and rejecting demands thrust upon them by those conventionally seen as their social superiors—rulers and officials. Specifically, we find the following behaviors repeatedly attributed to adepts:

Fails to marry

Avoids sexual intercourse

Takes multiple partners or successive spouses

Marries but fails to produce offspring

Leaves or ignores family (parents, spouse, and/or children)

Avoids social interactions; avoids speaking when addressed

---

33. This is not the place to enter into the long-standing (and often tedious) scholarly dispute over the meaning of this term. Suffice it to say here that *wu* is the designation applied, in early medieval hagiographies and anomaly accounts, to personnel attached to local temples who often spoke for the resident god and apparently managed temple affairs—a topic on which I plan to write. Whether these *wu* served as passive mouthpieces for the god (that is, as spirit mediums) or whether their own personalities remained intact while communicating with the god (in the manner of shamans) remains unclear, and this distinction is *not* prioritized in these sources.

34. Hagiographies are full of instances of this prerogative; for examples, see *TL*, 252–255 and 153. I return to this theme in Chapter 6.

Wears distinctive clothing, or less clothing than customary; sports unkempt hair;
  body covered with hair
Carries the insignia and travels with the accoutrements of a different, unseen
  administrative hierarchy
Interacts freely across family, gender, and status boundaries
Ignores etiquette; behaves with (apparent) rudeness at state functions, banquets
Refuses interviews with officials and rulers; refuses official appointments
Defies visibly, vocally, and dramatically the attempts of officials and rulers to control
Travels constantly; maintains no fixed abode

From an intrinsic perspective, texts have much to say about the insignia and secret protocols by which the adept wielded powers associated with the unseen administrative hierarchy of spirits—spells, talismans, inscribed swords, staffs, titles, and commands. But these protocols had extrinsic functions as well: adepts' use of imperial insignia and bureaucratic terminology made them resemble rulers and high officials, but adepts were also symbolically superior in that the beings they summoned, commanded, and directly petitioned were higher than those accessed by rulers and officials. Anna Seidel's seminal study of the roots of "Taoist sacraments" brilliantly demonstrates the numerous borrowings from the Han apocrypha. To use her language, "the Taoist religion" was created by the mimicking and piecing together of royal and imperial symbology into new configurations.[35] But three revisions now seem called for: (1) Seidel treats mostly of the Celestial Master tradition, whereas I would argue that the same points apply to the symbolic repertoire developed by practitioners of transcendence arts before and after that tradition arose in the late Eastern Han. (2) Seidel lumps distinct movements with distinct emphases together under a unitary "Taoist religion." (3) Seidel mostly misses the radical one-upmanship implicit in these various religious uses of imperial protocols and symbols. The hierarchy to which the adept appealed and to which he or she belonged, and the spiritual powers therefore wielded, were not simply borrowed from the imperial tradition, they *outranked* it.

Practitioners are repeatedly depicted, in texts both sympathetic and hostile to their claims, as refusing or ignoring the importunities of rulers and officials, occasionally going so far as to make a theatrically elaborate and humiliatingly complete mockery of their attempts at coercion. Adepts repeatedly claimed exemption from the rulers' sphere of command and asserted their right to deference from officials who wished to learn their secret arts, just as they claimed a higher cosmological status than the gods to whom rulers and their administrations were obliged to perform sacrifice. These repertoire features worked to dissociate adepts from a variety of social others:

---

35. Seidel, "Imperial Treasures and Taoist Sacraments."

Free from the constraints of: the family system, including the ancestor cult, "the rites,"
polite society in general, official culture in particular, deference to officials and rulers
most especially

On the other hand, these same features associate adepts with another important social role during the period, a role that was similarly marked by withdrawal from (and implied superiority to) all manner of normal social constraints and expectations, particularly those of official culture and political hierarchy:

On a par with: recluses[36]

ENDINGS

The endings of transcendents' careers as human adepts and their accession to transcendent status are portrayed in prescriptive texts, narratives, and visual scenes in a small number of conventional ways.

Evades the spirits who enforce pre-allotted lifespan (usually via "escape by means
of a simulated corpse")
"Departs," often to a noted mountain or to an unknown destination, or "departs
as a transcendent" (xianqu 仙去) without further specification
Ascends to become a celestial transcendent (tianxian 天仙)
Remains on earth but continues to roam as an earthbound transcendent
(dixian 地仙)

In the standard narrative pattern associated with the first "ending" repertoire feature, the adept announces he is ill or specifies the day on which he will depart; he "dies"; funeral rites are observed; later he is seen alive at a distant location; his coffin is found to be empty except for an object—a shoe, sword, staff, or talisman. In the third feature, the adept is witnessed rising up into the heavens on a celestial mount that has descended to bear him upwards. The fourth feature is another instance of secondary differentiation: earthbound transcendents, a type that seems to have been developed only after celestial transcendents began to be imaged in texts and tombs, are to their celestial counterparts as recluses are to human officials. They are often explicitly stated to have declined celestial transcendence because of the servile bureaucratic labors required of them on high and to prefer to remain on earth in humble but carefree circumstances.

Transcendence was not an abstract state and was not defined in terms of an escape from time or change. In early medieval China, dying was an event that set off a chain of specific social and ritual processes. Not dying, therefore, amounted to absenting oneself from those processes and from the larger systems that sustained them. Not dying meant, at a minimum: (1) opting out of the ancestor cult: if one

---

36. On the recluse as a social type, see Vervoorn, *Men of the Cliffs and Caves;* and Berkowitz, *Patterns of Disengagement.*

was not dead, one was not an ancestor and would not receive ancestral offerings;[37] (2) evading the horrific bureaucratic underworld, declaring oneself immune to its control; (3) becoming qualified to ascend to the heavens and take up a post in a celestial administration (whether one chose to do so or not)—in effect, becoming a sort of supergod, with a full array of divine powers and responsibilities but exempt from the need of most gods for sacrificial sustenance. A transcendent might, to be sure, be remembered by communities of the living in the same ways as the ordinary dead were remembered and might be treated by his own family as an ancestor; there are many instances of temples and shrines being established to transcendents and offerings presented in those sacred precincts, which amounted to treating a transcendent as a local or celestial deity. But, by virtue of the repertoire features we have seen, to be a transcendent was to be a distinct category of being: the *role* as such was unique, even if some who played that role were treated by others in ways that blurred this uniqueness.

Transcendents, then, were:

Superior to: the ordinary dead

Superior to: ancestors

Not subject to: the powerful bureaus of the underworld administration of the dead

This transcendence of death and escape from the fates awaiting all ordinary beings subject to death is, of course, the hallmark feature of the *xian*'s religious and cultural repertoire. But, as I hope to have shown, it was only the *xian*'s crowning glory. Many more traits were associated with his role than his final escape from the shackles of mortality.

The *Xian*-hood Seeker and the Wonder-Working Monk: A Digression

Beginning, so far as we know, in the fifth century, authors began collecting and recording stories about miraculous events in response to devotion to the Buddha, the bodhisattva Guanyin, the recitation of powerful sutras, and veneration of *stūpas*, images, and relics. The same bodies of tales included narrations of the wondrous exploits of Buddhist monks whose ascetic self-cultivation regimens had equipped them with mantic powers.[38] The texts preserving these tales fall outside the bounds of this study,

---

37. An ancestor might, however, receive offerings made to him in his status as a *xian*, thus blurring this distinction; the most salient example—but also a quite unusual one, at least so far—is the Fei Zhi stele, discussed in Chapter 8.

38. See *SW,* 321–334; Campany, "The Earliest Tales of the Bodhisattva Guanshiyin"; Campany, "The Real Presence"; Campany, "Buddhist Revelation and Taoist Translation in Early Medieval China"; and Campany, "Notes on the Devotional Uses and Symbolic Functions of Sutra Texts."

but I want to pause here to comment on the relationship between the role of wonder-working monk and that of the wonder-working adept seeking transcendence.

To anyone who charts the recurring patterns in the bodies of early medieval narratives surrounding these two types of figure, what must be most striking is the extreme degree of overlap, down to the level of detail.[39] Virtually every sort of feat attributed to adepts on the way toward transcendence was also attributed to one or more monks featured in collections such as Wang Yan's 王琰 *Signs from the Unseen Realm* (*Mingxiang ji* 冥祥記) or Huijiao's 惠皎 *Traditions of Eminent Monks* (*Gaoseng zhuan* 高僧傳). Clearly the fashioners of stories about wonder-working monks must have known and built upon the body of lore attached to their counterparts in the quest for transcendence. It is as if the corpus of stories of monks was carefully crafted to (among many other things) match transcendents feat for feat, marvel for marvel—as if story-fashioners were exercising care to assure that at least a small handful of monks would be on record as performing every last type of marvel that had previously been credited to transcendence-seekers. Put another way, it becomes evident that the role of wonder-working monk in China was prepared for by the much earlier construction of the repertoire of the transcendent-to-be. Much of the cultural, social, and narrative framework for the new role was already in place and was quite obviously borrowed by the fashioners of tales about monks.

This borrowing was so pervasive that even themes that might be thought distinctive to the quest for transcendence—such as the practitioner's extreme longevity (running to centuries or even millennia), avoidance of "grains" and of ordinary foods, and performance of escape by means of a simulated corpse—appear in narratives about monks as well. And what is striking about the borrowing of these features is that, to my knowledge, there was no intrinsic rationale for them in the prescriptive texts on which even the most self-denying monks were basing their ascetic regimens—no particular value placed on long life (and a strong negative value placed on attachment to one's own life), no early scriptural warrant for avoiding grains or foods entirely (even the extreme regimen known as *toutuo* 頭陀, a transliterative rendering of the Sanskrit *dhūta*, specifies that one is to eat once a day and eat only what is received by begging—but eat nonetheless!—and the Buddha had famously rejected extreme self-denial on his way to formulating the Middle Path), and certainly no method for *shijie*, nor any prescribed goal to which *shijie* could conceivably be conducive.[40]

---

39. For a comparison that has not much shaped my own, see Poo, "The Images of Immortals and Eminent Monks."

40. On *toutuo*, see Kieschnick, *The Eminent Monk*, 34–35; and Benn, *Burning for the Buddha*, 269 nn.62, 63.

This extraordinary degree of borrowing must have functioned extrinsically to associate the relatively unfamiliar type—the wonder-working monk—with the long familiar one of the transcendence-seeker. A few features in the monks' overall cultural repertoire, however, marked them as distinctive. A rather weak example is the emphasis in monks' hagiographies on celibacy—weak, because some seekers of transcendence were similarly said to have avoided sex or even the slightest contact with members of the opposite sex, despite others' inclusion of sexual arts of self-cultivation in their toolkit of methods. Two areas of stronger contrast are monks' production and veneration of relics (and other's veneration of their relics) and the practice, among a very small minority of monks, of self-immolation as a supreme act of devotion. Simply put, transcendents, in theory and in attribution, did not die, so—at least in the period before 350 C.E.—they could leave no bodily relics behind (although remnants of personal items were reportedly preserved and enshrined in otherwise empty tombs); and there was no warrant in the prescriptions for transcendence for adepts' sacrificing their lives and bodies as a devotional act. The statement we find in the section on "those who gave up their bodies" (*wang-shen* 亡身) in the *Traditions of Eminent Monks* hagiography of a self-immolating monk—"To save another person by dying is, in fact, to live on even in death"[41]—is simply inconceivable in an account of a transcendent.[42] Some transcendents and transcendents-to-be did work for the benefit of others, but they did not do so by dying themselves.[43]

Conclusion

What did transcendents transcend? The stock answer is death. But things are not so simple. A one-word answer leaves out of account the richness of what "death" meant, exactly, for Chinese people of the time, the sort of event it was imaginatively, metaphorically, ritually, and narratively constituted as being, involving much more than the mere cessation of life. It also fails to notice all the other things transcendents transcended—all the things they *were not* that made them what they alone *were*.

---

41. *Gaoseng zhuan* 404c: 以死濟人雖死猶生.

42. At least a transcendent in this period. It would not be surprising to find that the Buddhist value of self-sacrificing compassion was incorporated in later centuries into the repertoire of transcendents.

43. When comparing narrative motifs across these texts, it is significant to note, in a few cases, common behaviors with very different rationales. We find a Buddhist monk, for example, said to have cut off his consumption of food and eventually even of water—to this extent resembling a transcendence-seeker. But his reason for this behavior is his desire to avoid disturbing a bird's nest and harming the fragile young life inside it. See *Gaoseng zhuan,* "Wangshen" section, item 1.

More precisely, we might say that what it meant to be a transcendent was negotiated through complex strategies of differentiation and association. The role of transcendent was likened to certain other roles in certain specific respects and was distinguished from certain other roles in other respects, and this process of likening and distinguishing, worked out collectively by many hands over multiple generations of cultural work, created a cultural, social, and religious niche that was distinctive, enduring, and—to many at least—attractive. I have tried here to sketch the hologram-like array of vectors that together, and only together, constituted "transcendence" as a goal and role among others. Only by seeing transcendents in relation to these others can we fully see the significance of what they alone were.

CHAPTER 3

Deeper Repertoire Analysis
"Avoiding Grains"

BECAUSE THE EXTRINSIC functions of particular repertoire features can be complex and powerful, we may learn a great deal from deeper analysis of a single, important repertoire feature: the adept's claimed avoidance of "grains" (referred to by *duangu* 斷穀, "cutting off grains," and other terms). Such dietary regimens, whatever their details, directed the adept to minimize or entirely avoid eating things considered to be staple foods in the surrounding culture and to subsist on something else instead, something that, we might say, was precultural or natural, often pure *qi* (ingested in breathing exercises) or *qi* as available in certain rare herbal or mineral substances.

To appreciate the extrinsic meanings and power attached to the proclamation, "I do not eat grains," in early medieval China, we must first assess the significance and the range of meanings attached to grains in various texts and ideologies at the time. What roles did grains play in thought, myth, and ritual, such that renouncing them became a powerful thing to do? A sketch based on a few salient textual passages will suffice to show how deep the ramifications of a single feature in the repertoire of a type of holy person can go.[1]

Eating Grains and Cooking as Key Markers of Civilization

In the "Royal Regulations" chapter of the *Book of Rites* or *Liji* 禮記, which represents a Western Han or earlier viewpoint, we find the following discussion:

---

1. Each passage adduced was likely also circulated as a response to some opposed view, yet it is impossible here to do justice to each passage in its own argumentative setting. I treat these passages as articulating some of the baseline views and practices, from various ideological vantage points, to which cuisines of transcendence were crafted as alternatives.

The people of the five regions—those of the central kingdoms, the Rong, the Yi, [and so on]—each had their several natures, which they could not be made to alter. Those of the east were called Yi; they wore their hair unbound and tattooed their bodies, and some of them ate their food without cooking it. [The people of] the south were called Man; they tattooed their foreheads and had their feet turned in toward each other, and some among them ate their food without cooking it. [The people of] the west were called Rong; they wore their hair unbound and wore skins, and some of them did not eat grain. [The people of] the north were called Di; they wore feathers and furs and lived in caves, and some of them did not eat grain.

The discussion ends by noting how, in ancient times, people were redistributed into walled towns and fields, "so that there was no unoccupied land and there were no people left wandering."[2]

K.C. Chang astutely notes that, in this passage, not cooking and not eating grains are both markers of barbarism, but they are different markers. "One could eat grain but also eat raw meat or one could eat his meat cooked but eat no grain. Neither was fully Chinese. A Chinese by definition ate grain and cooked his meat"[3]— and, we might add, lived in a settled agricultural community. Unlike Chang, I read this passage as reflecting the views of its late Warring States or Han author-redactors, seeing it less as a Zhou ethnographic description than as ideology wrapped in the guise of description, and its message, hardly unique to this text, is that eating grains (the products of organized agriculture), cooking, and living in settled communities are among the traits that uniquely define human beings. Anything less counts as not fully human and should be modified by the instructive interventions of the paradigmatically human people whose norms fill the book's pages.

Many texts relevant to our inquiry take the form of what Bruce Lincoln has termed sitiogonies,[4] narratives on the nature and origin of food (from Greek *sitos* "food, bread, grain"—this term, like *gu* 穀 in Chinese, denotes both grain and grain-based staple foods in particular and, synecdochically, mainstream food in general, including the meat and wine that were the standard offerings in sacrifices to gods).[5] Consider, for example, the poem "Shengmin" 生民 in the *Book of Odes* (*Shijing*

---

2. *Liji zhengyi,* section "Wangzhi," 246–247, consulting Legge, *Li Ki,* 1:228–230.

3. "Ancient China," 42.

4. *Myth, Cosmos, and Society,* 65.

5. For evidence that "abstention from grains" meant the avoidance of normal food in general, and not simply of the five specific grains normally listed in the group (that is, two kinds of millet, hemp, rice, and beans, or, in a common alternate list, two kinds of millet, rice, wheat, and pulse), see *TL,* 23–24, 190. "Rice" (*fan* 飯) functions similarly in modern Chinese, just as "bread" sometimes does in English.

詩經), a text of Zhou origin (ca. 1000–600 B.C.E.). The poem opens by asking
how Jiang Yuan gave birth to "the people." After making an offering and praying
for a child, Jiang Yuan trod on the toeprint of Di 帝 (the sky god) and subsequently
gave painless birth to Hou Ji 后稷 or Lord Millet. For reasons unexplained, Hou Ji
was thrice abandoned, but oxen and sheep, woodcutters, and birds successively res-
cued him. After the birds' departure Hou Ji began to wail and crawl, and then, "so
as to receive food for his mouth," he planted beans, hemp, wheat, gourds, and millet,
and his crops flourished and fattened. With this produce he "created [or founded
or commenced] the sacrifices." Then comes a second question: "What are they, our
sacrifices?" The answer lists processes for the preparation of the grains and meats used,
then describes the divine response: "As soon as the fragrance rises, Di on high is very
pleased." The poem concludes by linking the textual present to this august past: "Lord
Millet founded the sacrifices, and without blemish or flaw they have been continued
till now."[6] Much could be said of this text, but I limit myself to two points.

First, the very origin and continued existence of the Zhou people are here
bound up with the invention of agriculture, and the invention of agriculture with
sacrifice. Agriculture and sacrifice have the same originator, Lord Millet (named for
what is both a chief agricultural product and a chief class of grains offered in sacrifice), and although he plants crops to feed himself, the first thing he does with the
produce is to found the sacrifices. Agriculture and sacrifice link the Zhou people to
Di in multiple ways, through repeated sacrificial ritual, through continuous sacred
history, and through divine/human descent (Di is Hou Ji's divine father, and Hou
Ji is the father of the Zhou people). Further, Hou Ji's human mother, Jiang Yuan,
gains procreative access to his divine father by means of sacrifice.

Second, the poem sets up a hierarchy of eaters and foods: the semidivine Hou
Ji and his human successors eat grains and vegetables (and, implicitly, meats) here
below on earth, via the mouth; the divine Di, above in the heavens, eats but the
rising fragrance of the cooked foods, via the nose:

	Lower position	Higher position
Eaters:	Hou Ji; people of Zhou	Di
Station:	earth	heaven
Foods eaten:	grains/vegetables and meats	fragrances
Organ of consumption:	mouth	nose

We find passages similar in this respect in later texts. In a seasonal schedule of
activities laid out in the *Guanzi* 管子, for example, during the autumn, "the son of

---

6. Consulting Waley, *The Book of Songs*, 241–243, in rendering *Shijing* 6:129–131; compare
Bodde, *Festivals in Classical China*, 247.

Heaven issues orders commanding the officer in charge of sacrifices to select suitable animals and birds from their pens and suitable offerings of early ripening grains to present for use in ancestral temples and the five household sacrifices. Ghosts and spirits will consume their *qi,* while gentlemen ingest their sapors."[7]

In the *Huainanzi* 淮南子 we find the following sitiogony:

> In ancient times people ate vegetation and drank from streams; they picked fruit from trees and ate the flesh of shellfish and insects. In those times there was much illness and suffering, as well as injury from poisons. Thereupon the Divine Farmer (Shennong 神農) for the first time taught the people to sow the five grains and diagnose the quality of soils—which were arid or wet, fertile or barren, highland or lowland. He tasted the flavors of the hundred plants and the sweetness and brackishness of streams and springs, causing the people to know which were to be avoided and which used. In the process he himself would suffer poisonings seventy times a day.[8]

Here Shennong leads society from a gathering to an agricultural stage. The narrative goes on to tell of how, subsequently, morality was first taught under Yao, how dwellings were first constructed under Shun so that people no longer had to live in caves, how Yu channeled the waters, and how Tang instituted regular hours of sleeping and waking and systems of caring for the dead, sick, and unfortunate. One argument implicit in this tale is that agriculture was a necessary condition for the flourishing of other, later aspects of civilization. A similar narrative, focusing on Yao, appears in the *Mencius.*[9]

A passage in the *Liji* portrays aspects of the origins of sacrificial rites for ancestors and gods. At first people lived in caves and nests. "[T]hey knew not yet the transforming power of fire, but ate the fruits of plants and trees, and the flesh of birds and beasts, drinking their blood, swallowing also the hair and feathers. They knew not yet the use of flax and silk, but clothed themselves with feathers and skins." Then came the use of fire, which allowed for the making of tools for advanced building arts and for specific cooking operations and the making of liquors. The

---

7. Text in Rickett, *Guanzi,* 126; my translation differs. Wang Chong's discussion of sacrifices in the *Lunheng* also attends to the idea that spirits might absorb them through smell and through the nose: see the passage in *Lunheng jiaoshi,* 4:1047–1055; and Forke, *Lun-hêng,* 1:509–515. The mention of "sapor," by emphasizing taste, emphasizes the mouth as the portal of ingestion.

8. *DZ* 1184, 26:1a–b, consulting Birrell, *Chinese Mythology,* 49. A similar account is found in Lu Jia's *Xinyu* 新語 and was perhaps a source for this *Huainanzi* text; see *Xinyu,* 1:1; and Puett, *The Ambivalence of Creation,* 153. On Shennong, see Graham, *Studies of Chinese Philosophy and Philosophical Literature,* 67–110.

9. 3A/4; Puett, *The Ambivalence of Creation,* 108–109.

burden of the passage is to argue that this development, along with textile work, made possible not only better living but also better care of the dead in ways that are perpetuated in rites performed down to the present; as the text puts it, "[The people] were thus able to nourish the living and send off the dead [properly], serving ghosts, spirits, and Di on high. In all these things we follow those beginnings."[10] Thanks to fire, cooking, and the fashioning of textiles, the dead may be properly housed in well-built tombs, clothed in fine garments, and fed with cooked foods and spirits—precisely what we find in excavated Han tombs.

In *Hanfeizi* 韓非子 we find the following sitiogony:

> In the earliest times . . . the people lived on fruit, berries, mussels, and clams— things that sometimes became so rank and fetid that they hurt people's stomachs, and many became sick. Then a sage appeared who created the boring of wood to produce fire so as to transform the rank and putrid foods. The people were so delighted by this that they made him ruler of the world and called him the Fire-Drill Man (Suiren 燧人).[11]

In chap. 16 of the *Zhuangzi* 莊子, perhaps datable to the third century B.C.E., Suiren is the first ruler mentioned in a series of what were usually taken to be civilizational advances but which are portrayed in the *Zhuangzi* as initiating an ever-farther departure from the natural Dao into systems of social constraint and culture (here criticized).[12] Similar in spirit is a passage found in the fourth-century C.E. *Uncollected Records* (*Shiyi ji* 拾遺記), which also features Suiren in this key role and also sees the use of fire as the beginnings of human descent into the balefulness of what passes for civilization.[13] Such counter-narratives—and others might be cited—agree that cooking and agriculture are key elements of the known social order and of ritual, and so, wishing to oppose this social order, the counter-narratives attack at those points.

Not all sitiogonic passages are sociomythic in character; a few are situated within five-phases, *qi*-based systematic cosmologies and cosmogonies, and here it is the exalted *qi* pedigree of grains, rather than their descent from the ministrations of an ancient culture hero, that is emphasized. Consider the opening passage of the "Inner Training" ("Neiye" 內業) chapter of the *Guanzi* (assembled ca. 26 B.C.E. from earlier materials[14]):

---

10. *Liji zhengyi* 21:416, consulting Legge, *Li-Ki,* 1:369–370.

11. *Han Fei zi jijie* sec. 49, p. 339, consulting Puett, *The Ambivalence of Creation,* 77; Knoblock, *Xunzi,* 3:29. Suiren as a marker of the first use of fire to cook food is mentioned in *Guanzi* (Rickett, *Guanzi,* 430–431) and *Xunzi* (Knoblock, *Xunzi,* 3:43).

12. Graham, *Chuang-tzu,* 171.

13. See *SW,* 64–67, 314–315.

14. Rickett, "Kuan tzu," 244.

In all cases the essence [*jing*] of things is what gives them life.
Below [or descending] it gives life to the five grains;
Above [or ascending] it creates the arrayed stars.
When it floats between the sky and earth, we call them ghosts or spirits;
When it is stored in the breast, we call them sagely persons.[15]

Beginning with the first item, and arranging the rest by degree of spatial elevation (with indentation marking the two subpairings, grains/stars and sages/spirits), we get the following hierarchical taxonomy:

In this station:	*Essence manifests as:*
Below (rooted in the earth)	Grains
In people's chests [stored state]	Sages
Between sky and earth [flowing state]	Ghosts and spirits
Above (hung in the sky)	Stars

The text makes the following analogies: grains are to the earth as stars are to the heavens; grains are terrestrial stars, stars are celestial grains, each holding an analogous place in its proper realm. Further, grains are to ordinary plants as sages are to ordinary people: just as sages have trained and cultivated themselves, carrying essence within their chests, so grains represent a form of plant life cultivated by human labor and thus harboring superior nourishment.

I know of no text that exalts grains more highly than the *Guanzi*. More than once we find it said that "the five grains and the eating of rice are the people's Director of Allotted Lifespans (Siming 司命),"[16] an extraordinary metaphor likening grains to the forbidding deity who already by the fourth and third centuries B.C.E. was held to enforce predetermined limits on people's lifespans.[17] Or again, in explaining why it is that "the altars to land and grain are more to be valued than parents"—a truly astounding statement—the text offers: "When city and suburban walls have been destroyed and the altars to Land and Grain no longer receive blood and food sacrifices, there will no longer be any live ministers. However, after the death of their parents, the children do not die. This is the reason the *sheji* are more to be valued than parents."[18]

---

15. Consulting Rickett, *Guanzi,* 39; and Roth, *Original Tao,* 46.

16. For text and translation (my own translation departs slightly), see Rickett, *Guanzi,* 2:377; n.6 gives a list of other loci where the same statement appears.

17. See Chard, "The Stove God and the Overseer of Fate"; and Campany, "Living off the Books."

18. Consulting Rickett, *Guanzi,* 2:438.

Some of the human or quasi-divine progenitors of agriculture, cooking, and
sacrifice were themselves honored with sacrifices. The cursory *Liji* passage on the
twelfth-month *zha* festival suggests year-end harvest thank-offerings to the First
Husbandman, the divine overseers of husbandry, and the hundred grains, as well as
to the gods of the fields and apparently both domestic and wild animals; it was a
calendrical moment in which sacrificial requital was made to the myriad things for
their feeding and support of humanity.[19] Furthermore, from the Han onward the
spring ceremony known simply as Plowing formed part of the imperial ritual system; it opened with an offering to Shennong, followed by the emperor and officials
ritually breaking ground in a sacred field where the grain used in court sacrifices was
grown.[20] The founding Han emperor also instituted regular sacrifices to Hou Ji.[21]

The Centrality of Agricultural Control, and of Sacrifice, to the State

It is clear that for many authors in the late Warring States, Qin, and Han a primary
function and prerogative of the state was to assure a good agricultural harvest and
then to manage it carefully. Legal documents found at Shuihudi dating to 217
B.C.E reveal the care taken by the Qin state to manage grain stores, even down to
the local level, and provide insight into the way in which foods of the sacrificial
system—here, wine and meat—bound ritual participants together. Wine and meat
consumed before the gods sealed legal bonds between parties.[22] The *Liji* portrays
the careful notation of annual grain harvests and the management of seed for the
coming year as key functions of the state.[23] Conversely, the "Monthly Ordinances"
chapter of the same text frequently mentions that if the ruler acts out of season, the
five grains do not germinate or mature properly. "Minister of fields" was a key high
office in the standard accounts of governmental structure of the era. Additionally,
state sacrifices requited the gods for timely rains and abundant harvests.[24] Political
authority, agricultural production, and state-sponsored sacrifice were inextricably
interwoven.

Indicative of the importance of grains in the mainstream cuisine and of the
centrality of the control of agriculture to the symbolic as well as economic capital
of the state were the meanings attached to the "altars to [the gods of] soil and grain"
(*sheji* 社稷)—altars to gods who were the recipients of sacrifices "to requite them

19. See *Liji zhengyi*, 26:499, 34:749a; Legge, *Li-Ki*, 1:431, 2:167; and Bodde, *Festivals in
Classical China*, 68–74.
20. *Hou Han shu*, 3106; see also Bodde, *Festivals in Classical China*, 223–241.
21. *Shi ji* 28:1380; *Han shu* 30:1211.
22. Yates, "State Control of Bureaucrats under the Qin," 352–357, 359–360, 361.
23. Legge, *Li-Ki*, 1:221, 293, 308.
24. Wilson, "Sacrifice and the Imperial Cult of Confucius," 251.

for the merit of having given birth to grains and living things," as Wang Chong put it in the first century C.E.[25] Along with the temple to the royal or imperial ancestors (*zongmiao* 宗廟), with which they were paired, these altars were the ritual and symbolic center of the realm, their safety synonymous with the state's. A healthy state was one in which the *sheji* "feed on blood";[26] the inability of a state's *sheji* to feed on blood sacrifice constituted a national disaster.[27] Setting up a new dynasty required eliminating the *sheji* of the preceding dynasty and erecting one's own;[28] inheriting the *sheji* or setting up new ones was tantamount to rulership.[29] The destruction of a dynasty's or kingdom's *sheji* spelled the end of its political reign, the cutting off of its people's descent lines, the overwhelming of its population.[30] To embark on a policy that endangered the *sheji* was to endanger the realm, so much so that the verb "to imperil the *sheji*" became a synecdoche for any calamitous undertaking.[31] In the *Liji*, two passages say that important events in the realm should be announced to the gods and spirits of the *sheji, zongmiao,* and mountains and rivers; military expeditions began only after offerings had been made at the *sheji* and *zongmiao,* and the commander had received his charge there.

Not only were the spirits of heaven, earth, mountains, rivers, soil, and grain fed in sacrifices orchestrated by the state, but the human dead were also fed by the living: the royal/imperial dead by the state, others by their living descendants. This obligation to feed the ancestral dead—notably in offerings of grains, wine (a grain product), and meat—was of course nothing short of foundational to Chinese society and is voluminously attested both in transmitted texts and in archeologically recovered documents and grave goods. Some grave goods include cooked meals laid out as if for a banquet and supplies of food and utensils for use by the dead in the tomb. The proper extent of this ritualized culinary service was perennially debated, with authors of various persuasions trying to curb excess—lavish offerings having become, among other things, a mode of conspicuous consumption and a status marker among the living[32]—but that the living were obliged to feed the dead was assumed by all parties, even those (such as the first century C.E. Wang Chong) who argued that the dead lacked consciousness and could not therefore receive or be grateful for food offerings. In numerous stories preserved in late Warring States,

25. *Lunheng jiaoshi* 25:1049; compare Forke, *Lun-hêng,* 1:510.

26. *Shi ji* 34:1562, 86:2536.

27. Ibid., 87:2549; *Han shu* 2:53.

28. *Shi ji* 8:370.

29. Graham, *Book of Lieh-tzu,* 170; *Chuang-tzu,* 207.

30. *Shi ji* 89:2573, 79:2403, 6:278; *Han shu* 50:2007; Knoblock, *Xunzi,* 2:229.

31. For example, *Han shu* 4:1910.

32. *Mozi jijie,* 6:156–172; Knoblock and Riegel, *The Annals of Lü Buwei,* 227–233; Riegel, "Do Not Serve the Dead as You Serve the Living"; Forke, *Lun-hêng,* 2:369–375.

Han, and early medieval texts, unfed ghosts complain about their lot or thank those non-kin who, out of compassion, offer to feed or rebury them.[33] Sometimes the dead are represented as making specific requests and having particular preferences regarding their food and clothing.[34] The unquiet dead who went without normal food offerings were a special object of anxiety and received special ritual attentions and feedings.[35]

Feeding the ancestral dead was an emotionally charged event in which sensory and verbal as well as commensal contact between the living and the dead was briefly but powerfully reopened. At the banquet table a living descendant acted as ritual impersonator (shi 尸) of the honored ancestor. Offerings were preceded by a period of seclusion, purification, and fasting. The Liji poignantly insists at several points that only after completing this fasting for the full period of three days will the sacrificer be able to see and hear the beings he is feeding,[36] a passage undoubtedly reflective of the often repeated yet misconstrued Confucian remark that one is to "sacrifice to the spirits as if the spirits are present." Note that here one temporarily abstained from food in order to purify oneself to see the spirits of the dead when presenting food to them and eating with them.

The chronological, ideological, and generic variety of the texts I have juxtaposed indicates the depth and breadth of cultural assumptions about the priority of grains, cooking, sacrifice (of meats and grains), agriculture and its products, and the extent to which these were central to political authority, social function, and cultural identity. With rare exceptions, the spirits of nature as well as the human dead were thought of as needing to eat, and it was the job of the living human community to feed them. What they were fed was "grains"—synecdochic for the products of agriculture—and meats. Grain was, in short, a symbol and summation of culture itself, or rather of nature acculturated, as well as of the fully human community. A natural locus of nutritive essence, grain nevertheless required cooperative, communal, differentiated stages of production to be transformed into food. Thus transformed, it was the most culturally celebrated food of humans (both living and dead) and of gods.

---

33. Campany, "Ghosts Matter"; SW, 377–384.

34. Forke, Lun-hêng 1:512; Harper, "Resurrection in Warring States Popular Religion."

35. Kleeman, "Licentious Cults and Bloody Victuals," 195; Chard, "The Imperial Household Cult," 241–242.

36. For example, Liji zhengyi 27:507, 49:830; and, most explicit, 47:805ff. (compare Legge, Li-Ki, 2:210–215): "During the days of vigil and purification, [the mourner] thinks on the place where [the departed] sat, thinks on how they smiled and spoke, thinks on their aims and views, thinks on what they delighted in, thinks on what they enjoyed. On the third day of such vigil and purification he will see those for whom he has been keeping vigil and purifying himself."

Alternate Cuisines for Superior Eaters

Many late Warring States, Qin, Han, and early medieval textual and visual representations depict or prescribe an array of culinary possibilities other than the mainstream (elite) diet. They do not offer these possibilities neutrally, as a simple expansion of the choices available to consumers of food and of texts, but rather they recommend them as superior and imply that those who practice them are superior.

EATING *QI* IS BETTER THAN EATING GRAINS

I begin with the following well-known passage from the oldest portion of the *Zhuangzi*, written ca. 320 B.C.E.

> Jian Wu put a question to Lian Shu: "I heard Jie Yu say something.... I was amazed and frightened by his words...."
>
> "What did he say?"
>
> "He said that on the distant mountain of Guyi a divine man dwells. His skin and flesh are like ice and snow. He is gentle as a virgin. He does not eat the five grains, but rather sucks wind and drinks dew. He rides the *qi* of clouds and mounts dragons, roaming beyond the four seas. When the spirits in him congeal, this causes creatures to be free from plagues and the year's grain crops to ripen.—I thought him crazy and did not believe him."[37]

Now it would be a mistake to lump this strange figure with those who would soon become known as *xian*. For one thing, his rhetorical function is to serve as one of a series of things beyond the ken of ordinary folk, not as the representative of a class of deathless beings. The passage does not suggest that readers should or can emulate the divine man (although he is clearly presented as admirable). And for all the divine man's remarkable properties, there is no mention of long life or immortality. On the other hand, each of the properties that do mark him as different from ordinary humans becomes part of the repertoire of transcendents within the next two centuries: (1) Taxonomically he is neither a spirit nor a man, but something in between, a "divine man," perhaps a hybrid or else one of a distinct class of beings. (2) He does not eat the five grains but subsists on wind and dew. We may infer that this diet accounts for his wondrously refined body and also, since he is a "divine man," that this diet is being claimed superior to one based on grains. (3) He dwells at a distant place, not in the Central Kingdom, and on a mountain, not on the agricultural

---

37. *Zhuangzi* chap. 1, lines 26–31 in the Harvard-Yenching ed., consulting Graham, *Chuang-tzu*, 46. A similar and clearly derivative passage occurs in the much later *Liezi*. See Graham, *Book of Lieh-tzu*, 35; and *Liezi jishi*, 2:44–46.

plains; he also roams beyond the known limits of the settled world. (4) He travels by riding *qi* and dragons, implying flight and ascension into the heavens. (5) Despite his extreme distance from the people of the Central Kingdom, by some unexplained mechanism his "spirit-congealing" activities benefit these people, warding off illnesses and aiding their agricultural labors. This being who does not cultivate or consume grains somehow helps grains grow by his own self-cultivation.

The song "Far Roaming" ("Yuanyou" 遠遊) in the anthology of Chu lyrics known as *Songs of Chu* (*Chuci* 楚辭) maps out a cosmic journey and a path of self-cultivation toward a specific sort of transcendence.[38] For our purposes it suffices to focus on two clusters of lines. The first reads:[39]

> I shall follow, then, Wang Qiao 王喬 for my pleasure and amusement
> Sup on the six *qi* and drink Drifting Flow
> Rinse my mouth with True Yang and swallow Dawn Aurora
> Conserve the limpid clarity of spirit illumination[40]
> As essence and *qi* enter in, pollution and filth are expelled.

Here, the poet, following the example of the noted transcendent Wang Qiao, begins a culinary regime based on *qi* and, by implication, no longer on grain food. By the final verse, the purifying effects of this regime begin to be evidenced. As Harper explains, the three types of *qi* named in the second and third lines are the beneficial *qi* of midnight, midday, and dawn respectively. The beneficial six types of *qi*, mentioned here as a class, correspond spatially to the four quarters, heaven above, and earth below, and temporally to the seasons, and later texts specify seasonal schedules by which to ingest them; there are also five types of *qi* to be avoided, already mentioned in some Mawangdui manuscripts.

After receiving instruction from Wang Qiao, the poet flies on "to the Feathered Persons [transcendents] at the Cinnabar Mound, loitering in the long-standing land where death is not," and proceeds to bathe at other mythic destinations in the cardinal directions till he "sucks in the dark liquor of the Flying Springs" (a site located at the western Mount Kunlun). He then declares:

---

38. This composition may date to the late fourth century B.C.E. at the earliest or to the early Han at the latest. Its more precise dating is irrelevant here.

39. *Chuci jizhu*, 5:2b–3b, consulting Kroll, "An Early Poem of Mystical Excursion," 159–160; and Harper, *Early Chinese Medical Literature*, 307 n.1.

40. *Shenming* 神明 is a term whose meaning shifts by context and by period, and a single English translation that would satisfy all specialists is impossible. In a later text one might justify rendering the term as "luminous body-gods," but here an interpretation closer to late Warring States and Han medical and meditational discourses is more appropriate; my understanding of *shenming* in those discourses is based largely on Harper, *Early Chinese Medical Literature*, 120–121, 128, 143.

Essence, becoming whole and unmixed, now took on strength
As my body, weakening and wasting, turned tender and listless
And my spirit, growing fine and subtle, was released, unrestrained.

The transformation of *qi* into sustenance sufficient to support life, rendering ordinary foods obsolete, is described with metaphors grounded in the processing of agricultural products and metallic ores. The poet's body is denominated as if it were the raw material of a smelting process in which the essence is purified and strengthened, the bodily form is melted away, and the spirit is released. This conception of what it means to transcend—that one's "essence" and "spirit" are released from the dross of the "bodily form"—is merely one of many and is sharply at odds with others that prioritize the preservation and strengthening of the body. It is congruent, on the other hand, with passages elsewhere that hierarchize the pair "spirit"/body.

A silk manuscript found at Mawangdui titled "Eliminating Grain and Eating *Qi*" ("Quegu shiqi" 卻穀食氣[41]) outlines a method for avoiding "grains" (presumably here again meaning the products of agriculture) by ingesting *qi* according to scheduled procedures and by consuming the herb pyrrosia, which was apparently used to treat urine retention while not eating. Modes of exhalation are prescribed, and seasonal and age-based guidelines for the practitioner's ingestion of the various types of beneficial *qi* are laid out, along with the five types of harmful *qi* to be avoided. The brief text twice posits a hierarchy of eaters, those who eat grain versus those who eat *qi;* in the first passage the basis for this hierarchy is not made clear, but in the second we read: "Those who eat grain eat what is square; those who eat *qi* eat what is round. Round is heaven; square is earth." No specific benefits of this regimen are promised—perhaps details on them are lost in the several lacunae—but the hierarchy is clear: eating grain is to eating *qi* as earth is to heaven.

Similarly, the Heshanggong 河上公 commentary to the second line of chap. 6 (in the received ordering of chapters) of the *Daode jing* 道德經, which reads "This is called the mysterious female," informs us:

> "Mysterious" refers to heaven; in people it is the nose. "Female" refers to earth; in people it is the mouth. Heaven feeds people with the five types of *qi,* which enter through the nose and are deposited in the heart. The five *qi* are pure and subtle, and they constitute [in people] the essence, spirit, intelligence, voice, hearing, and the five natures. Their ghosts are termed cloudsouls. The cloudsouls are male and come and go through the nose; they course through the way of heaven; this is why the nose is the Mysterious. Earth feeds people with the five sapors, which enter through the mouth and are deposited in the stomach.

---

41. Ibid., 305–309.

The five sapors are impure and turbid, and they constitute the form, skeleton, bones, blood, vessels, and the six emotions. Their ghosts are termed whitesouls. The whitesouls are female and come and go through the mouth; they course through earth; this is why the mouth is the Female.[42]

Here a hierarchy of foods is correlated with other hierarchies:

In this domain:	the higher position is:	and the lower is:
Cosmos	heaven	earth
Human facial apertures	nose	mouth
Foods	the five types of *qi*	the five sapors
Components of the self	spirit, essence, etc.	body, bones, etc.
"Ghosts"	cloudsouls	whitesouls
Gender	male	female

The manuscript known as "Ten Questions" ("Shiwen" 十問), which was found on bamboo strips at Mawangdui and was thought to have been copied between 180 and 168 B.C.E.,[43] reveals diverse techniques for the intake, circulation, and cultivation of *qi* that utilize breathing, stretching, and sexual intercourse. Here there is no mention of a need to avoid grains, and one passage implies that the method outlined for "eating Yin" prepares the body for the maximally advantageous intake of "drink and food"—although that food may be the otherwise unspecified "diet of elemental stuff" 橾食 mentioned earlier in the text and perhaps synonymous with the expression *sushi* 素食, used in the *Mozi* to indicate a diet of uncultivated plants gathered from the wild.[44] But a dialogue in this text sets up a hierarchy in which being "signless," "formless," and "bodiless" are pronounced superior to their alternatives; it is in these states that the "culminant essence of heaven and earth" is said to be born, and it is "signlessness" that the practitioner accumulates when he "cultivates *qi* and concentrates essence." As Harper points out,[45] the *Huainanzi* uses "formless" as an epithet for Dao or One and terms the person who cultivates the Dao "bodiless" as well as formless; the *Guanzi* attests to the notion that the Dao is "signless" and gives the oldest statement that obtaining the Dao is the key to life and losing it means death. Methods for eating *qi* and sucking "sweet dew" are then

---

42. *Daode zhenjing zhu* (*DZ* 682) 1:5a-b. Heshanggong was assimilated by some into the ranks of transcendents (*TL*, 305–307).

43. Harper, *Early Chinese Medical Literature*, 28–29.

44. See ibid., 385–387; *Mozi jijie*, 1:38; and note commentaries; Rickett, *Guanzi*, 2:223.

45. *Early Chinese Medical Literature*, 394 n.1.

outlined, and the text—alone among the Mawangdui medical manuscripts—closes by explicitly promising deathlessness to those who practice its methods. Successful practitioners will become spirits, achieve "release of the form" (*xingjie* 形解), ascend on high, and become as constant as heaven and earth, not dying.[46]

In the *Huainanzi* treatise on topography (2nd c. B.C.E.) we find a series of correlations between the types of soils prevalent in people's habitats and their dispositions, followed by a list of correlations between diets and dispositions. The last four items read as follows:[47] "Those who eat flesh are brave and daring but fierce. Those who eat *qi* are spirit-illumined and live long. Those who eat grains are knowledgeable and clever but short-lived. Those who do not eat do not die; they are [or become] spirits." Rearranging the order of the passage to reflect the ascending hierarchy it entails, we see that:

Those who eat:	Have these properties (positive + and negative -):	
Flesh	+ brave, daring	- fierce
Grains	+ knowledgeable, clever	- short-lived
Qi	+ spirit-illumined, long-lived	- [none]
Nothing	+ deathless; are spirits	- [none]

Feeding on *qi,* then, is clearly superior to eating flesh and grains and confers longevity. Even better is to eat nothing at all, which confers deathlessness and is a property of spirits. This claim that spirits need not eat seems novel for its time and suggests a new class of beings who would, it is implied, require no sacrificial ministrations from the human community.

At one point in the massive *Scripture of Great Peace* (*Taiping jing* 太平經), much of which was probably assembled in the second century C.E. incorporating older material,[48] we find an interlocutor posing the question: What are the functions or offices of the nine grades of persons? The Celestial Tutor gives an answer we can summarize in the following table, where left-hand entries are the types of persons mentioned and right-hand entries are what they are assigned to manage:[49]

---

46. Ibid., 392–399. I concur with Harper that this *xingjie* should not be equated with the *shijie* of somewhat later techniques.

47. *DZ* 1184, 7:8b; Zhuzi jicheng ed. 4:60; consulting Major, *Heaven and Earth in Early Han Thought,* 172.

48. The dating of the various strata of the *Taiping jing* has been the subject of much scholarly discussion, most recently in Hendrischke, "Early Daoist Movements," 143–145; and Hendrischke, *The Scripture on Great Peace,* 343–372. For present purposes, a more precise dating of the passages adduced is unnecessary.

49. *Taipingjing hejiao,* 88–91.

Formless divine persons of fine *qi*	Primordial *qi*
Greater divine persons	Heaven
Perfected persons	Earth
Transcendent persons	The four seasons
Persons of the great Dao	The five phases
Sages	Yin and Yang
Worthies	Writings/all transmitted speech
Ordinary people	Plants, trees, and the five grains
Servants and slaves	Material goods

Key for our purposes is the hierarchical opposition between two bundles of things: at the top, divinity, formlessness, and "primordial *qi*" (with other modes of divinity, perfected ones, transcendents, and "persons of the Dao" also in high echelons); second from the bottom, ordinary humanity, vegetation, and the five grains. We are next told that when each of the nine types of persons controls (or harmonizes) the corresponding type of *qi,* then the nine types of *qi* and yin and yang will be harmonized and the "inherited burden" from previous generations will be eliminated, and this brings about the coming of the eponymous Great Peace. Linked to this hierarchy is the directive that superior practitioners "must begin by not eating what has form but rather eating *qi* so as to unite with the primordial *qi.*" To do this they shut themselves inside a thatch hut, fasting, not looking upon anything evil or defiled, daily refining their forms and not grasping after what they desire, until they ascend to assist the transcendents and perfected ones in celestial rule based on primordial *qi.*

Elsewhere in this text one is enjoined to eat moderately, gradually replacing foods with *qi* and medicinals until one consumes only things without bodily form.[50] Or again:

> The question was asked: "What do the higher, middle, and lower beings who have obtained the way and surpassed the world (or survived their generation) eat?" The reply: "The uppermost rank eat wind and *qi,* the second rank eat medicinal sapors, and the third rank eat little [food], reducing what passes through their stomach and intestines." It was said further: "Heaven is extremely distant and knows no bounds. If one does not eat wind and *qi,* how can one travel quickly enough to circuit completely through the courses of heaven? Further, if one is to work alongside the spirit-envoys and be associated with them, one must eat wind and *qi.* At the next [lower] level, if one is

---

50. Ibid., 684, 466.

to match the essences of earth in one's powers, harmonize the five types of soil, look down from above on mountains and rivers, follow mountain chains and enter waterways, so as to have commerce with the changings of earth and eat and work together with [others of this level], then one cannot eat grains; one drinks water and practices [medicinal formulas]. At the next [and lowest] level, eating in moderation is the way. Although one does not thus firmly establish one's form, one [eats] less than ordinary people and is thus slightly different from them. Therefore even those who [merely] eat little so as to pass little through their intestines are people who are in the process of achieving the way."[51]

In other passages the *Scripture* provides instructions for specific methods of "eating wind and *qi*" to maximum advantage.[52]

By the first century B.C.E. the idea that some practitioners were abstaining from grains while practicing methods for consuming, directing, and cultivating *qi* as alternate nourishment was ubiquitous, whether the authors are advocating or criticizing it. In the *Shi ji* biography of Zhang Liang 張良, for example, we read that late in his life, having reached remarkable social heights, he declared himself ready to abandon the affairs of the human world and "simply follow Master Redpine [like Wang Qiao, an exemplary ancient transcendent] and go roaming," whereupon "he practiced grain avoidance, guiding and pulling, and lightening the body." But later the Han empress pressured him to eat (or force-fed him?), leaving Zhang "no recourse but to submit to compulsion and eat"—and the next thing we read of him is that he died eight years later.[53] Around 70–80 C.E. Wang Chong also documented that grain avoidance was widely claimed to be a route to transcendence, a claim he disputed:

There are many who take people who avoid grains and do not eat to be persons with *dao* arts. They speak of Wangzi Qiao and the like, who, in not eating grains and in eating differently than ordinary people, therefore also achieved a different longevity than that of ordinary people, exceeding a hundred [years of age], surpassing the world, and thus becoming transcendent persons. This too is false.

---

51. Ibid.,716–717.

52. Ibid., 259, 699–700.

53. *Shi ji* 55:2048. On Zhang Liang, see Lewis, *Writing and Authority in Early China,* 81, 341; Lewis, *Sanctioned Violence in Early China,* 99–103; and Loewe, *A Biographical Dictionary of the Qin, Former Han & Xin Periods,* 683–686.

Wang proceeds to argue that it is natural for people to eat since they were given mouths and teeth for the intake of food and alimentary canals for its digestion and the elimination of waste, then continues:

> People, when alive, use food as [the source of] their *qi,* just as plants and trees when alive draw *qi* from the soil. Pull up the roots of a plant or tree, separate them from the soil, and they will wither and soon die. Shut up a person's mouth so that he cannot eat, and he will starve and not live long. Masters of *dao* boast to others, saying, "The perfected man consumes *qi*" and making *qi* their food. Thus it is handed down that "those who eat *qi* live long and do not die"[54] [and that] although it is not on grains that they become full, they nevertheless fill themselves by means of *qi.* This too is false.[55]

The somber conclusion of Zhang Liang's story is reminiscent of the following poignant tale found in the Han *Traditions of Exemplary Transcendents* but reworked by Ge Hong or some intermediate redactor:

> During the reign of Emperor Cheng of the Han, hunters in the Zhongnan Mountains saw a person who wore no clothes, his body covered with black hair. Upon seeing this person, the hunters wanted to pursue and capture him, but the person leapt over gullies and valleys as if in flight, and so could not be overtaken. The hunters then stealthily observed where the person dwelled, surrounded and captured him, whereupon they determined that the person was a woman. Upon questioning, she said, "I was originally a woman of the Qin palace. When I heard that invaders from the east had arrived, that the King of Qin would go out and surrender, and that the palace buildings would be burned, I fled in fright into the mountains. Famished, I was on the verge of dying by starvation when an old man taught me to eat the resin and nuts of pines. At first they were bitter, but gradually I grew accustomed to them. They enabled me to feel neither hunger nor thirst; in winter I was not cold, in summer I was not hot." Calculation showed that the woman . . . must be more than two hundred years old. . . .
>
> The hunters took the woman back in. They offered her grain to eat. When she first smelled the stink of the grain, she vomited, and only after several days could she tolerate it. After little more than two years of this [diet], her body hair fell out; she turned old and died. Had she not been caught by men, she would have become a transcendent.[56]

---

54. Wang is here quoting a *Huainanzi* passage discussed above.
55. *Lunheng jiaoshi* 7:335–336; compare Forke, *Lun-hêng,* 1:347–349.
56. *NP,* 207.

Few narratives more succinctly summarize the argument that ordinary foods or "grains" prevent transcendence. Here, as often, avoiding them is assisted by ingesting a simple plant product gathered in the wilds; whether this regimen helps by virtue of its appetite-suppressing properties or its provision of superior nourishment is unclear. Elsewhere pine resin is said to transform in the ground into a marvelous, longevity-conferring herb.[57]

In *Traditions of Exemplary Transcendents* one adept is said to have avoided the five grains and fed on the flowers of various herbs instead; another, to have avoided grains, absorbed dew, and fed on pine nuts, asparagus root, and "stony fat" (the "marrow" of stalactites in caves); and still another have subsisted on sesame, which was still at the time considered an exotic import.[58] "Grain avoidance" continued to be a key marker of a person engaged in the pursuit of transcendence in Ge Hong's time and beyond, for he writes of contemporary practitioners he regards as charlatans who announce that they have "cut off [the ingestion of] grains" so as to attract followers.[59] Many of the adepts he regards as successful transcendents included grain avoidance and *qi* ingestion among their methods, though none of them is portrayed as reaching transcendence by these means alone (for the polemical reason that Ge Hong favored alchemy above other methods). In some contexts—such as in the opening pages of the fifteenth of Ge Hong's *Inner Chapters*—it becomes clear that "avoiding grains" is tantamount to not eating food at all (as the *Huainanzi* and some other early sources said that the highest spirits were able to do), merely swallowing saliva and *qi* and ingesting medicinal preparations to suppress appetite and strengthen the body. A number of adepts, including Dong Jing, are said to have accomplished this.[60] As a test of his arts, Zuo Ci was reportedly enclosed in a room by Cao Cao, denied food and permitted only water for one whole year; he emerged looking just as he had when he went in; elsewhere a method for surviving famine years by not eating is attributed to this same master, and other methods for not eating are attributed to other transcendents-in-the-making, such as Gan Shi, who also was reported to have gone a whole year without food.[61]

The extant *Scripture of the Five Numinous Treasure Talismans* (*Lingbao wufu jing* 靈寶五符經), a text assembled ca. 280 C.E. that conveys numerous arts of transcendence, features an exercise in which the cosmic "sprouts" of the pentacolored *qi* of the five directions are systematically ingested, leading to transcendence.[62] Following

---

57. *TL*, 25.
58. Kaltenmark, *Le Lie-sien tchouan,* 48–50, 65–67, 135–137.
59. *NP,* 346.
60. *TL,* 24, 300.
61. *TL,* 279–280, 150, 284, 151–152.
62. *DZ* 388, 3:12a-b.

its outline of this method, which is embedded within a narrative of its own initial revelation—in this case by three Transcendent Kings from the Heaven of Grand Purity to the Yellow Thearch in antiquity—the scripture continues:

> The three transcendent kings further declared to the thearch: "We formerly fed according to this method and thereby attained transcendence. Our former teacher had us increase the sweet spring within our mouths and then swallow to the following twenty-two word incantation: 'The white stones, craggy, proceed in order;[63] the spring, bubbling and pervading, becomes a perfected juice; drinking it, I obtain long life, my long lifespan becoming even longer!' You, too, can practice this. If you are able to continuously ingest the perfected One without ceasing, swallow the floriate pond[64] without resting, and keep your *qi* shut within you without flagging, then you will forthwith attain the Dao and you will have cut off grains; you need no longer follow the changes of the moon for completion.[65] The people of primordial antiquity lived long because they remained in leisure and did not eat grains. The Verse of Great Existence says: 'The five grains are bores that gouge out lifespan; they rot and befoul the five viscera [lit. the five storehouses] and shorten the allotted lifespan. Once this food enters the mouth, there is no further hope of great longevity. If you wish not to die, you must keep your intestines free of sediment. If you wish to live long, you must make the *qi* of your visceral storehouses clean and pure[66] [by] decanting the floriate juice into the body. You will then meet heaven with the jade liquid in your mouth, and you and heaven will reach the same longevity.'"[67]

---

63. This line refers to the teeth, which are to be ground together or pressed by the tongue in precise sequences throughout the ingesting of the sprouts (ibid., 3:21a-b).

64. "Floriate pond" here refers to the adept's own saliva.

65. This appears to mean that one need not depend on the lunar cycle for planting and harvesting grains; one is freed from the strictures of the agricultural year.

66. Compare a passage in Ge Hong's *Inner Chapters:* "The methods of transcendence call for the cessation and cutting off of anything foul and putrid, abstaining from grains and purifying the intestines, but in the case of the lords of men there is the cooking and slicing of fat pork and the butchering of all manner of living things" (*NP,* 18). Compare also a passage in Mei Cheng's (d. 141 B.C.E.) rhapsody "Seven Stimuli" in which rich foods (literally "things sweet, crisp, oily, and syrupy") are warned against as being "rot-gut reagents"; see the text and translation (which I here quote) in Mair, *Mei Cheng's "Seven Stimuli" and Wang Bor's "Pavilion of King Terng,"* 26–27 (and compare Frankel, *The Flowering Plum and the Palace Lady,* 186–211). I thank Victor Mair for bringing this passage to my attention.

67. *DZ* 388, 3:21b–22a, consulting but departing from Kohn, *Laughing at the Tao,* 101. As indicative of how inadequate it would be to speak of a single "Daoist" stance on grains, consider the passage quoted from the *Scripture on the Conversion of the Barbarians* in the Buddhist polemical tract *In Mockery of the Dao* (570 C.E.; see Kohn, *Laughing at the Tao,* 100–101). Consider also

Metaphors drawn from mainstream cuisine are here once again wielded to describe a discipline that overturns that cuisine. This is one of the earliest passages of which I am aware in which grains are attacked based on what we might call negative intrinsic reasons—that is, on the grounds that they harm the body in specific, theorized ways. Again we should beware of the sort of lumping that would read this passage as the implicit rationale underlying all of the passages on grain avoidance adduced above. In those earlier passages there is no hint of the notion that grains (that is, mainstream foods) actually harm the body;[68] the argument is rather that *qi* and other more refined substances, when ingested and circulated in esoterically prescribed ways, give superior, longevity-inducing nourishment. This argument in turn rested on a view of the body as a self-sufficient microcosm that could imbibe beneficial essences from the cosmos and then close itself off like a sealed reaction-vessel to further refine and recycle them, periodically "exhaling the old and inhaling the new" but otherwise drastically minimizing contact with the surrounding sensory, cultural, social world. From the same view of the body came ideas and practices of "embryonic breathing" or "breathing like a fetus" *(taixi)* found in many early texts.[69]

There is another, more particular theory of the body that may be related to early intrinsic rationales for the avoidance of grain. I refer to the theory that the body from its conception harbors biospiritual parasites known alternately as the "three worms" (*sanchong* 三蟲) or "three corpses" (*sanshi* 三尸).[70] Various early weft texts[71] and scriptures portray these beings in both zoomorphic and bureaucratic terms. They were said to appear as maggots in excrement and lack organs of sight and hearing, suggestive of tapeworms, but also to ascend monthly to report to register-keeping officials of their human hosts' misdeeds so as to hasten their deaths, leaving the corpses free to roam about stealing offering foods. In fourth-century C.E. and earlier texts are preserved dozens of methods for expelling these baleful

---

the narrative deployed by the apparently early-sixth-century C.E. scripture *Taishang Laojun kaitian jing* (as preserved in *DZ* 1437 and as anthologized in *DZ* 1032, 2:9a ff.; tr. in Schafer, "The Scripture of the Opening of Heaven"), in which the divine Laozi descends and instructs Shennong on agriculture so that he may teach the people to sow the five grains as an improvement over hunting and slaughtering and then again descends to show Suiren how to make fire for cooking.

68. The single line in Mei Cheng's "Seven Stimuli" is an exception, but the thrust of that passage seems to be that overly rich foods excessively consumed do harm, not that mainstream foods per se harm the body.

69. *TL,* 365 n.23.

70. Ibid., 49–52.

71. Weft texts were prophecies and other teachings staged as esoteric transmissions from Confucius and other ancient sages. See Lewis, *The Early Chinese Empires: Qin and Han,* 184–185; and Seidel, "Imperial Treasures and Taoist Sacraments: Taoist Roots in the Apocrypha."

parasites.[72] In only very few early texts of which I am aware, however, is it suggested that these beings feed on grains or are a by-product of their digestion.[73] One finds this notion clearly articulated in certain texts anthologized in the compendium *Yunji qiqian,* compiled ca. 1028 C.E.,[74] but these texts, of uncertain provenance, seem by their content and wording to postdate the fourth century.

FEEDING ON EXOTIC, RARE, MARVELOUS DELICACIES OF THE COSMOS
The idea that strange locales on the distant horizons of the known world harbor longevity- or transcendence-inducing substances is as old in China as the goal of transcendence itself. We find numerous references to the hope of finding these mysterious realms, penetrating their veil of mystery and ingesting their marvelous, potent products. In general, these products seem to fall into three sometimes fuzzy categories: (1) naturally occurring trees, herbs, or fungi, ready for gathering and consumption; (2) naturally found minerals; and (3) "elixirs" of one or another sort that imply some degree of prior human or divine processing of natural ingredients.

To the east, there were Penglai, Yingzhou, and other ocean isles, where transcendents and their herbs or elixirs of deathlessness were thought to lurk; Qin and Han rulers famously sent expeditions to search for them, and there were reports of sightings—but no successful imperially sponsored retrievals—of these island paradises' herbs and drugs. To the west, there were Mount Kunlun and the divine Queen Mother of the West, each associated with immortality-inducing products (and other paradisal delights) before becoming associated with each other.

---

72. Lévi, "L'abstinence des cereals chez les taoïstes," and "The Body."

73. A passage in *DZ* 388 (a text probably assembled around 280 C.E.), 2:11a, states that fasting for twenty days, ingesting only a prescribed herbal preparation, and otherwise avoiding food intake, will cause the *qi* of one's intestines to settle down and "the worms to depart." But the recipe for the herbal compound in this case includes rice. Another passage (2:23a) states that unless the adept first expels the worms and the ambushing corpses, he will find it hard to abstain from eating because he will have cravings for tasty food, and his thoughts will be disordered; presumably these cravings are induced by the worms and corpses, but again we do not find the explicit claim that the worms and corpses themselves thrive on the ingested "grains." In yet another passage (2:23b–24b), one that treats the corpses at greater length (and one that once again recommends the ingestion of *qi* and of the five cosmic "sprouts"), we read that the upper of the three corpses craves luxury items, the middle one craves the five sapors (that is, food), and the lower one craves the five colors. Even here, however, the claim is not yet explicitly made that the sole or primary reason to avoid ingesting grains is that the three worms thrive on them. It is rather that the presence of the worms in the body will cause cravings for lesser foods, cravings that will impede the adept's quest to shun ordinary foods and dine only on pure *qi*.

74. See, for instance, the texts cited in *DZ* 1032 at 83:2b and 10b.

The lore concerning these exotic locales and their products is well known.[75] For our purposes, three features are significant. One is that these strange realms, distant from the agricultural heartland, are imagined as the sources of ingestible substances that are longevity-producing alternatives to ordinary food. A second is that both Kunlun and the eastern isles are uniformly described in texts—and pictured in visual iconography and in functional objects such as censers—as mountains. This facet again emphasizes their difference from the topography of the agrarian plains and river valleys of the Chinese heartland: mountains were places where grains and other mainstream crops could not be grown, but where other life-prolonging products grew naturally without need of cultivation. The third feature that these locations all share is difficulty of access. Their spatial distance is a code for other sorts of barriers. To obtain the wondrous ingestible products they harbor requires initiation and training in esoteric arts, a fact which itself announces these products' superiority to domestic foods.

Closer to home—removed from the agrarian lowlands not horizontally but vertically—were the mountains of China, seen as dangerous zones where wild animals, semibarbaric ethnic groups, and aggressive spirits lurked and where humans from the plains fled to escape centralized bureaucratic control.[76] These nearer (though hardly domesticated) mountains, too, were portrayed as sources of exotic edibles with longevity-inducing, healing powers, capable of replacing grains, and also as restricted, perilous areas requiring mantic protection for safe entry. Both of these aspects of mountains are the sole subject of an entire essay by Ge Hong, and the second fascicle of the *Scripture of the Five Numinous Treasure Talismans* is devoted to scores of transcendence-arts recipes employing mountain herbs.[77] In this scripture and elsewhere, some of these herbs are explicitly recommended, among their other benefits, as replacements for grain food.[78]

Transcendents, then, were said to feed on exotic, longevity-enhancing substitutes for what in China was ordinary food, substances located only in zones removed (horizontally or vertically) by geographic distance and by barriers to access from the heartland of Chinese civilization. It is no wonder that transcendents were often represented in verbal description and iconic depiction as winged beings able to fly, and that the ability to travel long distances rapidly was one mantic art often mentioned as having been practiced by adepts.[79] One of the marvelous arts

---

75. See the overview of the evidence in Loewe, *Ways to Paradise.*
76. Kleeman, "Mountain Deities in China."
77. *NP,* chap. 17; *DZ* 388, fasc. 2; for a typical passage, *TL,* 26.
78. For example, *DZ* 388, 2:15a–b.
79. Campany, "Long-Distance Specialists in Early Medieval China"; *TL,* 125–146.

often attributed to adepts in hagiographies and prescribed in scriptures is the ability to summon the "traveling kitchen" to deliver exotic, longevity-inducing foodstuffs to the adept rather than the adept's needing to travel outward to the limits of the world to secure them. Such banquets displayed near to home the exotic cuisine of the cosmic periphery and of the heavens, and hagiographies record audiences' amazement at them.[80]

Conclusion

Why did the repertoire of the transcendence-seeker, from the very earliest mention of any transcendent-like figures in texts, feature the rejection of grains and other everyday foods? Why did the role of adept include the shunning of agricultural products in favor of *qi* or exotic flora and minerals, things not normally considered food at all? Why do we see such insistence on this point, across texts beginning as early as 320 B.C.E. and running up through 320 C.E. and beyond, texts that teach different methods and envision different conceptions of what it means to become a transcendent?

It would be simple, and less revealing, if the answer were, "Because grains were deemed unhealthy or polluting." But this answer is not well supported by the evidence. The texts we have reviewed offer very little by way of an intrinsic critique of grains or other everyday foods. They all recommend avoiding grains and offer what they tout as superior alternatives, but on the question of precisely *why* grains are such inferior nourishment they have little or nothing to say. What little intrinsic critique we do find comes quite late—apparently Eastern Han at the earliest—and does not seem well developed: ordinary foods, described as rotten and smelly, make impure a body that ought to be brought into *qi*-based resonance with heaven. We find an echo of this notion in Ge Hong's writings, but elsewhere we also find Ge Hong averring that "even the five grains can sustain people; when people get them they live, if cut off from them they die. How much the more, then, in the case of divine medicines of superior grade: how could their benefits to humans not be a myriad times that of the five grains?"[81] In most discussions, then, it is not that transcendence-arts texts portrayed ordinary food as harmful; it is rather that they offered what they considered superior alternatives.

On the positive side, we do find some intrinsic justifications for ingesting *qi*: these were notions concerning the benefits of its circulation and cultivation in the body, grounded in wider views of the microcosmic self and in cosmogonies and cosmologies. And we find many promises of the spectacular benefits of ingesting

---

80. For example, *TL,* 327.
81. *NP,* 71.

one or another herb. Usually, however, *why* diets of *qi* or rare herbs and minerals should be regarded as better than ordinary food remains unanswered; we are merely told, but told repeatedly, *that* they are superior.

Take, for instance, the Heshanggong commentary passage and the Mawangdui text on avoiding grains adduced above, or the assertion, seen in several texts, that it is better to eat what has no form than to eat "formed" food. For these texts, eating *qi* surpasses eating food because the binary pair *qi*/food correlates with a series of other pairs in which one member outranks or bests the other. Eating *qi* is better than eating food in the same way that heaven outranks earth or the formless outranks form; the superiority of eating *qi,* once placed among these other asymmetrical pairs, is self-evident. Without a grain-based cuisine, the proposed *qi*-based cuisine would have no rhetorical or ideological traction. The prestige of eating *qi* is a function of the contrast with its culinary other. Similarly, a major reason for the claim (and belief) that certain wild herbs from distant lands had such longevity-bestowing power may have been simply that they were exotic.

Why did the gaze of these writers and practitioners stay so powerfully fixed on the cuisine to which they were constructing alternatives? I suggest that "grains" were, to echo a passage from Claude Lévi-Strauss, "good to oppose" rather than being seen as intrinsically "bad to eat"[82] and that they were good to oppose because of all that they expressed, symbolized, and implied, all of the other cultural values and institutions to which they were attached. Providing an alternative to eating grains meant providing an alternative to all that eating grains entailed, invoked, and had been linked to.

If cultivating and eating grains, cooking, and dwelling in settled agricultural communities were seen by some as quintessential marks of human civilization, then it is surely no coincidence that cuisines of transcendence exhibit precisely the antitheses of these three traits: they are based on something other than grains (whether inhaled *qi* or *qi* as found in exotic foodstuffs gathered from the periphery), ingested raw (already "cooked" by the action of heaven and earth) or else prepared according to secret methods different from the standard cooking techniques, and consumed as part of a disciplined life partially lived in the mountains and partially spent roaming through the barrens of the cosmos, which resulted in a feathered, flying, deathless being that was no longer human. If the advent of agriculture was a necessary condition for the flourishing of key cultural values and arts, the rejection of agriculture's products entailed a rejection of those values often couched in terms of a return to natural simplicity. That grain cultivation was often featured (by its proponents) more than the cooking of meat as a marker of proper civilization perhaps explains why grains were singled out for replacement by the creators of

82. Lévi-Strauss, *Totemism,* 89.

transcendence paths; later, the Celestial Master movements would focus on meat
and blood as the key avoidances and would develop different contrastive ideologies
based in part on the valuation of life.

If the divine progenitors and overseers of the annual agricultural cycle were
thanked with elaborate, society-wide, imperially sponsored sacrifices, then adepts
able to thrive without consuming the products of this cycle were, in effect, absenting themselves from this entire sacrificial system. Even more momentously, to the
extent that these sacrifices implied that these gods needed or wanted to eat the
products of the agricultural system they sponsored, transcendence-quest adepts
were implicitly but unmistakably portrayed as superior to gods in their ability to
eschew agricultural products. If adepts required no ordinary foods, all the more did
successful transcendents require no sacrificial food offerings, unlike the gods and
spirits against whom they were constructed as a distinct category of suprahuman
beings.[83] No wonder, then, that adepts are repeatedly portrayed as uniquely able to
command spirits and gods and to ignore their demands for sacrifice—demands that
pressed ominously upon farmers and merchants but that the adept could afford to
dismiss.

To the extent that political authority was inextricably bound up with the
management of agriculture, and to the extent that the altars and sacrifices to the
gods of grain and soil were the symbolic and ritual center of the state, abstainers
from agricultural products and from sacrificial foods transcended these structures
of authority as well. No wonder, then, that adepts are repeatedly depicted, in texts
both sympathetic and hostile to their claims, as refusing the importunities of rulers
and officials, occasionally making a theatrically elaborate mockery of their attempts
at coercion. Adepts repeatedly claimed exemption from rulers' spheres of command
and asserted their right to deference from officials who wished to learn their secret
arts, just as they claimed a higher place in the cosmic hierarchy than the gods to
whom rulers and their administrations were obliged to perform sacrifice.

And what, finally, of the ancestor cult, that bedrock of civilization perhaps
even older and certainly more ideologically freighted than agriculture? Ancestors
needed to eat, as transcendents did not; more urgently, departed transcendents were
no longer available to continue ancestral offerings. The patrilineal family and the
core rites that sustained it depended for their continued existence not only on
the uninterrupted generation of male descendants and on their performance of
sacrifices but also on the continued death of ancestors. Large numbers of successful

---

83. This did not prevent offerings to transcendents in shrines and temples; but this practice
represents an appropriation of transcendents by practitioners of sacrificial religion and was not
something that advocates of transcendence arts approved (see, for instance, Ge Hong's attacks on
sacrifice in the ninth chapter of his *Baopuzi neipian*).

transcendents would undermine society in all three of these ways, removing people from the lineage system and disrupting its transgenerational continuity in pursuit of what others deemed a purely selfish goal. Opponents of the quest for transcendence were quick to attack it on these grounds, and proponents had a ready response.

We do not understand cuisines of transcendence if we consider only their intrinsic meanings and functions. Those cuisines were at least as profoundly shaped by everything they appear to have been exquisitely crafted not to be. What they were not, and *how* they were not what they were not, figures importantly in assessing what they were and what they meant. Zhuangzi's aphorism—"Without an other, there is no self" 非彼無我[84]—applies as much to the collective creation of traditions of discourse and practice, to religious roles and their repertoires of features, as it does to individual epistemology and metaphysics.

---

84. HY text, chap. 2, line 14; Graham, *Chuang-tzu*, 51.

CHAPTER 4

Secret Arts, Manifest Wonders

In many ancient and medieval cultures of secrecy (along with their modern descendants), knowledge was deemed powerful because access to it was restricted and access to it was restricted because it was deemed powerful. A gulf separates these cultures from those Steven Shapin and Peter Burke have recently argued arose only in early modern times (in Europe at least), wherein truth-telling and the art of civil conversation among gentlemen formed the basis of a new epistemological decorum, and where lying and secrecy came to be seen as violations of a code of honor.[1] Over the past century scholars beginning with Georg Simmel have attempted a "sociology of secrecy" or "sociology of esoteric culture"[2]—an enterprise perhaps possible only in an era when secrecy has come to seem unusual rather than normal. To quote one of the most useful contributions to this literature, Tiryakian's "Toward the Sociology of Esoteric Culture," "a crucial aspect of esoteric knowledge is that it is a secret knowledge of the reality of things, handed down, frequently orally and not all at once, to a relatively small number of persons who are typically ritually initiated by those already holding this knowledge." In

---

1. Shapin, *A Social History of Truth;* Burke, *The Art of Conversation.* Of course, esoteric and "magical" religious practices persisted in early modern Europe and still persist today; the culture Shapin documents did not so much replace earlier cultures of secrecy as it displaced them from positions of prestige. If applied to Chinese materials, an analysis of Shapin's type, combining sociocultural history with the history of epistemology and of cognitive and textual practices, might reveal the earlier rise of analogous cultures in China, though without the concomitant "rise of science" to which such cultures are linked in the West; such an analysis would constitute a methodological advance in the rather tired discussion of why no "scientific revolution" took place in China. I borrow the fine phrase "practically religious" from the title of Reader and Tanabe, *Practically Religious.*

2. See Simmel, "The Sociology of Secrecy and of Secret Societies" this essay also appears in Tiryakian, ed., *On the Margin of the Visible,* which contains other attempts at a sociology of esoteric culture. See also Tiryakian, "Toward the Sociology of Esoteric Culture."

progressively realizing this secret gnosis, which is often of a "participatory" rather than detached sort, "the subject develops internally and liberates himself from the strictures of everyday life." Because this knowledge is of "the real but concealed nature of things," its recipients must prove themselves worthy to receive it, so we often find "a series of trials and ordeals, in the course of which the adept becomes increasingly socialized into the esoteric culture and increasingly desocialized from the natural attitude of the exoteric culture." Since esoteric knowledge must be concealed from public dissemination, it is often "presented to the adept not directly but . . . symbolically or metaphorically, so that it has to be deciphered progressively by the neophyte who uncovers layers of meaning in stages of initiation." Correspondingly, "the social organization and handling of esoteric culture tends to take the form of secret societies, societies whose modes and codes of organization and membership lists are not publicly disclosed." Finally, "since [esoteric] secrets are those that reveal the ultimate nature of reality, the concealed forces of the cosmic order, . . . esoteric knowledge is an ultimate source of power, which must be shared and utilized by a relatively small group of initiates. Such power is never justifiable in terms of the enhancement of the material conditions of the esoteric knowers but rather in terms of broad impersonal ends [or] humanitarian ideals."[3]

At first blush, this list of features seems to fit the masters of esoterica (fangshi 方士) and practitioners of longevity and transcendence arts in late classical and early medieval China, with two adjustments. The first is that the most social organization such practitioners achieved was the formation of loose (and often only fictively and retrospectively constructed) lineages of transmission of texts and techniques. There were no exclusive brotherhoods, no "schools" or cross-lineage organizations, and no secret societies, only masters with (usually) small clusters of disciples who were free and often encouraged by their teachers to seek esoteric knowledge elsewhere as well.[4] The other necessary adjustment is that Chinese practitioners of this period rarely appealed to "broad impersonal ends" or "humanitarian ideals" to justify their practices.

However, I want to suggest a more fundamental revision to this "sociology of secrecy." To do so I will draw on recent work by scholars such as Beryl Bellman, Lamont Lindstrom, and Hugh Urban that approaches secrecy as a cluster of forms of discourse rather than as a type of content and that sees discourses of secrecy as strategies for accumulating a type of cultural capital.[5] I want to elaborate here on

---

3. Tiryakian, "Toward the Sociology of Esoteric Culture," 498–501 passim.

4. See the remarks in Harper, *Early Chinese Medical Literature,* 60–62.

5. See in particular Urban, "The Torment of Secrecy"; Urban, "Elitism and Esotericism: Strategies of Secrecy and Power in South Indian Tantra and French Freemasonry"; Lindstrom, *Knowledge and Power in a South Pacific Society;* and Bellman, *The Language of Secrecy.*

one particular strategy characterized by Urban as "advertising the secret," in which "the claim to possess very precious, rare, and valuable knowledge [is made], while simultaneously partially revealing and largely concealing it. For a secret is only worth anything if someone knows you have a secret."[6] In the course of charting the habit of secrecy among practitioners of esoteric arts, we come to notice the practitioners' habit of displaying their secretly transmitted abilities and observe the tension and feedback relationship between these opposing habits.

The Culture of Esotericism

A history of secrecy in early Chinese culture might begin with chap. 65 of the received *Daode jing* 道德經 ("Of old those who excelled in the pursuit of the way did not use it to enlighten the people but to hoodwink them"),[7] proceed to early "allegorical" and other understandings of the *Book of Odes* as veiled speech,[8] continue to the notion that Confucius hid his teachings in indirect sayings and allegorical chronicles requiring interpretations that were not at all obvious,[9] treat the role of deception and secrecy in rhetorical and military strategy,[10] and alight on the surprisingly strange hermeneutic applied to what had by then become the canonical works of the imperium in the Han weft texts, a hermeneutic that assumed that the classics spoke in code. And then it might take up works that were explicitly and self-consciously positioned as secret works containing secret teachings, some examples of which we will examine shortly. Such a history might weigh the implications of these facts: that books in general during this period—existing only in laboriously copied manuscripts, of course—were rare, treasured commodities, in many cases not available at all to private readers but rather locked up inside royal libraries; that even such (to us at least) apparently nonesoteric books as the

---

6. Urban, "The Torment of Secrecy," 235.

7. Our hypothetical historian would also find meat in such passages as "The instruments of power in a state must not be revealed to anyone" (chap. 36), "The sage in his attempt to distract the mind of the empire seeks urgently to muddle it" (chap. 49), and "[The sage] keeps the people innocent of knowledge and free from desire" (chap. 3, all of these in D. C. Lau's translation, *Lao Tzu Tao Te Ching*), sentiments worthy of the legalist philosopher Han Fei zi 韓非子 but not readily congruent with the wishful *Daode jing* readings of the New Age. For a superb and long overdue rereading of the *Daode jing* along these lines, see Cole, "Simplicity for the Sophisticated."

8. On which, see Van Zoeren, *Poetry and Personality;* and Saussy, *The Problem of a Chinese Aesthetic.*

9. See Durrant, *The Cloudy Mirror,* 58; compare the passage in Fan Ye's preface to his collection of biographies of masters of esoterica in *Hou Han shu,* 82B:2703 (lines 6–8), tr. in DeWoskin, *Doctors, Diviners, and Magicians of Ancient China,* 45; and note the new contextual spin it puts on *Analects* 8:9 ("The people may be made to follow it; they may not be made to understand it").

10. See Raphals, *Knowing Words,* 101ff.

texts of the ancient philosophers, including the *Zhuangzi,* were held in secret for fear of their dangerous effects on readers; and that there were no bookshops before the first century C.E.[11]

Books of esoterica were hedged about with even more secrecy, which was expressed and enacted in several ways. The first was in nomenclature. The key generic term used to denote esoteric arts, texts, and practitioners—*fang* 方, literally "recipes" or "methods"—itself already implies specialization and limited access, heightened by its occasional pairing with modifiers such as *mi* 密, "secret," and *jin* 禁, "prohibited."[12] More fundamentally, the content of these books created an aura of remote origins. Esoteric texts were written in ways that created a palpable sense of their own inaccessibility, rarity, and sacred power.

SELF-ESOTERICIZING TEXTS

Divine revelation and extreme antiquity are two types of remote origin commonly claimed by esoteric texts, often simultaneously. One of the rhetorically simplest ways in which such origins were claimed was to frame the text as a dialogue between beings widely recognized as divine, ancient, or both. Two of the medical manuscripts found at Mawangdui, for example, share this structure. "Ten Questions" ("Shiwen" 十問) presents itself as the record of dialogues between various ancient figures cast as disciples, notably including the Yellow Thearch 黃帝 and Yu 禹, and more authoritative and in some cases transcendent figures, including the Celestial Teacher 天師, Rong Cheng 容成, and Ancestor Peng 彭祖. "Discussion of the Ultimate Way in the World" ("Tianxia zhidao tan" 天下至道談) is framed as a dialogue between the "Yellow Spirit," identified with the Yellow Thearch, who again appears in the role of disciple, and a figure called "the Left Spirit" 左神.[13] The august identities of these interlocutors encouraged readers to embrace the methods divulged in the texts as supremely authoritative and divinely revealed and thus extraordinary and hard to come by.

---

11. See Loewe, "The Religious and Intellectual Background," 650; Demiéville, "Philosophy and Religion from Han to Sui," 811–812; Harper, "Warring States, Qin, and Han Manuscripts Related to Natural Philosophy and the Occult," 227–228; Harper, *Early Chinese Medical Literature,* 49 n.1 and 64; and Tsien, *Written on Bamboo and Silk,* 15.

12. *Mifang* are mentioned (with *daoshu,* "arts of the Dao") in *Hou Han shu* 47:1440. *Jinfang,* often used by speakers to characterize books in their own possession, are mentioned in *Shi ji* 12:464, 28:1391, 105:2785, 105:2794, 105:2796, 105:2815; *Han shu* 30:1224, 33:1332; *Hou Han shu* 91:2705. Studies of these arts, the content of which I am largely bracketing here, include Ngo, *Divination, magie et politique dans la Chine ancienne;* Li Ling, *Zhongguo fangshu kao* and *Zhongguo fangshu xukao;* and Kalinowski, ed., *Divination et société dans la Chine médiévale.*

13. For annotated translations, see Harper, *Early Chinese Medical Literature,* 385–411 and 425–438.

Other texts keep the format of a dialogue between divine or ancient personae, but add another esotericizing device: they tell the story of their own divine revelation. Often such texts employ an additional strategy: they explicitly stress their own rarity as well as the secrecy in which they should be held, sometimes specifying infrequent intervals and solemn rites for their transmission.[14] *The Scripture and Instructions on the Elixirs of the Nine Tripods of the Yellow Thearch* (*Huangdi jiuding shendan jingjue* 黃帝九鼎神丹經訣), for example, opens with the direct, rather workmanlike statement that "the Yellow Thearch received the ultimate way of the reverted elixirs from the Mystic Woman 玄女. (The Mystic Woman is a celestial female.) The Yellow Thearch synthesized and ingested [the elixirs] and thereby subsequently ascended as a transcendent."[15] The text then proceeds to quote the Mystic Woman on the indispensability of its own methods:

> The Mystic Woman declared to the Yellow Thearch: "Whoever desires to live long but does not obtain divine elixirs and potable gold only brings suffering on himself. Although it is true that inhaling and exhaling, guiding and pulling, expelling the old and ingesting the new, and the consumption of herbal medicines can extend one's years, they will not allow one to avoid death. Ingesting the divine elixirs causes one to transcend the world as a divine transcendent, coming to an end only with heaven and earth. [As such], one shares in the radiance of sun and moon, sees a myriad *li* in distance while merely sitting, dispatches ghosts and spirits, lifts one's entire household to rise into the void, flies without wings, rides clouds and harnesses dragons [as mounts], ascends and descends in Grand Purity (Taiqing 太清), in an instant journeys to the eight extremities without being restricted within the rivers, and is not cowed by the hundred poisons."[16]

The *Scripture* then resumes the transmission narrative: "The Yellow Thearch transmitted this text to the Mystic Master [or Mystic Son, 玄子], admonishing him as follows: 'This way is of the utmost gravity. It must be transmitted only to the worthy. If there is someone who is not the right person, though he amass a quantity of

---

14. The fact that we now possess some such texts shows that they were sometimes leaked, often eventually to be collected and canonized (see Harper's musings on such leakages in *Early Chinese Medical Literature*, 64); on the other hand, vast numbers of them have disappeared without a trace. A few, such as the Mawangdui "books of esoterica" studied by Harper, have been recovered from tombs—private storage sites never intended for the public eye. Some that do survive were recreated in later times from titles cited in early works.

15. *DZ* 885, 1:1a.

16. Ibid.

gold the size of a mountain a myriad *li* square, do not divulge this way to him.'"[17] Detailed ritual instructions for transmission follow. Further on in the scripture, in passages perhaps added later, we find narratives of the quests of the Yellow Thearch for divine teachings that recapitulate the opening claim that he received transmissions from the Mystic Woman (as well, here, from the Unsullied Woman 素女) and synthesized and ingested an elixir.[18] Injunctions to secrecy and warnings against unauthorized transmission are repeated throughout the text.

The *Scripture of the Five Numinous Treasure Talismans* opens with an elaborate, convoluted, and dramatic narrative of the process of its own revelation and early transmission.[19] The process begins with certain celestial officials, continues through Thearch Ku 帝嚳 and Yu the Great 大禹, and proceeds to a certain Recluse of Mount Bao 包山隱居, who, acting as an envoy of He Lü 闔閭, journeys deep within a cave and recovers the scripture placed there earlier by Yu (who had earlier recovered his copy from another mountain cavern where it had been placed by Ku). The king, not having been formally initiated into the text's secrets, cannot understand it, so he seeks the help of Confucius, but that sage replies: "Only transcendents may employ this script; even sovereigns and kings are not to obtain its methods. If the king were to screen his body in the illimitable, go far off to seek the natural, avoid the snares and shackles of the world in inaction, and free himself from contention through secluded living in the deep mountains, then, at such a time, he should inquire of me again and I will perhaps tell him the strange mysteries of this numinous script and the abstruse words of the Most High." The disappointed king, we are told, stored the scripture for a while in a spirit hall; later, after secluding himself, he took it out at sunrise to view it, only to find that, although the seal of the case was unbroken, the text had vanished. The story ends by admonishing: "Few are they who take possession of a spirit text without explanation and bestowal who do not meet with disaster. None of those who illicitly gather and transmit celestial writings escape punishment in the Mystic Capital."[20]

Even texts that say nothing of their origins manage to esotericize themselves by other means. One of these is the implied disclosure of the secret practices of ancient or divine figures. An example is the *Grand Purity Scripture on Guiding-and-Pulling and Nurturing Life* (*Taiqing daoyin yangsheng jing* 太清導引養生經), with its

---

17. Ibid.

18. In these narratives he is also claimed to have received revealed teachings from the *boze* 白澤, a mythical beast that taught him to identify the shapes and names of anomalous creatures; see Harper, "A Chinese Demonography of the Third Century B.C.," 491ff.

19. On the first and third fascicles of this text (*DZ* 388), see Raz, "Creation of Tradition."

20. *DZ* 388, 1:7b–11a; my translation follows that of Bokenkamp, "The Peach Flower Font and the Grotto Passage," 68–69.

elaborately detailed descriptions of the breathing and stretching disciplines supposedly used by ancient transcendents such as Master Redpine, Ning Fengzi 甯封子,
Ancestor Peng, and Wangzi Qiao 王子喬.[21] What is striking about this work, aside
from its praxological details, is that although it ties those details to iconic transcendents of old, the practices themselves, as well as their associations with the figures
in question are (implicitly claimed to be) disclosed in this text for the first time: the
work might be subtitled "What the Famous Ancient Transcendents Really Practiced, First Revealed Herein." Another, rather similar nonnarrative self-esotericiz-
ing strategy is the systematic correlation of known phenomena with unknown.
Here the sheer novelty of the revelations is part of the aura-generating mechanism.
Laozi's Middle Scripture (or perhaps *Scripture of the Center, Laozi zhongjing* 老子中經)
works along these lines. Each item in its list of fifty-five relatively familiar gods,
aspects of the somatic microcosm, and disciplinary practices, originally accompanied by a picture, comprises newly revealed information about these items' true
identities, correspondences, and stations, or about how to perform associated practices correctly—an esotericizing hermeneutic.[22] The Han weft texts deploy the
same strategy, announcing unexpected, esoteric, and otherwise unavailable meanings and correlations underlying familiar passages from the classics. It is as if such
texts are saying, "The commonly acknowledged X is actually Y, a momentous fact
of which only those reading this text will be made aware." Simply by possessing the
book, one is drawn into a circle of privileged insiders, and at the same time a much
larger group of outsiders is constituted: those who, not having this book in hand,
can only resort to the surface, conventional meanings.

HOW ESOTERIC TEXTS WERE KEPT ESOTERIC

When we move beyond the texts to the social world in which they were created
and which they also helped to create, we find, on analysis, at least five major ways in
which access to them was carefully restricted, or, perhaps more accurately, five ways
in which such texts were portrayed as being hard to obtain, the question of their
actual accessibility remaining an open (and difficult) one.

---

21. All these figures receive hagiographies in the *Traditions of Exemplary Transcendents*. The
text is *DZ* 818; Schipper ("Le calendrier de jade," 77) is of the opinion that it predates the Eastern
Jin (317–420 C.E.); compare Schipper and Verellen, eds., *The Taoist Canon*, 95–96.

22. The text survives as *Taishang Laojun zhongjing* (*DZ* 1168) is anthologized under the title
Laozi zhongjing in *YJQQ* 18–19; it is silently quoted at several points in *DZ* 388 and is apparently
listed under two variant titles in the *NP* bibliographic catalogue. On this text, see Schipper, "Le
calendrier de jade" and "The Inner World of the *Lao-tzu chung-ching*"; Schipper and Verellen, eds.,
The Taoist Canon, 92–94; and Robinet, *La révélation du Shangqing dans l'histoire du taoïsme*, 1:27.
On the possible meaning of its title, see Schipper, "Le calendrier de jade," 117. On esotericizing
hermeneutics, see Urban, "Elitism and Esotericism," 11–17.

First, some texts were said to be transmitted only seldom, sometimes according to scripturally mandated schedules. A salient expression of this idea is found in the hagiography of Kong Yuanfang 孔元方 collected by Ge Hong into his *Traditions of Divine Transcendents:*

> Kong bored into the embankment beside a river to form a cavern chamber a little over ten feet square in area. He would enter this chamber and abstain from grains for a month, sometimes two, then return home. He did not permit his family to visit him there. In front of the cave opening there was a cypress tree; it grew beside the path in the scrub growth. It hid the entrance, so that even when one of his disciples wanted to visit him at his cave about some urgent matter, the cave could never be found.
>
> Now there came a youth from the east whose name was Ping Yu.[23] He loved the Way. He watched Yuanfang, then went looking for his cave dwelling and managed to find it. Yuanfang said to him, "Many people have come out here, but no one has been able to find me. You have succeeded in doing so. You seem to be teachable." With that he bestowed on Ping Yu a silk text[24] in two fascicles, saying, "These are the essential sayings about the Way. This text is to be transmitted to only one person in every forty-year period. And if you cannot find a suitable person, do not recklessly transmit it just because the year limit is up. If in forty years there is no one to whom it may be transmitted, then within an eighty-year period there will be two people to whom it may be given. Receive those two persons promptly, for if there is an opportunity to transmit the text and you fail to do so, you block the Way of Heaven. If, on the other hand, you transmit it to someone who is not worthy to receive it, you leak the Way of Heaven. In either case you will bring disaster on your descendants. Now that I have accomplished the transmission, I am leaving here." And so Yuanfang abandoned his wife and children and entered the Western Marchmount.[25]

Among other things of interest (including the motif of "recognition"), we see here a carefully controlled textual scarcity: the text is not to be transmitted so frequently as to dilute its power and not so infrequently as to risk letting it disappear altogether. Elsewhere we read of a similar forty-year transmission cycle in the case of the *Esoteric Writings of the Three Sovereigns* (*Sanhuang neiwen* 三皇內文) and the *Charts of the Perfect Forms of the Five Marchmounts* (*Wuyue zhenxing tu* 五嶽真形圖) as cited by Ge Hong.[26]

---

23. I have no further information on him.
24. On what I believe to be the special sense of this term, see *TL,* 219 n.311.
25. Ibid., 315, with slight modifications.
26. See *TL,* 67, 136.

Second, we find a motif of the physical inaccessibility of texts. They are pictured as having been discovered deep within caves by adepts who have prepared themselves by performing austerities. Ge Hong writes, in connection with the two scriptures just mentioned:

> These [types of?] scriptures are found in all the noted mountains and the Five Marchmounts, but they are hidden inside stone chambers in inaccessible places. When one who is fit to receive the Way enters the mountain and meditates on them with utmost sincerity, the mountain spirits will respond by opening the mountain, allowing him to see them. Such was the case of Bo Zhongli 帛仲理, who obtained scriptures inside a mountain, raising an altar and surrendering silk [as pledge-offering]. Such adepts always make one copy [of the scriptures] and then depart.[27]

The Bo Zhongli mentioned here is Bo He 和, of whom a *Traditions of Divine Transcendents* hagiography reports:

> He went to Xicheng Mountain and served Lord Wang, who told him, "I will go for a period of time to the Oceanic Continent. You should remain here in this cave, carefully regarding the north wall. After a long time you will see that there are written characters on the wall, and if you study these, you will attain the Way." Only after Bo He had regarded the wall for three years did he see the words of the *Scripture of Grand Purity* [*Taiqing jing* 太清經], which some person of ancient times had carved there. He studied them and thereby obtained transcendence.[28]

Third, access to esoteric texts was restricted by means of formal rites of transmission centering on the recipient's sacred oath not to reveal their contents to the uninitiated. Many texts detail the dire punishments for unauthorized transmission

---

27. *NP,* 19:336; see *TL,* 136.

28. See *TL,* 135, for the context of the passage, important variant versions, and annotations to the details found here. The reader will further recall the opening narrative of the *Five Numinous Treasure Talismans* scripture (*DZ* 388), with its multiple secretions of the text in successive eras deep within mountains, the text's repeated recovery from caves in later ages, and the lengthy relating of a hermit's quest to retrieve it—only to have it disappear, after all these arduous labors, due to the ruler's lack of qualifications to possess it. In the Daoist patrology is preserved a scripture, seemingly of early provenance, titled *Grand Purity Records from the Stone Wall* (*Taiqing shibi ji* 太清石碧記, *DZ* 881, in three scrolls). The text, containing a large assortment of alchemical methods, lacks an opening narrative of its own origins, but based on the above evidence we may infer that the title means to imply the scripture was discovered on the wall of a cave.

and emphasize that unseen spirits guard the texts at all times. In the *Yellow Thearch's Inner Scripture* (*Huangdi neijing* 黃帝內經), a text of medical methods compiled by the first century B.C.E. but, like many early texts, now existing only in later recensions, we find the following narrative model for the transmission rite: after three days of ritual purification, with the Thearch in the role of master and the Thunder Sire 雷公 in the role of disciple, we read:

> The Yellow Thearch then entered the purification chamber with him. They cut their forearms and smeared the blood on their mouths. The Yellow Thearch chanted this incantation: "Today is a True Yang day. Smearing the blood I transmit the recipes. He who dares turn his back on these words will himself receive the misfortune." Thunder Sire bowed twice and said: "The little son receives them." The Yellow Thearch then with the left hand gripped his hand and with the right hand gave him the books, saying: "Take caution, take caution. I will explain it to you."

An oral explanation—necessary supplement to the written text—is then provided: in this case, a lecture on vessel theory and acupuncture.[29]

Similarly, the *Scripture on the Elixirs of the Nine Tripods of the Yellow Thearch* gives clear instructions for its own transmission. The book, with accompanying oral instructions, which may never be written down, is passed from master to disciple in a solemn rite featuring an oath of secrecy and attended by the divine revealer of the text to the Yellow Thearch, the celestial Mystic Woman 玄女.

> As a [token of an] oath, a golden human figurine weighing nine ounces and a golden figurine of a fish weighing three ounces are thrown into an eastward-flowing stream. Both figurines should be provided by the one receiving the Way. Purifications and ablutions should already have been performed. Beside the stream, in a place unfrequented by other people, a seat [or altar, *zuo* 座] for the Mystic Woman should be set up. Burn incense and announce to those on high: "I intend to transmit to so-and-so the Way of long life." Place the scripture on elixirs on a table, and place the seat next to it. When you are ready to transmit the Way, face north and prostrate yourself for an hour; if the sky remains clear and there is no wind, the transmission may proceed. At the transmission, master and disciple together sip the blood of a white chicken as a covenant. The oral instructions are transmitted together with the essentials on synthesizing the elixirs. Then throw the golden figurines into the stream. No matter how many

---

29. Translation adapted from Harper, *Early Chinese Medical Literature,* 63; the passage occurs in the *Lingshu* 靈書, one of three medieval recensions of the text. For a summation of this text's complex history, see Sivin, *"Huang ti nei ching."*

adepts may come along, if they lack the bones of a divine transcendent, then they will never be able to view this Way.[30]

Elsewhere we find differing lists of pledge offerings and explicit warnings of divine punishment for breaking the oath of secrecy, as in the following passage from the *Celestial Master's Oral Instructions on the Scripture of Grand Purity* (*Taiqingjing tianshi koujue* 太清經天師口訣):

> These oral instructions are the great instructions to all the scriptures of divine transcendence. If one wishes to seek divine transcendence, though he have a thousand methods and a myriad arts, lacking these instructions his efforts will in the end come to naught. The secrets of the spirits are of the utmost gravity and must not be transmitted [without authorization] even for ten thousand in gold. When they are transmitted, according to the original scripture [of *Grand Purity*], they must be handed down orally one by one and cannot be fixed in writing. In accordance with the book of protocols for covenants, one uses eight ounces of yellow gold, forty feet of yellow cotton, eight ounces of white silver, and forty feet of white silk as pledges.[31] Such transmission is limited to one recipient per every hundred years.[32] The covenant is sealed by smearing the mouth with cinnabar in an oath of secrecy. If one day one violates the protocol by transmitting [the instructions] to one not fit to receive them or by otherwise leaking their contents, the Celestial Thearch will banish him from transcendence and he must eternally confess his error on the road to darkness. The Great Mystic Transcendents' Capital [Taixuan xiandu 泰玄仙都] will render his mind confused and his thoughts muddled so that all his endeavors fail. The Nine Aged Transcendent Lords [Jiu laoxian jun 九老先君] will disturb his vital essence and spirits so that all his studies will not come to completion. The Overseer of Registers at the [palace of the] Grand Monad will not enter his name on the registers of life, and the Overseers of Allotted Lifespans of the Three Heavens will lessen his count and shorten his years. The fault will reach his seventh-generation ancestors; all will be punished in the Grand Mystic Capital [Taixuan du 太玄都].[33]

---

30. *DZ* 885, 1:1b2–10, consulting Pregadio, "The Book of the Nine Elixirs and Its Tradition," 586; my translation differs at points.

31. The colors yellow and white symbolize the alchemical process.

32. This schedule, if actually practiced, would surely result in the text's extinction and must therefore be read as hyperbole.

33. *DZ* 883, 1a-b, consulting Pregadio, "Nine Elixirs," 586–587; my translation differs. Note that the "Mystic Capital" as the site of punishment for the leakage of esoterica is also mentioned in the *Five Numinous Treasure Talismans* passage translated above. For further examples of oaths of secrecy concerning scriptures, see *NP* 19:336; *TL* 67, 136; and Strickmann, *Chinese Magical Medicine*, 15, 82, 98, 232.

A fourth kind of restriction on access to esoteric teachings was the use of "oral instructions" (*koujue* 口訣), essential supplements to the written texts, sometimes constituting keys to their deliberately arcane terminology. These were never to be written down but only passed orally from master to disciple. As just seen, some texts loudly proclaim the necessity of such secret oral supplements and warn against their leakage. The lack of them was a handy retrospective explanation of past failures, as seen in a passage in Ge Hong's *Inner Chapters* regarding a text compiled at the Huainan court of the Han prince Liu An 劉安 and the subsequent failure by the Han courtier and bibliographer Liu Xiang 劉向 to make alchemical gold based on its recipes:

> Accounts of the fabrication of gold are in all the collections on divine transcendents. The Prince of Huainan extracted from them to form his *Esoteric Book of the Swan's Jewel* [*Hongbao zhenzhong shu* 鴻寶枕中書]. Although this work does have written materials [on alchemical methods], it conceals the most essential writings on them, which can only be transmitted by an orally conveyed commentary on the text; only then can the gold be made. And the names of many of the medicinal ingredients mentioned in it have since changed, so that the text cannot be directly employed as it stands.[34]
>
> When Liu De, Xiang's father, came into possession of this book while in charge of the case of Liu An, he did not have it properly transmitted to him by a teacher. And so when Liu Xiang, who had no understanding of arts of the Dao in the first place, happened to encounter this book, he assumed that its meaning was conveyed exhaustively on the surface of the paper on which it was written, and that is why his attempt to fabricate gold [based on it] failed.[35]

A fifth way in which esoteric texts were portrayed as difficult to access consists of a bundle of ideas concerning the selection of those who receive them: that text-possessing masters will not yield their treasures to the unworthy, even on pain of death; that adepts are carefully selected by discerning masters before being chosen to receive texts; that they must withstand trials of their worthiness; that only prequalified adepts will successfully find esoterica-possessing masters to begin with; and that adepts who come into possession of esoteric texts must be fated to do so (and,

---

34. The tone of these comments suggests that Ge Hong had perhaps seen the text; and indeed a *Scripture of the Swan's Jewel (Hongbao jing)*, along with three texts whose titles begin with the phrase *zhenzhong* 枕中 (literally "in the pillow" and meaning "esoteric"), are listed in the *Inner Chapters* catalogue in chap. 19. This impression is strengthened by another passage in which Ge Hong mentions the *Hongbao* and *Wanbi* texts (*NP* 19:337).

35. *NP* 2:21–22.

conversely, that those not so fated cannot possess the texts no matter what their other qualifications). Each of these ideas was luxuriantly developed in narrative.

NARRATING THE DIFFICULTIES OF ACCESSING ESOTERICA

Stories of masters of transcendence arts often emphasize their care in transmitting their secrets only to "the right person" and their skill in discerning who was qualified.[36] Of Kong Anguo, we read in Ge Hong's *Traditions of Divine Transcendents* that "as a person, he was very serious. He guarded the essentials of his Way with unusual care and was unwilling to transmit them lightly. He examined for five or six years the character of those who served him, and only then made a transmission to them."[37] Were one to believe the esoteric texts themselves, such behavior was standard and not worth mention in a hagiography; that it is mentioned here suggests that some masters were not as strict in their transmissions as the scriptures said they should be. In its several versions, the story of "Cheng Wei's wife," as she is identified, in which the husband, Cheng Wei, attempts to bribe and force his wife to reveal her secret arts to him, is notable for its portrayal of her stubborn resistance—and equally notable as an instance of an attempt to force divulgence of esoterica. After bribery failed,

> Cheng Wei plotted with a friend to force her to submit by beating her with a cane. His wife, already realizing this, said to him, "The method must be transmitted only to the right person. Having found the right person, I would teach him the method even if we met by chance on the road; lacking the right person, or in the case of a person whose words seemed proper but whose heart was not, I would not reveal the method even though my body be cut to bits and my limbs severed." But Cheng Wei kept on pressuring her until she finally went mad. Running away naked, she smeared herself with filth, and later died.[38]

This end was doubtless less horrible than the dire punishments she would have suffered at the hands of spirits had she divulged her arts to Wei, who, we are told in this narrative, lacked the proper preallotment (*ming* 命) to receive them. Ge Hong's

---

36. The theme is not confined to arts of transcendence; it pervades most accounts of transmission of secret arts of all kinds, one example being the story of how Zhang Liang received a secret manual of military strategy from a mysterious old man, after passing tests of his character. It was this book of strategy that, in the dynastic legends, he used in advising Liu Bang on how to defeat the formidable Xiang Yu and thus establish the Han dynasty. See *Shi ji* 55:2033–2049 and Lewis, *Sanctioned Violence in Early China*, 99–100.

37. *TL,* 311. I return to the case of Kong Anguo in Chapter 8.

38. Ge Hong quotes this story from Huan Tan's *Xinlun* 新論 in *NP* 16:285; compare *TL,* 140–141.

Traditions of Divine Transcendents includes a happier version of her story that has her merely staging her death, using the technique of the simulated corpse, and thus escaping her unworthy husband.[39]

In the narrative of Kong Yuanfang and Ping Yu related above, at the moment when Ping finds Kong in his hidden cave, Kong responds by saying, "Many people have come out here, but no one has been able to find me. You have succeeded in doing so. You seem to be teachable." He then transmits an esoteric text to his new pupil. This *motif of recognition*—reflecting the larger cultural concern, throughout the Han and early medieval periods, to develop methods for recognizing latent talent and choosing those most worthy to advance in the official hierarchy—reflects an essential means by which narratives stress the difficulty of getting access to esoteric books and oral instructions and the arduousness of being deemed qualified to receive them.[40] The recognition moves in both directions: qualified would-be disciples are portrayed as uniquely able to discern a powerful master beneath his public disguise of ordinariness and the fact of their having located and identified him is itself taken as proof of their worthiness to be taught; masters are likewise skilled at evaluating candidates and choosing the uniquely worthy even when they are not the ones apparently most capable.

Consider, for example, the following narrative sequence in the *Traditions of Divine Transcendents* hagiography of Sire Gourd 壺公 and his disciple Fei Chang-fang 費長房:

> In Runan there was a man named Fei Changfang who served as market administrator. He noticed that the Sire suddenly arrived at the market one day from a distant region and set himself up as a merchant of medicinals. No one recognized him. . . . He always kept a gourd hanging above his stall, and each evening after the sun had set he would jump up into the gourd. No one was able to see this save for Fei Changfang, who noticed it from his upper-floor room. From this Changfang realized that the Sire was no ordinary man.
>
> So Changfang began going to the Sire every day, sweeping the ground before his seat and taking him offerings of steamed cakes. Sire Gourd accepted and did

---

39. See *TL,* 139–140. On "escape by means of a simulated corpse," see ibid., 52–60.

40. On this motif in early Chinese literature more broadly, see Henry, "The Motif of Recognition in Early China"; for more on the importance of recognizing talent in early medieval discourse, see Shryock, *The Study of Human Abilities;* and Mather, *Shih-shuo Hsin-yü,* xxii–xxiii and 248–273. Compare two *Traditions of Divine Transcendents* narratives (concerning the adepts Chen Anshi and Cheng Wuding, respectively) in which an official in a bureaucratically superior position recognizes the esoteric aptitude of an individual under his supervision and responds appropriately: see *TL,* 138, 361. In this last story, the official is aided by a "mirror for recognizing people's [latent] characteristics."

not refuse this treatment. This went on for a very long time, but Changfang did not flag in his efforts, nor did he dare ask for anything. Sire Gourd knew Changfang had faith, so he said to him, "At dusk, when there is no one else around, come back." Changfang did as instructed. The Sire then told him, "When you see me jump up into the gourd, do as I do and jump in after me. You will be able to enter without any problem." Changfang did as he was told, and before he even realized it, he was inside the gourd. From inside, it no longer seemed to be a gourd at all; all you saw was the realm of a transcendent's palace, with towers, belvederes, multiple-lintel gateways, covered corridors, and several dozen attendants along the way.

Sire Gourd then said to Changfang, "I am a transcendent. Formerly I was in charge of a celestial office, but because of my carelessness in an official matter I was found guilty and was therefore banished to the human realm. You are teachable, and that is why you were able to see me." Changfang descended from his seat, bowed his head, and said, "On the contrary, I am an ignorant person of mere flesh; my sins are many and grave, and yet I now have the absurd good fortune to be looked upon with pity. . . . You would give life to the withered and raise up the decayed, but I fear I am smelly and dirty, stupid and decrepit, not fit for service even as a messenger. To be taken pity upon would be the great good fortune of a hundred lifetimes!" The Sire replied, "Then be mindful of your great opportunity, but tell no one of this."

Initially, then, it looks as if it is Fei Changfang's unusual perspicacity that qualifies him for a favorable reception. But the master informs him that the reverse is (also?) true: Fei was in the first place able to recognize the master's extraordinariness only because he was already qualified as "teachable." Fei's story does not end entirely favorably, however. He fails the ultimate test of faith in his master—the master's order to consume a pile of maggot-infested shit—and so is found incapable of the path to transcendence; instead he is consoled with the title of "agent above the earth," assigned to quell demons by means of talismans.[41]

The same text's hagiography of Wang Yuan 王遠 and Maid Ma 麻姑 (or the Hemp Maiden) plays twice on the theme of the master's evaluation of prospective pupils and recognition of their latent talent. We first encounter the following story:

Passing through Wu, Wang Yuan came to the house of Cai Jing 蔡經 at the Xu Gate. Cai Jing was only a peasant, but his bones and physiognomy indicated that he was fit for [eventual] transcendence. Yuan realized this, and that is why he went to his home. Said Yuan to Jing: "By birth, you are destined to transcend the world; you will be chosen as a replacement for an office. But your knowl-

---

41. See *TL,* 161–168. For more on the title "agent above the earth" (*dishang zhuzhe* 地上主者), see ibid., 78–80.

edge of the Way is scant; your *qi* is slight and you have much flesh. You cannot ascend [directly] in this condition, but must avail yourself of *shijie* [尸解].[42] It's like passing out through a dog's hole,[43] that's all." Then Yuan declared to Jing the essential teachings, and left him.[44]

Here the discerning master, despite Cai Jing's lowly social status, recognizes by his "bones and physiognomy"—reckoned in some quarters to be the seat of destiny, character, and lifespan[45]—that he will eventually accede to transcendence, though his body first requires a remedial purification, and so he transmits the secret knowledge (presumably both a text and its accompanying oral instructions). As the narrative unfolds, Cai Jing proves worthy; meanwhile, Wang Yuan's evaluative skills are once again called upon:

Cai Jing had a neighbor whose family name was Chen; his given name has been lost. He had once served as a district-level commander.[46] Hearing that there was a divine personage at Jing's house, he appeared at the gate, knocking his head on the ground and seeking an audience. So Yuan directed for him to be brought forward. This man requested to be made a Supporting Express Courier[47] like Cai Jing. Yuan told him to stand facing the sun for a moment; while he did so, Yuan regarded him from behind. Then Yuan pronounced: "Whew! Your heart is perverse and not correct. You will never be able to be taught the Way of transcendence. [But] I will bestow on you the office of Agent above the Earth."[48] When he was about to depart, Yuan placed one talisman and one text in a small box and gave this to Commander Chen, declaring to him: "These will not cause you to transcend the world, but they will at least prolong your original lifespan to beyond the age of one hundred. You can [also] use them to dispel misfortunes and cure illnesses."[49]

---

42. Normally I render this term as "escape by means of a simulated corpse," but since a different method seems to be indicated in this description, I here leave the expression untranslated; see ibid., 60, 266.

43. A small opening in a house wall, too narrow to permit a person easy passage. In a passage in *History of the Jin,* a man must strip off his clothes and hat in order simply to get his head through such a hole to shout at people inside a house to which he has been denied entry through the door (*Jin shu* 49:1385).

44. See *TL,* 260, where further annotation is provided.

45. See Bokenkamp, "Simple Twists of Fate."

46. Unless otherwise noted, official titles (at least those in the bureaucracy of this world) are rendered as suggested in Hucker, *A Dictionary of Official Titles in Imperial China.*

47. An office in the bureaucracy of spirits and transcendents.

48. On this title (*dishang zhuzhe* 地上主者), see *TL,* 78–80.

49. Ibid., 263–264.

As in the case of Fei Changfang, a would-be adept shows some promise but fails to qualify for the arts of transcendence. He is accordingly sent off with talismans, an enhanced lifespan and a lesser assignment commanding spirits and dispelling demons on the behalf of clients. The talismans, the text adds, were a one-time-only dispensation, not transferable to anyone else.[50] Again the master shows his ability to gauge latent talent by reading somatic signs; here the sign-bearer is not "bones and physiognomy" but the candidate's very heart, examined by a sort of esoteric proto-X-ray procedure.

This brings us to another narrative strategy by which the receipt of esoteric texts and arts was constituted in the *imaginaire* of transcendence as something exceedingly difficult: the recounting of the initiatory trials adepts had to pass in order to qualify to receive the texts.[51] We have just seen examples in which candidates pass—or fail—an initial evaluation by the master and are then either rewarded with secret, ultimate teachings or sent away, in these cases, with lesser though still beneficial arts. The esoteric *Scripture of the Jade Seal* (*Yuqian jing* 玉鈐經), now extant only in fragments, stresses that an aspirant to celestial transcendence must complete an unbroken series of 1,200 good deeds in order for elixirs to have any effect; should he complete 1,199 of them and then commit a single evil deed, the count is reset to zero.[52] As may be imagined, the adept's trials were promising material for dramatic narrative elaboration. One rather extreme example will suffice here. *Traditions of Divine Transcendents* tells of how the master Li Babai 李八百, on arriving at the home of his potential disciple Tang Gongfang 唐公房, in order to test him first pretended to be a diligent servant and then, having earned Tang's respect, feigned illness. Implicit questions about Tang's character are thus posed by the narrative: how would this householder treat his sick servant? How far would his compassion extend? The reader knows, but Tang does not yet know, how much is at stake in the answers; as far as Tang is aware, Li is simply a diligent domestic.

> Tang hired a physician to compound drugs for him, spending several hundred thousand pieces of cash but not considering it a loss. Tang's concern for Li showed on his face. Li then manifested ugly ulcers on every part of his body;

50. See ibid.

51. Even the resolutely anti-esoteric *Taiping jing* 太平經 explains that the masters of heaven above send trials to first test the earthly adepts who will receive their teachings and texts—trials including onslaughts by illness-causing "deviant spirits" 邪神 and temptations by jade maidens—because the Way is weighty and hard to transmit to humans, and their grip on it must be strong; see *Taiping jing hejiao,* 288. I read the *Taiping jing* as, in part, a reaction against the culture of esotericism and an attempt at a religious alternative to it that is public but anti-sacrificial and relentlessly anti-esoteric in nature.

52. *NP* 3:53–54; for a translation of the passage see *TL,* 50.

these disgusting sores oozed blood and pus, and no one could bear to go near him. Tang shed tears for him and said, "You have worked diligently as a messenger for my household for many years; you were always speedy. I hired the doctor to try to cure you, and I have no regrets about having done so, but still you are not well. What else can I do for you?" Li responded, "My ulcers will not be cured unless someone licks them. That should work." So Tang sent in three maidservants to lick his sores. Li then said, "The maidservants' licking has not cured me. But I can be cured if you will do it yourself." So Tang licked him, but again to no effect. Li then said that it would be most beneficial to have Tang's wife lick him. Tang ordered his wife to do it. Afterwards, Li declared, "My ulcers will heal if I can obtain thirty *hu* of fine wine to bathe in." Tang prepared the wine for him, pouring it into a large vessel, and Li bathed in it; and now his sores were finally healed. His body resembled congealed fat, and he bore no trace of illness.

This, then, is the climactic point at which Li reveals to Tang, "I am a transcendent. . . . I will now transmit to you instructions for transcending the world." Appropriately, Tang's entire household shares the benefits of the transmitted arts.[53]

Finally, some narratives suggest that successful recipients of esoteric arts, or achievers of transcendence, must have had a life-allotment or destiny—must have had the *ming*—sufficient to allow them to reach these goals. We have already glimpsed this idea: for example, in the hagiographic statement that "Cai Jing was only a peasant, but his bones and physiognomy indicated that he was fit for transcendence." Correlatively, we find Ge Hong writing: "Of old, transcendent officials and perfected persons venerated and kept secret the Way [taught in certain texts]; unless one has a transcendent's name"—unless one's name appears in the celestial lists of those fated to achieve transcendence—"they cannot be bestowed on one."[54] Some esoteric texts similarly say that the one possessing these texts must have the *ming* to do so; an example is the *Scripture on the Elixirs of the Nine Tripods* passage that "[n]o matter how many adepts may come along, if they lack the bones of a divine transcendent then they will never be able to view this Way"[55]—the bones being the seat of *ming*. In his *Inner Chapters* Ge Hong at several points assumes, and alludes to scriptures on transcendence that say, that the appropriate *ming* is a necessary (though hardly sufficient) condition for any adept's pursuing the path to transcendence. That the assumption of a conditional relationship between *ming*

---

53. See *TL,* 215–216. We will see in Chapter 8 that there were other reasons Tang's family members needed to be mentioned in the narrative.
54. *NP* 19:336.
55. *DZ* 885, 1:1b

and the receipt of teachings was widely shared is shown by its appearance at several points in the anti-esoteric *Scripture of Great Peace.*

This assumption regarding *ming,* and its confirmation in various scriptures, must have made the authorized possession of scriptures a promise of eventual success as reassuring as the signs of election discerned by Max Weber in early Calvinism.[56] Equally importantly, any adept possessing such self-authenticating signs of election could represent him- or herself to others as one assured of supreme future religious achievement, endowed with rare divine favor, and invested by higher beings with impressive prerogatives and credentials—a person in whom they could place much confidence.

SELF-OCCLUDING MASTERS

Finally, practitioners possessing secret arts were often portrayed as going to great pains to withdraw from ordinary social contacts and obligations, either disengaging entirely or assuming disguises so as to appear unremarkable. By restricting access to themselves, they also restricted access to their arts. In this, the collectively constructed role of the master of *xian* arts overlapped with and partially drew upon the larger, multifaceted role of "the recluse" (*yinzhe* 隱者), and indeed we find that some of the adepts commemorated as masters of esoterica also show up in stories of noted recluses.[57]

Some esoteric methods emphasize the need for secrecy and social isolation. Two examples will suffice. The *Scripture on the Elixirs of the Nine Tripods of the Yellow Thearch* stipulates that alchemical work must be done in seclusion:

> If you wish to synthesize the divine elixirs, you must dwell deep in the mountains or in a great marsh, or in a vast, empty rural area where there are no people. It is also permissible to make them among people, but in that case you must remain behind thick and high walls so that nothing is visible between inside and outside. Your colleagues should not exceed two or three in number.[58]

Strict purity must be observed before and throughout the entire process, beginning with the ritual receiving of the scripture and oral instructions:

> You must first purify yourself [*zhai* 齋[59]] for seven days, bathing in perfumed water and attending carefully to cleanliness. Do not pass by filthy places or

---

56. Weber, *The Protestant Ethic and the Spirit of Capitalism.*

57. On the complexities of the traditions and discourse of "reclusion" and "recluses" throughout this period—by no means a simple or unitary type—see Vervoorn, *Men of the Cliffs and Caves;* and Berkowitz, *Patterns of Disengagement.*

58. *DZ* 885, 1:2a, consulting Pregadio, "Nine Elixirs," 585.

59. The general term *zhai* would have been understood to include not only bathing but also dietary and sexual restrictions—further intensifying social disengagement.

homes where mourning is being observed or where there are marriageable women.... Have no dealings with profane or dull-witted persons, and do not let those who are envious, long-tongued, and without faith in the Dao know [of what you are doing], lest the divine medicine not be achieved.[60]

Ge Hong's *Inner Chapters,* although not itself an esoteric text (despite the somewhat pretentious connotation of *nei* 內 in its title), similarly contains an entire chapter on self-protective methods for adepts entering mountains to pursue their sacred disciplines. The assumption was that virtually all practitioners of esoteric "ways," as well as others fleeing social disorder or wishing to seclude themselves from unwanted political service, repaired to mountains—zones even less inhabited than they are nowadays—to do their work. Protection was needed not only from predatory wild animals lurking there but also from untamed mountain spirits resentful of human intrusion.[61] Mountains and marshes were understood as antihuman, extracivilizational, liminal, and hence dangerous zones but also, for those very reasons, as sites of religious opportunity.

Stories of masters of esoterica and transcendents are replete with examples of their subjects' self-occluding ways. There are five major narrative motifs. Many practitioners are depicted as being offered official positions and declining; some are shown refusing invitations to even speak with officials interested in them.[62] Adepts are portrayed as being asked to divulge their arts to rulers or officials and refusing, sometimes on pain of death (or, according to their hagiographies, an apparent death that allows escape). A great many adepts are described as dwelling in physical seclusion, often on mountains, but in yet another example of ambivalence regarding social disengagement, just as many are shown living in ordinary surroundings or dividing their time between the mountains and their family homes. In a fourth motif, adepts hold office or otherwise interact in ordinary ways with people (often by selling goods in markets), but they disguise their unusual appearance and conceal their extraordinary abilities until someone recognizes them. Finally, among the frequently reported repertoire of esoteric skills are the powers of instantaneous disappearance and body concealment—powers of literal self-occlusion often

---

60. *DZ* 885, 1:2a and 2b, consulting Pregadio, "Nine Elixirs," 585. Compare the discussion of similar prohibitions at *NP* 4:84.

61. The *NP* chapter in question is 17; see the salient opening passage at *NP* 17:299, translated in *TL,* 61. On mountain deities, see especially Kleeman, "Mountain Deities in China."

62. An example of this latter motif is the *Traditions of Divine Transcendents* account of Sun Deng; see *TL,* 336. The tension between official service and reclusion is evident throughout the Han-period *Accounts of Exemplary Transcendents* and continues in *Traditions of Divine Transcendents;* it also figures greatly in Fan Ye's collection of "Traditions of Exemplary Transcendents of Wielders of Esoteric Arts" in the *History of the Later Han.*

invoked by adepts when needing to extricate themselves from situations of social pressure.

It is clear how heavily and by what a luxuriant variety of means the culture of esotericism in late antique China stressed that certain methods for the attainment of desirable goals—most notably transcendence and longevity, but also such boons as healing, prognostication, protection from danger, even securing the affection of a desired lover or finding a lost object—were extremely hard to come by. Notice was served that such arts existed, and their efficacy was promised, but access to them was insistently portrayed as almost impossibly limited. This is, however, only half the story.

Displaying the Fruits of Secret Arts

The secrecy surrounding esoteric arts was bound to have a paradoxical result. Given how hard it was portrayed to be to make contact with holders of esoteric texts, to receive such texts in an authorized transmission, and then to perfect the arts they contained, and given how desirable the benefits of such arts were, any adept claiming to possess such texts and demonstrating (or even suggesting) command of the secret knowledge and abilities they conveyed would, ipso facto, draw instant attention and acquire tremendous prestige. The restriction of access to esoteric knowledge, accomplished via multiple and mutually reinforcing textual representations and social practices, inevitably enhanced the status of such knowledge and the status of its possessors in the eyes of outsiders (at least those favorably disposed) not privy to its secrets. Secrecy itself drew attention and generated prestige, the opposites of secrecy. The much-bruited secrecy of the arts no more prevented outsiders from knowing or caring about them than the "reclusion" of individuals ensured their being forgotten by others in society. Quite the opposite: the aura of secrecy, along with displays of the impressive results produced by the arts, generated interest in them and their wielders, just as recluses became famous for (and by) shunning the quest for fame by usual routes. Recluses' social withdrawal did not preclude recognition but rather invited it, as has been voluminously documented;[63] claims of secrecy surrounding texts and arts did not stifle curiosity but aroused it. The basic dynamic is delectably captured in the following line from the *Traditions of Divine Transcendents* hagiography of Jiao Xian 焦先, whose various eccentric behaviors have just been narrated in the text: "Because of all this, the Governor . . . went out to see him, but Jiao Xian was unwilling to speak to him, which only convinced the Governor more that he was a worthy."[64]

---

63. See Vervoorn, *Men of the Cliffs and Caves,* index s.v. "fame"; and Berkowitz, *Patterns of Disengagement,* 118, 136–138, 173.

64. *TL,* 187.

Such patterns of "conspicuous self-exile"[65] are familiar from the dossiers of holy persons in other societies and should not surprise us; they have been documented, for example, by Peter Brown in the late antique Mediterranean world and by Stanley Tambiah in modern Thailand.[66] Some holy persons withdraw from ordinary social intercourse to an extraordinary degree, retreating to mountains, forests, or the desert, climbing poles or towers, penetrating caves; yet it is precisely these most reclusive spiritual virtuosi who attract the most attention and draw the largest crowds out to their hermitages.

In general, though, in order for people to respond thus to socially disengaged adepts or holy persons, three things are needed—things that underscore the fact that the status of holy persons is always socially constituted. First, the adept's sheer existence and proximity, and more, his holy-person-like behaviors or powers (however these are locally viewed), must be brought to other people's attention. The reclusive, disengaged one has to be a visibly placed individual; people must notice his reclusiveness, disengagement, and special powers or traits. Second, social networks must be in place along which word of the holy person's reputation can travel. Reputations are built via social discourse, the exchange of opinion and narrative. Third, there has to be a set of signals, codes, types, or standardized gestures in place, so that people can recognize an individual as a member of a type and not merely random noise; not just any unusual behaviors will do. Taking these three requirements together, we see that there must be an *audience* who will notice and talk about the fact that an individual has withdrawn from normal social roles and is behaving in ways that signal a different code, a code consisting of signs that allow the individual to be fitted into a recognized role. What those signs were for "transcendents" and aspirants to this status was the topic of Chapter 2; here I am simply returning to the idea that such an inventory is possible.

In sum: the content of esoteric texts and the methods of practitioners may have been secret (or at least were mandated to be kept secret), but their existence was hardly a secret, nor were their benefits: these were often loudly and colorfully advertised. Much was done to call attention to the existence, possession, and power of these secret methods; access to them was carefully managed, but part of that management was the incessant announcement of the methods' existence and of the possibility of accessing them given the right qualifications and conditions. The ensemble of behaviors, gestures, and practices we have reviewed, summarized in the single word "secrecy," was, then, itself a stance toward the larger society, not the absence of any relation to society. And, paradoxically, the frequent net effect of that

65. Gellner, *Plow, Sword, and Book,* 156.
66. See Peter Brown, "The Rise and Function of the Holy Man," 1971; and Tambiah, *The Buddhist Saints of the Forest and the Cult of Amulets.*

ensemble was to attract the attention of others, create an aura of authority, enhance
prestige, even to arouse desire for forbidden knowledge. As the authors of the *Daode
jing* sayings understood very well, artificially enhanced scarcity induces want, and
"goods hard to come by" tantalize those lacking them (chap. 12); if "not to display
what is desirable will keep the people from being unsettled of mind" (chap. 3), then
displaying it guarantees the opposite effect. The very gestures of esotericism suggest
a particular kind of display for an audience and *create* the conditions under which
the revelation of secrets becomes a powerful event. We can chart the recognition
these gestures earned and the patterns of their reception by the larger society in
the types of responses recorded in histories, hagiographies, essays, and other works.
Practitioners of the arts of transcendence were not members of a secret society
utterly invisible to others; even some of the most reclusive of adepts by their very
habits of reclusion drew attention to themselves, attracting the curious and the
needy. Hagiographies and other mentions in surviving texts are, of course, witnesses
to this phenomenon: a truly and utterly reclusive adept would have left no recorded
impressions at all.[67]

A case in point is the above-mentioned Jiao Xian, perhaps the most reclusive
of all the adepts eulogized in extant hagiographies from the period treated here.[68]
The version of his story found in *Traditions of Divine Transcendents* reads:

> Jiao Xian, styled Xiaoran, was a native of Taiyang in Hedong. People in this
> village over successive generations said that he had reached the age of 170. He
> habitually decocted white stones and ate the product, which he also shared with
> other people. When cooked, they tasted like taro.
>
> Every day he would go into the mountains and cut firewood, which he
> would distribute to people. He would start with an initial household in the vil-
> lage, then work his way around; when he had completed a circuit of homes, he
> would begin again. He would carry the wood and place it outside each family's
> gate. Whenever people caught sight of him, they would invite him to sit down
> with them on their mats and would set out food for him. At this, Jiao Xian
> would simply sit down and eat, saying nothing to them. If no one happened to
> see him when he carried the wood up, he would place it in the gateway and
> then simply depart. He did this for many years.

67. And it is, of course, possible that such adepts existed. But if they did, we can know nothing of them. It is only those adepts who were somehow known to others that we can characterize
in any meaningful way. Absent other evidence, I see no reason to doubt that these "known" adepts
constituted the vast majority.

68. Fang Hui 方回, the subject of a *Traditions of Exemplary Transcendents* hagiography, is represented to be almost as reclusive as Jiao Xian but is also—as is quite typical of that text—said to
have held a court office (see *DZ* 294, 1:4a-b).

At the time when the Wei accepted the abdication by the Han ruler [220 C.E.], Jiao Xian dwelt beside the Yellow River, knotting together reeds to make a hut in which he lived alone, without any bed or mats, using only grass for his bedding and seating. His body was filthy and stank like a stagnant puddle. Sometimes he would go several days on a single meal. Whenever he wanted to eat, he would hire himself out to work for people just long enough to obtain the cost of one meal, then depart. When walking, he did not use paths. He had no intercourse with women. When his clothes wore out, he would sell enough firewood to buy some used clothes, and wear these. No matter what the season, he wore only a single-layer gown. Because of all this, the Governor, Dong Jing, went out to see him, but Jiao Xian was unwilling to speak to him, which only convinced the Governor more that he was a worthy.

Once a wildfire was spreading toward the location of his hut. People went out to see what had happened, and they saw Jiao Xian calmly sitting inside the hut, not moving at all. Only when the fire had passed and the hut was completely incinerated did he get up, utterly composed. None of his clothing or belongings were so much as singed by the flames. He built another hut.

Another time, there was a sudden snowfall, and many people's homes collapsed. Jiao Xian's hut also fell in. People went out to look for him but could not find him. Fearing he had frozen to death by then, they pulled apart his hut searching for him. They found him sleeping soundly beneath the snow. His complexion was bright and his breathing was relaxed, like someone lying comfortably in a drunken repose on a hot day.

People then realized that he was unusual. Many wanted to follow him and study the Way, but Jiao Xian would say, "I have no Way." At times he would suddenly seem to age, then just as suddenly he would seem to grow young again, and this went on for over two hundred years.

Later on he bade farewell to people, and it is not known where he went. No one who asked him [for his teaching] ever obtained so much as a word [of instruction] from him.[69]

Although Jiao Xian is said not to have spoken with others, he is depicted as bringing them firewood and sharing meals with them. This and his other strange habits attract the attention of the governor; Jiao's unwillingness to speak only impresses the governor more. Despite the insistence that Jiao avoided normal contact with people, everyone knows the location of his riverside hut and rushes to check on him after fires and snows. After his reputation spreads, "many wanted to follow him," despite his disavowal of having any special methods and his steadfast refusal to

---

69. *TL,* 186–187; see that text for annotations omitted here.

transmit whatever methods he patently—given his longevity and special abilities—must have had. It is inaccurate, then, to say that Jiao was disengaged from his local community; rather, he was engaged with it differently than ordinary people. The locals are keenly aware of his presence at the margin of their community, and his reputation travels, *because of* his withdrawal from the usual modes of social intercourse.

Unlike Jiao Xian, most adepts are on record as being not nearly so retiring and modest. They are shown openly displaying the marvels their secret methods made possible. Here is, for example, the opening of the *Traditions of Divine Transcendents* story of the demon-quelling Luan Ba 欒巴:

> Luan Ba was a native of Chengdu in Shu commandery. When young, he studied the Way and took little interest in profane matters. The Governor of the district paid him a personal visit, asking to appoint him to his Labor Section and treating him as a teacher and friend. The Governor said, "I hear that you possess a *dao*, sir. May I see one marvel?" Ba answered, "Very well." Then, from a seated position, he entered the wall of the room; he became like a cloud of vapor, then vanished [into it]. People on the other side of the wall were heard crying, "Tiger! Tiger!" But when he returned, he was Ba again.[70]

Noteworthy first of all is that the governor takes interest in Luan and hears of him despite Luan's noncultivation of "worldly affairs"; Luan has come to the governor's attention precisely because of that noncultivation as well as his "possessing a *dao*." Second, the governor asks not for Luan's methods but simply for a display of what they can do. And third, although some other adepts in this situation decline to perform marvels and deny possessing any special arts, Luan simply and promptly complies by providing an impressive, collectively witnessed wonder.

The hagiographies of a few adepts stress their wonder-working abilities much more than their attainment of one or another grade of transcendence. The "arts" these adepts display often seem utterly incidental to attaining transcendence yet are narrated in great detail. Consider the following subnarrative found in the *Traditions of Divine Transcendents* hagiography of Jie Xiang 介象:

> Jie Xiang was capable of innumerable kinds of illusions and transformations of this sort. He once planted an assortment of melon and vegetable seeds for the ruler, and all of them sprouted and grew immediately and were ready to be

---

70. Ibid., 252, slightly modified here.

eaten. The Wu ruler and Xiang once got into a discussion on which variety of fish was best for preparing sashimi,[71] and Xiang said, "*Zi* fish[72] is best." The ruler replied, "I'm talking only about local fish. *Zi* fish comes from the ocean; how could we even get any?" But Xiang answered, "It's obtainable." He told someone to dig a square hole in the palace courtyard, fill it up with water, and find a hook. Xiang baited the hook and set his line in the hole, and in a little while he indeed caught a *zi* fish. Surprised and delighted, the Wu ruler asked him, "May we eat it?" Xiang answered, "I especially obtained it for Your Majesty to prepare a sashimi dish with. How would I dare catch a creature that was not edible?" So the ruler sent it to his kitchen to be sliced. Then he said, "I have heard that a messenger from Shu is coming. It would be perfect if we could obtain some Shu ginger for a sauce, but, regrettably, we have none of this just now." Xiang replied, "Shu ginger is easy to get, too. Why not notify the messenger to bring some with him?" So the Wu ruler designated one of his attendants and gave him fifty pieces of cash. Xiang wrote a talisman and placed it inside a green bamboo staff; then he had the messenger close his eyes and mount the staff, and he told him that when the staff stopped moving he was to buy the ginger and then close his eyes again. This man followed the instructions, mounted the staff, and in a moment, when it stopped, he found himself to be already in Chengdu. Only he did not know what the place was, so he asked someone; they said it was a market in Shu. So he bought some ginger there. Now at this time the Wu messenger, Zhang Wen, was already in Shu, and he happened to recognize [the messenger sent by Jie Xiang] in the market. Startled to see him there, Zhang Wen wrote a letter to his family for the messenger to carry back with him. Once this man had bought the ginger, he stowed the letter, shouldered the ginger, mounted the staff, and closed his eyes. In a moment he was already back in Wu, and the chef was just finishing the slicing of the fish.

An almost identical feat is attributed in the same text to Zuo Ci 左慈, except that Zuo makes the journey himself rather than sending an attendant.[73] Presumably an adept who could so easily procure ginger from a distant province could also procure herbs of deathlessness from Penglai or elsewhere, but here the sole function of this ability to travel long distances almost instantaneously seems to be to entertain crowds of courtiers and please rulers.

---

71. "Sashimi" translates *kuai* 膾 (Japanese *namasu*), raw fish or meat hashed and served with a hot sauce.

72. Japanese *bori*. I do not know whether the English "mullet" is a good equivalent.

73. On the cases of Jie Xiang and Zuo Ci, see *TL,* 191 and 280 respectively.

One of early medieval hagiography's most prolific wonder-working adepts is Ge Xuan 葛 玄, the great uncle of Ge Hong. The narratives of Ge Xuan are filled with accounts of his marvelous feats and strange spectacles, always performed before crowds of onlookers. A small sampling follows:

Once [Ge Xuan and his disciples] were traveling by boat when [one of the disciples] noticed a box [of Xuan's] containing several dozen talismans and other documents on wooden tablets. The disciple asked whether the talismans were effective, what they could do, and whether he could see a demonstration. Xuan replied, "What's the fuss about a talisman?" He then took one of them out of the box and cast it into the river, and it made its way upstream against the current. "What do you think?" Xuan asked. "Strange!" replied the student. Then Xuan took out another talisman and cast it into the river as well; it stood still and did not move. Then the downstream talisman came up, and the upstream one went down, and the two joined together in one place. Xuan retrieved them. There was a woman by the riverside washing clothes. Xuan said to the youths, "I'll send this woman running. How will that be?" The students said, "Great!" Xuan threw a talisman into the water, and at once the woman ran off in fright; she ran for several *li* without stopping. Xuan said, "I can make her stop." Again he threw a talisman into the water, and the woman at once stopped and returned. When someone asked the woman what had frightened her into running, she answered, "I myself don't know why I ran!"

Xuan often entertained guests. He would go out to welcome the late-comers, while, meantime, seated and talking with the other guests was another Xuan.[74] When sending guests off, he did the same thing. [Once] when the weather was cold, Xuan told his guests, "It is impossible in my humble abode for each of you to have his own fire, but I invite you to warm yourselves in common." He then opened his mouth and exhaled flames, which quickly filled the room. All of the guests felt as if they were under a bright sun, but neither were they too warm.

Xuan was once dining with a guest when the conversation turned to arts of transformation. The guest said, "After we've finished eating, could you per-

---

74. In Ge Hong's *Inner Chapters* (*NP* 18:325), Ge Xuan is mentioned along with Zuo Ci and Ji Zixun as possessing "the *dao* of body division" 分形之道. "In a single day they could go to several dozen places. And when guests were present at their residences, there would be one host talking with guests at the gate, another host greeting guests by the waterside, and another host casting for fish; the guests were unable to distinguish which was the real host."

form one special feat?" "Since you're able not to be in a hurry [to see it]," Xuan
replied, "you'll see it in a hurry!" With that, he spat out the food that was in
his mouth, and it turned into several hundred large bees which all alighted on
the guest's body but did not sting. After the space of a meal, Xuan opened his
mouth again, and the bees all flew back into it; Xuan chewed them up and ate
them, for they had once again become the food he'd been eating.[75]

Although Ge Xuan is unusual in the dramatic detail in which his marvelous performances are narrated and in the proportion of his hagiography devoted
to them, he is hardly unique in his ready display of marvels to audiences. Judging from the surviving narratives, such displays were the stock-in-trade of adepts,
regardless of how tenuous the apparent connection between the marvel-producing
arts and the ultimate goal of transcendence. Liu An is said to have asked for, and
received, prior demonstration of each esoteric art he received from his transcendent
guests—such skills as bodily transformation and the generation of clouds, wind, and
fog.[76] Wang Lie reportedly held archery contests involving large crowds wherever
he traveled.[77] To Sun Bo is attributed the following impressive dossier of wondrous
performances, no doubt to large audiences:

> Bo could enter into rock cliffs in the mountains or stone boulders on the
> ground. When he went in, one at first saw his back and ears protruding from the
> surface of the rock. Only after a long while would he be completely submerged
> in it. He could also swallow several dozen knives and swords, pass through walls
> as if there were openings in them, and stretch mirrors out to become swords
> and bend swords up to become mirrors; they would remain this way until Bo
> himself pointed at them, at which time they would return to their original
> forms.

Large crowds are explicitly said to have participated in the following additional
marvel:

> Whenever Sun Bo walked over a large body of water, not only did he himself
> not get wet but he could also cause his crowd of followers, consisting of several
> hundred, not to get wet either. He was capable of leading large groups of people
> out onto the surface of water, where they would spread out mats, drink, eat, and

75. *TL,* 152–159.
76. Ibid., 237.
77. Ibid., 339–340.

make music. He enabled the whole group to dance on the water without sinking or getting wet. They could amuse themselves the entire day this way.[78]

Our sense that such dramatic displays of marvels were routinely expected of adepts is reinforced by cases in which rulers or officials command them as a test of authenticity. One such case is that of Wang Zhongdu, as related in *Traditions of Divine Transcendents*:

> Once, on an extremely cold day, [Han] Emperor Wen ordered Zhongdu, wearing only a single garment, to gallop around Lake Kunming in the Upper Park with a team of four horses. The driver, who had dressed in fox furs, almost died of cold, but Zhongdu's color never changed. His body and breath remained as warm as if they were burning. He was also exposed to fire on a torrid day and never broke a sweat.[79]

The Tension between Display and Concealment

I have charted the adepts' habits of secrecy and self-concealment but also provided evidence to suggest that many adepts flaunted their abilities. Rather than interpreting these facts as indicating a problem in the sources or as a merely literary effect of hagiographies, I read them as suggesting that a specific tension existed in the religious practice and the social lives of adepts.

AN INITIAL EXAMPLE

In *Records of the Grand Historian* or *Shi ji,* the unprecedented Han-period attempt to gather up the Central Kingdom's past into one grand framework, masters of esoterica are portrayed as walking onto the stage of history—that is, as coming to the notice of emperors and court officials—most notably during the reigns of two

---

78. Ibid., 335. One reviewer of this book in manuscript commented on this passage: "It stretches one's credulity to believe that *xian* somehow performed mass walking on water. More likely this is the product of an imaginative writer or an inspired copyist. Or someone with an agenda willfully rewriting stories.... Perhaps you need some hermeneutic principles for deciding which accounts might reflect typical reality and which fabulous imagination." I reply: this is a move that, as I explained in Chapter 1, I am unwilling to make. There are many things in these accounts that strain my own personal capacity for belief; the list is quite long and does not begin or end with mass walking on water. I do not find it a meaningful or useful exercise to try to sort out what did or did not happen on this or that *specific occasion*. I simply do not think that these sorts of texts lend themselves to that sort of inquiry. The point, for our purposes, is that even a feat as remarkable as this was one that could be seriously attributed to an adept such as Sun Bo in the *imaginaire* of transcendence in early medieval China.

79. *TL,* 271.

particular emperors, Qin Shi Huang 秦始皇 (r. 221–210 B.C.E.) and Han Emperor Wu 漢武帝 (r. 141–87 B.C.E.), by means of a specific type of verbal and behavioral self-presentation at court. One of the most vivid of these narratives concerns Li Shaojun 李少君 or Li the Youthful Lord, said to have appeared at the court of Emperor Wu around 133 B.C.E. Let us observe how the *Records* narrative represents this adept's behavior.[80]

Claiming to possess methods of "dispelling old age" 却老 by means of sacrifices to the god of the stove, commanding spirits, and some unspecified dietary regimens, Li, we are told, concealed his true age and place of birth, always saying he was seventy years old. With no wife or children, he traveled among the seats of nobility at the time, speaking of his esoteric methods and, we can presume, putting on performances such as the following two recorded by the historian. In the first, while a guest of a certain marquis, he told one of the other guests, a man of over ninety, that he had once accompanied the man's grandfather to a certain place to practice archery—implying that Li himself was at least more than a century and a half old. The old man indeed recollected going to the place with his grandfather as a child. "All those seated were completely amazed." In the second instance, the Han emperor, perhaps as a test, asked Li about a certain bronze vessel at the court. Li answered that it was presented in the tenth year of the reign of Duke Huan of Qi, corresponding to 676 B.C.E. When the inscription on the vessel was consulted, it confirmed that the bronze had in fact belonged to the duke, with whom Li was therefore implied to have been personally acquainted. "All the palace was in shock, taking Shaojun to be divine, a person hundreds of years old." Further responses are recorded as well:

> When people heard Li could summon spirits and avoid dying, they intensified their presentation of foods and gifts to him, so that he always had a surplus of money, clothing, and edibles. Seeing that he always seemed affluent though he did no work, and not knowing anything of his origins, people believed in him even more and vied with each other to serve him.[81]

Having thus won the confidence of the ruler and his court, Li proceeded to explain his convoluted longevity method to the emperor. By sacrificing to the god of the stove, one summoned spirits; the spirits would convert cinnabar to gold; with the gold could be fashioned serving vessels whose use would prolong one's life; having prolonged one's life, one could visit the transcendents on the isle of Penglai 蓬萊 in the middle of the sea; and if, in doing so, one performed the *feng* 封 and *shan* 禪

---

80. Ban Gu's *History of the Han* also incorporates the story.
81. *Shi ji* 28:1385–1386; *Han shu* 25A:1216–1217.

sacrifices—the ultimate subject of the historian's discourse here, in which Li the Youthful Lord is only one of many characters—one would not die. This, he said, was the method used by the Yellow Thearch in antiquity.

At this point, as if to reintroduce his qualifications to speak of such arcane matters, Li is recorded as having told another story about himself:

> Your servant was once traveling on the sea when I met Master An Qi 安期生, and together we ate giant jujubes as big as melons.[82] Master An Qi is a transcendent who frequents Penglai. If he deems someone suitable, he will come to see him; if not, he will conceal himself.[83]

This last detail, perhaps added by a commentator, accomplishes four things at once: it confirms Li's own exalted status—for the clear implication is that Li has been deemed worthy of approach by An Qi; it serves to restrict access to the sources of such methods as Li prescribes; it establishes a precedent for the contemporary adept's withholding of esoterica from the unworthy; and it acts as a fail-safe just in case the emperor practices the method unsuccessfully. The ruler, his advisers, and contemporary readers of the *Shi ji* narrative would have recognized the name An Qi as that of a reputedly long-lived master of esoterica who was honored by the founding emperor of Qin and who helped inspire eastward sea excursions seeking methods of immortality during that ruler's reign.

The passage continues by noting that Emperor Wu indeed personally offered the prescribed sacrifice, attempted to fashion alchemical gold from cinnabar, and sent out a maritime expedition to find Penglai—none of which measures, the historian notes, proved effective. So complete was the ruler's confidence in Li Shaojun, however, that when Li grew ill and died, the Son of Heaven maintained that he had merely "transformed himself and departed, not died,"[84] and assigned a minister in charge of sacrifices, Kuan Shu 寬舒, to carry on with Li's methods. Meanwhile, if Li's presence at court did not result in the emperor's immortality, it did accomplish something else: "All manner of strange, dubious masters of esoterica from the seaboard areas of Yan and Qi came in [to court] telling of divine matters."[85]

---

82. Compare the following passage in *Han Wudi gushi* 漢武帝故事, item 10 (in Lu Xun's ordering in his *Gu xiaoshuo gouchen*, 340): "Li Shaojun said that the dates from the Dark Sea were as large as melons and that the plums from Mount Zhong were as large as jugs." On this text see *SW*, 48–49.

83. *Shi ji* 28:1385–1386; *Han shu* 25A:1216–1217.

84. As would be asserted by later hagiographers, starting—at least among extant texts—with Ge Hong's *Traditions of Divine Transcendents;* see *TL*, 222–225.

85. I have paraphrased and translated from the closely parallel accounts in *Shi ji* (28:1385–1386) and in *Han shu* (25A:1216–1217).

In essence, this is the story of what a master of secret arts had to say about them to all who would listen. It is a story of how he demonstrated the wondrous effects of those previously unheard-of arts in his own implied multicentennarian longevity, his personal visits to the paradisal eastern isles, and his contacts with distant transcendents, including the famed An Qi. In the narrative the very same verbal performances that announce how hard to come by the transcendence-techniques are—and that thus qualify the speaker (who possesses them) as an advanced practitioner of them—also reveal quite a bit about how they are supposed to work. And the master has, of course, presented himself at court as a mediator through whom access to the secret arts is promised. Equally striking is the audience's recorded response: astounded courtiers rush to offer the adept tribute, and the emperor credits his claims to the point of believing that he has not really died.

But although Li thus disclosed much about his methods and even more about what he had achieved with them—the "display" side of the coin—it also remains true that no one other than he himself (at least in the estimation of some nonskeptical contemporaries, including the ruler) reached those methods' promised goal. Having displayed his arts, in the end he took them with him either into transcendence or into death—the "concealment" side of the coin.

Now it is tempting to chalk up this inherent doubleness of the esoteric stance—the adept's disengagement and the secrecy of his arts on the one hand, the attention he and his arts commanded on the other—to a duplicitous motive. To do so is to set a research agenda to ferret out of the intentions of individuals, their degree of sincerity or deepest beliefs, from surviving snatches of written discourse. Seeing that so-and-so wrote, said, or did such-and-such, we ask, "is he sincere?"[86] Thus Alan Berkowitz speaks of the reduction of social disengagement to "a marketable pose, adapted and adopted by attention-seeking profiteers or insincere freeloaders."[87] On what grounds is a historian, at such a chronological and textual remove, to discriminate the sincere from the insincere? It is not an easy job even in our own lives, concerning people we know personally. Penetrating the true motives of historical actors seems not only impossible but also less interesting than charting the sets of gestures, the social attitudes and poses and mores, and the matrix of assumptions within which plural individuals—both the senders and the receivers of social signals—operated. For our purposes, it is fruitless to speculate whether such-and-such an individual "really meant it"—though we may note

86. As does Berkowitz, *Patterns of Disengagement*, 173. Compare Vervoorn's formulation in *Men of the Cliffs and Caves:* "an elaborate demonstration of lofty personal ideals *designed* to attract the world's attention" (139, emphasis added). The stance dates back to Lu Xun: see Vervoorn, *Men of the Cliffs and Caves*, 15.

87. Berkowitz, *Patterns of Disengagement*, 137.

contemporaries' recorded judgments on this question, if any, as an aspect of their reception of him—but it is important to see that there was a collectively sustained matrix of behaviors and expectations within which an individual's withdrawal from certain standard roles increased, rather than decreased, his visibility. That is, for the "pose" to be "marketable," it must first be recognizable as comprising the gestures expected of an individual of a certain already standard type. These structures of expectation, unlike individuals' motives, are recoverable.

It is not as if we must take Li Shaojun's claims at face value (although, in those quarters of contemporary religious studies that disapprove of any function for the scholar other than to repeat his subjects' claims, that would be the only remaining option); the author of the historical passage already registers a scornful skepticism. But on the other hand, to Gopal Sukhu's recent statement that a figure such as Li Shaojun "conned the emperor with some of the oldest ploys in the occult book," and that the emperor, "who was an easy mark," responded by promoting him to high court rank,[88] I would reply: the story we have is not of one person doing something to another, but of two people—in fact a group of people—doing something together, albeit playing different roles. The adept's words and acts did not occur in a vacuum; a successful confidence game implies and indeed requires a context of confidence, the attitude of the "mark" counting every bit as much as the artist's self-representations. This environment of confidence at the Han court made the "con" (if such it was) possible in the first place; at the court and throughout society there was a public, collectively fashioned structure of expectation and belief—an *imaginaire*—in which many more than the emperor participated and to which we have many more narratives than this one to attest.[89]

FURTHER *SHI JI* CASES
The same tension between the masters' display of the wondrous results of their arts or the tantalizing descriptions of the realms of transcendents, on the one hand, and their withholding from imperial patrons of the complete means for reaching the goal of transcendence, on the other, recurs in many other stories related in the *Records of the Grand Historian*.

---

88. See Sukhu, "Monkeys, Shamans, Emperors, and Poets," 160–161. Sukhu speaks here not of Li but of a similar practitioner, Luan Da, whom we will meet shortly.

89. Additionally, the dyad of the practitioner's sincerity vs. his cynical deceitfulness is too simple to fit the evidence; ethnographic accounts of indigenous shamans and healers show us much more subtle processes at work, processes of the practitioner's own gradually deepening understanding of arts of which he might initially have been skeptical. For a superb study of this theme, which to my knowledge has not been improved upon, see Lévi-Strauss, *Structural Anthropology*, 167–185 (I am indebted to Bob Hymes for the reference).

The sections of the *Records* dealing with the Qin and Han empires, and particularly those concerning the reigns of the First Emperor of the Qin and Emperor Wu of the Han, are replete with accounts of the activities at court of transcendence-seekers and other masters of esoterica. None of these adepts is represented as shy about revealing his possession of secret methods or reticent in touting their benefits. Each reveals much about the content of those methods, but each also inserts himself as a mediator between the rulers and transcendence, never permitting the rulers direct access to the exalted states and realms claimed to be accessible to adepts.

The methods vary. Li Shaojun's combined a preparatory alchemical phase with sacrifices and a pilgrimage to Penglai off the eastern shore. The adept Xu Fu 徐福 proposed, and received imperial funding and approval for, a maritime excursion to Penglai and two other eastern isles, Fangzhang and Yingzhou, to meet transcendents and retrieve the sacred herbs on which they fed. Li Shaoweng 李少翁, later described by Ge Hong as a disciple of Li Shaojun but not so identified in the *Records of the Grand Historian,*[90] demonstrated his ability to summon and make visible not only spirits of the dead but also the god of the stove; presumably the appearance of this deity would permit him to be supplicated for long life.[91] Luan Da 欒大 proposed sending high-ranking envoys, including himself, into the eastern seas to locate transcendents (as well as his own former teacher) and persuade them to come personally to the Han court. All of these figures received enthusiastic imperial patronage (though Shaoweng's prowess waned and he was eventually executed—but even in this case the historian notes that the emperor later came to regret executing him "before his methods had been fully exploited").[92] The "tall and handsome" Luan Da, in particular, became fabulously wealthy and won high rank, obtained the hand of a princess in marriage, and was constantly invited to courtiers' homes and showered by them with gifts and favors before he, too, was finally executed when his methods proved ineffective.[93]

Despite the variance in methods, most of the accounts of these adepts' exploits share a common structure: the promised goals of esoteric methods remain always on the horizon, not obtainable without further effort or adjustment yet nevertheless visible to a select few adepts and described by them for an audience.

For example, in the chapter on the *feng* and *shan* sacrifices, when the three elixir- and transcendent-harboring "divine mountains" of Penglai, Fangzhang, and Yingzhou are introduced, they are first described at a level of detail implying intimate familiarity.

---

90. See *TL,* 225.

91. On the reasons for this god's importance in the quest for long life, see Campany, "Living off the Books"; and *TL,* 49–52.

92. See *Shi ji* 28:1390.

93. The exploits of all these figures are set down in *Shi ji* 28.

We are then told, however, that although they are not far from China's eastern shore, they are unreachable, for, it is said, each time a boat draws near, winds arise to push it away "so that in the end no one [can] ever reach the islands." When those sponsored by the First Emperor of Qin failed to reach these isles, they cited these winds as the reason, but they also reported: "We were unable to reach the islands, but we could see them in the distance!"[94] Elsewhere we read: "Those who had gone to sea in search of Penglai said that the isles were not distant, and that their inability to reach Penglai was likely due to their not perceiving its *qi*. The Sovereign therefore dispatched a specialist in watching for *qi* to assist them in locating [the island's] *qi*."[95]

Again, according to the "Basic Annals on the First Emperor of Qin," Xu Fu, who had received imperial backing for his eastward expedition, returned to say: "The Penglai medicinals were obtainable, but we were constantly troubled by large sharks, so we were unable to get there. We ask for skilled archers to accompany us so that when we see the sharks we can shoot them with crossbows."[96] In the biography of the Han prince Liu An, we find a different account of these events, but one with the same structure of display and unreachability:

The Emperor sent Xu Fu out to sea in search of spirits and marvelous goods. Xu returned and gave the following false excuse: "I saw a great spirit in the midst of the sea, who said to me, 'Are you the envoy of the Emperor of the West?' When I replied that I was, he said, 'What do you seek?' 'I wish to ask for a medicine that will extend years and lengthen lifespan,' I replied. The spirit said, 'Your king of Qin is stingy with his courtesies! *You may see the medicine, but you may not take it with you.*' He then led me southeastward to Mount Penglai."[97]

We then read a brief description of Penglai's numinous herbs and its impressive towers, followed by an account of how Xu Fu asked the oceanic spirit what offerings he required: 3,000 boys of good family and beautiful girls, along with the products of skilled craftsmen, came the answer. The passage goes on to claim that the emperor equipped Xu Fu as requested but that Xu, when he reached the broad marsh at Pingyuan, halted, made himself king of the region, and never returned to Qin.[98]

---

94. Ibid., 28:1370.

95. Ibid., 12:467.

96. Ibid., 6:263, my translation partially borrows from that found in Nienhauser, ed., *The Grand Scribe's Records,* 1:154. Xu Fu's failure to reach Penglai is also mentioned in the hagiography of An Qi in the *Traditions of Exemplary Transcendents* (*Liexian zhuan* item 30; see *DZ* 294 1:14b–15a).

97. *Shi ji* 118:3086, emphasis added.

98. It should be mentioned that the context of this version of the Xu Fu story is an impassioned speech by Wu Bei attempting to dissuade Liu An from his planned uprising; Wu tells the

For his part, Luan Da told of having personally met An Qi, Xianmen Gao 羨門高, and other transcendents on the eastern sea, but of having failed to receive their secret teachings due to his lack of rank as well as to the fact that his patron at the time was only a feudal lord, not the Son of Heaven. He added that his unnamed teacher promised that "yellow gold can be fashioned, the breach in the He River dikes can be stopped, a medicine of deathlessness can be obtained, and transcendents can be summoned,"[99] but explained that he had earlier hesitated to come forward for fear of sharing Shaoweng's fate. The requested fix, then, was for the emperor to ennoble his envoy with sufficiently high rank so that the eastern transcendents would be impressed enough to come and for the emperor not to lose patience with the method. Luan was careful to mention that the transcendents still might not deign to come—that their presence at court could be humbly beseeched but not commanded. The emperor followed through to a point, sending feather-clad attendants to assist Luan and granting him inscribed jade seals of office, including one that signified that he was not considered a subject of the emperor but was rather a "general of the Celestial Dao" 天道將軍. The emperor's confidence was presumably bolstered by Luan's confirmatory display of powers that even *Records* concedes: without touching them, Luan caused chess pieces to move and attack each other. We are told at this point that Luan Da thenceforth regularly made offerings in his home at night, attempting to cause spirits 神 to descend but in fact attracting only a multitude of ghosts 鬼, whom he was able to control, and that later he packed and, it was said, headed out to sea to find his former master. A few pages later the story resumes:

> The General of the Five Benefits [Luan Da], who had been sent as an envoy, did not venture to put to sea, but [instead] went to Mount Tai to perform offerings. The Sovereign sent men to follow him surreptitiously and verify [any results]; in fact they saw nothing. [The General of] the Five Benefits falsely said that he had seen his master, [but] his methods were exhausted, for the most part having elicited no response. The Sovereign then executed him.[100]

Immediately after this denouement comes another story about Gongsun Qing 公孫卿, who claimed to possess a text traceable to the Yellow Thearch that seems

---

story as an instance of the ability of ambitious men to capitalize on popular dissatisfaction with the Qin regime, in contrast to the Han's current strength, which would doom any revolt.

99. *Shi ji* 12:462.

100. Ibid., 12:471. It is possible to understand the penultimate line differently than I have just indicated, as Luan's attempt to lay blame at his purported master's feet and thus buy more time (for the failure of one teacher's methods need not entail that of another's), in which case we might translate thus: "[The General of] the Five Benefits falsely said that he had seen his master but that his [master's] methods had been exhausted and had largely elicited no response."

to have been a key impetus for the performance of the *feng* and *shan* sacrifices as a means toward the emperor's own transcendence.[101] While "watching for spirits" 候神 in Henan commandery, Gongsun Qing saw "the tracks of a transcendent" atop the city wall. "A creature resembling a pheasant"—suggestive of a transcendent, since transcendents were often imagined (and imaged on tomb walls) as having avian features—was observed walking back and forth there. The Son of Heaven personally visited the city to observe the tracks, and when he expressed some skepticism and alluded to the recent unhappy fates of Shaoweng and Luan Da, Gongsun Qing assured him that much patience was required for the spirits and transcendents to descend.[102]

As a final example, a certain Master Lu 盧生 attributed his and other practitioners' failure thus far to find "excrescences, strange medicinals, and transcendents" to the fact that courtiers and officials knew the ruler's location. This, Lu said, for unexplained reasons discouraged the "Perfected Persons" 真人 from appearing and divulging their secrets. If the ruler would travel incognito and let no one know his whereabouts, exorcising demons as he moved about, then and only then would the "drug of deathlessness" be obtainable.[103]

To recap: Penglai and the other eastern isles are close to shore and have been sighted, but winds prevent landfall there. Penglai is close but its *qi* must be detected. Penglai's medicinals are obtainable but sharks prevent the vessels from landing. A spirit is encountered and Penglai's medicinals are personally glimpsed, but richer offerings are required before they can be secured. Transcendents are personally encountered but the adept holds insufficient envoy rank to receive their methods. The birdlike tracks of transcendents are glimpsed, even by the ruler himself, but patience is required for further appearances by the elusive feathered beings. Marvelous excrescences exist and may be found and a drug of deathlessness thus obtained, but first the ruler's movements must be concealed. In each case the goal is almost within reach; it is palpable, visible, tantalizingly described, confidently claimed to be obtainable, but actually acquiring it is postponed pending further measures. More precisely: the goal and the elusive beings who guard the secret ways to the goal are directly visible *only to adepts,* who then describe and narrate them to their imperial patrons; they are never directly accessible by rulers. The goal is displayed via narration and description and is promised to the audience if certain conditions are met, but its achievement—by the audience—is constantly deferred; access to the goal is restricted, mediated by the adept possessing the methods and the stories. But if this deferral and constant mediation breed skepticism in rulers, it is a skepticism con-

---

101. See ibid., 12:467–469.
102. Ibid., 12:472.
103. Ibid., 6:257.

fined to particular adepts and their claims; it never amounts to a sweeping dismissal of all claims concerning the eastern isles, drugs of deathlessness, and the existence of transcendents.

This pattern of display and concealment may be thought a by-product of Sima Qian's own expressed cynicism concerning transcendence-arts practitioners. But we find it in sympathetic accounts as well, and this convergence of representations across very differently motivated narratives suggests that the pattern was part of adepts' actual mode of social action.

SYMPATHETIC SOURCES

If in the unsympathetic *Records of the Grand Historian,* transcendence is implied to be unachieved because it is in fact chimerical, other, sympathetic accounts argue its reality and attainability. But in doing so these accounts nonetheless retain the basic structure we have observed: adepts withhold their methods from the uninitiated, blocking any attempts by rulers or officials to gain direct access to their methods, but they visibly and strikingly display the results of their methods to large numbers of clients and spectators, prominently including rulers and officials. Sympathetic accounts typically blame the adept's withholding of secret methods squarely on the inquirer's lack of qualification to receive them.

In hagiographies, rulers, upon witnessing the marvelous results of the esoteric arts, often ask (humbly or arrogantly as the case may be) to receive the arts and are refused. In the *Traditions of Exemplary Transcendents* story of Kou Xian 寇先, for example, we read that Kou fished by the River Sui and lived for over a century. When Duke Jing of Song (who must have been motivated by reports of Kou's longevity) asked him for his *dao,* Kou did not reveal it, so the duke retaliated by having him killed. Several decades later Kou was seen playing the lute by the gate of the city walls of Song, implying that, at the moment of his execution, he evaded death by means of a somatic decoy and escaped unscathed—an esoteric technique termed "escape by weapon" (*bingjie* 兵解) in later texts.[104] In the same work we read of Xiuyang gong 修羊公, "the Shepherd Sire": at first he lived on a mountain, subsisting on "yellow essence" or Solomon's Seal. Later he wanted to display his *dao* before Emperor Jing, who honored him and provided palace accommodations. After several years the Sire's *dao* had still proved unobtainable; an imperial edict demanded to know when he would manifest it again. The messenger had not finished delivering the edict before the Sire, on his bed, transformed into a white stone sheep. On its flank were inscribed the words: "The Shepherd Sire takes leave of the Son of Heaven." Later this stone sheep was installed on an imperial tower,

---

104. Item 27; see *DZ* 294, 1:13b; and Kaltenmark, *Le Lie-sien tchouan,* 107–108. On *bingjie,* see further *TL,* 59.

whereupon even it disappeared.[105] In this case, unlike that of Kou Xian, there is a clear statement of the adept's intention to display his abilities; but, whatever an adept's intentions, feats such as extraordinary lifespans and non-aging were bound to be noticed, and indeed in many hagiographies this mysterious non-aging is the first thing that draws others' attention to adepts.

We find the same pattern repeated and indeed expanded in the cycle of narratives attached to the figure of Han Emperor Wu in third- and fourth-century texts.[106] The basic story line, seemingly first developed in the probably third-century *Precedents of Han Emperor Wu* (*Han Wu* [*di*] *gushi* 漢武帝故事) and already deployed several times in that text, is that although Emperor Wu had some faith in the existence of transcendents and the attainability of deathlessness, and although he made some efforts and even had some partial success in this regard—culminating in a personal meeting with the Queen Mother of the West in a special palace tower constructed for the purpose—he himself did not succeed in transcending. On the other hand, in the course of the narrative several of his advisers in such matters, including Li Shaoweng, a certain unnamed dwarf, and most especially Dongfang Shuo 東方朔, are shown to have superior command of esoteric arts. Li Shaoweng, although apparently executed by the disappointed emperor, later turns up at a distant location and his exhumed coffin turns out to be empty except for a bamboo staff (a classic instance of escape by means of a simulated corpse). The dwarf turns out to be an envoy from the Queen Mother of the West, and he as well as the Queen Mother recognize Dongfang Shuo as a courtier of hers at Mount Kunlun and as an incarnation of the planet Jupiter who has been temporarily banished to earth for stealing the Queen Mother's peaches of immortality.

At several points in *Precedents,* Emperor Wu is shown as eager to receive and practice secret arts but ultimately found wanting. The apparently executed but in fact escaped Li Shaoweng, whom the emperor had welcomed and sponsored at court, sends him the message that, had the emperor persisted in the method a few days longer (rather than impatiently executing his adviser in esoterica), it would have succeeded. In response, the emperor regrets his mistake and summons masters of esoterica to court once more. The dwarf appears to instruct the ruler to maintain "purity and stillness" for five years as preparation for a personal visit from the Queen Mother, then vanishes; when the emperor asks Dongfang Shuo for more details of this method, Shuo answers evasively with the words, "Your Majesty should know it yourself." Later the Queen Mother does appear, and the first thing

---

105. Item 38; see *DZ* 294 1:18b–19a; and Kaltenmark, *Le Lie-sien tchouan,* 130–132.

106. On questions of dating of these texts, and for translations, I have relied on Thomas Smith, "Ritual and the Shaping of Narrative." See also Schipper, *L'empereur Wou des Han dans la légende taoïste;* and *SW,* 318–321.

the impatient emperor does, after showing her to her seat, is request the drugs of deathlessness; he is denied by the goddess on the grounds that he has not dispelled his passions. He is granted peaches of long life and retains their pits, intending to plant them, but is informed by the goddess that they do not grow on earth and in any case that their 3,000-year cycle of fruition is too long to do ordinary mortals any good. Immediately after these rebukes the text reveals Dongfang Shuo's true identity, as if to underline that Shuo, the initiated adept, has direct access to secrets the ruler can never obtain; the Queen Mother, in the course of telling the ruler who (or what) Shuo really is, also pointedly informs him that Shuo is not his subject.[107] The *Precedents* narrative concludes with the emperor's death and its dynastic aftermath.

Other texts, such as the perhaps fourth-century *Inner Traditions of Han Emperor Wu* (*Han Wu di neizhuan* 漢武帝內傳), build on this same narrative structure while adding more details. In the *Inner Traditions* version the Queen Mother bestows not merely peaches but also an ensemble of esoteric scriptures, but the ruler later loses possession of these in a palace fire that, the text tells us, was ordered by the goddess herself because the ruler had proved unworthy to possess the texts. This work insists repeatedly that the ruler's unchecked desires make him unfit to receive any secret teachings (although, interestingly, it also narrates the Queen Mother's bestowal of such teachings on him), but it then goes on to say that the emperor had made his divinely revealed texts available to courtiers, namely, Dong Zhongshu 董仲舒 and Li Shaojun, whose copies survived the fire and enabled the transmitted texts to be preserved. But only qualified adepts can read them, not the emperor, who had proven unqualified to retain them.[108]

Another text in the same tradition, the *Record of the Ten Continents* (*Shizhou ji* 十洲記), consists of Dongfang Shuo's lengthy discourse about the outlying isles and mountains and their many wonders, at the end of which he warns Emperor Wu not to disclose what he has revealed; but the text ends by noting that the emperor, although vouchsafed all of this precious information, could never completely learn the principles necessary for transcendence from Shuo, who spoke in jests and who, this text seems to suggest, was himself not fully cognizant of the highest methods. Furthermore, the *Record* contains an astonishing passage in which Emperor Wu is severely upbraided as self-indulgent and desire-ridden by a visiting envoy from a

---

107. The late-third-century *Treatise on Curiosities* (*Bowu zhi* 博物志) by the *fangshi* Zhang Hua 張華 (232–300 C.E.) includes a parallel account regarding the peaches and Dongfang Shuo. See *Bowu zhi jiaozheng*, ed. Fan Ning (Beijing: Zhonghua shuju, 180), item 8, p. 97. On this text, see *SW*, 49–52.

108. See *DZ* 292 and 293; Schipper, *L'empereur Wou des Han dans la légende taoïste;* and Thomas Smith, "Ritual and the Shaping of Narrative."

Western "barbarian" kingdom, who, along with his wonder-performing beast, mysteriously disappears before he can be questioned further.

The basic message remains the same: rulers may have their interest stoked by witnessing the effects of secret methods; they may even be fortunate enough to receive such methods; but they are not qualified to understand or practice them properly. Only initiated adepts are. Adepts are the necessary mediators between importunate rulers and the secrets they so desperately seek but do not deserve to receive and cannot wield effectively. Rulers' proper role is to enjoy the wonders produced by esoterica to which they lack direct access, and to provide patronage for the specialists who alone are qualified to produce such wonders.

Conclusion

The sociology of secrecy, then, requires revision. It is not always or strictly the case—perhaps, indeed, it is rarely or never the case—that "the magician is an isolated individual" operating in "alienation" from any surrounding community.[109] Tiryakian and others have well described the secrecy aspects of some esoteric traditions, but they have not dealt with their outward-looking faces. Masters of esoterica in late antique and early medieval China did not constitute a "secret society": they neither organized themselves into widespread horizontal groups nor, for the most part, did they attempt to conceal their possession of esoteric arts or the results of these arts. Quite the contrary. Even narratives that depict adepts as retreating behind a disguise of ordinariness also depict their eventual recognition as adepts by discerning others, and many stories make clear that some adepts flaunted the abilities they derived from their access to secret arts.

To dwell exclusively on the habits of secrecy of esoteric traditions, then, will not suffice. In the case of Chinese masters of transcendence arts, at least, we find something more complex: a set of discursive strategies and patterns of depicted behavior that worked to create a tension between secrecy regarding methods and texts on the one hand and a display of wondrous results on the other. Furthermore, not only the dramatic display of the arts' results but also the carefully maintained aura of secrecy surrounding their contents had the same effect: the enhancement of the practitioners' prestige in the eyes of many non–arts-practicing but nevertheless interested witnesses. We have seen something of the range and complexity

---

109. The quoted words are found in Graf, "Prayer in Magical and Religious Ritual," 195–196. Graf is invoking a familiar trope: the notion that "magic" implies a lack of communal or social context goes back to Émile Durkheim's *Les formes élémentaires de la vie religieuse* and earlier—but not to Marcel Mauss, who saw, in his work on magic, the fundamental importance of the public clientele in constituting the magician's power; see *A General Theory of Magic*, 132–144.

such strategies could take in the literate culture of late classical and early medieval China.

In social terms the net effect of this dynamic of display and concealment amounted to the staking of a claim to a separate domain of power that was beyond the control of rulers and officials and separate from the network of ritual obligations binding the imperium to the spirits of ancestors and of topography. It was a domain in which possessors and wielders of arcane arts were the sole masters. Anyone else desiring access to this domain, it was claimed, had to approach it through these masters and their texts, and through them alone.

CHAPTER 5

Verbal Self-Presentation and Audience Response

OTHER THAN in terms of the secrecy-and-display dynamic, how else did adepts perform their roles? How did they present themselves to others? And how did others receive these performances? In revealing the wide array of activities of adepts and the responses of others to it, I want to focus on one particular aspect of self-presentation: the adepts' storytelling and certain other verbal modes of interaction. Where possible, I also take note of other people's responses.

We have examined the socially interactive, collectively fashioned nature of narrative (even of first-person narrative). We have also noted the real-life effects of narration on practitioners and patients: a patient's recovery, for example, depends in part on his success in shaping a coherent self-narrative. As Bruner writes, "Our experience of human affairs comes to take the form of the narratives we use in telling about them."[1] If these premises are true, then we may expect the arc of the transcendence-seeker's experience to have resembled, to some considerable extent, the sorts of stories told about that quest, and vice versa. And the same arc described hearers' expectations of adepts. It will be worth attending, then, to the sorts of stories some practitioners are represented as having told about themselves (recognizing as we do so that practitioners were hardly the only ones who told stories about their exploits), the ways in which they are shown narrating their labors and ordeals to others, and the responses of those others, as well as the social contexts in which such oral exchanges are represented as occurring. How did these acts of speech and of reception shape adepts' reputations before audiences? How did they invest speakers with the authoritative personae of accomplished transcendence-seekers?

---

1. Bruner, "The Narrative Construction of Reality," 5.

Practitioners' Self-Narratives

Consider the following text from the *Traditions of Divine Transcendents:*

> When Han Emperor Wu was on a tour of inspection,[2] he saw an old man hoe-
> ing near the road. A white light several dozen feet tall was above his head. He
> summoned and questioned the man. [From up close,] the man looked to be a
> person of fifty-something, with the facial complexion of a youth and a glow of
> health that made him stand out from ordinary people. The man gave this reply:
> "When your servant was eighty-five, I was decrepit and aged and near death.
> My hair had gone white and my teeth had fallen out. A man of the Dao taught
> me to avoid grains, to eat [only] atractylis and drink [only] water, and also to
> make a pillow for the [internal] spirits. Inside this pillow are thirty-two objects,
> twenty-four of them corresponding to the twenty-four *qi,* eight of them cor-
> responding to the eight winds. I put all this into practice and reverted to youth.
> I became able to walk three hundred *li* in a day. Now I am ninety."[3]

I leave aside here the royal identity of the interlocutor, as well as the story's
conclusion, which says that the emperor bestowed fine silks on the old man, who
then entered Mount Tai, from which he visited his home village periodically over
the ensuing three centuries until finally ceasing to return. The story's basic structure is as follows: a person who practices no special longevity arts notices another
person's unusual appearance, which is described in detail; in reply to questioning,
the man of unusual appearance explains that it is due to his practice of longevity
arts and narrates his story, which depicts his initial condition of decrepitude and
near-mortality, tells of his all-important encounter with a teacher of life-prolonging
arts, adumbrates the methods vouchsafed, and announces the results gained by their
practice. What is here delivered in the first person is precisely the same sort of narrative often told in hagiographies written in the third person. This simple structure
exemplifies a *pattern of action* or *cultural schema*[4] that is commonly deployed in early
medieval texts describing how a person came to receive esoteric arts and with what
results, and that action pattern is repeated in both first- and third-person narratives
that have come down to us through the collective work of memory.

Note further how much of this entire passage—both the framing story of the
emperor's encounter and the inner self-story told by the old man—concerns the
adept's body: its imperfections, its signs of radiant health, its degree of vigor and

---

2. On this supposed practice and its associated institutions and meanings, see *SW,* 106–126.

3. *TL,* 337; see 338 for comments on the self-cultivational method described here. The
story is similar to that of Wu Yan in the same text (see *TL,* 345–346).

4. See Ortner, "Patterns of History."

special capacities. This too is utterly typical of narratives of *xian*-seeking adepts,
whether sympathetic or hostile in attitude. The observable condition of an adept's
body—the ease or difficulty of breathing, the color of the hair and condition of the
teeth and skin, the sharpness of the senses and acuity of mind—was indeed his coat-
of-arms, but in a sense not yet grasped in the Jean Lévi article with that phrase in its
title:[5] in a culture in which visual bodily and facial details were assumed to indicate
otherwise hidden, inward truths about individuals, and in which physiognomic and
medical manuals guided interpreters of somatic marks and symptoms, the adept's
appearance was the set of indicators read *by other people* to ascertain the authenticity
of an adept's claims and the power of his methods. Visual inspection of adepts (and
would-be adepts) was therefore crucial in interactions with them, and the many
hagiographic depictions of their subjects' enhanced bodies and distinctive styles of
dress and behavior were hardly incidental; the same was true in other parts of the
ancient world.[6] In similar fashion, a practitioner was likely to build his own story in
part around these same somatic reports.

Elsewhere we find more extended self-narratives delivered by a master to one
or more disciples, as, for example, in this passage from the *Traditions of Divine Transcendents* hagiography of Liu Gen 劉根:

> The adjutant Wang Zhen 王珍 secured several audiences with Gen, each time
> receiving a look of favor. So he prostrated himself and knocked his head on the
> ground, begging to study the fundamentals of transcendence with Gen, who
> said: "I once entered the mountains, and in my meditations there was no state
> I did not reach. Later I entered Mount Huayin. There I saw a person riding a
> carriage drawn by a white deer, followed by several dozen attendants, including
> four jade maidens each of whom was holding a staff hung with a colored flag
> and was fifteen or sixteen years old. I prostrated myself repeatedly, then bowed
> my head and begged a word. The divine personage said to me, "Have you heard
> of someone called Han Zhong 韓眾?" "Truly I have heard that there is such a
> person, yes," I answered. The divine personage said, "I am he." I then gave an
> account of myself, saying, "Since my youth I have loved the Dao, but I have
> not met an enlightened teacher. I have practiced [the teachings of] rather many
> books of esoteric formulae, but when I carry them out they are often ineffec-
> tive. [I thought that] it must be because, due to my allotted lifespan and my
> physiognomy, I was not fit to transcend the world. But my meeting today with a
> great divinity must be a fulfillment of what I wished for last night in my dream."

5. "The Body."
6. See, among other recent treatments, Frank, *The Memory of the Eyes,* 134–170; and Patricia
Miller, *Dreams in Late Antiquity,* 196–197.

I beseeched him to take pity on me and bestow on me his essential instructions, but the deity was not yet willing to tell me anything. So I wept and beat myself and pleaded some more.

The divine person then said, "Sit, and I will tell you something. You must have the bones of a transcendent; that is why you were able to see me. But at present your marrow is not full, your blood is not warm, your breath is slight, your brain is weak, your sinews are slack, and your flesh is damp. This is why, when you ingest medicinals and circulate *qi,* you do not obtain their benefits. If you wish to achieve long life, you must first cure your illnesses; only after twelve years have passed can you ingest the drug of transcendence. . . ."[7]

There follows a lengthy discourse on methods, ending with Liu Gen's declaration, "So I followed his instructions, synthesized [the elixir] and ingested it, and thereby attained transcendence."

The first thing we notice about this passage is that a master responds to a would-be disciple's request for teachings by telling the story of *his own* arduous quest for teachings from *his* former master. Furthermore, that story recapitulates the self-account that the current master and sometime disciple Liu Gen once offered to his master, Han Zhong. (Indeed, offering this self-account is the first thing that Liu Gen does after Han Zhong's identity is revealed to him.) The same story also encapsulates Han Zhong's discourse on methods to Liu Gen, which now also becomes Liu Gen's discourse on methods to Wang Zhen. Teaching a disciple about one's methods meant (among other things) telling the story of how one came to receive them and of what happened next; being a disciple meant (among other things) hearing one's master's story.

An important theme of the whole passage is the difficulty of encountering a true master of *xian* arts and gaining access to his secrets. This theme, as we have seen, works to emphasize the value of the methods and the status of anyone wielding them: the more difficult the methods are to access, the more status they accrue. In the first paragraph we read of not one but two would-be adepts prostrating and (in one case) pummeling themselves to demonstrate their resolve to the master. The drama suffusing such encounters is captured in the first line—"Wang Zhen secured several audiences . . . each time receiving a look of favor"—and in Liu's claim that his meeting with Han Zhong must be the fulfillment of a wish he expressed in the previous night's dream. In both cases the tension is broken by the master's finally agreeing to speak about his methods.

---

7. *TL,* 242–244. See the annotation for earlier textual loci on Han Zhong, and 243–246 for the rest of Han Zhong's discourse on methods (with notes explaining the details mentioned in the passage).

In the case of Liu Gen, we also note the importance of somatic evaluation and diagnosis as a prelude to receiving secret methods. Somatic signals and properties of particular kinds, that is, came into play not simply at the end of successful practice but also as a condition of it. Here, Han Zhong—apparently by a mere summary visual inspection (his ability to do this testifying to his advanced skill and discernment)—detects certain somatic imperfections in Liu Gen that must be overcome before a drug of transcendence can be essayed. Han Zhong also, however, presumes in Liu Gen a crucial somatic feature which, he claims, must account for their having met in the first place: "the bones of a transcendent," which is to say, the somatically imbedded predisposition to become a *xian* at some future point. This notion, also found in some scriptures on methods, rests on the idea, fundamental to early medieval physiology and embryology, that the bones are the seat of one's *ming,* or predetermined life allotment, understood both as a predicted lifespan and as a predisposition to a particular lot in life.[8]

Finally, the figure of Han Zhong invoked in this narrative would have been, to most any early medieval reader, instantly recognizable as a transcendent of antiquity, mentioned already in the "Yuanyou," the *Records of the Historian,* and other early texts. Liu Gen, in linking himself to this august figure, argues his own pedigree and that of the methods he bestows. By thus linking himself—and now, by extension, his pupil as well—to an authoritative past, he claims considerable authority in the present. He also assumes his listener will recognize the name and thus recognize his own authority. His own authority depends, in part, on this recognition. These hagiographically embedded transmission narratives parallel the self-narratives of transmission often found in scriptures, in which the text tells the story of its own divine origin in antiquity and transmission down to the present. Both sets of narratives share the functions of identifying and constructing lineages and filiations, grounding adepts and methods of the present in authoritative past times, and thus authenticating—for an audience and a readership—the transmitted methods or texts and their transmitters.[9]

Beyond such transmission narratives, we have records representing adepts' first-hand narratives of their purported experiences, tales not just of how they received their methods but also of the otherwise inaccessible wonders to which the methods afforded access. These tales allow the listener (or reader) glimpses of realms unreachable by ordinary mortals except by secret arts and must on that account alone have held early medieval audiences spellbound. Their essential rhetorical, illo-

---

8. For more on these ideas and related practices, see Bokenkamp, "Simple Twists of Fate"; and Campany, "Living off the Books."

9. The very same points could be made in detail of the *Shenxian zhuan* hagiography of Kong Anguo 孔安國 (see *TL,* 311–312), which I pass over here but take up again in Chapter 8.

cutionary function is to showcase the adept's status as long-distance specialist, one who has privileged access to distant or past wonders otherwise unavailable to listeners (and readers) except through his (and the narrative text's) mediation.[10] As the speaker opens those distant wonders to listeners, listeners—at least if they respond favorably—are drawn into the circle of approval and support that constitutes the base of the speaker's reputation as a skilled, successful practitioner.

Take, for example, the *Traditions of Divine Transcendents* hagiography of Shen Xi 沈羲.We first read a third-person account of how he and his wife were unexpectedly wafted up into the heavens one day, thanks to their unusual virtue, and then just as suddenly returned home more than four centuries later.The narrative continues:

> Shen Xi told his family that, at the time when he first ascended to Heaven, he did not see the Celestial Thearch but saw only Lord Lao. Lord Lao was seated facing east. Attendants ordered Xi not to decline [the honor] but merely to sit in silence. The palace was luxuriant. Cloud vapors in five colors [and] "mystic yellow"[11] [billowed about]; the scene was simply indescribable in words. There were hundreds of attendants, including many who were girls and many who were young men. In the courtyard grew trees of pearl and jade as well as profuse bunches of all sorts of herbs, and dragons, tigers, and other evil-dispelling creatures cavorted among them. The only audible sound was a *langlang* like bronze or iron, the source of which he could not discern. The four walls were fully covered in talismanic writings. As for the person of Lord Lao himself, he was about ten feet tall; his hair was tied up, and he wore a patterned garment. His body radiated light. In a little while, jade maidens brought out a golden table on which were jade cups filled with medicinals. They bestowed these on Xi, saying, "This is a divine elixir. Whoever drinks it will not die. There is one spatula's worth each for you and your wife. Drink it all and do not [out of politeness] decline it." After they had consumed this medicine, they were given two jujubes, as big as chicken eggs, and some strips of dried meat.
>
> Then, when Xi was sent back, he was told: "Go back to the human realm and cure the sick among the common people. Whenever you wish to return to this upper realm, write this talisman and hang it on a pole, and you will be welcomed back." Xi was then given one talisman as well as one text containing methods of transcendence. Then he suddenly felt as if he were asleep, and he was already back on earth.[12]

---

10. For further ruminations on this theme, see Campany, "Long-Distance Specialists in Early Medieval China."

11. *Xuanhuang* 玄黃, an alchemical term of shifting signification; for details, see *TL,* 257 n.52.

12. *TL,* 257–258.

Hearers and readers must have been fascinated by such a detailed recounting of the sights, sounds, smells, architecture, staffing, and etiquette of the divine Laozi's celestial palace, related by one who claimed to have traveled there. All narratives of *xian* served, in part, to construct, modify, and maintain the *imaginaire* of transcendence, an *imaginaire* that was the project of large segments of society (even those who took the trouble to oppose it in their writings); this particular story contributed to that project, in part, by supplying a detailed sensory description of Lord Lao's celestial court as well as an unusual reckoning of how a fortunate person might be selected for transport there (unusual in its stress on merit rather than the practice of any particular esoteric art).

It would seem that a good many practitioners of transcendence arts were accomplished raconteurs, and their fashioning of stories about their experiences no doubt played a key (though not necessarily determinative) role in forming their reputations as well as in their fashioning of their sense of themselves. Wang Chong mentions one such raconteur in his *Lunheng,* a certain Xiang Mandu 項曼都, who reportedly set off to practice transcendence arts, abandoning his family, only to return three years later. When his family asked what had happened, he replied:

> "At the time of my departure I lost consciousness. I suddenly found myself lying down, and several transcendents took me up into the heavens until we were a few *li* from the moon. I saw that above and below the moon it was so dark that I could not tell east from west. At the place where we stopped near the moon, it was bitter cold. I was feeling hungry and wanted to eat when a transcendent gave me a cup of Flowing Aurora (*liuxia* 流霞)[13] to drink, after which I was not hungry for several months. I don't know how long I've been gone, nor do I know what fault I committed, but I suddenly found myself lying down, having been brought back down here." People of Hedong called him the Banished Transcendent (*chixian* 斥仙).[14]

Again we find detailed, purportedly firsthand sensory descriptions of celestial realms rumored among, but otherwise scarcely accessible to, ordinary mortals. Here it is the specific detail supplied in the narrative rather than any visible somatic effects or abilities that authenticates the report. The speaker's identity as a "banished transcendent" furnishes an etiology for his lack of any somatic badges of authenticity. It also signifies his having been deemed by a large community to have achieved

---

13. For a later mention of this term, see Bokenkamp, *Early Daoist Scriptures,* 315, where it clearly connotes ingestible sunlight. For a study of related terms, see Schafer, "The Grand Aurora."

14. *Lunheng jiaoshi,* 325.

transcendence, despite his now-compromised status in that role (a notoriety that may only have served to create more interest in him).

Ge Hong recounts a more robust version of Xiang Mandu's tale, based on what source we do not know—a tale that circulated widely enough to be preserved in variant versions two and a half centuries apart and to have earned its teller a reputation throughout Hedong.

> In Puban in Hedong there was a certain Xiang Mandu, who with one of his sons entered the mountains to practice [arts of] transcendence. Ten years later he returned home. When his family asked him why, Mandu said: "We meditated in the mountains for three years. Then a transcendent came to welcome us, and together we all mounted a dragon and ascended into the heavens. After a while I lowered my head to look down at earth, which appeared dim and dark; we had not even reached anywhere above but were already extremely far from earth. The dragon raced along, its head raised and tail lowered, causing us who were on its back to feel frightened and in danger. When we reached heaven, we first passed through purple halls where the beds were of gold and the tables of jade, gleaming and shining—truly a luxurious place. A transcendent then gave us a cup of Flowing Aurora, after drinking which we felt no hunger or thirst. Suddenly I thought of home, so that, when we were brought before the Celestial Thearch, I bowed in a way that violated protocol, and we were therefore banished and sent back with an order to continue our self-cultivational efforts so that we may eventually return. In former times Liu An, Prince of Huainan, ascended to heaven and had an audience with the Thearch on High, but he sat with his legs spread, talking big and referring to himself as the 'single man,' so he was punished by being put on guard duty at the celestial latrine for three years. Who am I, then?"[15] People of Hedong therefore called Mandu the Banished Transcendent.[16]

This telling of Xiang's story, with its vivid depiction of flight and of heaven's splendors and its narrative device of the wayward thought of home as the reason for the protagonist's return to earth, reminds us of the many poetic narratives of ascensions and encounters with transcendents. Modern literary historians usually treat

---

15. This form of self-reference was an imperial prerogative; it reflects both Liu An's political ambitions while on earth and his failure to give due deference to the celestials in whose august presence he rudely sat; sitting spread-legged implied contempt. The sense of the last line is that to be banished from heaven for violations of protocol can happen very easily to one such as Xiang if it happened to one so venerated as Liu An; the rhetorical intent is to minimize the shame attached to Xiang's demotion.

16. *NP* 20:350.

such poems as allegories,[17] although there is not the slightest tinge of allegory in this closely similar narrative, presented as a personal experience recounted literally. Whether the poems are best understood allegorically or not—and one suspects that the binary "allegory/non-allegory" may be too blunt an interpretive instrument— they and the first-person prose narrative collected here clearly tapped into the same cultural repertoire, and many in contemporary society, at many social levels, clearly believed such journeys had really been made by a fortunate few. We see here again the mention of a famous former figure as a means whereby the speaker in the present links himself to a prestigious past—but here the past figure is not a transmitter of texts or methods, and it is thus not a lineage that is claimed, but simply an off-stage association being brought to the attention of hearers and readers.

It is our ironic good fortune that both Wang Chong and Ge Hong preserved versions of a tale they saw as exemplifying the fraudulent claims made by (for Ge Hong some, for Wang Chong all) seekers of *xian*-hood.[18] But there is absolutely nothing to distinguish the account—in tone, substance, or the reported situation of its telling, an adept's return home after a long absence—from the narrative we saw ascribed to Shen Xi above, whom Ge Hong regarded as an authentic transcendent. When we find sympathetic and hostile witnesses thus testifying to precisely the same sorts of behavior, we may be confident that the reports reflect ways adepts were actually behaving. We may conclude that stories such as these were the stuff of lived social interaction; they were actively exchanged on the ground as part of the work of collective memory, not simply made up in writers' studios, and their exchange, as Malinowski said of myth, was not an idle exercise but "a hard-worked active force."[19]

Ge Hong preserves two other similar accounts, both of which he attributes to named practitioners he regards as false claimants of transcendence (though he concedes to one of them, at least, an advanced age and some degree of self-cultivational achievement). The tales they told are worth lingering over, as are the accompanying accounts of audience response, and it is intriguing to notice that although Ge Hong disdained these individuals—for the reason that he saw them as falsely claiming great longevity and thus spinning bogus tales of their exploits—he recorded the sorts of stories they told in great detail for posterity. His rejection of their claims to longevity and thus also of the truth of their self-narratives, when so many others

---

17. For one example out of dozens that could be cited, see Kwong, "Naturalness and Authenticity," 60.

18. Note that in Ge Hong's case, there is nothing in the content of these stories that he necessarily finds fraudulent; for him they are fraudulent simply because the person telling the stories has not achieved the longevity he claims to have achieved.

19. See Strenski, ed., *Malinowski and the Work of Myth*, 82.

(according to him) credited them, is also a good example of the differential reception of adepts by their audiences.

One of these figures was a certain Gu Qiang 古強. Ge Hong's source of information on him was none other than Ge's contemporary and friend, Ji Han 嵇含, who had personally conversed with Gu and observed him in action; Gu's activities thus come to us via a secondhand relating of an eyewitness account, and this relating, and the oral or written telling it is based on, are themselves examples of the sort of intimate narrative exchange that is my focus here. Ji Han, furthermore, an official who served (among other posts) as governor of Guangzhou, who was killed in 306, and who was a great-nephew of the famous Ji Kang 嵇康 (223–262), shared with Ge an interest in medicinal herbs and esoteric practices; he left a rhapsody on the preparation known as "cold victual powder," in which he claims it cured his ailing son when other treatments had failed. He also authored the *Records of the Plants and Trees of the South* (*Nanfang caomu zhuang* 南方草木狀), a major botanical treatise.[20] No wonder, then, that Ji, upon hearing of a practitioner and raconteur such as Gu, went to meet him at Yidu, an administrative seat located at the time at the confluence of the Yi and Yangzi rivers. The pains Ji took to meet Gu attest to the sort of reception Gu and others like him sometimes received in upper-middle-rank circles of officialdom.

Thanks to this meeting we learn that Gu Qiang practiced herbal and sexual regimes and was still vigorous and clear-headed for his eighty-plus years. Because he appeared relatively youthful (note again the authenticating function of bodily signs) yet was quite old and because he practiced macrobiotic regimens, "people called him a *xian* or 'the thousand-year-old old man.'" (The appellation is, again, testimony to his reception by listeners and tale-circulators.) He said of himself that he was 4,000 years old and told what Ge Hong calls "fables" (*xuyan* 虛言) "in great detail, as if they were factual." Ge gives an extensive record of the sorts of details he spoke of. He offered intimate, personal descriptions of the ancient rulers Yao 堯 and Shun 舜, including information about their unusual, sagely appearance (Yao's strange eyebrows, Shun's double pupils) and Yao's capacity for alcohol, correcting two widespread misapprehensions about Yao.[21] (Here again an adept enhances his own authority by narratively associating himself with famous past figures.) He

---

20. His official biography appears in *Jin shu* 89:2301–2303; and see also *Jin shu* 72:1911; the rhapsody is anthologized in *YWLJ* 75:1292; see further Ōfuchi, *Shoki no dōkyō*, 501–502; and Sailey, *The Master Who Embraces Simplicity*, 286–288. The botanical work has been translated in Li Hui-Lin, *Nan-fang ts'ao-mu chuang*.

21. This corrective function parallels that of some return-from-death accounts, where protagonists newly returned from the realm of the dead correct misunderstandings among the living. For examples, see Harper, "Resurrection in Warring States Popular Religion"; and Teiser, "Having Once Died and Returned to Life."

described in detail Confucius' appearance and physiognomy, relaying the master's comments on his fondness for the *Book of Change*. And he told stories of the founding emperors of the Qin and Han. The most remarkable thing about his narrations is their intimate and vivid immediacy. Gu claims that he had known each of these figures personally and had advised them on portents, recounting conversations they had shared. Of Confucius he said, "Still today I can remember his countenance down to the last detail." Ge's characterization of his style of speech is apt—"in great detail, as if factual"—and it was no doubt this verisimilitude, "fictive" like the archival narratives studied by Natalie Zemon Davis,[22] combined with Gu's reputation for being a transcendent, that explains some listeners' recorded reactions: "Those at the time who recognized [what Gu was doing] treated it as a joke and laughed, but when ordinary people (*fanren* 凡人) heard him, they all believed his words."[23] This recorded bit of audience response reminds us that not all who participated in the circles of clients and listeners surrounding adepts were the same in knowledge, experience, attitude, or need. Some more seasoned audience members might remain skeptical of an adept who, in the eyes of others, rose to be acclaimed as successful. Such differential reactions are hardly unexpected; they must have greeted every performance of every adept—in this case we simply have a close-to-the-source record of the difference.

Ge Hong also tells of a certain Cai Dan 蔡誕, said to have been active in Wuyuan.[24] Here, too, Ge names his source, one Wu Wen 吳文, governor of Chengdu; unfortunately no information on him seems to have survived, and we cannot even be sure when Wu Wen lived: perhaps he, like Ji Han, was Ge's contemporary and acquaintance, or perhaps he had lived earlier and Ge was drawing on some now-lost written account. In any case, Cai Dan, we are told, devoted himself to reciting scriptures Ge Hong considered ornate and nonessential because of their lack of *xian* recipes, including the *Yellow Court Scripture* (*Huangting jing* 黃庭經); he taught that if one recited them a thousand times one would receive whatever was asked for.[25] Perhaps spurred by tension with his family over his devotion, he left home, saying he had completed the path of transcendence, and headed into the mountains; but, knowing no methods for using mountain herbs as substitutes for ordinary food,

---

22. See Natalie Davis, *Fiction in the Archives*.

23. *NP* 20:347–348.

24. There were several places known by this name, including ones in what are now Shanxi and Gansu provinces, as well as a Han frontier commandery in what is now southern Mongolia. On the commandery's founding, see Yu Ying-shih, "Han Foreign Relations," 390.

25. This is a mode of textual piety familiar elsewhere in the period, as seen, for example, in several recently translated Mahāyāna sutras. See Campany "The Real Presence"; "The Earliest Tales of the Bodhisattva Guanshiyin"; and "Notes on the Devotional Uses and Symbolic Functions of Sutra Texts."

he barely subsisted by selling firewood until returning home three years later, so darkened and emaciated that he seemed inhuman. When his family inquired where he had been and whether he had not, after all, attained transcendence, he claimed that he was as yet unqualified to ascend to heaven and was an earthbound *xian,* and that he must first hold lowly positions, serving more advanced transcendents, before he could rise through the ranks. He had thus been assigned to shepherd several of Lord Lao's dragons, he said, including his favorite, a dappled mount, but had carelessly allowed his charge to escape, engrossed as he was in games of "sixes" (*liubo* 六博[26]) with other low-ranking transcendents, and for this lapse had been consigned to weed a large area at the foot of Mount Kunlun for ten years. Finally Woquanzi 偓佺子 and Wang Qiao 王喬—well-known figures eulogized in the Han-era *Traditions of Exemplary Transcendents*—had come to inspect his conduct and, thanks to their patronage, he had been released to return home, where he was expecting to continue his self-cultivation and later to depart once more. But in fact, Ge Hong writes, he then died of old age.

I here interrupt my paraphrase to point out that Cai Dan's self-claimed lowly status as an earthbound transcendent (*dixian* 地仙) neatly explains his lack of somatic signs that would authenticate his claims. His detailed narration of the wonders he had seen and of his patronage by two noted transcendents of old (whose names would have been easily recognized by his eager family as well as by Ge Hong's readers) serves to compensate for his lack of somatic credentials and links him to an ancient lineage of sorts.

Ge Hong then proceeds to relay samples of the stories Cai Dan told upon his return home, prompted by his family's insistent inquiries. Unlike Gu Qiang, who regaled his listeners with tales of ancient sages, Cai specialized in vivid, catalogue-like descriptions of the wonders of Mount Kunlun. He describes its height and distance from the bottom of the sky; the "tree grains" that cap its summit, a single stalk enough to fill a cart; trees of jade, pearl, *langgan* 琅玕,[27] and other gems; shiny jade fruits, melons, and plums, washed in jade well water; the music produced by all these wondrous trees when the wind blows through them; the numerous gateways and towers of Kunlun, guarded by fantastic animals such as enormous serpents and hornets; the rivers that flow down from its slopes; and the names of the gods who bar the gates to ordinary folk, Cai having been able to enter thanks to his posses-sion of talismans and tallies bestowed by Lord Lao. As in the case of Gu Qiang, it was apparently the level of detail that created an aura of verisimilitude sufficient to

---

26. The translation is that of David Knechtges. On the game and its connections to tran-scendence lore, see Yang, "A Note on the So-Called TLV Mirrors and the Game *Liu-po*"; and his "An Additional Note on the Ancient Game *Liu-po.*"

27. For a study of this term's referents, see Schafer, "The Transcendent Vitamin."

convince Cai's audiences. Ge Hong comments, "When people heard Dan speak of these matters in such great detail, many believed him"[28]—another fleeting glimpse of a realistically differential audience response.

It was with such tales of distant wonders personally seen that some practitioners of *xian* arts—or some who claimed to practice such arts—regaled audiences. Their performances drew crowds. What they spoke of also resonated widely throughout early medieval Chinese culture. The distant wonders narrated by practitioners became part of the mental furniture, the cosmological *imaginaire,* of Chinese culture, just as, in a feedback loop, that *imaginaire* continued to inspire and serve as a resource for new practitioners. The distant wonders of *xian*-dom ended up depicted on the inner walls of tombs, on coffins, on incense burners and money trees and mirrors and other household objects.[29] They were routinely mentioned in poems—many such songs composed orally on the spot during drinking games and parties—that otherwise had nothing to say about transcendence.[30] Officials, generals, and rulers joined in telling tales of far-off roaming, whether their own or others'.

Seven poems attributed to Cao Cao 曹操 (155–220 C.E.) that can be said to belong loosely to the *youxian* 遊仙 or "wandering-as-a-*xian*" genre, for example, have come down to us.[31] None of them unambiguously claims transcendence for its author, and some express a wish for divinely granted methods of long life or a desire to climb mountains and sojourn with transcendents, implying not that the speaker has achieved transcendence but precisely the opposite. One poem narrates the speaker's mountaintop meeting with a "triply aged" man but laments his departure

---

28. *NP* 20:348–350.

29. For *xian* imagery incorporated into mirror designs, see Cammann, "The 'TLV' Pattern on Cosmic Mirrors of the Han Dynasty," 165–166; and Brashier, "Longevity Like Metal and Stone." On money trees, see Erickson, "Money Trees of the Eastern Han Dynasty." On incense burners, see, for example, Schipper, "Taoism: The Story of the Way," 37. *Xian* were even referenced as the name for a part of the lute ("*xian* shoulders") and in some tonal terminology; see van Gulik, *The Lore of the Chinese Lute.*

30. Examples are almost innumerable; see, for example, Rushton, "An Interpretation of Hsi Kang's Eighteen Poems Presented to Hsi Hsi on His Entry into the Army," 180, 186, 188; Ho, Goh, and Parker, "Po Chu-i's Poems on Immortality"; Kwong, "Naturalness and Authenticity," 60–61; Westbrook, "Landscape Transformation in the Poetry of Hsieh Ling-yun," 252; Hightower, "Allusion in the Poetry of T'ao Ch'ien," 20; Frankel, "Fifteen Poems by Ts'ao Chih," 6–7; Hartman, "Stomping Songs," 25; and Huntington, "Crossing Boundaries." On the convivial contexts of poem composition, see, for example, Cutter, "Cao Zhi's (192–232) Symposium Poems."

31. The songs are: "Moshang sang" 陌上桑; "Qi chu chang" 氣出唱 (three songs by this title); "Qiu Hu xing" 秋胡行 (two songs by this title); and "Jing lie" 精列. They are anthologized in Lu Qinli, ed., *Xian Qin Han Wei Jin Nanbeichao shi,* 345–355; Jean-Pierre Diény provides complete translations with text-critical comments (*Les poèmes de Cao Cao,* 67–103). English translations of two poems are available in Balazs, *Chinese Civilization and Bureaucracy,* 173–186.

and inaccessibility; another decries the brevity of life; and one calls attention in its last lines to the contexts of oral performance in which such songs were composed and performed, mentioning guests seated at a banquet, wishing them long life and numerous descendants. Based on these songs, some have attempted inferences about Cao's personal beliefs concerning the attainability of transcendence.[32] I regard such attempts as a blind alley for research, and would rather see the poems as an example of how an important figure—a busy military commander and administrator whose audience knew full well that he had no time to pursue transcendence methods—employed elements of his contemporary culture's repertoire in skilled oral performances that would surely not, in the contexts in which they were uttered, have been taken literally as claims of personal transcendence.[33] For our purposes these and similar songs are valuable in that they attest to the wide distribution, and the deep place in the contemporary *imaginaire,* of imagery and lore concerning transcendence and particular past figures (such as, in Cao's poems, the ubiquitous Master Redpine and Wang Qiao) deemed to have achieved it. Also, for such a man to compose a poem claiming his own transcendence, even ambiguously, fictively, or half in jest, was ideologically significant: in a society in which practitioners of esoterica often guarded their arts from the prying inquiries of rulers and officials while nevertheless displaying the fruits of those arts in public, a leader reciting such stanzas was an attempt, in part, to co-opt a bit of the cultural status that normally came with the ability to narrate such journeys in the first person.[34] Cao was thus, among other things, perhaps playfully invoking Qin Shi Huang and Han Wudi, august predecessors who had famously sought (and, in Wudi's case, according to some narratives, at least temporarily attained) access to techniques of transcendence normally reserved for ascetics—precedents that Cao and his audience would have known well.

Self-Authenticating Remarks

Practitioners of *xian* arts are often represented as also making briefer remarks that imply or contain the kernel of a story and that function—in addition to amusing

---

32. For two recent, useful studies, see Li Gang, "Cao Cao yu daojiao"; and Diény, *Les poèmes de Cao Cao,* 67–103.

33. This is a classic instance of the importance of a statement's context in constituting its meaning, a meaning that requires what Gilbert Ryle famously termed "thick description" in order to arrive at a full accounting. For a recent reevaluation of this notion, see Gallagher and Greenblatt, *Practicing New Historicism,* 20–48.

34. A parallel maneuver is the claim by certain later rulers to be living buddhas or bodhisattvas—claims that few contemporaries could have taken seriously as declarations of actual religious achievements but that accrued symbolic capital and brought certain prerogatives along with them. I return to this theme in Chapter 7.

and astonishing their audience—to authenticate the practitioner as someone skilled in esoterica, or at least to stake a claim to such authenticity, a claim that was then subject to audience evaluation.

Sometimes these remarks take startlingly direct form. "Li Gen 李根 told his disciples: 'I have not obtained the instructions for the great *dao* of any divine elixir. All I have obtained is methods for attaining earthbound transcendence. Although I have not attained equality with Heaven and Earth, at least I will not become one who descends into the earth'"[35]—a self-assessment that manages to be at once self-promoting and self-deprecatory. Tucked into the hagiography of Ge Xuan 葛玄 is the following subnarrative:

> Once there was a practitioner of the Dao from the central region who had some ability to cure the sick. He was deceiving people by saying "I am several hundred years old." Ge Xuan knew he was lying, so, at a time when many people were sitting at hand, Xuan said to a friend, "Would you like to know this gentleman's age?" "Certainly!" Suddenly a group of people descended from the heavens, sitting upright [in midair] and gazing watchfully about them. After a while they settled on the ground. They wore crimson gowns and promoting-the-worthy caps. They came into the group, approached the practitioner, and said to him, "The Celestial Thearch has ordered that we ask you your actual age, since you have lied to commoners about it." Terrified, the practitioner got down from his couch and prostrated himself before them, saying, "Please forgive me! Really I am seventy-three." At this, Xuan clapped his hands and laughed heartily. Then suddenly the crimson-clad persons vanished. The practitioner was greatly ashamed, and it is not known where he went after that.[36]

It is altogether typical that this dramatic unmasking of a boastful practitioner's actual age is performed as a vivid spectacle "at a time when many people were sitting at hand." We begin to form a picture of a society in which many practitioners with some facility in healing or other arts that would attract a respectful following went about saying to large, enthusiastic gatherings that they were centuries old. The man portrayed here had the misfortune to have been exposed, this encounter forming part of the dossier of feats by which his exposer—Ge Hong's great-uncle—established his own claim to authenticity. This story of a public challenge to an adept's claim affords another glimpse of the differences among audience members, who were sometimes critical of adepts' actions and statements.

---

35. *TL*, 220.

36. Ibid., 155. "Promoting-the-worthy caps" were worn by certain classes of officials in the Later Han and Jin courts. This narrative detail thus indicates that the visitors are from the highest celestial court.

More often, however, adepts are represented as making much less direct remarks, uttered in passing, that invite listeners to infer an extreme longevity (or other remarkable feats) that they do not claim explicitly. These passages are among the more fascinating samples of discourse attributed to practitioners of esoteric arts.

Let us begin with two incidents involving Li Shaojun. These were already recorded in the *Records of the Grand Historian;* I quote from the closely similar version in the *Traditions of Divine Transcendents,* adding emphasis relevant to this discussion:

> Li Shaojun was once drinking and dining with the Marquis of Wu'an. In the group was an elderly man over ninety. Shaojun asked his name. *He then commented that he had once traveled with the old man's grandfather, that he had one night seen a little boy following after the grandfather, and that the two of them were consequently former acquaintances.* All present at the time were astonished. Also, during Shaojun's audience with [Han] Emperor Wu, he noticed an ancient bronze vessel nearby. Recognizing it, *he remarked, "Duke Huan of Qi* [reigned 455–405 B.C.E.] *displayed this vessel in his chamber of repose."* The emperor checked his words against the inscription carved into the bronze, and it did indeed turn out to be an ancient Qi vessel. From this he realized that Shaojun was several hundred years old. But he looked to be around fifty. His facial complexion was excellent, his flesh smooth and radiant, and his mouth and teeth were like those of a youth.[37]

The *Records of the Grand Historian* was a hostile witness to such behaviors and practitioners; it reports these events not as proofs of the reality of transcendence but as instances of the extravagant claims some rulers and courtiers were apt to believe, and in that work Li Shaojun's story ends with his death—although it was a death that the emperor refused to acknowledge as such, believing that Li must have "transformed" and transcended. In the *Traditions,* these vignettes are recontextualized to do the opposite work, and there Li successfully ascends.[38] Here again we see the adept's implicitly claimed status authenticated both by somatic signs (Li's youthful and healthy appearance despite his fantastically advanced age) and by narrated or implied association with past figures (Li's strategy in this respect being closely similar to Gu Qiang's). In the *Records* treatment of these claims we also see two things:

---

37. *TL,* 222; see also the quite similar passage in *Shi ji* 28:1385–1386, in which the old man confirms Li's recollection of their meeting many decades earlier (a passage paraphrased in Chapter 4). Compare the *Shenxian zhuan* passage in which a servant girl or consort surreptitiously reads Li Gen's "silk text" and learns that, according to Li's own notes, he must be over 700 years old (*TL,* 219–220).

38. *TL,* 223.

many affirmed them, but the author of the passage in which such responses are preserved for posterity bucks this trend, rejecting the claims.

It seems to have been essential to these self-authenticating remarks that they be delivered offhand, in passing; otherwise they might be received as too blatantly boastful and self-promoting. They are often related in short, self-contained subnarratives in hagiographies, nuggets that depict the sometimes startling, eccentric behavior of adepts, attesting to their longevity or special powers. Cheng Wuding 成武丁

> was once sitting with a group of people when the calls of a flock of sparrows were heard, and he laughed at them. When the others asked why he was laughing, he answered, "East of the market, a carriage full of rice has overturned, and the sparrows are calling to each other to go and eat it." Someone was sent to inspect, and what he had said was confirmed.[39]

Of the exorcistic healer Fei Changfang 費長房 we are told: "Whenever he sat and conversed with people, he would often break into angry shouts and curses; when asked why, he would answer, 'I'm only shouting at a demon.'"[40] Ge Xuan had been traveling with the emperor's entourage when the party encountered a storm, capsizing boats, including Ge's; afterwards he could not be found. A week later he was seen emerging from the water and rejoined the ruler, "still smelling of liquor. He apologized to the emperor, saying, 'I should have been in attendance these last few days, but Wu Zixu [伍子胥] detained me and I could not get away. I am sorry to have troubled you with the storm and water.'"[41] All who heard this story would have known that Wu Zixu was a famous ancient minister who had drowned himself and around whom legends and temple cults had accreted.[42] The dual implication is that Wu Zixu had joined the ranks either of transcendents or of gods and that Ge Xuan kept company with such august figures, even when they dwelled underwater.[43]

All three of these brief accounts share the same fundamental narrative structure: a figure in conversation momentarily breaks off communication with his interlocutors, seemingly so as to converse with others who are invisible, distant, or otherwise offstage; the subsequent explanation of his odd, seemingly impolite behavior confirms his contact with distant beings. Sharing this structure are the half-dozen or

---

39. Ibid., 361.

40. Ibid., 163.

41. Ibid., 156.

42. See Johnson, "The Wu Zixu *Pien-wen* and Its Sources," 93–156, 465–505; Durrant, *The Cloudy Mirror*, 74–98; and *SW,* 88, 195.

43. For other passing remarks of this kind, see the examples of She Zheng 涉正 (*TL,* 332) and Ma Gu 麻姑 (*TL,* 261–262).

more stories of the type where an adept, often during a state ritual or banquet, spits out wine or water, and explains that he did so to extinguish a fire hundreds of miles distant; later reports from the distant locale confirm his statement.[44] Practitioners of *xian* arts, it seems, were apt to disengage from social scenes in the here and now due to some sort of long-distance contact. Such behavior was one of the patterns of action and speech expected of those who played this role in society.

Another incident involving a relative of Ge Hong's, in this case his father-in-law, Bao Jing 鮑靚, is related as follows: "There was one Xu Ning 徐寧, who served Bao Jing as his teacher. One night Xu heard the sound of lute music coming from Jing's room. He asked about it and was told, 'Ji Shuye 嵇叔夜 formerly left a trace at the eastern market, but actually he achieved 'escape by weapon' (*bingjie* 兵解)."[45] Here again we have a passing remark that has the rhetorical effect of associating a living adept with a famous, former figure. In addition, in this case it reveals that figure's actual status as a transcendent. Shuye was the style (*zi* 字) of Ji Kang 嵇康, renowned frequenter of salons, poet, essayist, debater, and lute virtuoso, who was, according to historical records, executed in 262. The sense of this passage is that Ji Kang's execution was actually a staged event that allowed him to evade the other-world agents of death, an instance of the "escape by weapon" acknowledged in scriptures as an esoteric method employed by adepts as well as a hermeneutical device by which the untimely deaths of self-cultivators could be interpreted and explained. That Ji Kang would have been privy to such techniques might have seemed plausible to some in light of his having written defenses of the possibility of transcendence "nourishing life" against detractors.[46]

With the exception of Li Shaojun in the *Records of the Grand Historian*, the examples of self-authenticating remarks we have reviewed are preserved in texts sympathetic to the quest for transcendence. But in addition to the *Records* passages, there are others that are either hostile to that quest in general or else seek to debunk specific claimants as frauds. In an informative passage, Ge Hong complains of certain practitioners in his day:

> Those capable of understanding the essentials of the path desire nothing among things and do not seek praise from their generation. How could they be willing to display themselves before the common types? But the shallow are given to

---

44. Two examples of such stories in the *Shenxian zhuan* may be found in *TL*, 254, 362; other such tales appear in the *Hou Han shu*, in *zhiguai* collections, and elsewhere.

45. *TL*, 295. On Ji Kang (also known as Xi Kang), see Holzman, *La vie et la pensée de Hi K'ang*; Henricks, *Philosophy and Argumentation in Third-Century China*; Knechtges, *Wen xuan, or Selections of Refined Literature*, 3:278–301, 390–392; and further comments in Chapter 8.

46. Elsewhere, however, Ge Hong disparages his accomplishments in this area (as discussed in Chapter 8).

boasting and self-promoting talk. They adorn their empty claims with bright colors and rare sounds sufficient to deceive those who come to the practice late in life, daring to make big claims. So they will say that they have ascended noted mountains and seen transcendents. Those who rush to listen to them but are unable to arrive at clear estimations seldom realize their deceit. I have often seen various sorts of *dao* practitioners heading to the gates of nobles expressly for the purpose of having their followers inflate their reputation by saying, for example, that they were four or five centuries old. But if someone tries asking them their age directly, they pretend not to have heard the question, or, looking around, they say eighty or ninety. Then suddenly they will say of themselves, "I once went without food for fifty years on Mount Huayin, then again on the Lesser Chamber peak of Mount Song for forty years, then again on Mount Tai for sixty years, then again I was with so-and-so on Mount Ji for fifty years," saying all this so that those in league with them can sum up the amounts of time mentioned and calculate their age at several hundred years. Then those who are enamored of this sort of thing all congregate and converge at the man's gates.[47]

But, as we have seen, some adepts Ge Hong regarded as authentic are recorded as behaving precisely as described here. It is not the dropping of self-authenticating hints per se that troubles Ge Hong but rather the doing so by people who hint falsely and thus lay implicit claim to achievements that are not, in fact, theirs. This passage, a remarkable sketch of the poetics and psychology of reputation-forming, confirms the hagiographic portrayals: it appears that many practitioners of *xian* arts spoke in these ways in their social intercourse with others. It also vividly documents the audience enthusiasm that sometimes greeted such performances.

Or consider the example of Gan Shi 甘始, another adept of whom we are fortunate to have an eyewitness account. His hagiography in the *Traditions of Divine Transcendents* is quite terse:

> Gan Shi was a native of Taiyuan. He excelled at circulating *qi*. He did not eat [a normal diet] but ingested [only] asparagus root. In curing the sick, he made no use of needles or moxa. He remained in the human realm for three hundred years, then entered King's Chamber Mountain and departed as a transcendent.[48]

But Cao Zhi had met him personally, thanks to the fact that his father Cao Cao had summoned many adepts to court, where he had tested them and incarcerated

---

47. *NP* 20:346.
48. *TL,* 150–152, 400.

many. Cao Zhi recorded his impressions in a passage in his *Disputations on the Dao* (*Biandao lun* 辯道論):

> Gan Shi, although old, had a youthful face. All the masters of arts flocked to him, but although what he said [to them] sounded complex, it had little substance to it. I once spoke with him privately without all those attendants, and I asked him what he practiced, using a familiar manner and fine words to try to draw him out. He told me: "My original teacher was surnamed Han and named Ya. I once made gold with him in Nanhai; altogether we performed several sessions. We threw several myriad catties of gold into the sea." He also said: "During the flourishing of the Liang family [ca. 150], barbarians from the western lands came and submitted fragrant wool belts and jade-cutting knives as tribute. I regret not taking any of these things at the time." He also said: "In the western land of Kucha [Jushi, a tribal confederation in what is now Xinjiang], the males are born with their spleens protruding from their backs. This makes them prone to eat only a little but to be angry often." Again he said: "If you take a pair of five-*cun*-long carp, coat one of them with [a certain] medicine, and throw both of them into hot oil, the one that is medicated will swim about freely as if in a pond; the other will quickly be cooked and ready to eat." At this point I asked him: "Can we try this out now?" He replied, "This drug is located a myriad *li* away from here. One would have to go out beyond the pass. Unless I were to go to get it personally, it cannot be obtained." And what he spoke of was not only these things; it is rather hard to record them all, so I have selected only the most bizarre.[49]

Cao Zhi later seems to have reversed his position, writing a treatise touting *xian* arts in general and Gan Shi in particular.[50] Even here, though, Cao grants Gan Shi an apparently authenticating somatic feature (his youthful face despite advanced age) while debunking his mentions of the sorts of vivid, detailed wonders of distant and past phenomena we have also seen attributed to several other figures. And for our purposes, one of the most significant things about this passage is its portrait of an adept at work, surrounded by attendants and supporters, invited by a high-ranking aristocrat into a private conversation in which the adept tells of the distant marvels to which he has gained access by dint of his ascetic disciplines.

Once again we note that both sympathetic and hostile texts depict adepts making the same sorts of remark. It is difficult to see why such habits of speech

---

49. Cited from Cao Zhi's "Biandao lun" by Tang commentators in *Hou Han shu* 82B.2750. Compare the similar, third-person passage in Zhang Hua's 張華 (232–300) *Bowu zhi* 博物志 5 (item 180 in Fan Ning, ed., *Bowuzhi jiaozheng*), written perhaps twenty years before *Traditions*.

50. See Holzman, "Ts'ao Chih and the Immortals."

would have been so widely attributed to practitioners by writers both sympathetic and hostile unless many practitioners were known to speak in these ways in actual social discourse. Such speech seems to have been essential to the ways in which many practitioners of *xian* arts presented themselves to others and hoped to be recognized and received—and often *were,* but sometimes *were not,* so recognized and received—by others *as* successful practitioners.

Conclusion

Let me now summarize the rhetorical functions of adepts' verbal self-presentation to audiences. By telling their stories and making suggestive passing remarks to others in their self-presentation, adepts did the following kinds of work.

They gave particular narrative and dramatic shape to the quest for transcendence, thus shaping the *imaginaire* in certain directions. They stressed the difficulty of encountering a teacher and qualifying to receive his instruction, which was also a way of arguing the rarity of esoteric methods and the prestige of teachers who controlled access to them. They threw a certain sort of narrative frame around their bestowals of methods on their disciples. They linked themselves and their methods to well-known, prestigious *xian* from the past, constructing lineages and filiations as ways of authorizing themselves in the present. They described their personal experiences of distant marvels in believable terms, thus convincing audiences of varying social levels of their authority and acceding to the prestige and acclaim that audiences were prepared to bestow in response. They positioned themselves as the sole and necessary mediators between distant, otherwise inaccessible wonders—distant in space as well as in time and to which audiences desired access—and the here and now. They helped create desire for access to these distant wonders and hence also desire for access to adepts themselves.

Audiences, for their part, responded variously, as is only to be expected: some believed, others doubted; some clamored for access and offered material support, others scoffed and offered only scorn. The one sort of audience response never mentioned in these accounts is indifference.

One irony is that the records of verbal self-presentation we have analyzed were themselves preserved only thanks to the labors of many people—most of whom will always remain faceless and nameless to us—who intervened between adepts and ourselves. These were the people who spoke about, wrote down, circulated, transmitted, and preserved records of adepts' doings. Who were these people, and what was the shape of their relationships with the adepts whose memories they shaped and kept?

CHAPTER 6

Adepts and Their Communities

SCHOLARS HAVE LONG portrayed *xian* and would-be *xian* as socially withdrawn. When they have commented at all on the social contexts of the quest for transcendence, it has usually been to point out that histories record a keen interest on the part of certain rulers in esoteric arts, or to note that adepts shunned ordinary society and lived as hermits on mountains, or that in their training they were subject to certain poorly documented ethical rules, or that the only communities they formed were master-disciple lineages.[1] These characterizations (with the exception

---

1. Henri Maspero, in his discussion of the quest for immortality, pioneered in his coverage of the range of techniques used, but he did not so much as mention its social aspects except to note that numerous acts of virtue are required of the adept; see *Taoism and Chinese Religion,* 263–298, 319–346. Joseph Needham and his associates, in their first pass at the topic, spoke of a separate paradisal world (distinct from this "ordinary world," which successful *xian* might revisit) for which individual adepts prepare themselves, then moved on immediately to discuss the methods by which they do so; see *Science and Civilisation in China,* vol. 2, *History of Scientific Thought,* 139–154. On returning to the topic, they provided a more nuanced account. While still focused squarely on the techniques and goals of the individual's quest for material immortality, they at least mentioned "the deep interest of emperors and the highest of their officials, to say nothing of all kinds of princes and patricians," in those techniques and pointed out the apparent challenges they posed to the ritual service of ancestors; but their exploration of the social world of transcendence-seeking ended there; see *Science and Civilisation in China,* vol. 5.2, *Chemistry and Chemical Technology: Spagyrical Discovery and Invention, Magisteries of Gold and Immortality,* 103 (for the quoted phrase), 111–112 (on the issue of ancestors). Max Kaltenmark and Holmes Welch spoke of biospiritual techniques and final goals without mentioning the social environment of the transcendence quest (Kaltenmark, *Lao Tzu and Taoism,* 117–132; Welch, *Taoism,* 105–130). Qing Xitai notes that among the several distinct paths to transcendence adumbrated in the *Liexian zhuan,* one consists of performing good works and acts of moral-ritual reciprocity (*bao* 報); he also summarizes several hagiographies that portray adepts as heavily engaged in social activities, but undertakes no analysis or inference from these materials toward a cogent reconstruction of adepts' social roles; see *Zhongguo daojiao shi,* 1:59, 226–233. Ren Jiyu and his collaborators approvingly summarize the stereotype, explaining that practitioners of esoteric arts worked alone or formed master-disciple lineages, in contrast to the way of the Five Pecks of Rice with its kitchens and assemblies; see *Zhongguo daojiao shi,* 69. When they come to discuss Ge Hong (73–109), they treat only his statements on methods of practice.

of the blanket statement that adepts shunned society) are true to an extent, but all of them omit what I will show were key elements of adepts' relations to local communities. Even Isabelle Robinet, in her magisterial history of Daoism, while she mentions the need for adepts to follow moral guidelines and (nevertheless) to withdraw from ordinary social contacts and notes also the danger of incurring punishment for misdeeds by one's family members, passes in silence over the social roles played by adepts.[2] In an example of the odd juxtapositions one is apt to encounter in discussions of *xian,* she writes that "immortals prefer to live in hiding, far from the world, withdrawn into the mountains and often living in caves," and then a few lines later she says that "as healers, they compound drugs and practice respiratory and gymnastic exercises."[3] It is hard to see how *xian* (or adepts pursuing that goal) could function as healers if they supposedly lived "in hiding, far from the world." The tendency, begun by Yü Ying-shih,[4] to resort to a Weberian language of "otherworldliness" when describing adepts only exacerbates the difficulty in seeing what in the Weberian conceit are termed their "this-worldly" aspects.[5] Only Kristofer Schipper has broken from the norm. In his brief discussion of the wider social meanings of the ubiquitous technique of "avoiding grains," and in his studies of two Eastern Han stele inscriptions concerning individuals who were reputed to have achieved transcendence and who were recipients of local cults, and whom he does not hesitate to call "saints," Schipper has opened a path toward a new understanding of adepts that focuses not only on their esoteric practices and goals but also on how they related to others in society.[6] It is this path that I follow further

2. *Taoism,* 78–113. Her other extended treatment of the subject may be found in "The Taoist Immortal."

3. *Taoism,* 49.

4. In his important early article, "Life and Immortality in the Mind of Han China," esp. 89. At least Yu recognized early on that there was a "worldly" type of "immortality," though what he means by "worldly" involves an emphasis on pleasure and the continuation of family ties; he does not attend to the social context of adepts except to note their activities at the Han court.

5. This tendency is continued by Livia Kohn when she characterizes the realm of transcendents as "outside and beyond the known world" (*Early Chinese Mysticism,* 85). Most recently, the article "Immortality and Transcendence" by Benjamin Penny in the *Daoism Handbook* devotes but two short paragraphs to adepts' social contexts (115–116).

6. See in particular "Le culte de l'immortel Tang Gongfang"; "Une stèle taoïste des Han orientaux récemment découverte"; and *Le corps taoïste,* 216–226. I agree that adepts fully functioned as a type of holy person in late antique and early medieval Chinese society, but the analogy of "sainthood" is potentially misleading, primarily on the grounds that the esoteric nature of the arts of Chinese adepts sets up a dynamic (seen in Chapter 4) importantly different from the European societies thus analogized. Schipper also points out several times that successful transcendents were *gods.* I believe the matter is more complex, in that (among other things) their divinity was a matter of social perspective and ritual attribution, not an intrinsic property independent of point of view: they claimed to be superior in status to temple gods, but their communities of clients assimilated

here. I will sketch the social environments of the quest for transcendence (up until the mid-fourth century C.E.), focusing here on relations between practitioners and local communities.

Spectacles, Stories, and Audiences

Many practitioners of transcendence arts, for all their alleged secrecy and social disengagement, were visible, talked-about public figures. They attracted large audiences even, or especially, when they tried to remain secluded, just as other noted recluses in early medieval China (and elsewhere, too) drew attention precisely because they so conspicuously vacated normal social relations and official roles.[7] Withdrawal from normal patterns of interaction did not constitute the absence of any relation to society. The very secrecy of adepts' methods was itself one of the things that got noticed, stoked curiosity, and enhanced the cultural capital of adepts who possessed such arcana. And many self-cultivators, far from (or in alternation with) hiding in mountain caves or chambers of quietude, performed vivid wonders and told marvelous tales to crowds of onlookers. Indeed any of the hundreds of marvels and spectacular abilities mentioned in the hagiographies presuppose an audience: there is no point in performing a marvelous feat unless someone is watching. These aspects of the quest for transcendence are so ubiquitously attested in the hagiographies that almost any narrative chosen at random can serve as an example.

It is in these innumerable interactions between adepts and their audiences, and in the audiences' responses, that adepts' reputations were forged, challenged, and maintained. In imagining what these social contexts, so distant from us historically, must have been like in practice, it is helpful to turn to an ethnographic portrait of analogous recent situations. Louis Golomb's study of practitioners of mantic healing arts in contemporary Thailand is instructive in this regard, not least because our adepts also functioned prominently as healers. Golomb shows how "curer-magicians" in multiethnic areas of Thailand are situated in sociogeographic systems of information exchange. Controls on the flow of information about unsuccessful cures enhance these specialists' reputations, while reports of positive outcomes are shared along referral networks. Specialists and clients often live a considerable

---

them to the category of gods (or, more precisely, *shen* 神) when they built shrines for them and made offerings to them there.

7. For examples of attention-attracting recluses in China, see Vervoorn, *Men of the Cliffs and Caves,* index s.v. "fame"; Berkowitz, *Patterns of Disengagement,* 118, 136–138, 173; Tian, *Tao Yuanming and Manuscript Culture,* 27 (a superb example); and the section on recluses in *Shishuo xinyu.* For examples elsewhere, see Peter Brown, "The Rise and Function of the Holy Man in Late Antiquity," and Tambiah, *The Buddhist Saints of the Forest and the Cult of Amulets.*

distance apart, and this distance restricts the two parties' relationship to a single dimension. This lack of broad-based relationships works to enhance the practitioner's reputation—as does a cultural predisposition to respect, even fear, such figures. And, unlike the situation in modern times with its widely available option of Western medicine, practitioners of esoteric arts in early medieval China were even more heavily relied on because they were a major source of services we would now call "medical," and there were few other options.[8] Golomb goes on to characterize as follows the matrix of reputation-maintenance in which Thai practitioners operate:

> The curer-magician is in an excellent position to represent himself as a competent, if not omnipotent, figure. He may overstate his prowess with impunity; no client would think of gainsaying his boastful accounts of former triumphs or prying into a possibly spotty record of successes. When outside clients pass through a practitioner's community they are free to inquire about his talents among his neighbors. The latter generally withhold pejorative remarks from strangers and may in fact echo many of the magician's claims. This support is readily forthcoming, especially when the practitioner in question is a venerated monk or religious scholar. The typical successful curer-magician can count on supportive neighbors to proliferate accounts of his achievements while omitting any mention of his shortcomings. It is often these very neighbors who, during their travels or while entertaining outsiders, initially propel a practitioner's reputation beyond the confines of his native district. . . . Since word of a practitioner's prowess is primarily broadcast through a diffuse network of supporters and satisfied clients, there is little likelihood that reports of his failures will reach the same audience of potential clients. Even if a disgruntled former client were to wage a vindictive campaign to expose the shortcomings of a particular respected magician, the reverberations of such activity could hardly penetrate most of the widely dispersed communities from which new clients are likely to be drawn.[9]

We may imagine the reputations of transcendence-quest adepts being similarly formed and maintained.[10] We must not forget that it is particular versions of those reputations as created, revised, filtered, honed, and preserved through dense social

---

8. See the apt comments in LaFleur, "Buddhism in a Fail-Safe Mode," 229.

9. Golomb, *An Anthropology of Curing in Multiethnic Thailand,* 251–253.

10. The main difference from Golomb's observations may have been a higher proportion of *written* exchanges between interlocutors in the Chinese case, at least among literate segments of adepts' clientele. I do not see how, in an era before mass media, this would have dramatically changed the dynamics, however.

networks and countless unrecorded verbal acts of estimation and narration that finally came to be preserved in the texts and fragments that have reached us today. Our texts stand at the endpoints of long processes of multifaceted interaction and narrative percolation, much of it oral, some of it conducted in the exchange of letters, some of it posted publicly in inscriptions. For the most part it is only our imagination that can supply a picture of these background activities of interaction, talk, storytelling, among interested parties. But occasionally our texts allow us passing glimpses of them in the background.

The reader will recall how Ge Hong complains of the excited groups drawn to two men that he—but not the crowds—considered false claimants to the title of transcendent, Xiang Mandu and Gu Qiang. Another up-close portrait of a more or less contemporary adept's activities and the public's response to them can be seen in Ge's comments on the figure of Li Kuan 李寬. A careful reading of this account shows us more about the social worlds in which adepts moved and the ways in which their reputations were formed. It begins:

> There was a man surnamed Li and named Kuan who arrived in Wu speaking Shu dialect. He achieved some successful cures with incantation water 祝水, and at news of this everyone near and far agreed in identifying Kuan with Li A 李阿, and so they all began to call him Li Eight Hundred 李八百, but in fact he was not Li A.[11]

The new arrival's success in curing and, more importantly, his Shu dialect lead locals in Wu to assimilate him to a figure they had already heard of, Li A (himself the subject of a *Traditions* hagiography).[12] This represents a confusion, for not only was Li Kuan not Li A, as Ge Hong notes, but Li A also was not Li Eight Hundred. According to *Traditions* at least, these were two distinct individuals, although both were from Shu. This detail is highly significant for our purposes, however, for it indicates the readiness with which the lay populace, already familiar with the reputation of an earlier figure, knowing of the propensity of such figures to change their names periodically,[13] and presuming that that figure was likely to live a very long time and perhaps to travel to other areas, might identify an adept newly arrived in their area with the familiar one. This phenomenon is attested elsewhere as well.[14] We note also that the newcomer attracts notice at first because he is credited with an impressive rate of cure among sick patients he treats, a point to which I return below.

---

11. *NP* 9:174.
12. See *TL,* 212–215.
13. On the reasons for this, see ibid., 52–59.
14. As in the case of Bo He 帛和, on which see ibid., 137.

The account continues:

> From the high officials on down, all flocked to his gate in droves. Later he
> turned haughty and no longer permitted others to call on him at all times.
> Visitors and guests were so awed by him that they would simply bow outside
> his gate and withdraw. Refugees from government labor forces who attached
> themselves to him as disciples regularly numbered near a thousand. But even
> those who managed to "ascend into the hall," "enter into the chamber," and
> advance to the highest ranks [of initiation] got nothing more than incanta-
> tion water, three talismans,[15] and [methods for] guiding-and-pulling and daily
> and monthly *qi*-circulation—nothing essential to regulating the body, no divine
> medicinals to be ingested, no ways of extending one's years and halting [the
> enforcement of] one's preallotted lifespan or of not dying. . . .[16]

Here we note, first of all, the social level of Li's would-be clients and disciples: "from
the high officials on down" 自公卿以下. Then we see their numbers: "in droves,"
"regularly near a thousand." Li is hardly a hermit, even allowing for a bit of annoyed
exaggeration on Ge Hong's part. The mention of "refugees from government labor
forces" 避役之吏民 suggests a possibly frequent demographic pool of disciples;
their "attaching themselves" 依 to the adept was perhaps a way for them to elude
official detection (to which they would be subject if they returned home) but
still have a respectable status and access to material and cultural resources.[17] The
language of "ascending into the hall" 升堂, "entering into the chamber" 入室, and
"advancing to the highest ranks" 高業先進 suggests degrees of ritual initiation.
Any enterprising adept would reveal his secrets to disciples only by stages, thus
lengthening their span of ritual service and material support.
      Ge Hong then writes:

> I am personally acquainted with many who have approached and seen Kuan.
> They all have said that he was decrepit, emaciated, and haggard, his breathing
> labored whether standing or sitting, his eyesight and hearing failing; that he had
> lost his teeth and his hair had gone white; and that gradually he became more
> muddled, sometimes forgetting who his sons and grandsons were, just like any
> ordinary person. Even so, people maintained that Kuan was intentionally acting
> in ordinary ways so as to deceive others; but how could that be?[18]

---

15. In the phrase *sanbu fu* 三部 符 here, *bu* seems to function as a counter word for the
number of talismans. I thank Terry Kleeman for this suggestion.

16. *NP* 9:174.

17. This seems to prefigure later exemptions from taxation and government labor granted
to Buddhist monks.

18. *NP* 9:174.

As we have seen, an adept's physical appearance was a key indicator of his authenticity, a set of signs carefully read by other people to weigh the adept's claims and assess his methods. Visual contact with adepts was therefore a crucial element of interaction with them, and the many hagiographic depictions of their subjects' enhanced bodies and distinctive styles of dress and behavior document audiences' keen interest in these aspects of adepts' self-presentation. Elsewhere Ge Hong writes of the adept Gu Qiang that, at an age of over eighty, "still had his wits about him and had not much aged, so people at the time began calling him a transcendent person, and some styled him the thousand-year-old man."[19] In Li Kuan's case, his aging body worked against his claims, at least in the eyes of skeptics such as Ge Hong and perhaps others. On the other hand, as we have seen, for many others Li Kuan was obviously convincing enough in his role, and, further, there is a fascinating detail added in the last sentence: since adepts were sometimes known to conceal their true abilities behind ordinary façades, their true names behind false ones, and to fake their own deaths in order to continue living past their predestined life limits, any decrepit or ordinary visage, any name, and any apparent death could be interpreted by a crowd of interested onlookers as merely a front, part of the expected performance.

We see this hermeneutic in play as the narrative concludes:

> Then there came a time when a great pestilence spread through Wu; more than one in two died. What Li Kuan entrusted himself to was his *dao* chamber, which he termed a "hut." Kuan, too, contracted the epidemic disease, whereupon he put out word that he had "entered his hut to fast and keep the precepts." He proceeded to die inside this hut, but his followers said that he was a "transcendent who had transformed his body and escaped by means of a simulated corpse" and that his death was not real.[20]

Elsewhere I have speculated as to whether what is being described here is perhaps the response to the plague of a Celestial Master follower from Shu, not yet recognized as such in pre-317 C.E. Wu.[21] Here, however, I am focusing on the adept in his social environment. For any practitioner of longevity arts to contract an illness constituted a serious public relations problem. Li Kuan manages this by "putting out word that" 託言 he was withdrawing into his "hut" 盧 for ritual reasons. Then, even after he dies, his disciples stick to the alternative set of meanings of their master's doings: his apparent demise is actually to be read as a successful performance of *shijie* 尸解. The adept's behaviors, right down to his death, were constant subjects of interpretation and discussion on the part of disciples, clients, and other interested

---

19. *NP* 20:347.
20. Ibid. 9:174.
21. *TL*, 216–218.

(and sometimes skeptical) parties. It was in the crucible of these social representations, interpretations, and evaluations that his reputation was forged and the collective memory of his achievements was rooted. Perhaps, if he was successful, his reputation would become fixed onto the landscape in the form of a commemorative stele and a shrine or temple, and perhaps he would even find inclusion in a translocal hagiographic collection such as *Liexian zhuan* or *Shenxian zhuan*.

In sum, many adepts presented audiences—sometimes quite large audiences—with visual and verbal spectacles. Even some of the most reclusive among them were public figures: people knew who they were and what they were capable of, knew where to find them, talked often of them, and sought their help on many occasions.[22] This sort of presence before a community of others was not incidental but rather was central to adepts' recognition as successful transcendents, and it consumed a large portion of their time, energy, and attention.

Healing

Of Cui Wenzi 崔文子, the *Liexian zhuan* tells us that he was a native of Taishan district (one version adds that he lived during Qin times) and belonged to a family that had practiced Huang-Lao arts for generations.[23] After having lived for a time as a hermit at the base of the mountain, he made a yellow powder and red pellets at the place that would later become the site of a shrine to him. He sold drugs in area markets and said of himself that he was three centuries old. Later, during an epidemic in which people died by the tens of thousands, magistrates went to him seeking help. Raising a red banner and carrying his yellow powder, he visited people's homes; whoever drank his potion recovered at once. He thus saved the lives of myriads. After this he departed and sold his powder in Shu. This, the story concludes, is why Cui's red pellets and yellow powder have been so highly valued, seen by many as divine.[24]

Here we see an adept from a family with a multigenerational history of practicing esoterica undergoing a period of social withdrawal, to be sure. But later he sets himself up as a seller of medicines in markets and does not hesitate to mention

---

22. It is also of course quite possible that there existed some truly and totally reclusive adepts who never interacted with nonpractitioners. Since there can, by definition, have been no record of such persons, we will never know. We cannot assume that because our stereotype of adepts portrays them as completely solitary, they must therefore have always been completely solitary. We also cannot assume that because records show adepts interacting with other people in manifold ways that all adepts interacted with others in these ways.

23. For introductions to what these arts may have entailed, see Csikszentmihalyi, "Han Cosmology and Mantic Practices," 57–58; and Yates, *Five Lost Classics.*

24. *Liexian zhuan* item 40; see Kaltenmark, *Le Lie-sien tchouan,* 134–135; and *DZ* 294, 1:19b–20a.

there his extraordinary longevity. Between the lines of the story we can sense a reputation forming, because the next thing we read is that officials are coming to Cui for help in an epidemic: word of his abilities has spread and confidence in him has solidified to this extent. Cui's ministrations to masses of patients have their dramatic effect, and it is this service to the people that accounts for the shrine later erected in his memory. Cui moves to the distant region of Shu and sets up shop again. His recipes become a legacy cherished by further generations, not just of his own family but presumably of all in the areas where he operated.

Cui's case is hardly unique; much evidence corroborates this portrayal of adepts' social relations with others. Practitioners of longevity and transcendence arts (and other esoteric methods[25]) often functioned as healers. They cured the sick of all social levels, sometimes in great numbers. Healing, including diagnosis, is the service adepts are most frequently depicted as providing for other people. It was a natural outgrowth of their mastery of medicinal products and spirits and of skills lending themselves to diagnostic purposes (such as divination, physiognomy, inner vision, and the ability to see the true forms of spirits). But here I will focus on the social aspects of adepts' curing activities, bypassing commentary on the methods used.

It will be convenient to analyze the material into themes. Several passages emphasize the large scale of adepts' healing activities. In extraordinary cases they were credited not just with a discrete number of efficacious cures but even with saving masses of people from epidemics or simply with having cured thousands or myriads of patients over a long period. The case of Liu Gen is especially vivid in this regard; a public official appeals to Liu Gen for help during an epidemic, and the adept's response—an esoteric procedure to be followed, delivered by the adept from a distance—proves strikingly effective.[26] Other accounts make clear that certain adepts were identified and remembered as the source of curative practices or substances long after their own departures.[27]

---

25. Not every adept treated in this section was recognized as a transcendent, but the social environments in which healing adepts are portrayed as operating are the same in both sets of cases, and most of my examples concern practitioners to whom great longevity was attributed.

26. *TL*, 240–249. Other examples include Shen Jian in the *Shenxian zhuan* (see *TL*, 333) and Fu Ju xiansheng in the *Liexian zhuan* (item 63; Kaltenmark, *Le Lie-sien tchouan*, 174–176; *DZ* 294 2:12a–b).

27. Examples include "Cassia Father" in *Liexian zhuan* (item 31; Kaltenmark, *Le Lie-sien tchouan*, 118–120; *DZ* 294 1:15a–b) and "Sire Gourd" in *Shenxian zhuan* (see *TL*, 161–164). Aside from medicines and recipes, adepts also left legacies of other kinds. Customs, land features, and place names, as well as texts, were attributed to their previous activities. Examples include: (1) Dong Feng's apricot grove; (2) 9/9 customs traced to Fei Changfang's apotropaic advice to a particular family (*TL*, 168, from *Qi Xie ji*); (3) the texts bestowed by Wang Yuan and preserved by a certain Chen and his family "for generations" (see *TL*, 264); (4) text and method left behind by Wei Shuqing and his son (see *TL*, 274); (5) place name (see *TL*, 368).

We may infer from the narrative evidence that some adepts traveled about from region to region or door to door, curing patients, while others could be found selling medicinal ingredients and preparations in city markets. Examples of marketplace merchants of medicinals are numerous.[28] A particularly striking example of itinerancy is the case of the Holy Mother of Dongling, who "knew how to heal sicknesses and cure people, and she visited some of them at their homes. This enraged [her husband] Du even more, so he filed an official complaint against her, stating that she was lecherous and wicked and was not attending to her proper domestic role. She was therefore arrested and imprisoned."[29] A woman visiting and treating the sick at their homes was a powerfully aberrant phenomenon, but it was probably not a phenomenon unique to the woman who became known as the Holy Mother of Dongling.[30]

We have here a story concerning Ge Xuan, great-uncle of Ge Hong:

> He was especially adept at curing illnesses. Ghosts and demons would all manifest their forms before him; some of these he would send off, others he would execute....
>
> Ge Xuan once stayed as a guest in someone's home while passing through Wukang. The host was sick and had commissioned a female spirit-medium to

---

28. Merely in the *Liexian zhuan* we find these statements: (1) Xiaqiu Zhong sold drugs in Ning for over a century. (He also took care to remain occluded.) When he appeared to die, a layperson stole his medicines, then quaked with fear when Zhong returned to reclaim them, very much alive (item 32; *DZ* 294 1:15b–16a; Kaltenmark, *Le Lie-sien tchouan,* 120–121). (2) Master Anqi sold drugs by the eastern sea. Later he returned (or retired) to Penglai, where Qin Shihuang, who had interviewed him for three days, sent maritime parties led by Xu Fu and others to try to find him, to no avail (item 30; *DZ* 294 1:14b–15a; Kaltenmark, *Le Lie-sien tchouan,* 115–118). (3) Fan Li sold drugs in Shandong for several centuries (item 25; *DZ* 294 1:12b–13a; Kaltenmark, *Le Lie-sien tchouan,* 102–104). (4) Ren Guang sold cinnabar in a market in the capital and in villages (item 34; *DZ* 294 1:16b–17a; Kaltenmark, *Le Lie-sien tchouan,* 123–124). (5) Dongfang Shuo after leaving court was seen in Guiji selling drugs in the Five Lakes area (item 42; *DZ* 294 2:1b–2a; Kaltenmark, *Le Lie-sien tchouan,* 137–138). (6) Lupi gong (The Sire Clad in Deerskin), after a century or more spent in a tower, came down to sell medicines in the market (item 48; *DZ* 294 2:4b–5a; Kaltenmark, *Lie-sien tchouan,* 2:4b–5a). (7) Chi Fu (Red Axe), a red-headed Rong tribesman, sold "Yu's leftover provisions" (a mineral) that he had gathered on Huashan at several places in a large region (item 61; *DZ* 294 2:11a–b; Kaltenmark, *Le Lie-sien tchouan,* 171–172). (8) Huang Yuanqiu periodically would come down from his mountain residence to sell medicinals in the market (item 65; *DZ* 294 2:13b–14a; Kaltenmark, *Le Lie-sien tchouan,* 179–180). (9) Xuan Su sold medicinals in the capital market (item 70; *DZ* 294 2:16b–17a; Kaltenmark, *Le Lie-sien tchouan,* 191–193). In the *Shenxian zhuan,* in Gan Ji's hagiography, Hu gong and Bo He are described as selling medicines in markets, where they are met by future disciples.

29. *TL,* 146.

30. Other examples of itinerant healers include Feng Heng in the *Shenxian zhuan* and the adept featured in *Yiyuan* 異苑 item 9.18 (on this text see *SW,* 78–80).

call down a god on his behalf, to whom he was making offerings. Through the medium, the god commanded Xuan to drink some wine, which Xuan refused to do, and otherwise spoke rudely to him. At this, Xuan grew angry and shouted, "How dare you, you perverse demon!" Xuan then commanded the Five Earls[31] to apprehend the god [through the medium], take him out, tie him to a post, and whip him. The medium then seemed to be led outside by invisible beings. Upon reaching the courtyard, the medium hugged a pillar as her gown was removed, then fell to the ground as a whipping sound was heard, and blood was seen flowing from her back. Then, in a demonic voice, the god through the medium begged for its life. Xuan said, "If I pardon you for this capital offense, can you cure this living person's illness?"

"I can," said the god through the medium.

"Very well, I will give you three days' time. If this sick man is not well by then, I will deal with you." The medium was then released, and the host recovered from his illness.[32]

Here the conflict between two modes of religious power is dramatized. The adept himself does not heal the patient directly; rather, in a gripping public display, he wields his spiritual authority by commanding unseen spirits, demonstrating the superiority of his station to that of a god. The god must be accessed through a medium, as well as through an economy of exchange, via the making of offerings, but the adept shows himself as standing outside and above this web of obligation, tapping into a higher structure of power.

Quite a few narratives are, like this one, at pains to argue the efficacy and power of adepts' healing techniques and, in some cases, their supremacy over rival curative regimes. Through these stories we glimpse a society in which practitioners competed with each other for clients, their reputations dependent on the perceived and reported efficacy of their arts.[33] Even a statement as simple as this one concerning Gan Shi 甘始—that "in curing the sick, he made no use of needles or moxa"—is neither idle not neutral; the point is that his own methods, which

---

31. I am uncertain of the identities of these 五伯. They may be the martial, demon-subduing spirits of the Spring and Autumn period kings known variously as the Five Earls or Five Hegemons (*wuba* 五霸); for more on these figures (but nothing on their deification), see *DKW* 1:505a, 506a. The spirits of deceased, warlike kings and generals were often domesticated by being incorporated into priestly pantheons, usually as relatively low-ranking but potent and fierce guardians or exorcistic attackers.

32. *TL*, 153.

33. Especially clear examples include those of Dong Feng and Liu Ping in the *Shenxian zhuan* (see ibid., 141–145 and 319–321). Bo He is also mentioned as having healed Gan Ji by esoteric means (ibid., 301–302).

the text leaves mysterious, were superior to these more common ones.[34] Similarly contrastive comments about transcendence-quest-adepts' methods are made elsewhere as well.[35]

Let us examine now the following statement concerning Li Changzai 李常在: "Whenever he treated those who were seriously ill, they would recover within three days; lesser cases would recover in a single day. Those whom he could not cure he did not go to treat at all."[36] The first sentence underscores the efficacy of Li's healing work; the second, however, may come as a surprise. A similar statement occurs in another hagiography:

> Chen Chang remained on Linen Island[37] for over six hundred years. People who lived on the mountain built a dwelling for him, and every season they made offerings to him. But Chen Chang neither ate nor drank and did not practice any special regimens. Whenever any of the people who served him were ill, they took vessels and asked for some offering water 祭水 from him; on taking it, they would be cured. *But if according to their allotted lifespan they were due to die, Chen Chang would give them no water.*[38]

These statements can be read in several ways at once. It can indicate these adepts' respect for allotted lifespan, which they often altered in their own cases but perhaps could not alter in the case of others; it can show their prescience about *ming* and hence their skill as prognosticators as well as healers (and their need to work within the limits of the *ming* they could discern); and perhaps it is an unintended glimpse, through the text, of a way in which adepts carefully managed their social reputations as healers, taking only those cases where they stood a good chance of succeeding, *ming* being a convenient explanation for refusal or failure of treatment, since to clients it was inscrutable.

Narratives of successful transcendents display their subjects' healing powers by means of various other rhetorical devices as well. One of these is the claim that only those helped by the master escaped an otherwise general threat.[39] Another is the depiction of an initially skeptical patient who is won over by the striking

---

34. See ibid., 150.

35. Examples include Wang Yao (ibid., 342–343) and Sun Bo (ibid., 334–335).

36. Ibid., 316–317.

37. This is a small isle off the coast of Guiji, mentioned (along with other small isles in the same area) in Ge Hong's *Inner Chapters* (*NP* 4:85) as a good place to pursue arts of transcendence if one cannot get to a major inland mountain. It is also sometimes known as Mount Linen Island.

38. *TL,* 297–298, emphasis added.

39. An example appears in the *Shenxian zhuan* hagiography of Yin Gui (*TL,* 347–349).

efficacy of his treatment; such an outcome is so much the better if the patient in question is a famous intellectual on record as having argued that transcendence is impossible. The story is told of how Li Shaojun produced a medicine whose potency convinced Dong Zhongshu that he had been wrong to doubt the efficacy of longevity arts.[40] Polemical though the story is, we can once again glimpse behind it a certain social world. The entire episode takes place at court and at the highest levels of society. The adept and the patient are friends. The adept, as usual for those seeking transcendence, deploys not the standard sorts of remedies but extremely exotic ingredients (the narrative goes to lengths to stress this) prepared under special conditions of ritual purity. The patient finally takes the long-neglected medicine, despite his skepticism, when his memory is jogged by a conversation about the departed adept. Belief in its efficacy is then handed down from father to son.

Prognostication

Another service lay clients sought from adepts was accurate prediction of fortunes—of individual clients, families, whole communities, ruling houses, armies, and kingdoms. Once again we will leave aside the methods by which adepts are depicted as arriving at such predictions.[41] Our concern is to recognize a social environment in which prognostication, of whatever sort, was a service laypersons often sought from adepts in esoteric arts of longevity and transcendence.[42]

The ability to prognosticate (as well as to "see" past events by various means) seems to have been ubiquitous among adepts, although the methods by which they foretold the future varied considerably, and such ability apparently had no direct relation to attaining deathlessness. Prognostication simply was something a religious adept of almost any kind was expected to be able to do, and the narrative motif of the adept's strikingly successful prediction is a staple of hagiographic literature across

---

40. The story appears in Li's *Shenxian zhuan* hagiography; see *TL,* 223–224; and is discussed further in Chapter 8. Independent evidence corroborates that Dong Zhongshu did in fact argue the impossibility of transcendence. See, for instance, *Han Wudi gushi* 漢武帝故事 item 10 (tr. Thomas Smith, "Ritual and the Shaping of Narrative," 403–404), which is based on *Shi ji* 12:456; *Shi ji* 28:1386; and *Han shu* 25A:1218.

41. For more, see *TL,* 72–75; Kalinowski, ed., *Divination et société dans la Chine médiévale.* We do well to recall that prediction per se may not be the heart of divination in many cases, that it is (also) "an imaginal and poetic appropriation of aspects of the natural world (including human relationships and activities) toward the construction of a language of signs" (Patricia Miller, *Dreams in Late Antiquity,* 7).

42. It was also a service some adepts provided on their own initiative without having been commissioned; an example is the case of Yin Gui (see *TL,* 347–349).

several traditions. Unelaborated claims of skill in this area are sprinkled through the hagiographies.[43]

Some narratives stress that it was the adept's face that laypersons particularly scrutinized for signs of their own fortunes: "Li Yiqi seldom spoke. If someone asked him something, he would make no reply. But when people of Shu had troubles, they would go to him and ask him to speak about the inauspiciousness or auspiciousness of their situations and then wait. They could divine simply from his facial expression whether it would be sad or happy."[44] The adept simply *knows* or *can see* the future without resort to any procedures; spectators then come to know what the future is by scrutinizing the adept's facial expression as if it itself were a diviner's board.[45]

Another motif is that of the adept who, commissioned by a ruler or official to divine political or military fortune, merely acts out the bad news without speaking it directly. This seems to have been a standard story type.[46] Another was that of the adept who, becoming aware of a fire hundreds of miles away while attending a formal banquet or other function, spits out wine to quench it; others questioning his

---

43. Examples include: (1) Qilong Ming ("Cry of the Dragon-Mounter [or Dragon Mount]") warns of imminent flood (*Liexian zhuan* item 45; *DZ* 294 2:3a–b; Kaltenmark, *Le Lie-sien tchouan*, 144–146). (2) "Several times, You Bozi helped members of the Su clan avoid disaster or attain good fortune" (*Liexian zhuan* item 29; *DZ* 294 1:14a–b; Kaltenmark, *Le Lie-sien tchouan*, 114–115). (3) Yin Si divines by lunascopy (*Shenxian zhuan;* see *TL,* 370). (4) Cheng Wuding understands the speech of animals (*Shenxian zhuan;* see *TL,* 360–363). (5) Guo Pu divines the cause of an illness; it lies in the fact that someone in the client's family history once cut down a great tree and killed the snake that they found inside it (*Soushen ji* 搜神記 3:15). (6) "When Bo Shanfu spoke of any person's fortunes from past times onward, of their good and bad deeds, their successes and disasters, it was as if he had seen them himself. He also knew whether what was about to happen was auspicious or inauspicious" (*Shenxian zhuan;* see *TL,* 297). (7) "Liu Jing knew the auspiciousness or inauspiciousness [of future events]" (*Shenxian zhuan;* see *TL,* 249–250). (8) "Wang Yuan broadly studied and mastered the Six Classics, but had especially good understanding of celestial patterns and the essentials of the He and Luo River Charts and [other] prognosticatory weft texts *(chenwei).* He could predict the flourishing and decline of all beings in the heavens and among men and could foretell fortune and misfortune in the nine provinces as easily as if he were gazing at them on his palm" (*Shenxian zhuan;* see *TL,* 259–264).

44. *TL,* 228–229; a similar passage appears concerning Li A in both *Shenxian zhuan* and *Baopuzi neipian* (see *TL,* 212–215).

45. This use of divination sets these adepts in contrast to the early Celestial Masters religion, which banned divination as an illicit attempt to cheat fate. See Nickerson, "Shamans, Demons, Diviners, and Taoists," 45–47; Andersen, "Talking to the Gods," 7–8; Hendrischke and Penny, "The 180 Precepts Spoken by Lord Lao" (note precept nos. 16, 78, 114). Both Nickerson and Andersen also document ways in which this prohibition was relaxed sometime after the early period of the movement.

46. We have stories of this type concerning Li Yiqi and Sun Deng (see *TL* 228–229 and 336 respectively).

apparently impolite behavior reveals its true purpose, and later fact-checking confirms its long-distance efficacy. (The fact-checking involves either sending an emissary to the distant location, or exchanging letters, which attest to ways in which news of adepts' doings could be spread over long distances.) Closely similar narratives of this kind are recorded concerning Guo Xian and Fan Ying in the "Fangshu liezhuan" section of *Hou Han shu;* of Luan Ba and Cheng Wuding in *Shenxian zhuan;* and, for that matter, of Fotu Deng in *Traditions of Eminent Monks.*[47]

People continued to seek prognostication in transcendents' temples after their departure, as evidenced in the following odd story regarding the Shangqing progenitor Mao Ying in the *Shenxian zhuan:*

> Near and far, people established temples to Lord Mao and served him. He would converse with them from inside a screen. In his comings and goings, sometimes he would ride on a normal horse; sometimes he would change himself into a white crane. When people were ill, they would come [to his temples] to ask for his blessing. They would always bring ten cooked eggs and place them inside the screen. In a moment, he would throw them back out, one by one. The people would take them home and crack them open. If there were no yolks inside them, it meant that the patient would recover; if there was soil inside them, it meant the patient would not recover. This was a constant predictor of the patient's fortunes. The eggs were always returned just as they had been before; they had not been opened anywhere.[48]

Managing Local Gods and Demons

In Eastern Han, Wei, and early Jin China, people often made offerings at temples to accompany their prayers to deities for protection, health, good harvest, timely rain, healing, and the like. We have many stories of gods who rewarded the pious for their devotion; we also have stories of gods—or other classes of beings, "demons" denoted by one or another Chinese term, masquerading as gods—peremptorily demanding offerings in exchange for not harming the populace, gods who essentially commissioned their own temples and founded their own cults. It is well known that the early Celestial Master community objected to such behavior on the part of gods as well as their human representatives, the spirit-mediums, invocators, and other personnel of local temples. It is less well known that, probably beginning before the rise of the Celestial Master movement in Sichuan in the mid–second century C.E., adepts in quest of transcendence similarly opposed what they in

---

47. *Hou Han shu* 82A:2709, 2722; *Gaoseng zhuan* 386b.
48. *TL,* 328.

effect portrayed as divine protection rackets. We have stories of their efforts to quell local cults, thereby relieving the people of the need to make excessive offerings and demonstrating their own hierarchical superiority to temple gods. By means of such efforts, they both served client communities and enhanced their reputation.

The following three narratives are all drawn from the *Shenxian zhuan* and arranged to show a progression: the first simply emphasizes the adept's spiritual authority over temple gods; the second echoes this, but with the added mention of the god's depredations on the community, depredations stopped by the adept; and the third adds explicit justification—submitted in the form of an official memorial—of the adept's god-quelling in terms of its benefit to communities that have long suffered the demands of an overweening god and his temple personnel.

1. Ge Xuan once passed by a temple, the god of which often forced travelers to dismount [and present offerings] when within a hundred paces [of the temple]. Inside the temple grounds were several dozen trees which were the home of many birds which no one dared molest. Xuan, riding a carriage, passed by without getting down. In a moment a great wind swirled up toward Xuan's carriage from behind, scattering dust up into the sky. Those following him all scattered, but Xuan only became incensed and cried, "How dare you, you little demon!" He raised his hand as if to stop the wind, and it died down at once. Xuan then rode back and threw a talisman up into the temple treetops. The birds there all fell down dead, and within a few days, all the trees had withered even though it was the height of summer; and soon thereafter a fire broke out in one of the temple rooms and burned the temple completely to the ground.[49]

2. There was an old temple, and inside the compound was a tree above which a light would often appear. Many who stayed beneath that tree met violent deaths, and birds and beasts did not dare to nest in it. So Liu Ping exorcised it. Although it was midsummer, the tree withered and died, and an enormous serpent, seventy or eighty feet long, was found hanging dead in its branches. After this there were no more disturbances there.[50]

3. Later, Luan Ba was nominated as a Filial and Incorrupt, appointed a Gentleman of the Interior, and then promoted to the post of Governor of Yuzhang district.[51] Before he was made Governor of Yuzhang, there had been a god in the temple at Mount Lu,[52] who would converse with people, drink liquor, and

---

49. Ibid., 153.

50. Ibid., 321.

51. Its seat was located in modern Nanchang district, Jiangxi Province.

52. This temple, located in the Yuzhang jurisdiction (Mount Lu is located in Jiujiang district, Jiangxi Province), was a powerful and prominent regional temple during the early medieval period.

throw its cup in the air. The god could make the wind blow on Lake Gongting in two directions at once, so that travelers in either direction would have the wind in their sails. But, a couple of weeks before Ba arrived at his post, the god in the temple no longer made a sound, and no one knew where it had gone. When Ba arrived, he personally submitted a memorial[53] saying that this "temple demon" had falsely arrogated the title of a celestial official and had been duping and depleting the common people for a long time. It was time for the demon to be punished for its crimes. The memorial asked that notice be given to the personnel evaluation sections [of all districts] that he was personally going to be pursuing and capturing this demon; for, if it were not controlled and punished, he feared it would continue to roam about the world, eating blood sacrifices wherever it went, visiting sickness on the good people without due cause in order to increase the offerings made to it.

And so he set out, inquiring in many areas in the shrines at mountains and rivers, seeking the tracks of this demon. He traced it to the Qi domain,[54] where it had assumed the form of a student. The Governor of Qi had granted this student an audience and had been impressed with his physical beauty, his talent for disputation, and his knowledge of and ability to discuss the classics and expound on their meaning. In fact, he had made a widespread impression in Qi; everyone knew of him. The Governor, furthermore, not knowing that this was really a demon, had given him his daughter in marriage, and a son had been born of the match.

When Ba arrived, after exchanging greetings and pleasantries, he said to the Governor, "I have heard that your son-in-law knows the Five Classics and the philosophers. May I meet him?" The Governor invited his son-in-law to join them, but he declined to come out, saying he was ill. Ba then repeatedly insisted on seeing him. In their quarters, the son-in-law told his wife, "If I go out there today, I will surely die." The Governor's daughter thought it all very strange and did not know what to make of it. Meanwhile, Ba, knowing he would not come out voluntarily, asked for an official proclamation tablet and a brush. He wrote a talisman on it and gave it to the Governor, saying, "Give this to your son-in-law,

---

For a study, see Miyakawa, "Local Cults around Mount Lu at the Time of Sun En's Rebellion." Further studies of Daoist (often as compared with Buddhist and Confucian) relations with local cults and the gods, temples, and shamans of the common religion include Rolf Stein, "Religious Taoism and Popular Religion from the Second to the Seventh Centuries"; Miyakawa, *Rikuchō shi kenkyū,* 191–235; Miyakawa, *Rikuchū shūkyō shi,* 356–365; Schipper, "Purity and Strangers"; Lévi, "Les fonctionnaires et le divin"; Kleeman, "Licentious Cults and Bloody Victuals"; and Kleeman, "Mountain Deities in China."

53. It is unclear whether he does so to the court or to the unseen hierarchy (or perhaps both).

54. The seat of this domain was located in modern Linzi district, Shandong Province.

and he will come out on his own." When he had received the talisman, the son-in-law wept, gave some parting instructions to his wife, and came out. On seeing Ba from a distance, his body already changed into that of a fox, but his face was still that of a human. Ba cursed him in a stern voice: "How dare you, you dead fox! Why do you not revert to your complete, true form?" With that he turned completely into a fox. Ba spoke again: "Let him be executed!" At once, but without Ba's lifting a hand to cause it, the fox's head was severed and fell to the floor. Ba then ordered that the baby fox be brought out. The boy to whom the Governor's daughter had given birth had already changed back into fox form. It, too, was executed. Ba then took his leave and returned to his commandery.[55]

All such accounts emphasize the drama of the confrontation between adept and temple god; the contest takes the form of public theater, with visible results confirming the adept's success. In such scenes, the adept challenges the most potent spiritual force most of his clients have had contact with and emerges victorious. It was in such public performances that adepts displayed the potency of their arts and won their reputations for spiritual power. And, as we see, adepts themselves could also step in to provide the services once offered by the vanquished local god.[56]

Other Kinds of Help

Transcendence-seekers are on record as having provided a striking variety of other services for their clients. Most often mentioned among these is the control of weather—ensuring good harvests and preventing flooding and drought.[57] A few adepts are mentioned as having resurrected recently deceased clients, usually by a combination of medicinal ministrations to the corpse and administrative wrangling in the unseen world of spirits. These narratives afford fascinating glimpses into early medieval understandings of the workings of the afterlife; they also clearly testify to the extraordinary powers adepts were credited with by others. One such story

---

55. *TL,* 252–254; this narrative accounts for the bulk of Luan's *Shenxian zhuan* hagiography.

56. Adepts battle local gods in many other narratives, both in hagiographies and in the *zhiguai* literature.

57. Adepts control rain or other weather events in a great many narratives, including *Shuyi ji* (by Ren Fang) 1:72, 2:2; *Bowu zhi* 8:7, 8:8; *Soushen houji* 10:3; *Soushen ji* 1:20, 1:22, 1:23, and other items; *Liexian zhuan* items 11, 17 (where rain is said to be procurable by offerings at Peng Zu's shrine in Liyang), 21, 41 (the latter involving weather prediction); *Mingxiang ji* 13, 56 (examples of Buddhist adaptations of the motif); "Fangshu liezhuan" section of Fan Ye's *Hou Han shu,* item 4; and, in the *Shenxian zhuan,* the hagiographies of Hu gong, Dong Feng, Fan furen, Ge Xuan, Yuzi, Liu Ping, Liu Zheng, and Ge Yue.

appears in the *Shenxian zhuan* hagiography of Dong Feng.[58] Another was told of Wu Meng:

> During the Jin there lived one Gan Qing, who died without having been ill. At that time the master of esoteric skills Wu Meng said to Gan Qing's son, "I estimate that Gan's count was not yet used up. I am going to make an appeal on his behalf based on his allotted lifespan. Do not hold his funeral yet." The body was laid in a chamber of purity; only a place beneath the heart remained warm. After thus lying in state for seven days, with the weather quite hot, Qing's body was about to decay when, the next morning, Wu Meng burst in, commanding the relatives to watch for Qing's breath and have water ready for him to bathe and rinse out his mouth with. Then he departed again. Around noon, Qing revived. At first he opened his eyes and mouth but could not make a sound. His household was both sorrowful and delighted. Wu Meng again commanded that he take water in his mouth and be sprinkled with it. Then Qing rose, vomited several *sheng* of putrid blood, and gradually became able to speak. Three days later he was back to normal. He said that at first he saw a dozen or so men arrive; they bound and shackled him and took him to prison along with a group of a dozen or so others. They were being called by turns to face [the magistrate], and his turn had not yet come when suddenly he saw Lord Wu facing north pleading for his release. The king therefore released him from his shackles and ordered him to return. [On the way back] they were welcomed and received at whatever offices and bureaus they passed, and everyone extended invitations to Lord Wu, who acted as if he were of equal status to them all. He did not even know which gods they were.[59]

---

58. See *TL,* 142–143. Feng Gang, Mao Ying, and others are also credited with this ability in the *Shenxian zhuan.*

59. *Youming lu* 幽明錄 74; my translation is based on a comparison of the composite version in LX, 217–218 with its two sources, *TPGJ* 378:8a–b and *TPYL* 887:5a. *Soushen ji* 1:26 contains a quite summary version of this story, with a few differences of detail; for a translation (in which Gan's name is mistranscribed as "Ch'in"), see DeWoskin and Crump, *In Search of the Supernatural,* 13. Another story involving interaction between Wu Meng and Gan Qing occurs in the *Daoxue zhuan,* compiled in the last quarter of the sixth century; see Bumbacher, "The Fragments of the *Daoxue zhuan,*" 162, based on a fragment quoted in *TPYL* 666:7a–b: here Gan Qing is said to have loved to hunt, despite having been warned not to by Wu Meng; on one occasion Wu Meng went into the grass as the hunters' fire closed in from all sides, and the animals of the area all flocked to him for protection, the fire unable to reach them—at which point the terrified Gan Qing repented. This story is simply set during the Jin, but other tales concerning Wu Meng more specifically represent him as having been active in the second through the fourth decades of the fourth century, which would have made him a contemporary of Ge Hong.

We see here the expected afterlife elements—the notion of "counts" as determinative of lifespan, the forbidding "earth prisons"—but also the adept's remarkable skill in negotiating his way through this bureaucratic system on his client's behalf and, of course, the vivid spectacle provided in the client's telling of the story of his experiences in the other world.

As we have seen, one of the earliest depictions of a transcendent-like being, in the first chapter of the received text of the *Zhuangzi,* credits him with somehow aiding the ripening of the people's crops. The same sort of work on behalf of the people continued to be credited to adepts in later texts, including both collected hagiographies (for example, Jie Xiang in the *Shenxian zhuan*) and stele inscriptions (for example, the Fei Zhi stele).[60] Adepts possessed and transmitted potent means of protecting themselves from attacks by wild animals and mountain spirits (and often the texts seem to conflate these two categories of dangerous beings into one), as is well known; Ge Hong discusses talismans and other methods for this purpose. They also, however, are recorded as having provided such protection for their disciples and clients.[61] Yet another benefit adepts were recorded as providing for lay clients was assistance in legal and administrative matters.[62] Like the holy men of the Late Antique Mediterranean world studied by Peter Brown, they were well situated to provide leverage in such situations since they were often outsiders who lacked normal family or official ties to the communities in which they operated.[63]

We should not forget that adepts also provided the less tangible benefits of entertainment and the incitement of wonder. They allowed clients to glimpse the marvels to which they had privileged access. Consider the following narrative:

Atop Mount Lu are three stone beams several hundred feet long. Looking down from them, the depth is so great there seems to be no bottom. During the *xiankang* period [of the Jin, 335–343 C.E.], the Regional Inspector of Jiangzhou, Yu Liang,[64] went out to meet Wu Meng. Meng took [Yu and] his disciples up the mountain on a sightseeing excursion. Thus they passed by these beams. [While doing so] they saw an old sire sitting beneath a cassia tree using a jade cup to receive sweet dew. He proffered it to Meng, who passed it around to all the disciples. Then they proceeded to a place where they saw ranks of towers and capacious buildings, jade rooms and gold chambers, tinkling and sparkling;

60. On Jie Xiang, see *TL,* 189–194; on the Fei Zhi stele, see below.

61. An example appears in the *Shenxian zhuan* hagiography of Yin Gui (*TL,* 347–349).

62. In the *Shenxian zhuan,* Liu Ping and Yin Gui are credited with this sort of performance (see *TL,* 319–321 and 347–349).

63. See Peter Brown, "The Rise and Function of the Holy Man in Late Antiquity."

64. He receives a biography in *Jin shu* 73:1915–1924 and is frequently mentioned in the dynastic histories of the Song, Qi, and Liang dynasties and the *Nanshi.*

the radiance dazzled the eyes, and there were too many precious gems and jade vessels to recognize or name.[65] They saw several persons conversing with Meng as if they were old acquaintances. They were served "jade salve" all day long.[66]

Here, a notable client on a sightseeing excursion is afforded temporary access to a mountain world of wonders—access that can be gained only through the adept's mediation. We glimpse a society in which well-placed patrons made such pilgrimages to the mountainous areas that had long been the bases of operations of adepts in esoteric arts. And, thanks in part to such pilgrimages, many other people were able to hear stories of the exploits and strange doings of adepts.

Economies of Exchange

We find adepts selling goods or services in markets or, in a few cases, simply frequenting markets, or begging in them; a few are even said to have amassed wealth in this way.[67] These adepts' participation in normal economic activities seems unremarkable—except in that it belies the stereotype of practitioners as socially aloof. Markets were clearly one standard place where adepts in esoterica could be encountered.[68] Some accounts emphasize that adepts in the marketplace had an ordinary appearance, betraying no signs of their esoteric abilities, and hence they were recognizable as practitioners only by those qualified or fated to serve

---

65. *TPYL* 663 has: "There were vessels and objects [or creatures] that were unrecognizable," more strongly suggesting the strangeness of the place.

66. *Shuyi ji* by Zu Chongzhi (429–500 C.E.), as collected in LX, based on *Fayuan zhulin* 31:521b; *TPYL* 41:5b–6a; and *TPYL* 66:1a–b. The story is also picked up in *Shuijing zhu* 39:493, where it is cited from the topographic treatise *Xunyang ji* 尋陽記. On the *Shuyi ji,* see *SW,* 83–85.

67. Already in the *Liexian zhuan* we note, for example, that: Chijiang Ziyu sometimes sold string in the market (item 4); Xiao Fu, when young, was a shoe repairman in the market at Quzhou (item 13); Ge You sold sheep that he carved from wood (item 23); Kou Xian, a fisherman, sold some of his catch, ate some, let some go (item 27); Jiu Ke (The Alehouse Guest) was an employee in a wine shop in the market of the capital of the state of Liang and made excellent wine there (item 33); Zhuji weng (The Old Man Who Summoned Chickens) sold chickens and eggs, but later abandoned his considerable earnings and left to raise fish elsewhere (item 36); Zhu Zhong sold pearls in the Guiji market (item 37); Duzi (The Herder) was seen at the foot of a mountain selling peaches and plums in winter (item 44); Chang Rong sold a purple herb to dyers (item 49); Yin Sheng was a beggar in the market (item 53); Fu Lü sold pearls, jewels, and jades he had collected on Fangzhang Isle (item 56); Nü Ji (Lady Ji) sold wine in the market at Chen, and later, after acquiring a manual on sexual arts from a master, she practiced those arts with young male clients at her tavern (item 66).

68. For brief, suggestive comments on the markets of Jiankang, the southern capital, in early medieval times, see Liu, "Jiankang and the Commercial Empire of the Southern Dynasties," 39, 42.

them as disciples.[69] Unlike the case of Buddhist monks and nuns, with their quite distinctive appearance, dress, and physical accoutrements, transcendents-in-training often had no distinguishing marks—except, that is, for their remarkable speech or behavior.

But adepts' provision of services was not always an economic exchange. Chen Chang, as reported in the *Shenxian zhuan*, "remained on Linen Island[70] for over six hundred years. People who lived on the mountain built a dwelling for him, and every season they made offerings to him. But Chang neither ate nor drank and did not practice any special regimens. Whenever any of the people who served him were ill, they took vessels and asked for some offering water 祭水 from him; on taking it they would be cured."[71] The people in this case respond in a familiar way—a response indicating the level of authority they recognize in Chen. A specialist provides a valuable service; they reciprocate by providing "offerings," presumably gifts of food and drink of the sort that might be offered to gods or ancestors. However, with the statement, "But Chang neither ate nor drank," the normal, reciprocal exchange is disrupted: the people here are dealing with a being who, unlike a god or ancestor, has no use for their offerings, and who thus announces himself to be of a still higher order of authority than the one they are accustomed to. Yet he goes on providing his service anyway.

Or we have the case of the Box-carrying Master as narrated in the *Liexian zhuan*:

> Fuju xiansheng 負局先生 [the Box-carrying Master] always carried on his back a box [with equipment] for polishing mirrors; he frequented the markets of Wu asking to polish mirrors and *contenting himself with one coin as payment for this service.* He would ask his clients if anyone in their families was sick. If so, he dispensed purple pills or a red drug; those who took these always recovered. He kept this up for several decades. Later, during an epidemic, he went to the doors of all the households to give out his drugs, *saving myriads without accepting any money at all.* The people of Wu thus began to grasp that he was a perfected person. Later he withdrew to a promontory on Mount Wu from which he dispensed drugs to people by lowering them down. When about to depart, he said to those below, "It is my desire to return to Mount Penglai. *I'm going to make a divine spring for you up here.*" One morning, water of a whitish color flowed

69. For more on this theme, see Chapter 5.

70. A small isle off the coast of Guiji, mentioned (along with other small isles in the same area) in Ge Hong's *Inner Chapters* (4:85) as a good place to pursue arts of transcendence if one cannot get to one of the major inland mountains. Also sometimes known as Mount Linen Island.

71. *TL,* 297–298.

down between the rocks. Most of those who drank of it were cured of their illnesses. Shrines were established for the master in over a dozen locations.[72]

Here too we see an adept who performs valuable services for the populace without accepting payment. He also establishes a healing legacy that will continue after his departure for Penglai. The people respond in their usual reciprocating way, erecting shrines, but it seems clear that the departed adept neither requests nor has any need for such offering sites, in striking contrast to local gods, who in the same period are often represented as requesting or demanding offerings.[73]

As we survey the corpus of surviving hagiographies, a pattern emerges that is clearly not the result of the accidental habits of one or two unusual adepts. Many practitioners of esoterica disengaged from the usual economy of exchange and instead practiced an alternative economy—performing healing and other services gratis, distributing largesse to the poor, giving goods without regard to the other party's ability to pay.[74]

What accounts for this? Some early scriptures specify that esoterica must not be revealed for money but only to the right person under the correct ritual protocols,[75] but, to my knowledge, there is no code in any extant early scriptures that specifies an alternate set of economic behaviors for seekers of transcendence. There are later codes of moral rules and taboos for practitioners of transcendence arts, such as the ones collected in *Yunji qiqian*,[76] but these cannot be assumed to preserve early material. There are early moral codes from the Celestial Master community (such as the 180 Precepts[77]), but these cannot be assumed equivalent to any codes that practitioners of older esoteric arts may have possessed, nor should they be assumed to amount to any sort of generalized "Daoist" codes followed by all. We have an intriguing account of a master of divination arts in Eastern Han times; born to a wealthy family, he gave away his family's money and treasures after his father's death,

---

72. *Liexian zhuan* item 63 (*DZ* 294 2:12a–b; Kaltenmark, *Le Lie-sien tchouan,* 174–176), emphasis added.

73. For examples, see *SW,* 369–377; also Kleeman, "Licentious Cults and Bloody Victuals."

74. Examples are numerous and include, in the *Liexian zhuan,* the hagiographies of Fang Hui and Chang Rong; in the *Shenxian zhuan,* the hagiographies of Sire Gourd, Dong Feng, Peng Zu, Sun Deng, Li A, Li Yiqi, Li Zhongfu, Jiao Xian, Yin Changsheng, and Yin Gui; and the stele inscription of Fei Zhi (on which more below).

75. For example, Schipper, "The Inner World of the *Lao-tzu chung-ching,*" 117; *Taishang Laojun zhongjing* (*DZ* 1168) 2:15b, 2:20b; and so forth.

76. See, for example, scroll 33, which collects *Sheyang zhenzhong fang* 攝養枕中方 by Sun Simo.

77. On which, see *DZ* 786, 2a–12b; Schipper and Verellen, eds., *The Taoist Canon,* 131; and Hendrischke and Penny, "The 180 Precepts."

alluding to the rhyming *Laozi* maxim "Too much store is sure to end in immense loss" 多藏必厚亡 (in chap. 44 of the received text) and saying that "Hoarding wealth is something that masters of the *dao* shun" 盈滿之咎, 道家所忌.[78] Again, however, we cannot assume that it was the *Daode jing's* injunctions against hoarding that motivated the behaviors portrayed in the narratives above.

There is, however, one fragment of a now-lost weft text preserved in Ge Hong's *Baopuzi neipian*, the *Scripture of the Jade Seal* (*Yuqian jing* 玉鈐經), that directly enjoins the sorts of behaviors we have seen here, that explicitly addresses itself to practitioners of esoteric arts, and that supplies a clear warrant for the alternate behaviors that is not only ethical but also metaphysical and theological in nature:[79]

> *Interlocutor:* Is it not correct that those practicing the Dao must first establish merit?
>
> *The Master Who Embraces the Unhewn:* Yes. According to the middle chapter of the *Scripture of the Jade Seal*,[80] "Establishing merit is of the utmost importance, and eliminating faults is next. *Dao* practitioners *should consider saving people from distress, causing them to escape misfortune, and protecting them from illness so that they do not die before their allotted times to be acts of the highest merit* [為道者以救人危使免禍, 護人疾病, 令不枉死, 為上功也]. For those seeking transcendence it is essential that they consider loyalty, filiality, harmoniousness, obedience, humaneness, and trustworthiness as fundamental. *No one who does not cultivate meritorious acts but only wields esoteric arts will achieve long life.* For major evil deeds, the Director of Allotted Lifespans deducts a mark; for lesser faults, he deducts a count. Just as infractions are heavy or light, so are the deductions greater or lesser. Each person receives an initial length of life based on his allotted lifespan. He will thus have an original number [*benshu* 本數]. If this number is large, then the marks and counts will not easily use it up, and death arrives slowly. If the original allotment is small, and if infractions are many, then the marks and counts quickly use up the allotment and death arrives early." The *Scripture* also says: "A person wishing earthbound transcendence must establish three hundred good deeds; a person wishing celestial transcendence must establish twelve hundred. If a person has established 1,199 good deeds and then happens

---

78. *Hou Han shu* 82A:2720–2721, the biography of the diviner Zhe Xiang.

79. This text is also mentioned in the *Liexian zhuan* hagiography of Lü Shang (item 12). In that narrative a copy of the sacred text is found in the adept's coffin after his feigned death but before his burial—in other words, it is the object that magically replaces his corpse long enough to allow his escape. See *DZ* 294, 1:6a–b; and Kaltenmark, *Le Lie-sien tchouan*, 71–74.

80. "Middle chapter" translates *zhongpian*. In the *Traditions of Exemplary Transcendents* passage cited above, the text is said to have had six chapters. It is likely that the text had either suffered losses or been rearranged by the time it came into Ge Hong's hands.

to commit one evil deed, all of the prior good deeds are wiped clear and one must begin once again to accumulate merit." . . . Again the *Scripture* says: "If your accumulation of good deeds is not yet complete, then not even ingesting an elixir of transcendence will be of benefit. On the other hand, if one does not ingest an elixir of transcendence but practices good deeds, although one will not yet attain transcendence one will at least avoid a sudden [premature] death."[81]

It was perhaps this sort of scriptural passage, and no doubt others like it now lost, that provided the main intrinsic rationale for adepts' enactment of an alternate economy in their relations with their clients. We can also readily identify a powerful extrinsic rationale: by behaving in these ways, adepts extricated themselves from the network of moral reciprocity or *bao* 報 and the locative structures of obligation that accompanied it. Unlike temple gods and ancestors, who *were* fully implicated in these structures, adepts and transcendents showed themselves to stand outside it and thus implicitly claimed hierarchical superiority to these other categories of unseen beings.[82]

Lay Patronage

Yet the adept was not, in actual practice, entirely free of the obligations incurred in the host-guest relationship. We read, in the *Shenxian zhuan:*

> Ling Shouguang . . . at the age of over seventy obtained a method for [making] "efflorescence of vermilion" pills. These he synthesized and ingested. . . . By the first year of the [Later] Han *jian'an* period [196 C.E.] he was already two hundred and twenty years old. Later, without having shown any signs of illness, he died at the home of Hu Gang in Jiangling. Over a hundred days after his

---

81. *NP* 3:53–354, emphasis added. There is also the *Chisongzi zhongjie jing* 赤松子中誡經 (*DZ* 185, 5:282ff.) to consider. Kohn (*Monastic Life in Medieval Daoism,* 203–205) considers it a third- or fourth-century work now extant in a Song edition; but in Schipper and Verellen, eds., *The Taoist Canon* (319) it is treated as a work written in the Song in imitation of, or inspired by, an ancient work with a similar title, *Chisongzi jing* 赤松子 經, as paraphrased by Ge Hong (*NP* 6:125–126). Whatever the date of *DZ* 185, this and other scriptures paraphrased in the relevant *Baopuzi neipian* passage (and elsewhere in the *Baopuzi* and *Shenxian zhuan*) sketch the workings of the divine rewards-and-punishments system in ways similar to those seen in other early texts and then go on to list a large number of positive and—in much greater numbers, typical of religions everywhere!—negative precepts adepts should follow. Among the positive precepts we find these: "commiserate in the sufferings of others, help others in distress, aid the poor" (*NP* 126).

82. For elaboration of this point, see Chapters 2 and 3.

funeral and burial, someone saw Ling in Xiaohuang. This person sent a letter to Hu Gang, who, upon receiving the letter, dug up the coffin and looked inside. It was empty except for an old shoe.[83]

Narrative details such as these suggest that interested laypersons of means sponsored some practitioners of esoterica, providing them with material support, food and other goods, and living space, whether inside or outside their domestic compounds. This is an as-yet untold story, and it provides another example of how certain features of later Daoist movements—in this case, the Shangqing movement in particular, with the adept Yang Xi working on behalf of and sponsored by the Xu family being the primary instance—were foreshadowed by the quest for transcendence.

The case of Ling Shouguang and his patron Hu Gang is by no means unique. In the hagiography of Wang Yuan 王遠, for example, a lay patron, one Chen Dan 陳耽, constructs a "dao chamber" 道室 for the adept; twice daily pays his respects, which surely entailed the making of offerings to him 且夕事之;[84] merely asks for the master's blessings, not for his esoteric arts 但乞福未言學道也; receives blessings in the form of health and flourishing livestock and crops (this detail reminiscent of the early Zhuangzi passage on the "divine man"); and, like Hu Gang, is instrumental in orchestrating the departed adept's mock funeral, all the while aware that Wang Yuan has attained transcendence. The passage also suggests that some lay patrons were deemed to have attained transcendence in their own right: "A little over a hundred days after Wang Yuan died, Chen Dan died, too. Some said that Dan had obtained Yuan's dao and so [merely] transformed and departed; but others said that Yuan knew Dan was destined to die soon, so he abandoned him and departed."[85] We have to deal with a society in which a person's apparent death was always potentially interpretable as having been, in fact, a departure into transcendence, so a case like this one must have sparked many conversations. This passage also suggests another way—aside from the receipt of "blessings"—in which lay patrons benefited from hosting adepts: whether by actual practice or simply by reputation, they might come to share in the glory of their departed guest.

The same pattern appears across a number of collected hagiographies. Sometimes it is the ruler, but more often a local or regional official, who steps into the role of lay patron, providing living quarters, funerary expenditures, and often other goods and services.[86]

---

83. See TL, 232–233.
84. Thus TPYL; the corresponding passage in TPGJ has 且夕朝拜之.
85. TL, 260.
86. Various permutations of the pattern occur in the hagiographies of Cheng Wuding (TL, 360–363), Jie Xiang (TL, 189–192), Dong Feng (TL, 141–145), Sun Deng (TL, 336), Ji Zixun

We see the pattern also in inscriptions. A stone stele dating to 169 C.E., unearthed in 1991 from the antechamber to a small tomb near Luoyang,[87] opens by narrating the exploits of the master of esoterica and transcendent Lord Fei 肥君. It then shifts focus to his lay patron, one Xu You 許幼, employing the following terms: "The meritorious officer and Grandee of the Ninth Order, Xu You, a native of Dongxiang in Luoyang, served Lord Fei with the rites due a transcendent master and with warmest reverence invited him to reside in his home. By following the Lord, You was able to 'surpass the world' [*dushi* 度世] and thus departed."[88] The ensuing section of the inscription makes clear that Xu You's son, Jian, is the one who erected the stele. Whether *xian*-hood or merely longevity is being claimed for Xu You with the expression *dushi* is unclear—not surprisingly, since we have learned to expect some vagueness and variance of opinion on the status of the patron as compared with that of the adept. What is clear is that we have here a depiction of the patron-adept relationship that was carved on a tombside stele and has been archeologically recovered, not transmitted in any received hagiographic or historiographic text, a provenance that supports the notion that such patron-adept relationships were a feature of lived social practice, at least among the official classes, and not merely a trope of hagiographic collections.

Such inscriptions, as well as the transmitted hagiographies of which inscriptions constituted one important source, were works of collective memory. What is striking in these accounts is that patrons were often remembered alongside the adepts they sponsored. This preservation in collective memory was a share of a sort of immortality for the patrons, whether or not they also achieved personal transcendence.

Depictions of these sorts of adept-lay relations are not confined to hagiography. And the fact that they were also rendered in passages decidedly hostile to the behaviors depicted further confirms that they were a fixture of actual social practice and no mere hagiographic wish. We find Ge Hong reporting that when Gu Qiang, whose elaborate stories we saw in Chapter 5, and whom Ge regarded as a false claimant to extraordinary longevity, died of illness at the home of one Huang Zheng in Shouchun, Huang "suspected he had transformed and departed. A little

---

(*TL*, 169–171), Li Gen (*TL*, 218–220), and Chen Anshi (*TL*, 137–138). Some of the officials mentioned also appear in extant historical records; others do not.

87. I discuss this stele further in Chapter 8.

88. Here is the entire line: 功臣五大夫洛陽東鄉許幼 仙師事 肥君恭敬 丞丞解止幼舍 幼從君得度世 而去. I have translated following the photoreproductions and transcriptions of the text in Little, ed., with Eichman, *Taoism and the Arts of China*, 150–151; Schipper, "Une stèle taoïste des Han orientaux récemment découverte," 246–247; and Wang Yucheng, "Dong Han daojiao diyi keshi Fei Zhi bei yanjiu," 15–16. I have also benefited from consulting the translation in Raz, "Creation of Tradition," 54–57.

over a year later he tried boring into the coffin to have a look. The corpse was quite intact there."[89] Clearly Huang had heard stories of adepts performing *shijie,* assisted by their lay patrons. Having had an adept in his home as guest, he now wanted to step into the role of empty-coffin-discoverer and thus attach his name to a successful, celebrated transcendent. How disappointed he must have been to find Gu's corpse—the real thing, not a simulacrum—still in its coffin!

More generally, cases of aristocrats (and perhaps also some commoners, though the evidence for this is scanty) "serving" and presenting gifts and offerings to adepts are well documented as far back as the *Shi ji;* Sima Qian complains that men he regarded as false claimants to longevity grew wealthy from the gifts their admirers piled up.[90] Ge Hong similarly complains about phenomena he has witnessed. Although he regards the particular practitioners in question as charlatans, their behaviors are no different from those attributed in hagiographies to successful transcendents—more confirmation that the depicted behaviors were actual social practice, not mere literary conceit. The passage repays close scrutiny:

> Stupid and shallow people of recent times become attracted by a self-lauding person who says, "I possess secret books," and so cherish and serve him. Many ordinary people and even children openly claim to possess a *dao,* their reputations, thanks to their boasting and deceit, exceeding their actual attainment, while within they harbor greed, intent only on profit. When they are asked to act on someone's behalf, they utter sighs, nod, bend and rise, creating the impression of someone in possession of precious secrets so deep as to be unobtainable. When the other party insists, they accede to the request, nodding and smiling, sometimes saying [the results] might take a while. They thus cause their unaware clients, who may want to stop but cannot, to say of themselves that their service is not yet diligent enough, that the gifts they have offered are still insufficient. Then those of trusting heart become still more respectful and solemn, presenting costly novelties as gifts, and undertake the duties of a servant [for the adept], not declining to shoulder heavy burdens over long distances, not avoiding dangers and risks, hoping by their accumulated labors to bring about the desired effect. They submit to suffering and grief hoping to hear of something extraordinary. They waste the passing months, neglecting the care of their parents, abandoning their wives and children without a care, enduring cold and frost while following [the adept] for years until, their resources exhausted and their strength gone, they still have achieved nothing....

---

89. *NP* 20:348. I have no further information on Huang Zheng.

90. *Shi ji* 28:1385–1386, the passage concerning Li Shaojun, discussed in detail in Chapter 4.

I have personally seen several [self-claimed adepts] of this type, perhaps a dozen. They sometimes give themselves high titles, claiming to have lived through many generations. The world sometimes says of them that they are three or four centuries old but have lived under different names; they are falsely claimed to be sages and, their reputation thus built up by others, many of them come to receive the services of other people. . . .

People of the world generally chase after those with a reputation, but few are able to check [reputation] against reality. Whey they hear that so-and-so has as many as a hundred or more disciples, they decide that he must have something extraordinary, and so they rush off in their conveyances to join the group of followers gathered round him. . . . These sorts of *daoshi* of false reputation . . . ashamed of their own ignorance and pretending that their knowledge is broad and sufficient, in the end are unwilling to seek instruction from those better than they are. . . . But they will not content themselves with remaining silent, but will become spiteful toward those who really possess a *dao* and slander them, fearing that those others' reputations will overtake their own.[91]

This is a vivid eyewitness portrait of a common social situation, even of the motivations and psychology of clients who undertake gift-giving and service to adepts; it is also an insightful sketch of the social poetics of reputation-shaping. We see again the key role played by the *secrecy* of the adept's methods: secrecy is what stokes the curiosity and faith of clients and makes possible the constant deferral of results. Yet we also see adepts arrogating titles to themselves and boasting of centuries-long lifespans. In the final passage we glimpse an environment of competition among adepts, in which the rise or fall of their reputations, as measured against the reputations of other adepts, could make or break careers.

In another passage Ge Hong reports on an eyewitness interview his friend Ji Han had with the adept and skilled raconteur Gu Qiang, who, Ge Hong informs us, was eighty-something years of age and a practitioner of macrobiotic and sexual regimens at the time:

He still had his wits about him and had not much aged, so people at the time began calling him a transcendent person, and some styled him the thousand-year-old man. . . . He had the aura of someone who was truly knowledgeable of distant matters and had not yet revealed all he knew. Because of this, curiosity-seekers, hearing of him and spreading word, like shadows following images flocked to him in droves, vying with one another in singing his

---

91. *NP* 14:256–258.

praises. Gifts of food came to him in profusion, and he always had a surplus of money.[92]

Nor are mentions of these sorts of patron-adept relationships confined to the *Shenxian zhuan, Baopuzi,* and the Fei Zhi inscription. In the "Fangshu liezhuan" section of the *History of the Later Han*[93] we find mention of a wealthy man who seeks to bestow riches on a hermit-adept skilled in divination, and in *Shishuo xinyu* we read of a layperson who habitually sponsored recluses.[94] A *Liexian zhuan* hagiography portrays a lay patron learning an esoteric method from a transcendent who "often stayed" at his home.[95] The *Shenxian zhuan* also mentions cases of adepts' staying as guests in the homes of lay hosts while traveling. In two instances the adepts perform valuable service to the host family before leaving, in one case offering a lifesaving prediction, in another curing the household head of illness.[96]

Individual officials and their families are not the only ones who provided patronage for adepts. Large groups or whole communities of "commoners" are said to have "served" (*shi* 事) them, sometimes over several generations.[97] Judging from details mentioned in such passages, this "service" must have included the provision

---

92. Ibid., 20:347. The passage was previously discussed in Chapter 5. In a second passage, Ge narrates the stories told by one Cai Dan upon his return from a stay in the mountains. This passage, too, was discussed in Chapter 5, but I return to it here from this different angle. According to Ge Hong, his stay there was a disaster since he knew no esoteric methods and only pointlessly chanted some texts; but Cai Dan represented himself to his own family as having ascended to the heavens, only to be banished temporarily back to earth for a minor infraction. For present purposes, the key line in this account is this: "When at first Dan returned and said he had come back from Kunlun, his family members all vied with one another to question him" (*NP* 20:349). The social climate was such that many people were disposed to take such self-narratives seriously and to react with intense interest, excitement, and—as we observe in other, nonfamilial cases—offerings of gifts and services. A third, more briefly sketched case is that of an adept claiming to be Bo He, in which we read: "There was a man in Hebei saying he was Bo He, and at this people from far and near vied with each other to go to him and offer service to him [往奉事之], so that he received many gifts and became wealthy" (*NP* 20:350).

93. *Hou Han shu* 82B:2730.

94. See Mather, *Shih-shuo Hsin-yü,* 338.

95. Item 50; see *DZ* 294 2:5b–6a; and Kaltenmark, *Le Lie-sien tchouan,* 154–155.

96. The former is Yin Gui, the latter Ge Xuan; compare also the hagiography of Zuo Ci for a story in which the adept, passing by the home of another practitioner, is at first denied hospitality.

97. Examples may be seen in the *Shenxian zhuan* hagiographies of Chen Chang, Wang Lie, Li Changzai, Lü Gong, and Zhang Ling, among others; in the *Liexian zhuan,* in the case of Gui Fu (item 31); and compare the story of Shi Men (item 14). Since we have no artifacts produced by these "commoners" themselves, we can take such statements at best as anecdotal support for the participation of unlettered groups in the social and narrative circles surrounding adepts.

not only of food but also of shelter and other material gifts—sometimes while the adept was living on the margin of the local community, in other instances after his departure. If the adept had departed, the community is usually depicted as raising shrines where offerings were presented.

What are we to make of these various depictions? I know of no extant scriptural passage that mandates this sort of sponsoring relationship between lay patron and adept; nor do we find any technical vocabulary for the lay role, such as the Buddhist *jushi* 居士 or "householder,"[98] or any theorized articulation of its responsibilities and benefits. But from their repeated mention in narratives such as these, along with the fact that they are never explained, we may infer that such relations were common enough in the second, third, and early fourth centuries—and perhaps earlier—so that contemporary readers needed no elaboration of the point.

Shrines and Offerings

Hagiographies of *xian* typically end in one of three ways: the adept is seen flying up into the heavens; he leaves, announcing that he is headed into mountains; or he is seen departing for some unspecified destination, often after performing *shijie*. But relations of communities with adepts did not end after the adepts' departure. The communities often erected shrines (*ci* 祠) and temples (*miao* 廟)[99] to preserve the memory of adepts and to serve as a place where offerings might be made to them in their transcendent state. We can now see the great extent to which this entire set of activities is simply an extension of the way in which laypersons related to adepts while they were physically present in or near the community. From the community's viewpoint, the purpose of establishing a shrine or temple was to provide a place of access to the departed adept's spiritual efficacy, a place where they could host the adept with offerings of food and drink and make their requests for help. From the insider point of view, which is projected in the methods texts for those pursuing transcendence, *xian* had no need of shrines or offerings, and they are (to my knowledge) never depicted as demanding or requesting them, in sharp contrast to local gods, who often are. In other words, communities, by erecting shrines to *xian* and presenting food offerings, were, in effect, assimilating them to

---

98. This term is used in one, and only one, quite late-attested *Shenxian zhuan* passage to designate a lay sponsor. To my knowledge, the term *jushi* was coined by Buddhist authors, and this late-attested passage represents an anachronistic appropriation of what had by then become a standard term for the layperson's role.

99. Both terms are used to designate structures dedicated to the memory and ritual service of *xian* and of gods in the period; so far, my research suggests that the terms were interchangeable in this period and that if there was a distinction between what they designated, it was only a difference of scale, with *miao* being larger and more elaborate structures.

the role of temple gods; but adepts and transcendents, in depicting themselves (or being depicted) as indifferent to such treatment, were, in effect, resisting this assimilation and claiming (or being claimed) to be their own distinct, superior category of beings, ones who did not depend on offerings after their departure (just as they did not depend on normal food during their lives in the visible world). In either case, temples and shrines functioned as sites where the memory of adepts was kept alive, celebrated, and contested. Stele inscriptions preserving versions of their stories and recording (or claiming) their spiritual achievements were also erected, and, as I have argued elsewhere, these texts on stone must have constituted an important source for the transmitted hagiographic collections that have come down to us, just as Buddhist inscriptions have been shown to have formed an important basis for received hagiographies.[100]

Many seekers of transcendence, like Buddhist monks, stood out from the majority of the population because they were mobile, not tied to particular localities by family relations or official obligations. Local communities, however, tended to try to forge links with particular practitioners, both while they were present nearby and after their transcendence. The erection of shrines and stelae can be seen as a community's attempt at binding adepts to their locales, controlling access to their spiritual power, gaining status by association with them, and shaping the ways in which they were collectively remembered.

When extant sources mention the location of shrines to *xian,* they are usually described as located at the top or foot of a mountain. A few are said to have been situated near the mouth of a cave. Most shrines were probably situated neither directly within local communities nor too far from them. Master An Qi is said to have been honored with shrines along the coast in Langye "at ten or more places," and Qin Gao's followers were instructed to await him with offerings along a riverbank.[101] What all of these locations have in common is liminality: *xian* shrines seem to have been situated in outlying areas. The strong association with mountains is hardly surprising since *xian* themselves were similarly associated; nor is the coastal location of An Qi's shrines surprising, since that adept was fabled to have made his way to Penglai off the eastern coast. There are, however, exceptions to this pattern, including a small number of shrines said to have been set up by rulers inside palace precincts, as well as one or two shrines mentioned as having been established in cities.[102]

---

100. See Shinohara, "Two Sources of Chinese Buddhist Biographies"; on inscriptions as a source for hagiographies of *xian* and other transmitted texts, see *TL,* 106–108; and *SW,* 187–198.

101. In the *Liexian zhuan,* see items 30 and 26 respectively.

102. Palace shrines include those of Gouyi furen, Xiaoshi, and Nong Yu, all in the *Liexian zhuan.* The same text claims that many people in Qu city made offerings to Xiao Fu. Gil Raz ("Creation of Tradition," 57, 77) suggests that the stele to Fei Zhi, with the cup-shaped hollows on its base designed to hold offerings, originally stood in the home of the Xu family that sponsored his cult.

Narratives that mention *xian* shrines often describe anomalies observed at the site, indicating the active, numinous presence there of the august beings to whom the altars were dedicated. Offerings for rain at Peng Zu's shrine in Liyang were said to always win a favorable response, and this ancient transcendent's presence and authority were indicated by tigers, whose tracks could be observed in the nearby soil. At the Phoenix Maiden Shrine to Xiaoshi and Nong Yu, the sound of a flute was sometimes heard, indicating the invisible presence of the shrine's guests; similarly, at the shrine to Hanzi in Shu "often there was the sound of drums, pipes, and exchanged calls."[103] Departed *xian* were sometimes reputed in hagiographies to visit their shrines periodically.[104]

Shrines to *xian* were, as I have mentioned, sites where the collective memories that families and communities had of departed practitioners coalesced and were preserved; stele inscriptions durably preserved and disseminated certain locally (or sometimes centrally) authorized versions of the stories of adepts. Shrines were also, of course, the sites of devotional activities directed to *xian*. The Xu family's stele narrating the exploits of the transcendent Fei Zhi contains three hollows on its base, clearly designed as receptacles for offerings or perhaps for votive oil lamps. The inscription itself mentions the family's periodic offering of libations and prayers to the departed *xian*.[105] An inscription on a stele that apparently once stood at a shrine to the fabled ancient transcendent Wangzi Qiao 王子喬 lists musical performances, offerings, prayers for good fortune, meditation, and pilgrimage as among the activities focused at the shrine.[106] Descriptions in later texts such as *Zhen'gao* 真誥 and *Shuijing zhu* 水經注 show that some of these Eastern Han and early medieval shrines stood for centuries, the cults in some cases as long-lived as the transcendents themselves were claimed to be.[107]

---

103. All of these instances may be found in the *Liexian zhuan*.

104. For example, Gu Chun in *Liexian zhuan* item 52; there are also several instances in *Shenxian zhuan*.

105. Raz, "Creation of Tradition," 56. I discuss this and other inscriptions further in Chapter 8.

106. The inscription has been translated and discussed in Holzman, *Immortals, Festivals, and Poetry in Medieval China;* see also the helpful discussion in Raz, "Creation of Tradition," 99–101; and the excellent diachronic study by Bujard, "Le culte de Wangzi Qiao ou la longue carrière d'un immortel."

107. Shrines and offerings to adepts are mentioned in the cases of Xiao Fu, Qiu Sheng, Peng Zu, Ma Dan, Ping Changsheng, Ge You, Qin Gao, Kou Xian, Wangzi Qiao, Anqi xiansheng, Xiaoshi and Nong Yu, Jiu Qiu jun, Cui Wenzi, Gouyi furen, Yuan Ke, Chang Rong, Gu Chun, Zi Ying, Fu Lü, Zi Zhu, Fuju xiansheng, Huang Ruanqiu, and Hanzi in *Liexian zhuan;* Dongling shengmu, Mao Ying, and Wencheng jiangjun in *Shenxian zhuan;* and in many *zhiguai* and geographic texts as well.

Conclusion

We may conclude the following:

- Withdrawal from normal social roles and obligations did not mean that adepts lived in isolation; they—at least those of whom we have any record—did not simply disappear into oblivion. In fact, they operated in a public arena under intense social scrutiny. Their words, mannerisms, appearance, and behaviors attracted close attention and provoked powerful responses in onlookers. Some of them, at least, played their role in a way calculated for maximum effect, attracting large crowds of followers and onlookers. There were certain standard ways in which an adept was expected to comport himself: to be a practitioner of arts was to inhabit a definite social role, with attendant precedents, expectations, and conventions.
- Adepts operated in an environment of intense competition for acclaim and patronage, in which reputation was determinative and in which controlling one's reputation would therefore have been a paramount concern, at least to those adepts interested in "succeeding" in their socially defined role. Giving the appearance of not caring about succeeding in this role was one of the most important ways of succeeding in it.
- People sought certain services from adepts, especially healing and prognostication, but also occasionally a wide array of other sorts of help. From the point of view of a nonpractitioner, these powers to heal, predict, and otherwise help clients were surely the most important feature of adepts. These lay clients included people from many levels of society, from rulers down to local officials and probably—though here the evidence is less clear—to commoners as well.
- These clients expected to offer compensation for the services of adepts, but adepts often refused payment or else distributed the proceeds to the poor. They perhaps did so in light of a scripturally described system of celestial rewards of merit for such good deeds (and punishments for bad ones). Distributing their payment also extricated them from networks of reciprocation and obligation that were in effect not only among living persons but also between persons (and communities) and their gods and between families and their ancestors.

From the perspective of the society at large:

- Laypersons often responded to the presence of such persons (or to the news of one operating at some distance away) by eagerly seeking proximity to them, spreading word of their accomplishments, and, when access had finally been gained, offering them gifts.

- This gift-giving often included the daily provision of unspecified offerings and other supplies, and sometimes went as far as building special lodging for the adept within the family compound of whichever lay supporter was fortunate enough to win the competition to offer hospitality.
- While some laypersons sought to receive and practice some of the adept's secret methods, many were content with the "blessings" his presence and his self-cultivation brought and, no doubt, the added social status and cultural capital for which they were willing to trade some material resources.
- Patterns of access to living adepts were continued after their departure into transcendence, primarily at shrines founded to perpetuate and localize versions of the communities' collective memory of the adepts and their achievements. The making of offerings to accompany requests for help continued (along with conversation and the exchange of stories) to be the primary way in which the vast majority of people related to departed *xian*.

One other thing is clear: whether they acknowledged it or not, adepts relied heavily on the support of their patrons and clients and on the less immediate but no less palpable presence and support of the wider public from whose ranks they rose and before whom they played out the dramas and achieved the victories essential to their role. This was the public they served and in contrast to whom they defined themselves. The relationship between adepts and the public was one of mutual benefit and mutual dependence. Peter Brown's comment on the holy person of late antique Europe applies equally to early medieval China: "Power gained in this way had to be seen to exist.... The *potens* needed a crowd."[108]

---

108. "The Rise and Function of the Holy Man in Late Antiquity," 94.

CHAPTER 7

Adepts, Their Families, and the Imperium

THE STEREOTYPE holds that practitioners abandoned society to pursue their esoteric arts, but as we have seen their relations with local communities were, in fact, exponentially more complex than that. They functioned in society as a type of holy person, in part by absenting themselves from normal patterns of social interaction and taking up instead the behaviors identified with the role of *xian*-hood-seeker, but these behaviors included many relations with others. We now turn to the social relations of practitioners with their own families and with representatives of the imperial bureaucracy.

Adepts and Their Families

The patrilineal family and the body of ritual that sustained it—the cult of ancestors—depended for their continued existence not only on the uninterrupted generation of male descendants and on their performance of sacrifices but also on the continued death of ancestors. Large numbers of successful transcendents would undermine society in all three ways, by removing individuals from the lineage system, disrupting its generational continuity, and leaving the elderly uncared for. From the early Han onward, unfiliality was thus one standard complaint against the quest for transcendence. At the beginning of the Han, for example, we find Lu Jia 陸賈 (ca. 228–ca. 140 B.C.E.) protesting: "If a man treats his body ascetically and tires out his form by going deep into the mountains in search of divine transcendence, [if he] leaves behind his parents, casts aside his kindred, abstains from the five grains, gives up classical learning, thus turning his back on what is cherished by Heaven and Earth in quest of a *dao* of 'not dying,' then he gives up any way to communicate with this world or to prevent what is not right from happening."[1]

The mid-second-century B.C.E. *Huainanzi* minces no words:

> Wang Qiao and Chi Song left the realm of dust, separated themselves from the wicked mass, inhaled the harmony of Yin and Yang, consumed the essences of Heaven and Earth, expelled the old when exhaling while taking in the new in inhaling, raised themselves up to tread the void, rode clouds and coursed through the mists.[2] They can be said only to have nourished their natures; they cannot be said to have been filial sons.[3]

Even a recovered fragment of the *Scripture of Great Peace,* a work containing many sections advocating transcendence and prescribing methods for it, lays out three grades of "those who practice *daos.*" Those of the highest grade assist rulers and, out of their regard for living beings, amass merit (by doing good works for others) and thus live long. Those of the middle grade desire to save their families. Those of the lowest grade liberate only themselves.[4]

Ge Hong was well aware of these and other literary precedents. In his *Inner Chapters,* he has an interlocutor pose the problem bluntly:

> If upon examination it turned out that divine transcendence could be achieved by study, that people could thus fly upwards into the empyrean, would they not turn their backs on ordinary life and quit this world, so that none would any longer perform the rites of offering food? And then would not the spirits of the ancestors, if they possess consciousness,[5] go hungry?[6]

---

1. *Xinyu,* 10–11; my translation relies on (differing only slightly from) that in Yu Ying-shih, "Life and Immortality in the Mind of Han China," 93. The *Xinyu* is said to have been presented to Gao Di, first of the Han emperors (r. 202–195 B.C.E.); see Loewe, "Hsin yü."

2. These phrases summarizing the practices of Wang and Chi are all standard descriptions of transcendence-quest disciplines. Wang and Chi are the two most fabled transcendents of ancient times.

3. *Huainanzi* (Zhuzi jicheng ed.), 20:353–354. The passage, and the one from *Taiping jing* about to be discussed, serve once again to remind us how utterly misguided it would be to speak of any single "Daoist" stance on these matters.

4. 上士學道，輔佐帝王，當好生積功乃久長。中士學道，欲度其家，下士學道，脫其軀. *Taipingjing hejiao,* 724, recovered by Wang Ming from *TPYL* 659. In many other passages in this scripture (for example, 685–686), even in sections oriented to the personal quest for transcendence rather than total societal reform, filiality is strongly insisted on; see Hendrischke, *The Scripture on Great Peace,* 351.

5. Here and below in Ge Hong's reply, it is possible to understand this phrase not as a conditional but as an affirmation that ancestral spirits do in fact possess consciousness.

6. *NP* 51.

This was a most serious charge. Ge Hong's response, reminiscent of one typical Buddhist monastic reply to the same challenge, was to claim that the adept's achievement of his religious goal constituted not a lack of filiality but a higher form of it:

> I have heard that preserving one's body free of injury is the ultimate in filiality. Does not the attainment of the Way of transcendence, long life and everlasting vision, coming to an end only when Heaven and Earth do, surpass by far the returning intact to one's ancestral lineage that which one had received whole? For one could thereby ascend into the void, tread amidst phosphors, ride in a cloud-chariot with a rainbow canopy, sup on mist from the aurora of dawn, inhale the purified essence of "mystic yellow." What one drinks there is liquor of jade and juice of gold; what one eats is excrescences of blue and efflorescence of vermilion; one dwells in halls of agate and chambers of jasper; for travel, one roams aimlessly in Grand Purity. If the spirits of the ancestors have consciousness, then they would share in one's glory, perhaps serving as advisers to the Five Thearchs, perhaps overseeing the hundred numina. They would receive such stations without requesting them. For food, they would dine on floriate rarities; for position, they would oversee Luofeng;[7] their prestige would be sufficient to rebuke Liangcheng. . . .[8] None among them would go hungry.[9]

Underlying this passage is the ancient view that merit, guilt, and fortune were not only matters for individuals but were also collectively shared by the family, and not only its living but also some of its dead members.[10] Hence, although in the short run from the family's point of view there might appear to be grave costs in one of its members neglecting filial duty (not caring for his aging parents and failing to produce offspring to continue the family line) by cultivating himself in the hills, the benefits of his attaining transcendence would spread to all members of

---

7. Another appellation of Fengdu. By the early fourth century this was one of the standard destinations of the ordinary dead.

8. This is Xiang Liangcheng 項梁成, reckoned in some texts to be a high official of the underworld; see Bokenkamp, *Ancestors and Anxiety,* 43–45, whose translation of the phrase in question I have incorporated here, and Wang Ming's helpful textual note in *NP* 66 n.147.

9. *NP* 51–52. Technical terms in this passage are explained in the annotations to my translation of it in *TL,* 88–89. For an especially clear example of the Buddhist parallel—the argument that the monastic life is not the abrogation of filiality but its higher fulfillment due to the succor the successful adept is able to give her parents (and, in this case, to all other living beings as well)—see Wright, *Studies in Chinese Buddhism,* 69–72. Compare Teiser, *The Ghost Festival in Medieval China,* 65.

10. For a recent discussion of this theme, see Strickmann, *Chinese Magical Medicine,* 10–50.

the patriline, even the dead, whose afterlife lot in both of the major categories of concern—food and otherworld office—would thereby markedly improve. The claim is striking. To my knowledge, no modern scholar has drawn any connection between the pre-Shangqing search for transcendence and the concern for aiding the familial dead,[11] but Ge Hong is here quite clearly claiming a sort of transfer of merit from the transcendent to his ancestors. No special mechanism or explanation is required (unlike the Buddhist system for transfer of merit, which had to surmount the prima facie obstacle of karma's strictly individual basis); the distribution of benefits in the other world works just as it would in this one—all relatives share in the honor of a court appointment, whether the court is celestial or terrestrial.

A similar defense of the pursuit of transcendence against charges of unfiliality, this time involving an adept's still-living parents, appears in the *Traditions* hagiography of Mao Ying 茅盈, one of the brothers Mao who would become key figures in the Shangqing revelations forty-odd years after the writing of *Traditions*. I emphasize the key line for our purposes:

Lord Mao . . . practiced a *dao* in Qi, and after twenty years, when he had completed it, he returned home. His father and mother, on seeing him, were enraged, saying, "You are unfilial! You have not personally supported us! Instead you have gone seeking deviant things, dashing about in all directions!" They were on the verge of caning him when he knelt and apologized, saying, "I have received a command to ascend to Heaven. This means that I am to attain the Way. I could not follow two paths of service at once. But although I have been lax in my support of you, and although the days have been many when you received no benefit from me, *I am now in a position to bring peace and security to our household.* But the inspectors who oversee your lifespan will not permit you to whip and insult one who has completed his *dao.* I fear this is no small offense." This last statement enraged his father even more. He seized his staff and made toward Lord Mao. Just as he was raising it to strike, it fragmented into dozens of small segments. . . . This made his father stop. Lord Mao said, "Consider what I just said. This is the sort of thing that will happen; you will only cause injury to others." His father asked, "You say you've attained a *dao.* Can you, then, raise the dead?" Lord Mao answered, "If the sins of dead persons are grave and their wicked deeds many, they cannot be brought back to life. But if they have had their lives cut short by injury, they can be raised." His father arranged for him to do this, and his ability was confirmed.[12]

---

11. And, arguably, not merely the familial dead: as seen in Chapter 6, a few adepts are on record as having revived recently deceased relatives of their lay clients.

12. *TL,* 326–328.

Mao Ying goes on not only to ascend to the heavens in a grand community send-off but also to become the guest of honor at many regional temples founded in his name, where he *and his family* receive offerings from a populace grateful for his services of healing and prediction. He thus makes good on his bold claim, "I am now in a position to bring peace and security to our household."

Nevertheless, it is clear that the short-term challenge of the transcendence quest to filiality worried the makers of stories about adepts, for the hagiographies seem at pains to explore this problem. More broadly, they reveal various facets of the tension between self-cultivation and family life, a tension Ge Hong remarked on personally: "Sometimes I get oral instructions for an essential method, or meet an uncommon teacher, but still I cling to my wife and children and long for the hill where the fox and hare run. . . . Knowing that long life can be achieved, I cannot undertake its practice. . . . Why? Fond and familiar feelings are hard to leave behind, and it is never easy to realize the aim of breaking with common practice."[13] How do the hagiographies represent, and probe, this tension?

At one extreme are the very few adepts who are explicitly said not to have had any children. In *Traditions of Divine Transcendents*, these include Li Yiqi 李意期, Wang Yuan 王遠, and Wang Yao 王遙. At the other extreme is a figure such as Yin Chang-sheng 陰長生, who, having received from his teacher the *Scripture of the Divine Elixir of Grand Purity* (*Taiqing shendan jing* 太清神丹經), a key alchemical scripture in the textual tradition Ge Hong held in highest esteem, made the elixir it prescribed but "took only half a dose so as not to immediately finish the process of ascending to Heaven. . . . He traveled all around the world, with his wife and children in tow; his whole family all achieved longevity without aging,"[14] though whether they also became celestial *xian* is left vague by the story's ending. At this same extreme, Tang Gongfang 唐公房 (in a stele inscription) and Liu An (in widespread legend reported in several sources, including Ge's *Traditions*) are said to have taken their whole families with them into transcendence by sharing their elixirs; in Liu's case, even his chickens and dogs ascended with the family by scavenging traces of elixir from the vessel.[15]

Between these extremes lies a spectrum of more complex negotiations between familial and ascetic demands. Each is situation-dependent, making a neat typology impossible.

In both Ge's *Traditions* and the "Traditions of Exemplary Transcendents of Eso-teric Arts" ("Fangshu liezhuan") incorporated into the *History of the Later Han*, the adept Fei Changfang 費長房, known for his demon-quelling prowess but not, in

13. *NP* 2:18–19.

14. *TL,* 275.

15. Both of these cases and their sources are discussed further in Chapter 8.

fact, for attaining transcendence (his teacher, Sire Gourd, reportedly deemed him unfit in the end), is portrayed as aspiring to the self-cultivational life but fearful about his family's reaction. Sire Gourd equips him with a method of "escape by means of a simulated corpse" so that his family will think he has died.[16] The clear implication is that Fei would rather his family think him dead than realize he has left them to seek transcendence. Fei's story also reveals an unexpected, indeed rather shocking facet of *shijie* methods of transcendence: if relatives perceived them as having died, adepts did not have to face their families' vehement objections to their leaving home.

Kong Yuanfang 孔元方 is portrayed as following a periodic practice, maintaining a family but strictly separating it from his place of retreat: "He bored into the embankment beside a river to form a cavern chamber. . . . He would enter this chamber and abstain from grains for a month, sometimes two, then return home. He did not permit his family to visit him there."[17] Cai Jing 蔡經, disciple of Wang Yuan, returns home twice after departing on his quest, once a decade later, then again after several decades, in order to rendezvous with his teacher there.[18] Of the "Old Man of Mount Tai" it is said that, after his departure to the mountains, "Every five or ten years he would return to visit his home village; then, after more than 300 years had passed, he returned no more," the implication being that he had finally ascended.[19] A number of adepts, once having completed their practice, return home to bid a final farewell to their families before departing for the mountains or the heavens for good. Of Lu Nüsheng 魯女生, for example, *Traditions* says that

> once his *dao* was complete, he bade farewell to his family and friends, saying he was going to enter Mount Hua. Fifty years later, one of these acquaintances ran into him in a temple on Mount Hua. His complexion had reverted to a youthful condition, and he was riding a white deer followed by a train of thirty jade maidens. He asked with great specificity that this person carry his regards to each of his relatives and friends.[20]

Others are implied to have completed their entire practice at their ancestral home and only then departed, as did Dongguo Yan 東國延, who "was in his village for over 400 years, and did not age. One morning several dozen persons riding tigers

---

16. *TL,* 161–168.

17. Ibid., 314–315. Other adepts depicted in Ge's *Traditions* as following a similar periodicity of practice include Kong Anguo and Peng Zu.

18. Ibid., 259–270.

19. Ibid., 337–338.

20. Ibid., 323–324.

and leopards came to escort him, and they all ascended to [Mount] Kunlun," fabled haunt of transcendents.[21]

Several hagiographies wrestle vividly with the propriety and emotional costs of abandoning spouse and children for full-time ascesis. In the story of Wang Yao, who is pointedly said to have had "a wife but no children," the adept is invited one rainy night by transcendents to join them in the mountains. A wrenching scene ensues:

> A hundred days later, on another rainy night, Wang Yao suddenly began packing. For some time he had had a light linen garment and a linen kerchief. In over fifty years he had never once worn them, but on this night he took out and donned them. His wife asked, "Do you mean to abandon me and leave?" Wang answered, "It's only for a short trip." "Aren't you taking Qian [Wang's disciple] with you?" she asked. "No, I'm going alone." With that, his wife wept and said, "Can't you stay a little longer?" "I'll be back soon." With that, he himself shouldered the bamboo box and departed. He never returned.[22]

Li Changzai 李常在, on the other hand, said to have fathered two boys and one girl, waited until they were all married before taking on disciples and leaving home to wander the mountains. Dong Feng 董奉, who fathered a daughter but no son, finally left his wife and daughter to soar up into the heavens; but he left them an enormous apricot grove, the proceeds of his long-standing medical practice, by which to earn a living.[23]

Two hagiographies further highlight the emotional and moral tensions between self-cultivation and family life. One is that of Huang Chuping 皇初平, found both in Ge's *Traditions* and in a scripture Ge esteemed, the *Numinous Treasure Five Talismans*.

> Huang Chuping . . . at the age of fifteen was made to tend sheep for his family. There was a master of the Dao who, noting his goodness and attentiveness, took him to a cave in Goldflower Mountain. *For more than forty years Chuping did not miss his family. Meanwhile his older brother,* Chuqi 初起, *searched for him without success.* Then one day there was a master of the Dao who excelled at divinations performing in the market nearby. Chuqi approached and requested a divination [of his brother's whereabouts]. The master said, "There is a shep-

---

21. Ibid., 300–301. The same is implied of Ge Yue, who is said to have "lived to be 280 years old when, one morning, he said farewell to his family, mounted a dragon, and departed" (ibid., 303).

22. Ibid., 342–343. The bamboo box mentioned in the passage contained reed organs that had previously been played by Wang's transcendent tutors.

23. Ibid., 316–317 and 141–145 respectively.

herd lad on Goldflower Mountain. I wonder if it might be your brother?" So Chuqi followed the master [to the mountain], where he searched for and [at last] found his brother. They had mixed feelings of joy and sorrow on seeing each other. Chuqi then asked where the sheep were. Chuping replied, "They're close by, on the eastern side of the mountain." Chuqi went to look, but he saw no sheep there, only countless white rocks, so he returned and said that there were no sheep. "The sheep are there, it's just that you didn't see them," Chuping responded, and so they went together to have another look. "Sheep, get up!" Chuping shouted, and at this the white rocks all stood up and turned into several myriad head of sheep.

Chuqi then said, "Brother, if you've obtained divine powers like these, might I study them as well?" "You need only love the Dao and you can obtain them." *So with that Chuqi abandoned his wife and son and stayed with Chuping.* Together they ate pine resin and *fuling* fungus.[24] When they had done this for 5,000 days, they could disappear at will; they cast no shadows in sunlight and had the complexions of youths.

Later they returned to their home village, but all their relatives had died. So they left. They transmitted their techniques to Nan Boda. *They changed their surname to Chi* 赤. Chuqi changed [his style] to Luban 魯班; Chuping changed his to Songzi 松子.[25] Those who came after them and received transmission of the [technique of] ingesting these medicinal substances, and thereby attained transcendence, numbered several dozen.[26]

The brothers' change of surname and names, as well as their consumption of a mixture of pine resin and *fuling,* exactly follows the procedure outlined in the scripture, which promises that, having done so, "one can come and go as one pleases . . . and enter August Heaven."[27] It is striking that the Huang brothers, due to their extraordinary longevity, outlive their entire extended family; it is therefore to an outsider, the otherwise unknown Nan Boda, that they transmit their arts. Chuping, engrossed

---

24. Standard items in the adept's alternate cuisine.

25. I have no information on Nan Boda. Lu Ban was a carpenter of almost otherworldly skill; he is mentioned in several texts of the Warring States era. Master Redpine, mentioned in the *Zhanguo ce* and the *Chu ci,* receives a hagiography in *Traditions of Exemplary Transcendents* (see Kaltenmark, *Le Lie-sien tchouan,* 35–42), where he is placed in the primordial era of the Divine Husbandman. Not a word is breathed there of what the scripture and Ge Hong's *Traditions* hagiography here claim was his former identity as Huang Chuping.

26. *TL,* 309–311. In the last line, the parallel text in *DZ* 388, 2:14a6–7, has "several thousand" for "several tens." The texts in *Traditions* and in the scripture are otherwise virtually identical. I have added emphasis at points relevant to this discussion.

27. *DZ* 388, 2:13a7–8.

in his religious quest, is portrayed as not missing his family even after four decades, while Chuqi, still at home, continues to search until finally finding Chuping and then himself joining the quest and abandoning his wife and son. Perhaps most astonishing of all is the brothers' change of surname: no gesture more powerfully expressed the radical extent to which some adepts, at least, abnegated the lineage and ancestor cult altogether.

This change of names bears further comment. For one thing, their choice of the surnames of two figures familiar from antiquity can be read in one of two ways. If we take the story to imply that the Huangs preceded (Chi) Luban and Chi Songzi in time, then we must understand it as a rewriting of the origins of these two figures known from legends in old texts familiar to contemporary readers, a revelation of their true identities—an esoteric rewriting or correction, as it were, of an old and widespread understanding on the part of literati. This rhetorical strategy was often deployed in esoteric and later Daoist texts, where claims of new revelations about old matters could always be made. If, on the other hand, we assume that the story intends that the Huangs followed the two historically older figures in time, then we must view them as having adopted these old personae as if donning masks. In either case, the name change clearly has the effect of concealing the brothers' true identities. But from whom, and why? From the spirits, we can only surmise, who keep the registers of life and death and who come to summon individuals when their lifespans have run out. Like imperial census recorders, these spirits were pictured as keeping track of people by their names and ancestral places of residence. In the same era, instructions for performing "escape by means of a simulated corpse" directed adepts to flee their homes for distant areas (especially mountains, away from settled areas where the registering spirits presumably focused their baleful work) and change their names after they had staged their own death, thus allowing them to live on past their allotted date of death.[28]

The other hagiography that highlights tensions between family life and self-cultivation, albeit differently, is that of Li Changzai 李常在, where we see a paradigm case of what Victor Turner would call a "social drama"[29] vividly played out:

---

28. For further discussion, see Cedzich, "Corpse Deliverance, Substitute Bodies, Name Change, and Feigned Death"; *TL*, 52–60; and Campany, "Living off the Books."

29. "During my fieldwork I became disillusioned with the fashionable stress on fit and congruence.... I came to see a social system or 'field' rather as a set of loosely integrated processes, with some patterned aspects, some persistences of form, but controlled by discrepant principles of action expressed in rules of custom that are often situationally incompatible with one another. This view... I came to call 'social drama analysis....'" Then, quoting someone else's comment on his own work, Turner writes: "These situations—arguments, combats, rites of passage—are inherently dramatic because participants not only do things, they try *to show others what they are doing or have done;* actions take on a 'performed-for-an-audience' aspect" (*On the Edge of the Bush,* 179).

At home Li Changzai had two sons and one daughter. After they left home to be married, he took in one son each from the families of [some of] his disciples, the Zeng and the Kong households. Each of the boys was seventeen or eighteen. The families did not know where Li Changzai intended to go, but they sent their sons anyway.[30] Changzai gave each of the boys a green bamboo stave and sent them back home with instructions to place them at the spot where they slept at home and not to speak to any family members on their way in or out. The two boys did as told and took the staves to their homes. No one in the families saw the boys, but after they had gone, they saw on the beds the boys' dead bodies. Each family mourned and buried its dead member.

Over a hundred days later, some of his disciples were going to Pi District[31] when they met Li Changzai, who was traveling with these two boys. The boys and the disciples wept and talked for a long time. Each of the boys wrote a letter home to his family; their coffins were opened and inspected, and only a green bamboo stave was found in each. So the families realized that the boys had not died.[32]

Some twenty years later, Changzai [and disciples] dwelled on Earth's Lungs Mountain. At this time he took another wife. But his former wife and one of his sons went searching for him. When they were ten days away, Changzai told his second wife, "My son will come here looking for me. I must go. Give him this golden disk." The son indeed arrived, asking where his father was. The second wife gave him the gold piece, to which the son responded, "My father

---

30. Compare the following case, which may or may not reflect a similar practice and body of ideas: After several of Eastern Han Emperor Ling's children had died at the palace, Empress He bore him a son. The boy was entrusted to the care of Shi Zimiao 史子眇, a "master of the Dao" (*daoshi* 道士); the emperor *"did not dare give the child a formal name" (bu gan zheng ming* 不敢正名). Later the child became known as Lord Shi 史侯. See *Hou Han shu* 10B:449; and Yü Ying-shih, "Life and Immortality in the Mind of Han China," 117. Yü also points (118) to the case of the poet Xie Lingyun, who just after his birth was sent to a Daoist family for fosterage because the Xie family had not produced many offspring. Xie did not return to his own family until the age of fifteen. Yü cites *Shipin* 詩品 as his source; the same anecdote is preserved in the *zhiguai* text *Yiyuan,* item 7.33 (item 5.10 in the same text also tells of his father's death at the hands of a rapacious local deity). What Yü fails to note is that it was in part the *change of name and household* that must have been thought to protect the child, for it was by name and address that the spirit overseers of lifespan registers kept track of people. Masters of the Dao took on the role of caretaker in such situations, we may surmise, because they were the ones who understood the workings of the otherworld registration system and could explain to families how to elude it.

31. An area west of the Shu commandery capital at the city of Chengdu and on the way to the sacred mountain Qingcheng shan; this entire story is set in that region.

32. A closely similar episode is related in Ge Hong's *Inner Chapters* 2, but there it is attached not to Li Changzai but to Li Yiqi.

abandoned me several decades ago. Night and day I have been thinking of him. Having heard that he was here, I traveled a long distance to investigate. I am not seeking money." He stayed thirty days, but his father did not return. The son then said wistfully to the wife, "My father is not coming back. I am leaving." When he got outside he hid in some brush.

Li Changzai returned and said to his wife, "My son spoke falsely. He will come back. When he does, tell him that, since he is grown, he no longer needs me, and that according to the procedures I am not to see him anymore." Then he left. Soon the son did indeed return, and the woman told him what Changzai had said. Knowing he would not see his father again, the son wept and departed.

More than seventy years after this, Changzai suddenly left [again]. [Afterwards] some of his disciples found him living on Tiger Longevity Mountain, where he had taken yet another wife and had had sons. Generations of people kept seeing him, always the same as before, so they called him Ever-Present.[33]

Li seems to be following an unspoken esoteric method that requires him periodically to shed old identities—including residences and families—and acquire new ones. Judging from the telling line, "According to the procedures (*fa* 法) I am not to see him anymore," the method forbade any subsequent contact with relatives tied to the adept's former identities, perhaps because such contact risked putting the spirit-enforcers of lifespan limits back on his trail. The emotional costs to all concerned are highlighted in the narrative. This method, whatever else it entailed, seems to have constituted one way of perpetuating the ancestral lineage while cultivating oneself. Multiple sons are produced who will marry and have offspring; one has disciples, but they are not one's own sons, so one's family lineage remains intact.

On the other hand, we also have instances of intrafamilial transmission of esoteric techniques (either from father to son or skipping one or more generations)—another of the many ways in which tension between family and self-cultivation was negotiated. Ge Hong himself is an example of this pattern: his great-uncle Ge Xuan transmitted the Grand Purity alchemical scriptures to Zheng Yin 鄭隱, who subsequently transmitted them to Ge Hong. Other examples include Lü Gong 呂恭 and Wei Shuqing 衛叔卿.[34] Nor were esoteric methods transmitted intrafamilially only to males. The *History of the Later Han* biography of one Li Nan 李南, a native of Ge Hong's home area of Gourong (an epicenter of early medieval esoteric and Daoist textual production), records that "his daughter also understood the family's arts," which were primarily those of divination by means of "wind

---

33. *TL*, 316–318.
34. Ibid., 250–252, 271–274, 451, 464–467.

angles" *(fengjiao* 風角*)*. One day a strong wind blows through her mother-in-law's
kitchen and she begs leave to return home to her own family, as the wind is a sign
that she (the daughter-in-law) is about to die. She explains that she knows this
because "my family has transmitted esoteric arts for generations."[35] Another case of
family transmission to a woman occurs in the *Traditions* hagiography of Bo Shanfu
伯山甫, in which Bo dispenses a medicinal compound (and presumably the recipe
for making it) to his niece, who lives past the age of 230 years, appearing to be a
girl, and eventually departs into the mountains—implicitly, as a *xian*.[36]

Two ways in which domestic structures of authority that were the early
medieval norm are reversed in certain stories of transcendents clearly imply that
the pursuit of a *dao* of *xian*-hood trumps such hierarchies as master/servant and
husband/wife.

The *Traditions* tells of Chen Anshi 陳安世, a servant in the home of Guan
Shuben 灌叔本. Chen displays a love of all living things; Guan, for his part, "loved
the *dao* and meditated on spirits." *Xian* disguised as students come to test Guan's
worthiness to be taught their secret arts. The servant, Chen, proves more deserving,
"so they gave him two pellets of a drug and admonished him as follows: 'When
you return, do not eat or drink anymore, and live in separate quarters.'" Chen
obeys their instructions, to the growing wonderment of his master Guan. The story
concludes:

> Guan began to suspect that Chen was no ordinary person, and he knew that
> he had proved unworthy, so he sighed and said to himself: "The Way is vener-
> able, and its Power is honorable, but these have nothing to do with seniority.
> My father and mother gave me life, but I can be caused to attain long life only
> by a teacher. And one who has already heard of the Way is qualified to be my
> teacher." And so he adopted the ceremonial behavior of a disciple, and did
> obeisance to and served [Chen] both night and day, sweeping and cleaning for
> him. When Chen had completed his *dao,* he ascended into the heavens in broad
> daylight; but on the verge of his departure he transmitted his essential arts of the
> *dao* to Guan. Guan, too, later departed as a transcendent.[37]

Thus, the story argues, are rewarded those in positions of domestic power who are
humble enough to recognize their religious betters and act accordingly.

Even more dramatically, three extant hagiographies in *Traditions* portray female
adepts as displaying biospiritual mastery superior to that of their husbands. They

35. *Hou Han shu* 82A:2716–2717, translated in Ngo, *Divination, magie et politique dans la
Chine ancienne,* 94–95; and in DeWoskin, *Doctors, Diviners, and Magicians,* 57–58.
36. *TL,* 297, 485–486.
37. Ibid., 137–139.

are sometimes resented and persecuted for this and ultimately flee their marriages and homes. In each case the hagiography implicitly praises them for this behavior, without a whiff of criticism. Cheng Wei 程偉, the text records, pursued alchemy unsuccessfully. He wanted access to his wife's superior methods, but she refused to transmit them, saying his "bones and physiognomy" showed he was unfit—a common reason for such refusal. "He relentlessly pressured her, so she 'died,' escaped by means of a simulated corpse, and departed," her story concludes.[38] The Holy Mother of Dongling 東陵聖母 possessed healing and other esoteric arts and went so far as to visit the sick in their homes, enraging her skeptical husband, who filed an official complaint charging that "she was lecherous and wicked and was not attending to her proper domestic role." Imprisoned, she flew out the window and departed, crowds watching as she soared aloft. The people built temples and made offerings to her.[39] The story of Lady Fan 樊夫人 and her husband, Liu Gang 劉綱 portrays them both as practicing adepts. They stage a contest to determine who has reached the higher level of mastery. Lady Fan wins the marital competition most convincingly. In the end they ascend together into the heavens as transcendents, but Liu, still the lesser adept, has to work harder at levitating than his wife does.[40]

Adepts and the Imperium

Just as there was considerable tension between the quest for transcendence and the demands of family and ancestral lineage, so there was also tension between transcendence and empire.[41] Here the dynamics were even more complex; the relevant textual material is abundant, and some of it is already well known. What I provide, therefore, is not a history of the topic but a sketch of its shape.

The empire was, among other things, a religious system for the maintenance and control of relations with divine powers. Its legitimacy was linked to the observed rhythms of the stars and planets; omens in the sky and on earth were collected and interpreted as signaling cosmic approval or disapproval.[42] The gods by whose sanction the empire ruled the people, from whom it drew its legitimacy, and whose signs of approval it carefully collected and published, needed and expected ritual service in the form of offerings. It was the state's job to feed the gods regularly. The empire claimed many other functions for itself, of course, but feeding the gods on

---

38. Ibid., 139–141.
39. Ibid., 146–147.
40. Ibid., 147–148.
41. For an excellent historical overview of relations between the imperial state and various religious groups and institutions, see Anthony Yu, *State and Religion in China.*
42. See Pankenier, "The Cosmo-Political Background of Heaven's Mandate"; Lippiello, *Auspicious Omens and Miracles in Ancient China;* and *SW,* 116–119.

behalf of the people was perhaps its core legitimating purpose. The scale of this imperial sacrificial system was staggering. Michael Loewe summarizes as follows the numbers involved *solely* in the cult of imperial *ancestors* during one Western Han emperor's reign (Emperor Yuan, r. 49–33 B.C.E.), a list that does not include any of whole other classes of deities serviced by this system:[43]

> There were 167 shrines established for [the cult of imperial ancestors] in 68 provincial divisions of the empire; and at the capital city 176 sites of worship were kept to the souls of the departed ancestors. At each one, four daily offerings of food were made in funerary chambers; 25 sacrifices were performed annually in the main temples, including the oblation of animals; and services were held in the side chapels at each of the four seasons. In addition there were a further thirty sites where reverence was paid in similar fashion to the empresses. According to the *Han shu* the total number of meals offered annually was 24,455; the sites were guarded by 45,129 men; and the priests, cooks and musicians totaled 12,147, not counting the servicemen engaged in looking after the sacrificial animals.[44]

The emperor, titled August Thearch 皇帝 or Son of Heaven 天子, headed this vast system of sacrifice and omen-collection. Its success in theory depended on his carrying out these ritual roles as well as on his personal virtue. In short, the role of emperor was inextricably bound up with the system of sacrifice and the maintenance of dynastic continuity, as implied in the title Son of Heaven: in his person was located the vital link between the divine cosmos and humanity, metaphorically and ritually cast as a father-son relationship.[45]

This system, as I have argued, is among the things that transcendents transcended. Bypassing the emperor's personal mediation between humanity and heaven, *xian* ascended directly to heaven themselves; they withdrew from the agricultural economy and the divine-human exchange of blessings for sacrificial offerings on

---

43. The Han, Wei, and Jin states officially recognized a changing, hierarchically ordered but messy pantheon of deities, from nature gods of particular locales up to such cosmic and rather abstract powers such as Heaven, Earth, and the Grand Monad 太一, as well as the ancestors of the regnant imperial family and various sages and culture heroes of past eras, and they attempted to maintain strict sanction over who was authorized to sacrifice to these deities and how. See Loewe, "K'uang Heng and the Reform of Religious Practices (31 B.C.)"; Bujard, *Le sacrifice au ciel dans la Chine ancienne;* and Puett, *To Become a God,* 311.

44. Loewe, "K'uang Heng and the Reform of Religious Practices (31 B.C.)," 19.

45. The emperor's "sonship" under Heaven, entailing a filial duty to obey and sacrifice to Heaven, was explicitly articulated at many points, for example in a memorial submitted to the throne by Wang Mang (see *Han shu* 25B:1264–1265).

which that economy was based. They eschewed something on which even the gods depended and something whose production and management was a central state function—agricultural food—touting their access to superior nourishment.

No wonder, then, that writers both ancient and modern have seen the roles of emperor and *xian* as deeply incompatible. At mid-Han, Yang Xiong 揚雄 (53 B.C.E.–18 C.E.) in his *Exempla (Fa yan 法言)* dismissed the quest for transcendence by saying, first, that it is simply impossible since whatever is born must die; second, that *xian,* if they did exist, would be "a kind of person that is of no benefit" to society; and third, that sages do not take *xian* as masters: their techniques are different.[46] Gu Yong 谷永, sometime late in the reign of Han Emperor Cheng (r. 33–7 B.C.E.), submitted a lengthy memorial, preserved in the *Han shu,* that gives a colorful summation of the courtly quest for transcendence down to his time and argues that fascination with such matters, as well as with uncanonical sacrifices to all manner of ghosts and spirits, was not becoming to an emperor; a ruler who was properly "clear as to the nature of heaven and earth" and "understanding of the essentials of the myriad things" could not be led astray by "spirit anomalies" or "things out of their proper kinds," but would instead cleave to "the correct path of benevolence and righteousness" and "the exemplary sayings of the five classics." The purported methods of transcendence, Gu argued, many of which he ticks off in an impressive list, were

> all things with which wicked men deceive many, men who use sinister arts and make false claims to fool the ruler of humanity. Hearing them talk, their copious words fill the ear and it seems as if [their promised goals] can be obtained, but when one carries out [their methods] everything is vast and formless as if one were trying to tie up the wind or capture a shadow, and in the end nothing is achieved. These are matters that a wise ruler will keep his distance from and not listen to, that the sage [Confucius] cut off and would not speak of.[47]

The sitting emperor reportedly agreed with Gu's finely crafted words. Even a modern scholar such as Martin Kern, with no ideological axe to grind on the question, has justly observed, "The two notions of personal transcendence and dynastic permanence are mutually exclusive: the first is narrowed to the individual

---

46. *Fa yan* 12:3940. See the very brief discussion in Nylan, *The Canon of Supreme Mystery,* 59. On the text's history, see Knechtges, "Fa yen."

47. *Han shu* 25B:1260; compare the partial translation in Needham et al., *Science and Civilisation in China,* 3:36–37. The memorial is a rhetorical masterpiece articulating a Western Han–style classicist view of proper rulership.

yet transcends the social realm; the second is within this realm yet not restricted to the individual ruler."[48] This incompatibility of roles, however, did not stop some emperors—including two who were among those most responsible for shaping imperial rule, Qin Shi Huang and Han Emperor Wu—from seeking (or at least being charged with seeking) transcendence for themselves, sponsoring adepts at court, inquiring after their methods, and commissioning expeditions to the eastern isles to seek drugs and herbs of deathlessness.[49] The stories of these emperors' quests are well known, thanks especially to the rhetorical work of Sima Qian and Ban Gu, whose annals of both reigns, as well as their treatises on sacrifices, featured these rulers' search for immortality while bitterly criticizing it as chimerical and the adepts who enabled it as duplicitous charlatans.

What astonishes is that these holders of the sacred office of Son of Heaven, guarantors of timely sacrifice and dynastic (and familial) continuity, apparently considered it possible while filling this role to also seek *xian*-hood for themselves—a goal that, if obtained, would absent them from the imperial sacrifice system and their own ancestral lineages and would render them no longer merely sons of Heaven but outright occupants of transcendent offices in the heavens. We might, as fellow mortals, empathize with their desire not to die (even if we might not, on reflection, share it), but how, in the *imaginaire* of the time, was this role-jumping maneuver construed as possible? On what repertoire of cultural resources and precedents did its advocates draw for support? Explicit and quite creative attempts to bridge the roles of emperor and transcendent focused on three nodes of repertoire-tweaking activity: the figure of the Yellow Thearch or Huangdi 黃帝, the myth of ancient sacrifices known as the *feng* 封 and *shan* 禪, and a courtier's masterful poetic composition, "Rhapsody on the Great Man" ("Daren fu" 大人賦).

We would be hard-pressed to name more than a few cultural inventions that had not, by the middle of the Han era, been mythically associated with the figure of the Yellow Emperor or the Yellow Thearch—Huangdi 黃帝—of hoary antiquity. God of war, weaponry, and storm; world conqueror; demon queller (invoked as

---

48. *The Stele Inscriptions of Ch'in Shih-huang,* 160. The contrast between the imperial project as seen in Qin Shi Huang's stele inscriptions, on the one hand, and the personal mode of transcendence attributed to him by Sima Qian and other authors, is very clear and is nicely presented by Kern.

49. They were hardly the only rulers to whom the quest for personal transcendence was attributed in the period before 350 C.E. Even Wang Mang, at great cost, reportedly sponsored the construction of an "eight winds tower" and the carrying out of "the Yellow Thearch's grains technique for becoming a *xian*" at the palace, under the advice of the master of esoterica Su Le 蘇樂, and "several times issued edicts saying that he should become a *xian*." See *Han shu* 25B:1270 and the translation in Needham et al., *Science and Civilisation in China* 3:37.

such in the travel sacrifice, funeral processions, and exorcism rites[50]); inventor of boats and oars; lord of the dead, keeper of the registers of the living and of allotted lifespans; master of esoteric arts of rulership—these were among his many roles and associations. For our purposes what is most significant is that he was an ancient figure reputed to have managed to become, *as ruler*, a transcendent, and that he was the *only* figure to whom this dual feat was widely attributed.

He is granted a hagiography in the Han-period *Traditions of Exemplary Transcendents,* which runs as follows:

> The Yellow Thearch was titled Xuanyuan. He could summon the hundred spirits to court and command them. As an infant he could already speak; sagely, he knew the future and understood the natures of things. He considered himself master of clouds and had the appearance of a dragon. He selected the day of his disappearance and took leave of his courtiers. When he died [as predicted], he was returned to Mount Qiao and buried there. [Later] the mountain collapsed, revealing his coffin to be devoid of a corpse; only his sword and shoes were within. The "Book on Transcendence" (*Xian shu* 仙書)[51] says: The Yellow Thearch collected copper [or bronze] from Mount Shou and with it cast a tripod at the foot of Mount Jing; when it was complete, a dragon with a long trailing beard descended to welcome him, and the Thearch thus rose into the heavens. His courtiers and ministers seized hold of the dragon's beard and thus followed the Thearch upward; but because they had kept hold of the Thearch's bow, the dragon's beard was pulled out and the bow fell to earth along with [some of?] them. Those courtiers who were thus unable to follow the Thearch gazed up at him and uttered cries of despair. This is why later generations take this place to be Tripod Lake and call his bow the Crow's Cry.[52]

There is scant focus here on the Yellow Thearch's rulership, though the mention of court and courtiers makes it clear that this text assumes him to have been ruler. The focus is rather on his tripod-making as the apparent method of transcendence; on

---

50. See Lewis, "The *Feng* and *Shan* Sacrifices of Emperor Wu of the Han," 59, an essay on which I often rely in the next few pages; and Csikszentmihalyi, "Reimagining the Yellow Emperor's Four Faces."

51. It is unclear whether this is a generic term ("book(s) on transcendence") or a title; Ge Hong uses the same phrase in a similarly vague way.

52. "Crow's Cry" puns on a common expression meaning "alas!" My translation is based on the Chinese text and French translation in Kaltenmark, *Le Lie-hsien tchouan,* 50–53 (item 5). Another ancient ruler associated with cosmographic, palladia-like tripods (but not transcendence) was the flood-tamer Yu; see *SW,* 102–106.

the tomb, its location and mysterious lack of a corpse;[53] and on the strange celestial ascent scene, already alluded to in the "Yuanyou."[54] Meanwhile, both before and after this account was recorded, the Yellow Thearch was identified as an ancient wielder of esoteric arts of many kinds and was often credited with the initial human receipt of their revelation from gods and goddesses; both received texts (in the Daoist canon and elsewhere) and recovered manuscripts, including some found at Mawangdui, associate him with secret arts of healing and divination as well as with sexual, macrobiotic, and alchemical techniques of self-cultivation.[55]

By the early fourth century C.E., Ge Hong, clearly aware of the *Liexian zhuan* narrative (which he cites by name), mentions the Yellow Thearch in several con-nections: he is the only ruler to have attained transcendence thus far; he journeyed to many mountains to secure various transcendence arts from multiple teachers; the purpose of his tripod-making was the fashioning of an elixir, which was the means of his ascension.[56] Ge Hong takes up the matter of the Thearch's tomb: an interlocutor asks why, if he attained transcendence, he has a tomb on Mount Qiao; Ge responds, apparently paraphrasing two old texts, that the Thearch's ministers, to commemorate him, built a temple to house his chair and staff and made offerings there, while others preserved his hat and robe by burying them.[57]

A second attempt to bridge the roles of emperor and transcendent was the mythology of the *feng* and *shan* sacrifices. This mythology was closely linked to the Yellow Thearch since, according to historical accounts, during the Qin and Han he was frequently cited by masters of esoterica as an exemplary ancient performer

---

53. Very often in hagiographies a coffin subsequently found to be lacking a corpse is a standard narrative trope indicating an adept's use of some sort of *shijie* method, but, to my knowl-edge, this relatively low-ranking method was not attributed to this august personage, and, as we will see, other explanations than his only apparent death were offered for the existence of his empty tomb.

54. Line 53 in Kroll, "An Early Poem of Mystical Excursion," 159: "Xuanyuan may not be caught up and held on to."

55. For numerous examples, see Harper, *Early Chinese Medical Literature;* Wile, *Art of the Bed-chamber;* Pregadio, *Great Clarity; DZ* 283, 284, 285, 1020, 1018, 885, and so forth.

56. *NP* 12:224 (the only ruler to have attained transcendence), 13:240–241 (his peregrinations; which arts he studied where from whom; why, if he transcended, he has a tomb on Mount Qiao; summary of *Liexian zhuan* account; critique of Ru scholars' silence on his case and on transcendence generally); *NP* 18:323–324, based on *DZ* 388 3:16b–23b (again his peregrinations, what arts he got from whom on what mountain).

57. *NP* 13:241. The two texts cited are *Jingshan jing* 荊山經 and *Longshou ji* 龍首記; both texts are listed in Ge Hong's catalog in *NP* 18, and there is a *Huangdi longshou jing* preserved as *DZ* 283 apparently dating back to the Han (see Schipper and Verellen, eds., *The Taoist Canon,* 84–85).

of these sacrifices.[58] The *feng* and *shan*, though claimed to be ancient, were in fact newly created along with the recently constructed empire itself;[59] they are a classic instance of an invented tradition—the manipulation of collective memory to justify something new by claiming it to be very old.[60] The Yellow Thearch himself was added as a recipient of offerings in the imperial cult system, along with thearchs of the other four directions, during this same period.[61] Masters of esoterica repeatedly explained to rulers, particularly Han Emperor Wu, that performing the *feng* and *shan* was the very method by which the Yellow Thearch had transcended. One factor stimulating Emperor Wu to follow his example was the report from a master, Gongsun Qing 公孫卿, of a certain previous Master Shen 申公, an acquaintance of the renowned ancient transcendent Master Anqi 安期生, who came into possession of the tripod forged by the Yellow Thearch, a tripod now said to bear an inscription predicting that the Han dynasty would rise and that Emperor Wu would perform the ancient sacrifices; Gongsun also claimed that, of seventy-two ancient rulers who attempted them, only the Yellow Thearch had performed them successfully.[62] And so the emperor made the sacrifices near Mount Tai in the northeast, stopping on the way to present offerings at the Yellow Thearch's corpse-free tomb at Mount Qiao and donning yellow during the *feng* and *shan* sacrifices as well as the preliminary sacrifice to the Grand Monad (Taiyi 太一). Upon hearing Gongsun Qing's tale announcing the possibility of all this, Emperor Wu is recorded to have

---

58. In Sima Qian's treatise on the sacrifices, this claim is first made in a speech to the ruler of Qin during Warring States times (*Shi ji* 28:1361), though that passage does not yet link the performance of the *feng* and *shan* with personal transcendence. Such linkages later come thick and fast, however, beginning with Li Shaojun's promise to Han Emperor Wu that if, after many preparatory measures, he performs the two sacrifices, he will never die, and that "this is what the Yellow Thearch did" (*Shi ji* 28:1385). Puett correctly notes that, for Sima Qian, "imperial power and a certain mode of religious worship are directly interconnected. . . . The rise of a particular mode of religious worship and the emergence of centralized state institutions are thus presented as linked" (*To Become a God,* 307). And Puett notes that each stage in the development of this imperial sacrificial system was instigated by *fangshi,* who repeatedly held up Huangdi as the chief exemplar. What Puett does not discuss is that the *fangshi* recommended this system not only as an expression and generator of sovereignty but also as conducive to the ruler's personal transcendence, and that it was personal transcendence on the part of a ruler, among other things, that Huangdi was held to exemplify.

59. As is made clear in Lewis, "The *Feng* and *Shan* Sacrifices of Emperor Wu of the Han," 52–53.

60. For studies on the theme, see Hobsbawm and Ranger, eds., *The Invention of Tradition.*

61. *Shi ji* 28:1364, 1386, 1394, and so forth.

62. Ibid., 1393–1394. This convoluted speech, which I here only summarize, is typical of the lengthy explanations offered by masters of esoterica at court.

exclaimed, "If only I could become like the Yellow Thearch, I would think no more of my wife and children than I would of a castoff slipper!"[63]

As imagined by *fangshi* advising Qin Shi Huang and Emperor Wu, then, the *feng* and *shan* were some sort of sacrifice to the gods—the details of which were deliberately left quite vague[64]—that was claimed to lead to transcendence for the sacrificer. They were, furthermore, a type of sacrifice that only rulers could perform and only a few specially qualified rulers at that. Thus was fashioned the possibility of an imperial, sacrificial way to personal transcendence—the only such transcendence method of which we have any record.

Perhaps the boldest attempt to bridge the roles of emperor and transcendent was the "Rhapsody on the Great Man" or "Daren fu" 大人賦, a poetic composition submitted by the Han courtier Sima Xiangru 司馬相如 (ca. 179–117 B.C.E.) to Han Emperor Wu (r. 140–87 B.C.E.).[65] This work charted in elegant, culturally authoritative verse a mode of transcendence fully compatible with rulership.[66] Emperor Wu is said to have been delighted by it, declaring that it made him feel "as if he were drifting away on the *qi* of clouds and already roaming in the space between heaven and earth."[67]

The "Daren fu" is clearly modeled on, and at times quotes, the *Chuci*'s "Far Roaming" ("Yuanyou" 遠遊) but it places the emperor in the role of cosmically itinerant protagonist. This intertextual relationship itself already signals to readers that *xian*-hood is attainable not just by disaffected literati (as in "Far Roaming") but

---

63. Ibid., 1394. This emperor too, like Ge Hong's imaginary interlocutor later, reportedly asked why the Thearch had a tomb if he had not in fact died, and received the explanation that the ancient ruler's cap and robe were interred here by his ministers to commemorate him (ibid., 1396).

64. Lewis emphasizes that we know very little about what the sacrifices actually entailed; they were an "empty center" of which we have only tantalizing clues involving their names, their relations to mountain cults and acts of conquest, their tie to imperial processions, their status as responses to divine omens, and, as I have discussed, their links to transcendence and to the Yellow Thearch, a figure in whom these various themes converged.

65. The poem is quoted in full in *Shi ji* 117:3056–3062, as part of that work's biography of Sima. The only complete English translation of which I am aware is in Watson, *Records of the Grand Historian: Han Dynasty II*, 296–299. For helpful biographical notes on Sima Xiangru, who also numbered among the courtiers urging Emperor Wu to perform the *feng* and *shan* sacrifices, see Loewe, *A Biographical Dictionary of the Qin, Former Han and Xin Periods*, 487–488.

66. Lewis suggests that since Han Emperor Wu read Sima Xiangru's works and since those works were written for him, they may be the best extant expression of the ruler's own views of transcendence. This may be so, but the rhapsody remains significant for our purposes as a bid to craft an imperial route to transcendence, whether or not it expressed Emperor Wu's or other rulers' personal views.

67. *Shi ji* 117:3063.

also by rulers themselves. The poem is introduced in Sima Xiangru's *Shi ji* biography with the statement that Xiangru wrote it because "he felt that the transmitted traditions of transcendents portrayed them as living in the mountains and marshes, their bodies and countenances greatly emaciated, but that this was not the idea of transcendence held by emperors and kings."[68] Let us see how this intertextual work of poetic imagination—not a representation of its protagonist's progress on an already existing royal route to celestial transcendence but rather an agent in the *construction* of such a route[69]—charts a path and goal for the ruler.

Saddened by the world's vulgarity, the protagonist, beginning on the Central Continent, embarks on a cosmic airborne journey. He first flies east, then north to Taiyin 太陰, seeking perfected persons; he greets gods of the Northern Dipper and employs the Five Thearchs to clear his way. Returning to the Taiyi 太一 asterism, he follows the transcendent Ziming of Lingyang 陵陽子明.[70] He then is described as having two celestial deities riding to either side of him and two others riding fore and aft. He has two other named transcendents (one of them Xianmen 羨門[71]) as his footman and page, while the physician Qi Bo, who served the Yellow Thearch in this capacity, prepares a superior recipe for him. The god Zhurong 祝融 goes ahead to clear the path of noxious *qi*. Riding in a cortege of a myriad cloud-topped chariots, he summons the god Goumang 句芒[72] to go along with him as well. With this growing entourage he then turns south, visiting Yao and Shun on their respective mountains (the mountains named are the places where these ancient sage rulers were held to be buried). The ruler and his party press on to encounter the creatrix Nügua 女媧; Pingyi 馮夷, god of the Yellow River, is summoned to chastise the lords of wind and rain when the sky grows threatening. Gazing toward Mount Kunlun, they knock on Heaven's gate and enter the Celestial Thearch's palace, then depart, taking jade maidens with them. The protagonist then spies the Queen Mother of the West, a white-haired crone living in a cave lair, a three-legged crow her only servant, and utters the most ideologically significant line of the poem: "If it is thus that one must attain long life and not die, though one survives then thousand eras, it does not suffice to bring joy." This is a sharp critique not of the pursuit

---

68. Ibid., 3056.

69. Drawing here on Greenblatt, *Hamlet in Purgatory*, 51.

70. A figure who receives a hagiography in *Liexian zhuan* (item 67; see Kaltenmark, *Le Lie-hsien tchouan,* 183–187), which makes clear that the Lingyang element in his sobriquet derives from his having frequented the mountain by that name for over a century.

71. Another figure known from several early sources, though not the subject of a *Liexian zhuan* hagiography; see *TL,* 289–291. A *Zhen'gao* passage later (presumably between 364 and 370 C.E.) provided the location of his empty tomb.

72. On the early lore surrounding this deity, whose name may also be read Jumang, see Riegel, "Kou-mang and Ju-shou."

of transcendence tout court but of ascetic methods for attaining it; the protagonist enjoys a more luxuriant, free-roaming path toward this goal.

Having thus in effect traced the ascetic path to transcendence to its divine source on Mount Kunlun, the ruler now turns his chariots about, making for Buzhou and Youdu in the north, inhaling and ingesting vapors, dining on excrescences, blossoms, and gem flowers. This brief passage is the point at which the protagonist engages in the core macrobiotic practices that render him deathless. He then quickly presses on, leaving the bounds of the known cosmos to continue northward, going out through the Dark Pass and Cold Gate at the northern extremity of reality. Earth vanishes beneath him, Heaven recedes above, gazing into the blackness he can see nothing, listening in the silence he can hear nothing; "mounting the void, he ascends on high, surpassing all, companionless, to dwell alone." The protagonist's end state, merging with primordial emptiness, echoes that of the protagonist of "Far Roaming."

This triumphalist tour of the heavens in the company of celestial gods and transcendents is saturated with imperial imagery, drawing on items from the repertoire of the ancient (and recently revived) tradition of the tour of inspection of the ruler's far-flung domains; it is, as Puett observes, "a claim of absolute power"[73]—of rulership over the cosmos. But it is, at the same time, an explicit claim to an imperial route to transcendence—not just mastery over the realm of forms, but also escape from it. The rhapsody charts a path that does not require rulers to give up their throne or pursue austerities full time in order to ascend into the heavens and achieve deathlessness, and it does so while fully aware of the ascetic path to which it offers an alternative. By this means, the poet argues, rulers can be both rulers and transcendents at once.

In the face of these arguments that rulers qua rulers could attain transcendence, other parties—many of them forever unknowable to us by name—insisted there were limits on the ability of emperors and officials to practice transcendence arts successfully. For the most part these critics did so not in direct, expository style, which perhaps would have been too risky, but through a large body of narratives that both reflect and participated in a running ideological struggle that went on for centuries. I concluded Chapter 4 by noting how adepts' display-and-concealment of secret arts opened a domain of power that was beyond the control of rulers, unplugged from the network of ritual obligations binding the imperium to various spirits—a domain in which possessors of arcane arts were the sole masters and to which they were the self-appointed gatekeepers. This claim of exclusive access to esoteric arts worked to limit the ability of rulers and officials to tap into these sources of prestige. It was supported by an array of narrative patterns recurring in

---

73. Puett, *To Become a God*, 242.

hagiographies, tales of anomalies, pseudohistoriographic works, and similar genres. Repeatedly we see in stories, for example, that rulers impatiently summon adepts to their courts, hoping to learn something of their esoteric methods and exert some measure of control over their activities and movements; that rulers unsuccessfully press adepts to reveal their secret arts; and that, even when rulers and officials receive such secret texts, they prove unqualified to practice their arts or unable to understand their strange contents.[74] A few examples will suffice.

Quite early on, perhaps even predating the *Traditions of Exemplary Transcendents* compilation, there appeared in chap. 11 of the *Zhuangzi* a counternarrative concerning the Yellow Thearch. This narrative clearly presupposes and responds to the view that the Yellow Thearch was a ruler of considerable self-cultivational attainment, though whether its makers were aware of the specific attribution of transcendence to him is not clear. It seeks to put him in his proper place by portraying him as arrogant in the face of a superior master of esoteric arts and as deluded in his priorities as a ruler as well as by comparing him unfavorably to his teacher, Guangchengzi 廣成子, and by leaving off any claim of the Thearch's eventual attainment of transcendence: he simply receives Guangchengzi's words on quiescence, and there the narrative ends, leaving open the question of the Thearch's own attainments, if any.[75] A shortened version of this narrative appears in Ge's *Traditions* as a hagiography of Guangchengzi, though whether it was incorporated there by Ge Hong or by later hands is unknown.[76] Its main impact in this hagiographic setting is to underscore the superiority of adepts to rulers.

Much blunter is the story of the River-Dwelling Sire or Heshang gong 河上公 in *Traditions of Divine Transcendents:*

> No one knows the real name of the River-Dwelling Sire. During the reign of Emperor Jing of the Han,[77] the Sire bound up grasses to make a hut for himself by the banks of the Yellow River, and there he busied himself in studying the *Scripture of Laozi*. Emperor Jing was fond of Laozi's sayings. . . .[78] But there

---

74. Some of the most explicit and dramatic narratives of this type collected around Han Emperor Wu and his court; these were discussed in Chapter 4.

75. See Graham, *Chuang-Tzu*, 177–179; for an analysis of the passage, see Roth, "The Yellow Emperor's Guru."

76. Its inclusion does not seem fully compatible with the Yellow Thearch's treatment in *Baopuzi,* but that does not prove much.

77. Reigned 157–141 B.C.E. Some versions of the text give Emperor Wen (r. 180–157 B.C.E.) as the ruler with whom the master interacted.

78. This statement is echoed in official histories and other documents of the time, which speak of Han Emperors Wen and Jing—the husband and son, respectively, of Empress Dou (d. 135 B.C.E.)—favoring the teachings of the *Lao zi* (or of Huang-Lao, the "teachings of the Yellow

were passages he did not understand, and no one could explain them satisfactorily. Having heard that the River-Dwelling Sire was studying the *Laozi,* the Emperor dispatched someone to inquire of him about the misunderstood matters. The Sire said: "The Way is venerable; its Power is honorable. They are not things that can be asked about from a remote distance."

The Emperor then rode out personally to be his follower. The Emperor said [to the Sire]: "There is no place under Heaven that is not the King's land. There is no one who lives on this land who is not the King's subject. 'In a realm there are "four great things," and the King is one of these.'[79] So, although you possess the Way, you are still one of my people and cannot subsist independently. Why then are you acting so haughtily?"[80]

Here we have the imperial challenge to adepts' esoteric power, stated as baldly as possible. Everyone in the realm is, in principle, the ruler's subject and is hence bound to obey his commands. The ruler has requested instruction. The adept should simply comply. But the story argues otherwise:

At that, the Sire clapped his hands, sat down, and then rose straight into the air until he was several dozen feet above the ground. Looking down, he made this reply: "Above, I do not reach as far as Heaven; in between, I do not become entangled with other people; below, I do not dwell on the earth. How can I be considered one of your subjects?"[81]

Here, then, in *its* baldest form, is adepts' reply. Their authority is of a different order. Unlike ordinary citizens, they are not bound by custom or law; they are not fixed to particular points on the landscape or limited by particular social roles whether familial or political (save the role of transcendent, which in theory escapes all other roles); they are not bound up in the locative system of power over which the emperor presides. Rulers therefore have no basis on which to command obedience, much less insist on receiving transmission of esoteric techniques from adepts. All of this is as graphically demonstrated as possible when the adept literally rises into the air, standing on no place in particular, hovering above the ruler. And so the battle

Thearch and Lao zi"). For more information, see *Han shu* 88.3592; *Han shu* 97A3945; Twitchett and Loewe, *Cambridge History of China,* 1:139, 801–810; and Emmerich, "Bemerkungen zu Huang und Lao in der frühen Han-Zeit."

79. The ruler here presumes to quote Laozi's scripture to justify his claim to obedience. His quotation tallies verbatim with a passage found in chap. 25 of the received text (that is, the one edited by Wang Bi in the third century C.E.) of the *Daode jing.*

80. *TL,* 305–307.

81. Ibid.

is joined, and the next move is the ruler's. In this case, he responds with what the story argues is proper deference: he dismounts, bows, utters humble words, and asks for instruction rather than demanding it. Having now behaved appropriately, he receives a text from the master. "The emperor paid it"—or him, or both—"the highest honor."[82] To this narrative from a sympathetic source we may compare Sima Qian's decidedly hostile record of a curious ritual—performed at night (perhaps so it would be observed by as few onlookers as possible)—in which an imperial envoy presented the adept Luan Da with a seal investing him as "General of the Celestial Way" (*Tiandao jiangjun* 天道將軍), the envoy and the investee dressed in similar feathered ritual costumes and standing alike on white rushes: "This was done to indicate that [Luan Da] was not being treated as [the emperor's] subject."[83] Here we see a careful ritual protocol invented to emphasize that some adepts, at least when they had their own way, were treated as envoys from another realm, on an equal footing with the Son of Heaven.

It is this same basic argument that we find in the *Traditions* hagiography of Zuo Ci 左慈. But here the adept's autonomy is flaunted to the point of publicly humiliating and enraging rulers, in scenes that must have either delighted or outraged readers and hearers depending on their ideological persuasion. After a typical opening in which the subject's abilities are said to have been evident from an early age, the hagiography declares: "Seeing that the fortunes of the Han house were about to decline, Zuo sighed and said, 'As we move into this declining [astral] configuration, those who hold eminent offices are in peril, and those of lofty talent will die. Winning glory in this present age is not something to be coveted.' So he studied *dao* arts."[84] With this opening, rulership and all it entails are already relativized by juxtaposition with a distinct, higher pursuit. We next read of the methods Zuo received and practiced (most of them alchemical in nature), that resulted in his gaining the ability, not to ascend into the heavens—that is not where the narrative's focus will rest—but "to transform into a myriad different forms." It is this art of transformation that Zuo will now put to vivid use.

Over the bulk of the ensuing story, Zuo works his way successively into the presence of the three most powerful men in China in his day, each of them the head of one of the three kingdoms into which the Han empire had by now been divided. The first to be mentioned is Cao Cao:[85]

---

82. See *TL,* 305–307, 494–495. The unnamed text mentioned is the *Daode jing* commentary attributed to this figure.

83. 以示不臣也, *Shi ji* 28:1391.

84. *TL,* 279.

85. Cao Cao (155–220 C.E.) never assumed the title of emperor except posthumously; he was a highly successful official and general who was largely responsible for creating the conditions for the proclamation of the dynasty shortly after his death by his son, Cao Pi, in 220.

When [the ruler] Cao Cao heard about Zuo Ci, he summoned him to court. Cao had him incarcerated in a room and placed under surveillance; he denied him grains and other foods for a period of year, allotting him only two *sheng* of water per day. When Ci was brought out, his appearance and complexion were just as they had been before. Now Cao maintained that there was no such thing as a way of not eating that could be viably practiced by any living person; the fact that Ci had done this, he claimed, must mean that his was a way of the left.[86] It was then that Cao began planning to have him killed.[87]

It is quite telling that food intake, with its many ideological associations, here forms the crux of the conflict. Cao Cao cannot allow the possibility of viable human life outside the network of agriculture, sacrifice, and commensality; precisely this possibility is what Zuo Ci has, seemingly miraculously, demonstrated. So he must be dealt with. But killing an adept with Zuo's skill set proves quite difficult, even for this famous general.

The next scene shows us Zuo at a state banquet hosted by Cao. Zuo performs a type of feat elsewhere attributed to other adepts: from a great distance he rapidly procures rare or seasonally unavailable products for the ruler's table.[88] Next, by means of a trick involving a floating wine cup, he creates a diversion allowing him to escape the court and return home, while the enraged Cao Cao, we are told, was now even more determined to have him killed. The subsequent sequence of dramatic and at the same time comedic scenes only drives home the impression of Zuo Ci's power and Cao Cao's helplessness to control him in any way whatsoever.

Ci fled into a flock of sheep, and his pursuers, losing sight of him, suspected that he might have transformed himself into one of the sheep. They had the sheep counted. Originally there had been an even thousand of them, but now there was one extra, so they knew that Ci had indeed transformed himself. They announced: "Master Zuo, if you're in there, just come out; we won't hurt you." Then one of the sheep knelt down and spoke words, saying, "Who would have thought I'd be pardoned?" When the pursuers tried to seize that one sheep, all of the others knelt down and said, "Who would have thought I'd be pardoned?" So the pursuers [gave up and] left.

Later on, someone learned Ci's whereabouts and informed Cao, who once again sent men to apprehend him, and they captured him. It was not that Ci

---

86. *Zuodao* 左道, meaning a deviant, heteroprax religious path. The term has overtones of malicious intent.

87. *TL,* 279–280.

88. A theme on which I elaborate in "Long-Distance Specialists in Early Medieval China."

could not have escaped; he deliberately allowed himself to be arrested in order to demonstrate his divine transformations. He was taken into prison. When the guards there were ready to torture and interrogate Ci, there was one Ci inside the cell door and another Ci outside it, and they did not know which one to torture. When Cao was informed, he despised Ci even more, ordering that he be taken out of the city and killed. As they were leading him out, Ci suddenly vanished. So they locked the city gates and searched for him. It was announced that [they were searching for a man who] was blind in one eye and wearing a linen cloth wrapped on his head and a one-layer gown. The moment this announcement was made, the entire city full of people, numbering several tens of thousands, all turned into men blind in one eye wearing a linen cloth on their head and a one-layer gown. So in the end no one knew which Ci to seize.

Cao then put out an all-points order that Ci was to be killed on sight. Someone saw and recognized Ci, so they beheaded him and presented [the head] to Cao. Cao was overjoyed. On inspection, however, it turned out to be only a bundle of straw. When someone went back to search for Ci's corpse, it had vanished. Later, as someone was traveling in from Jingzhou, they saw Ci [alive].[89]

It is as if narrators of the era could not resist piling on more and more stories of this kind—stories of the adept as a powerful, wily trickster, running circles around powerful men and upending the most fundamental of social hierarchies.[90] In the same hagiography Zuo Ci is credited with similar elusive tricks in the presence of Liu Biao and, finally, in front of Sun Ce, head of the Wu kingdom in the southeast, which culminates in the following dramatic scene and hagiographic send-off:

Ci then went to see the ruler of Wu, Sun Ce, who also wanted to see Ci killed. Later Sun went out traveling and invited Ci to accompany him; he had Ci walk ahead of his [Sun's] horse, intending to kill him by running him through from behind. Sun then whipped his horse and brandished his spear as he chased Ci. Ci, who was wearing wooden clogs, plodded slowly along leaning on his bamboo stave all the while, but neither Sun nor his troops could catch up with him. Then, realizing that Ci really did have arts [of the Dao], Sun gave up.

---

89. *TL*, 280–281. Jingzhou was located in modern Xiangyang district, Hubei Province. This episode constitutes a sort of liberation by means of a "corpse"; the straw-headed figure is Zuo Ci's substitute body, and the place where he is next seen after his "execution" is far away, fitting the *shijie*—or in this case *bingjie*—pattern.

90. On the ludic aspects of the reputations of adepts, see Strickmann, "Saintly Fools and Taoist Masters (Holy Fools)."

Late in the Construction of Peace period [196–220 C.E.], Ci crossed the Yangzi River, searching for [suitable] mountains, and entered a cave in Lesser Gua Mountain. His countenance and complexion [at that time] were outstanding.[91]

Having thus mocked each of China's contemporary leaders by turn, the adept vanishes from the stage to pursue his higher goals free from imperial interference. The example of Zuo Ci was clearly constructed to amuse, but it also portrays the adept not as comfortably domesticated but rather, if not quite dangerous, then certainly far outside any known realm of etiquette or social control.

Meanwhile, other narratives vividly made the point that, just as imperial officers have their subordinate functionaries, so do adepts have theirs—and the adepts' outclass those of the imperial officers. Such stories also emphasize the fearsome, not merely the trickster-like, aspect of the adepts' power:

Yan Qing often returned from his disciples' homes after dark. One time the Commander-in-Chief ran into him after dark. The Commander demanded, "Who is it who travels after dark?" Yan Qing also asked in a stern voice, "And who are *you* to be out walking at night?" The Commander, not realizing it was Yan Qing, answered him angrily and ordered his guards to arrest this night traveler. Qing also barked an order to his attendant spirits: "Tie up all of these night travelers!" Qing then went on his way, leaving the Commander and all his men and their horses, several dozen in all, immobilized there. The next morning, passersby asked the Commander what he was doing there on the path, and the Commander told them what had happened. The passersby said, "It must have been Master Yan." The Commander told them, "I am unable to move. Please inform my family." As soon as his family learned of it, they went straight to Qing, knocking their heads on the ground and begging forgiveness from him, explaining that the Commander had not realized the previous evening that it was Qing who was on the path. Upon hearing this, Qing loudly proclaimed: "Release all those who were detained last night for traveling after dark!" Only then was the Commander able to go. From then on, whenever he encountered someone walking about past dark, he was always careful to ask first if he was Master Yan.[92]

We must always bear in mind that these arguments for adepts' autonomy from modes of imperial control—modes ranging from ruler's direct commands to the importunate pressures that could be applied by a pushy local official—coexisted

---

91. *TL,* 281–282.
92. Ibid., 346–347, 528–529.

alongside adepts' bid for imperial and official-class patronage. Some of the earliest datable textual representations of adepts, predating the Qin, situate these figures not on distant mountains or isles but in the courts of rulers.[93] It was a balance delicately maintained, precisely because the adepts' independent access to powers not otherwise available to rulers is what made their arts attractive and seemingly worthy of sponsorship. On the other hand, it was the promise of eventual access that kept sponsors interested; too much autonomy on the adept's part risked an indifferent or hostile response from a potential patron.

Finally, we should note that a good many practitioners of transcendence arts were men who had held office or were qualified to do so. The duties of officialdom, like those of family, figure in many narratives as obstructions to proper ascetic practice (although much less so in *Liexian zhuan* than in *Shenxian zhuan,* perhaps due to the increasing prestige of reclusion between the dates of compilation of the two texts), and the hagiographies reflect (or propose) many ways of negotiating this basic tension, on a spectrum ranging from total withdrawal from officialdom and from almost all contact with officials, on the one hand, to simultaneous office-holding and arts-practicing, on the other, with a great many other possibilities in between.[94] Ge Hong at several points acknowledges the tension between esoteric practice and official life, as, for instance, when he writes: "When a sagely and enlightened one is on the throne, only the worthy are treasured. Yet those who pursue transcendence

---

93. Among these are two passages in the *Han Fei zi* dating to the mid- to late third century B.C.E.—stories cited as examples of successful "persuasive discourse." In one, a "guest" at the court of the Prince of Yan teaches his host something of "a way of not dying," only to die before he can finish teaching it fully to some men sent by the prince to learn it. The text not unreasonably assumes this way was bogus since it did not preserve its very teacher from his own demise. *Han Fei zi jijie, pian* 32, p. 201; see also the translation and discussion in Needham, *Science and Civilisation in China,* 5.2: 95. On the other hand, the scenario sketched in this narrative closely fits later hagiographic cases in which it is claimed that the adept-guest feigns his death to escape the patronage and hence the control of his royal or official-class host—cases discussed further below. The other story also concerns a guest at the court of a prince, here the Prince of Jing. The guest presents a "drug of deathlessness" to the prince. But, as the chamberlain is taking it into the palace, the gate guard asks if it can be eaten and, upon hearing that it can, snatches and eats it. The angered prince sentences the guard to death, but the guard sends someone to persuade the prince. This man argues, in part, that if the prince executes the guard he will render the "drug of deathlessness" a "drug of death," thus exposing the guest's claim as a lie, but that since it was not worth a man's life to prove the guest's deceit, the guard should be freed. The prince relents. *Han Fei zi jijie, pian* 22, p. 130; see also the translation and discussion in Needham et al., *Science and Civilisation in China,* 5.3:7. The story was also collected into the *Zhanguo ce* (compiled late in the first century B.C.E. from earlier materials) in slightly modified form: see Crump, *Chan-kuo Ts'e,* 258.

94. Representing the extreme of disengagement, perhaps, is the Jiao Xian of *Traditions of Divine Transcendents,* and representing the extreme of simultaneous engagement is Luan Ba in the same text.

are unwilling to enter office. If everyone cultivates a *dao,* who will help any longer with affairs of governance?"[95] His response is to defend "reclusion," that is, refusal of office, as an authentic cultural option, citing many authoritative precedents from old annals.

Pursuing transcendence, then, existed only very uneasily as a goal alongside the sociopolitical hierarchy of the imperium and the solemn obligations of kinship, and hagiographies and other narratives were the primary media in which these tensions were reflected and negotiated.

---

95. *NP* 8:151–152.

CHAPTER 8

Hagiographic Persuasions

> If one says that X influenced Y it does seem that one is saying that X
> did something to Y rather than that Y did something to X. . . . If we
> think of Y rather than X as the agent, the vocabulary is much richer
> and more attractively diversified: draw on, resort to, avail oneself of,
> appropriate from, have recourse to, adapt, misunderstand, refer to,
> pick up, take on, engage with, react to, quote, differentiate oneself
> from, assimilate oneself to, assimilate, align oneself with, copy, address,
> paraphrase, absorb, make a variation on, revive, continue, remodel,
> ape, emulate, travesty, parody, extract from, distort, attend to, resist,
> simplify, reconstitute, elaborate on, develop, face up to, master, subvert,
> perpetuate, reduce, promote, respond to, transform, tackle.
>
> —Michael Baxandall, *Patterns of Intention*

EVERY INSTANCE of discourse about a holy person, whether oral or written, is,
among other things, an attempt at persuasion. This feature is not unique to hagiographic writings, nor is it their only feature worth examining. But it is important to
ask: in hagiographies, who was attempting persuade whom of what, and how? What
interests and outcomes were at stake in these persuasive efforts? How do extant
texts use rhetorical strategies and reflect social contexts of attempted persuasion?
We saw some partial answers in Chapter 5, regarding the stories adepts were said
to have reported about themselves. Here I shift the focus to other agents to discuss
hagiographic persuasion in both senses of "persuasion": how texts attempted to
persuade readers (and what they tried to persuade them of) and the ideological
persuasions (or sets of interests) from which they did so.

It may be true, as some have said, that collective memory tends to be conser-
vative in nature.[1] But it is not a static, monolithic, or uncontested thing. In fact it

---

Epigraph: Patterns of Intention, 59.
1. Castelli, *Martyrdom and Memory*, 14.

is not a thing at all: rather, "collective memory" is a convenient label for the always ongoing social processes (and the products of those processes) by which people appropriate, shape, and transmit elements of the past. One of the many things narratives about *xian* (or any sort of holy person in any society) attest to is how people with varying interests shaped and reshaped memories of these figures.[2] Just as the reputation of a practitioner of *xian* arts during his or her lifetime was continually being forged, managed, received, and contested by many interested parties, including the practitioner, so, too, these evaluative and persuasive processes continued after the practitioner's departure, carried on by the same parties except for the practitioner.[3] And, as the Michael Baxandall epigraph suggests, it is more empirically accurate—more closely descriptive of what in fact happens in human cultures over time—to think of ourselves as studying what various shapers of narrative did with available material than to imagine ourselves as documenting what "influence" an earlier "version" had on a later one. We will see how proponents of the quest for *xian*-hood reprised and recast earlier figures, in an attempt to persuade others of, and by means of, these recastings. In some cases the evidence points to deliberate, creative misprision, even violent misreadings on the part of the crafters of collective memory.[4] I have argued above that early medieval hagiographies were not fictions in the modern sense of being made up from whole cloth. Here, however, I argue that neither were they neutral receptacles into which past stories were poured. They were something more complex: they were *reworkings* of earlier material and thus of reputations. In many cases this reworking escapes our notice because we have no other stories, or no significantly different stories, of a particular adept for comparison. But sometimes we do have sharply rival stories to compare, and here we catch glimpses of the hagiographic reshaping process at work.

---

2. Long-range diachronic studies of such hagiographic reshapings include Bujard, "Le culte de Wangzi Qiao ou la longue carrière d'un immortel," a superb work of scholarship; and Kirkland, "The Making of an Immortal."

3. Except (from the point of view of the *imaginaire*) in cases where *xian* were claimed to return periodically to their old homes or to the temples dedicated to them. Of course, we may also choose to see such reports as themselves simply another strategy by which others sought to shape the reputations of departed virtuoso practitioners.

4. I draw the phrase "violent misreadings" from the title of a recent article by Michael Puett that provides a striking example of what it describes: a group of authors present a surprising, even disconcerting interpretation of a passage in an earlier text; this is not due to their somehow having misunderstood the earlier passage and thus "gotten it wrong" despite their efforts, but is instead a rhetorical strategy deliberately deployed to advance their own argumentative and persuasive goals by reshaping the passage in a direction that suits them. As Puett puts it, "The authors were aware of the discrepancy and were actively playing on that discrepancy in order to develop their claims" ("Violent Misreadings," 36).

As elsewhere, the question of authorship arises: exactly who was responsible for this textual portrayal of an adept? It may be that the compilers of the extant hagiographies and the authors of the relevant histories are themselves directly responsible for many of the rewritings these works contain. But I suspect that in many cases these reshapings had been done already by hands unseen to us, and the compilers were more or less quoting materials now lost. In almost all of the cases I will discuss,[5] and in virtually all others as well, we simply cannot know the ultimate sources of the traditions that the author-compilers report. But by comparing differ- ent stories of the same figure we can see processes of contestation now otherwise hidden, the sorts of processes that generated all the texts we have and in which these texts themselves participated.

Persuasive Effects

Certain features of hagiographic narratives seem especially designed, whatever their other functions, to persuade readers or hearers of their veracity. We had occasion to note this reality effect[6] in Chapter 5, for example, when we saw Ge Hong sug- gesting that it was the level of graphic detail in some accounts of celestial palaces or distant mountains that convinced audiences of their truthfulness. The more precise the descriptive detail, the more real the narrative seemed. Of the many other fea- tures of hagiographies that could be pointed out as functioning similarly, I will note only one: some stories build in characters who doubt the truth of an adept's claims or the efficacy of his arts. Events then unfold in a way that convinces the skeptic inside the story, and hence, the story argues, any doubters in the audience should be similarly convinced.

One particularly dramatic example of this rhetorical strategy occurs in the hagiography of Liu Gen preserved in *Traditions of Divine Transcendents*. It allows us to glimpse the sort of struggle for status that must have been waged on the ground between local officials and adepts, as well as the awesome powers adepts were often believed to wield and the vivid, hair-raising spectacles they could mount for audi- ences. It reminds us that transcendents could be objects of fear and dread, and it shows us ways in which they created such impressions. But, in addition, it also constitutes a textual attempt to persuade readers of something.

---

5. With the possible exception of stele inscriptions, whose sponsors are named in the inscrip- tions. Even here we cannot assume that these named individuals were the ultimate originators of the stories they commissioned to be chiseled in stone, but we do know that they were happy enough with the textual portrayals to have paid to have them carved and erected.

6. A phrase I draw from somewhere in Stephen Greenblatt's writings.

Commandant Zhang, the new governor, took Gen to be a fake, and he sent lictors to summon him, plotting to have him killed. The entire district remonstrated with Zhang on Gen's behalf, but Zhang would not drop the orders. The lictors reached Gen, intending to order him to return with them, but Gen would not comply. Then Zhang's envoy reached Gen and invited him to return. Gen replied, "What does Commandant Zhang want with me that he sent you all here? I fear that if I do not go back with you, you will all be accused of not daring to come here to summon me." And so Gen went to the Commandant's offices that day. At the time of his arrival, the offices were filled with visitors. The Commandant ordered over fifty men brandishing swords and pikes to tie Gen up and stand him at attention. Gen's face showed no change in color. The Commandant interrogated Gen as follows: "So, do you possess any *dao* arts?" "Yes." "Can you summon ghosts?" "I can." "Since you can," said the Commandant, "you will bring ghosts before this chamber bench at once. If you do not, I will have you tortured and killed." Gen replied, "Causing ghosts to appear is quite easy."

Gen borrowed a brush and an inkstone and composed a memorial. [In a moment,] a clanging sound like that of bronze or iron could be heard outside, and then came a long whistling sound, extremely plangent.[7] All who heard it were awestruck, and the visitors all shook with fear. In another moment, an opening several dozen feet wide appeared in the south wall of the chamber, and four or five hundred armored troops could be seen passing orders down the lines. Several dozen crimson-clad swordsmen then appeared, escorting a carriage straight through the opened wall into the chamber. The opened wall then returned to its former state. Gen ordered the attendants to present the ghosts. With that, the crimson-clad guards flung back the shroud covering the carriage to reveal an old man and an old woman tightly bound inside. They hung their heads before the chamber bench. Upon examining them closely, the Commandant saw that they were his own deceased father and mother. Shocked and dismayed, he wept and was completely at a loss. The ghosts reprimanded him, saying, "When we were alive, you had not yet attained office, so we received no nourishment from your salary. Now that we are dead, what do you mean by offending a venerable official among divine transcendents and getting us arrested? After causing such a difficulty as this, aren't you ashamed even to stand among other people?" The Commandant came down the steps and knocked his head on the ground before Gen, saying that he deserved to die and begging that

---

7. Skill in whistling was often associated with transcendents (see Edwards, "Principles of Whistling"), and whistling, as here, was also a method for controlling spirits.

his ancestors be pardoned and released. Gen ordered the five hundred troops to take out the prisoners and release them. As the carriage moved out, the wall opened back up; then, when it was outside, the wall closed again and the carriage was nowhere to be seen. Gen had also disappeared.[8]

Not satisfied with recounting this vivid proof of Gen's powers, the story ends with an even more explicit caution against presuming to question adepts' abilities:

> [After this,] the Commandant was rueful and vacant-minded and looked like someone who had gone mad. His wife died soon after, then revived and said, "I saw your ancestors. They were incensed and were demanding to know why you offended the venerable officials of the divine transcendents. They said they had seen to it that I was apprehended and that next they would come to kill you." A month later, the Commandant, his wife, and their son all died.[9]

The prospect of having one's own deceased family members seek one's death for having offended a transcendent must have struck fear in the hearts of many listeners and readers: here was yet another way to run afoul of potent, sometimes menacing ancestors. Such a fate might, this story implies, befall anyone who questioned or threatened a capable adept. All narratives in which an authority figure challenges or tests an adept, only to see the adept's powers vindicated, share this basic rhetorical structure.[10]

Contested Endings

In their book *Living Narrative,* Ochs and Capps document how stories and counter-stories often spring up together; even interlocutors who were present at the same event often oppose each other's narrative renderings. "In each conversational inter-

---

8. *TL,* 241–242.

9. The tale is recounted in Ge's *Traditions;* see ibid. For more on the religious, narrative, and psychological relations between ancestors and descendants, see Bokenkamp, *Ancestors and Anxiety.*

10. Several emperors are on record as having tested the arts of adepts. The most elaborately documented episode was Cao Cao's summoning to court of several known practitioners, probably between 216 C.E., the year Cao was ennobled as king of Wei, and 220, the year of his death. Zhang Hua's third-century *Treatise on Curiosities* records the names of sixteen adepts who were summoned. Their arts, prominently including abstention from "grains" and circulation of *qi,* are listed; Zuo Ci, whom we met in Chapter 7, is described as having emerged in good health from a room after a year of ingesting only water. Cao Cao's son Cao Zhi left eyewitness reports of some of these practitioners, some favorable, others debunking; see *Bowu zhi* 5, items 178–184, pp. 61–63; *SW,* 287–293; *TL,* 150–152, 279–286; Goodman, *Ts'ao P'i Transcendent,* 85; Holzman, "Ts'ao Chih and the Immortals." As we saw in Chapter 7, Cao Cao reportedly attempted to kill the adept Zuo Ci, who was shown making a mockery of Cao's and other rulers' attempts to control him.

action, a prevailing narrative meets resistance through a counter-narrative, which in turn may be adopted or resisted."[11] It is hardly surprising, then, that surviving texts preserve conflicting viewpoints on the authenticity of particular adepts, their success, and the meaning of their apparent deaths or departures, each seeking to persuade readers of its veracity. What would be shocking would be if this were not so, if the texts spoke with unanimity on particular adepts. This aspect of the texts no doubt reflects a similar multiplicity of views in oral narrative and in the ongoing extratextual discourse on particular figures.

Perhaps the earliest recorded disagreement about a particular adept's success is found in the *Shi ji* narrative of Li Shaojun. Sima Qian, writing a few decades after the events in question, states flatly that Li died, but he also reports that the emperor maintained Li had simply transformed and departed, a claim echoed in later hagiographies.[12] To this case we might compare a subnarrative in the hagiography of Wang Yuan that tells of Wang's lay host, one Chen Dan, who served Wang for over thirty years. Having assisted at Wang's departure into transcendence, Chen himself died a hundred days later. "Some said that Chen Dan had obtained Wang Yuan's *dao* and so [merely] transformed and departed; but others said that Yuan knew Dan was destined to die soon, so he abandoned him and departed."[13] Two facts characterize both Li's and Chen's cases: rival interpretations of a practitioner's apparent demise begin immediately, and surviving texts mention both opposing sides.

There are many other textual examples of such rival views; most of them, however, do not portray the disagreement but instead participate in it. The survival of contesting story lines in extant texts must reflect to some extent a wider clash of views that took place outside those texts. This topic is worthy of sustained consideration elsewhere, but here it suffices to mention a few examples. Luan Ba, a learned official known for his efforts to promote education and standardize ritual, is recorded in both Fan Ye's (398–446 C.E.) *History of the Later Han (Hou Han shu)* and in Ge Hong's *Traditions of Divine Transcendents* as having abolished the temples of rapacious local deities. Fan's *History,* however, records Luan as having killed himself while under guard[14] while Ge's *Traditions* maintains that Luan ascended into the heavens as a transcendent, a reputation developed in subsequent scriptures, in the Shangqing revelations collected by Tao Hongjing in *Declarations of the Perfected (Zhen'gao),* and in temple inscriptions.[15] The female adept known simply as "Cheng

11. Ochs and Capps, *Living Narrative,* 16.

12. See *Shi ji* 28:1385–1386; and *TL,* 222–228.

13. *TL,* 259–260.

14. He had opposed an imperial tomb project because it would displace many commoners' graves, and he had protested the murder of two officials, which angered the sitting emperor.

15. *Hou Han shu* 57:1841–1842; see further *TL,* 252–255 and 452–453.

Wei's wife" died, according to Huan Tan's 桓譚 *New Discourses* (*Xin lun* 新論), but Ge's *Traditions,* while telling her story in a similar way, states she performed *shijie* and departed into transcendence.[16]

These contested endings dovetail with instances of *shijie,* "escape by means of a corpse substitute," and *bingjie,* "escape by weapon." In a culture where such methods were the stuff of common lore (if not in their details, then certainly in their basic formats), the death of a known practitioner of esoteric arts must have assumed an indeterminacy; it might always have been an apparent death, an instance of *shijie.* No wonder, then, that we find it said by the adept Wang Yuan's lay supporter, Chen Dan, on the occasion of Wang's death: "Chen knew Wang had departed as a transcendent and so did not dare bury his body in the ground."[17] Similarly, when the adept Gu Qiang, whose elaborate recountings we saw in Chapter 5, died of illness at the home of one Huang Zheng, Huang "suspected he had transformed and departed. A little over a year later he tried boring into the coffin to have a look. The corpse was intact there."[18] Clearly Huang had heard stories of adepts performing *shijie;* one imagines him debating whether to risk[19] opening Gu's coffin, finally giving in to temptation, hoping to find it corpse-free.

Persuasions in Stone

Persons deemed to have become *xian* were sometimes eulogized in inscriptions on stone stelae placed in homes, before shrines, and (at least in one known case) in tombs.[20] I here discuss two examples of such stele-inscribed hagiographies,[21] one dating to 169 C.E., and the other almost certainly Eastern Han as well. Both have been rather frequently studied, but I examine them as attempts to persuade audiences.

First, however, let us consider some general rhetorical aspects of stele inscriptions in this period.[22] It was essential to how they conveyed meanings that they

---

16. See *TL,* 139–141.

17. Ibid., 260.

18. *NP* 20:348. I have no information on Huang Zheng.

19. Contact with death and the dead was normally considered ritually polluting, so opening a coffin was not something that would have been undertaken lightly.

20. It is possible that some were also placed *in front of* tombs that were claimed to be empty. The one known case of entombment of such a stele is discussed below.

21. A third, not discussed here but mentioned in Chapter 6, was dedicated to Wangzi Qiao; see Holzman, *Immortals, Festivals, and Poetry in Medieval China;* and Raz, "Creation of Tradition," 96–108.

22. Helpful overviews include Ebrey, "Later Han Stone Inscriptions"; Zhao, "Stone Inscriptions of the Wei-Jin Nanbeichao Period"; Ch'en, "Inscribed Stelae during the Wei, Chin, and Nan-ch'ao"; and Wong, *Chinese Steles,* 1–41. I learned of Miranda Brown, *The Politics of Mourning in Early China,* only after I had completed work on the manuscript for this book.

were erected at particular places. Whatever else they did, they claimed that the figures and events they recounted should be seen as connected to the place where they stood. This connection was not inevitable or given, if only for the reason that it risked being forgotten by successive generations; the words on the stone served to keep the connection green, transforming an otherwise generic place into the site of a specific memory. As a consequence, these stone inscriptions, like transmitted texts, were quintessentially works of collective, public memory, functioning within a memorial culture to preserve—and persuasively shape in particular directions— the memory of significant past persons and events. This was necessary—the point is obvious, but worth remembering—because the persons and events were otherwise no longer present or accessible. The inscription gave a local habitation and a name to phenomena otherwise at risk of being reduced to airy nothings. In addition, the inscribed words were often recited aloud by visitors. Remembrance was vocalized and performed on the spot, the words on the stone serving as prompts.[23] The stones did not just refer to past events: they made a bid to orchestrate the lived, vocalized performance of memory of those events on the site and to evoke other sympathetic responses from visitors.[24]

Every narrative, like every religious virtuoso known to history, has its *sponsors:* people with an interest in putting the story before others, making its messages known, supporting the points made by the story, spurring others to remember and themselves talk about a spiritual achiever or significant past events. One of the most important aspects of stelae is that, unlike most transmitted narratives, they often record the names (and sometimes the titles and residences) of the individuals who sponsored their making. Someone had to pay for the stone and the skilled carving (as well, in some cases, as the elegant words of the eulogy carved there); paying for these things was a sign of proper respect, which was in turn a sign of virtue and hence a reputation-enhancer in its own right; and so sponsors wanted it known that they had contributed to the memory site upon which the public gazed. Like the mention of the names of particular aristocratic patrons of transcendence-seekers in transmitted hagiographies, these carved listings of donors' names are one of the few direct testimonies we have concerning who was directly and concretely involved in sponsoring the memories and reputations of individuals.

So much for sponsors; what about the audience? The primary audience of stele inscriptions was anyone, local resident or pilgrim from afar, who stood at the spot, looked upon the stone, and perhaps recited its words. But the audience potentially

---

23. For this and the previous point I draw in particular on Brashier, "Text and Ritual in Early Chinese Stelae."

24. We have records from the period of literati standing before stelae and weeping; for an example, see Tian, *Tao Yuanming and Manuscript Culture,* 54.

extended far beyond the immediate site. Inscriptions were *locally installed* but publicly available declarations that could be copied, recorded, or otherwise remembered and reproduced (perhaps with alterations) *translocally* by far-flung parties with widely varying interests. These could range from admirers of virtuosi
to collectors of the lore of a locality to collectors of antiquities or connoisseurs
of epigraphy.[25] Most of what we know about early medieval inscriptions comes
from such translocal collectors and their transmitted texts; relatively few actual
stones survive, but large numbers of records of inscriptions have come down to
us.[26] Li Daoyuan's 酈道元 (d. 527) important topography, *Annotated Classic on
Waterways* (*Shuijing zhu* 水經注), preserves explicit quotations of dozens of stelae
observed at specific locations, but many other early medieval texts drew silently
on inscriptions for source material. This has been particularly well documented
for early medieval Buddhist hagiographies;[27] it was true for many other texts,
particularly narrative compilations, as well. Our documentation of the *reception* of
stele inscriptions, although destined to remain woefully incomplete, consists largely
of the various transmitted translocal texts that explicitly recorded or silently quoted
or paraphrased them. This reception, of course, was a function of the interests
not of the inscriptions' sponsors but of their readers. In a very rough way we
might say that the more often and widely a particular inscription was taken up,
quoted, and used or responded to in various translocal texts, the more successful
it was in propagating its message to audiences. An inscription only recently
unearthed, whose specific content of persons and events is totally unknown in
the received record, is one that, absent further evidence, we must conclude did
not succeed as well in spreading awareness of its topic beyond its immediate local
environment.[28]

What were the persuasive aims and interests of inscriptions? These vary by
case, but in general we can say that one aim of erecting a stele at a particular place
was to enhance the prestige of that place while promoting its sponsors' reputations.
A stele memorializing a person sought to associate that person with the place in
question. It also associated the memory of its departed subject with the memory
of those sponsoring the inscription: the sponsors became part of the story and
inserted themselves by name into what was remembered at the site. Naturally the

---

25. For a study of writings about particular localities in this period, see Chittick, "The
Development of Local Writing in Early Medieval China."

26. Ebrey, "Later Han Stone Inscriptions," 326–327, makes the point with particular clarity.
By the Song, the making of *rubbings* of old stelae had come into vogue, but at this writing I am
uncertain how far back this practice has been documented.

27. See Shinohara, "Two Sources of Chinese Buddhist Hagiographies."

28. Of course, this argument from silence only goes so far, since a great many transmitted
texts have been lost over the centuries.

view advanced in the inscription of the persons or events in question depended quite directly on the viewpoints and interests of the stele's sponsors. But counternarratives, oral or written, could always be sponsored by others.

Let us now turn to two stele inscriptions concerning individuals claimed to be transcendents. The first was found in a tomb near Luoyang in 1991 and has drawn considerable scholarly attention. It is a relatively small stele (98 cm, or slightly over three feet tall) and was erected in 169 C.E. Near its rounded crown, the place of honor, are carved the names of the two Eastern Han emperors with whom the subject of the stele was claimed to have interacted.[29] I intersperse the following translation with running comments.[30]

> Stele of Lord Fei 肥君 of Anle in eastern Liang district, Henan. Officer in Waiting in the Lateral Quarters [of the palace] under the Han, the Lord's personal name was Zhi 致, his style Changhua 萇華. He was a native of Liang district. As a youth he embodied the freedom of naturalness; as an adult he displayed conduct that distinguished him from the profane.[31] He often dwelled in seclusion, nurturing his resolve. The Lord habitually dwelt atop a jujube tree, not descending for three years. [Thus] he roamed free and easy with the Dao and by his conduct established his reputation. Word of him spread everywhere within the seas. Crowds of gentlemen came to look up at him, gathering like clouds.

From the opening lines we learn that Fei Zhi at some point held (or at least was here claimed to have held) a sinecurial palace appointment. We also see a pattern familiar from earlier chapters: an adept goes into reclusion (in this case vertically, by dwelling atop a tree[32]) but, precisely because of that gesture, he draws large crowds who clamor for access to him. Word spreads as people talk about this strange, impressive figure.

---

29. These are Emperors Zhang (r. 75–88 C.E.) and He (r. 88–106 C.E.).

30. I have translated following the photo reproductions and transcriptions of the text in Little and Eichman, *Taoism and the Arts of China,* 150–151; Schipper, "Une stèle taoïste des Han orientaux récemment découverte," 246–247; and Wang, "Dong Han daojiao diyi keshi Fei Zhi bei yanjiu," 15–16. I have greatly benefited from consulting the translations in Schipper, "Une stèle taoïste des Han orientaux récemment découverte," 240–242; and Raz, "Creation of Tradition," 54–57.

31. My thanks to Terry Kleeman for his assistance with my understanding of this and other passages in the inscription.

32. Jujubes are commonly mentioned as a preferred item in transcendents' cuisine. Dwelling atop trees or columns is a feat attributed to ascetics in many cultures and times; the adept Chaofu is claimed in the *Liexian zhuan* to have done so.

Now at this time a red *qi* accumulated and filled the skies. From the ministers and directors down to the hundred officials there were none who could dispel it. When the ruler heard that in Liang there was a man of the Dao atop a jujube tree, he sent an envoy to invite the Lord with due ceremony. The Lord, out of loyalty, hastened in[33] to protect the ruler and produced a timely calculation that dispelled the calamitous anomaly. He was honored with the post of Officer in Waiting of the Lateral Quarters and an emolument of a million in coin, but the Lord declined [the position] and did not accept [the cash].

The imperial invitation is delivered respectfully; this, then, will begin as a story of an adept's loyalty to an emperor (the term mentioned is *zhong* 忠, a vassal's faithful obedience to his lord) rather than a lesson in the adept's autonomy. But, after the adept dispels the miasma[34] by means of some divinatory technique, he refuses the imperial rewards of cash and office, thus reaffirming his autonomy after all: he will not be drawn into the usual network of reciprocal obligation. On the other hand, the inscription opens by claiming that he did at some point serve in the palace. The relative chronology of it all is quite vague, perhaps deliberately so.

In the middle of the eleventh month, the ruler longed for fresh mallow. The Lord thereupon entered his chamber and after a little while emerged holding two bundles of mallow. The ruler asked the Lord, "Where did you get these?" The response was, "I procured them from the governor of Shu commandery." A courier was sent to make inquiries at the commandery, and the commandery reported back, "At dawn on the fifteenth of the eleventh month, a red-carriaged envoy arrived and plucked two sprigs of fresh mallow." Thus was confirmed the Lord's spiritual power.[35] He penetrated the mysterious and wondrous, now emerging from the abyss, now entering the dark realms, his transformations hard to recognize! He traveled several myriad *li* in less than the space of a single day; he wandered out to the eight extremities, resting in transcendents' courts.

Fei's long-distance mastery exactly resembles that attributed to many adepts (including Jie Xiang and Zuo Ci) in transmitted hagiographies. These lines estab-

---

33. The expression *xiangran lai* 翔然來 here could be understood literally—"he flew in"—since the capacity for flight was often attributed to transcendents.

34. Schipper ("Une stele taoïste des Han récemment découverte," 242) suggests it is not baleful *qi* but an auspicious celestial anomaly signaling Fei's own active presence in the world, but the officials' attempts to "dissolve" it and its characterization as a "calamitous anomaly" (*zaibian* 災變) make this seem very unlikely.

35. His *shenming* 神明, a term of multiple connotations, sometimes literally signifies the brightness of a practitioner's indwelling spirits, but sometimes not, and is very difficult to render into intelligible English.

lish Fei's ability to roam laterally throughout the cosmos, a quintessential attribute of transcendents. He procures the mallow from within his "chamber," making clear that the mechanism of retrieval was a meditative journey of the spirit (whether he himself made the spirit-journey or sent an envoy). This feat also, we are told, "confirmed" (yan 驗) Fei's spiritual powers—a loaded word implying initial doubt of his ability successfully reversed by an incontrovertible demonstration, a convincing and tangible reality effect carried out before an audience. Just as the feat convinced the audience described in the text, the story-makers hope that the feat will now convince skeptical readers of the stele.

> The Lord took Zhang Wu 張吳 of Wei commandery, Yanzi 晏子 of Qi, and Huang Yuan 黃淵 of Haishang as his teachers, and was befriended by Master Redpine 赤松子. While still living he was hailed as a perfected person, and in his age he had no peer.

Here is established a lineage for Fei—whether actual or fictitious we will never know. Of the four figures mentioned, only Redpine, here marked as a friend rather than a teacher proper, is clearly known from other sources.[36] The insertion of a figure as widely heralded as Redpine is a bid to impress viewers of the stele: if they knew anything at all about xian, Redpine was a xian they would have heard of. Here as elsewhere in the text we see the sort of grandiosity expected in such a document.[37] Taking it at face value, we would assume its subject was widely known throughout the empire and ubiquitously mentioned in transmitted texts of many kinds.

> The meritorious officer and Grandee of the Ninth Order, Xu You 許幼, a native of Dongxiang in Luoyang, served Lord Fei with the rites due a transcendent master (xianshi 仙師) and with warmest reverence invited him to reside in his home. By following the Lord, You became able to surpass the world[38] and so departed.

Here is a clear instance of the pattern of lay patronage discussed in Chapter 6. In this case the lay patron becomes a disciple and apparently transcends—or at least

---

36. Scholars have surmised that two of the other names mentioned, Yanzi and Huang Yuan, are perhaps variants of figures known from received literature, but these identifications must remain speculative.

37. Writers of stele texts were quite aware that they were exaggerating their subjects' virtues and expressed shame at doing so; see Brashier, "Text and Ritual in Early Chinese Stelae," 255–256.

38. Dushi 度世, perhaps meaning to surpass one's own generation in age, implies at least longevity if not outright transcendence; here, at least, its meaning is a bit vague, perhaps deliberately so.

attains great longevity—in his own right. The patron is remembered alongside the adept by being named in the adept's story. A place is thus reserved for him in the body of collective memory surrounding Fei.

> I, [Xu] You's son Jian 建, styled Xiaochang 孝萇,[39] out of a compassionate heart and filial nature, long constantly for [these] numinous beings.[40] In the second year of the Establishing Peace era [*jianning* 建寧 2, that is, 169 C.E.], when Jupiter was in the *jiyou* position, on day *bingwu,* the fifteenth of the fifth month,[41] I, Xiaochang, erected for the Lord a provisional altar.[42] Morning and evening, my entire family, diligently and without daring to let up, reverently approach Lord Fei with offerings appropriate to the season.[43] The divine transcendent [then] retreats into silence, solemn as a submerged dragon.[44] Though we wish to pay obeisance to him and see him, there is no route by which to reach him. I respectfully erect this stone to make known our profound veneration and to set forth what is recounted above to instruct and exhort the young.[45] The lyrics[46] say:

---

39. Literally "filial to Chang"; in so naming his son, Xu You expressed his devotion to Lord Fei.

40. That is, on Lord Fei and Xu You, both of whom are now claimed to be transcendents. The line may also, less probably in my opinion, be understood as meaning "long constantly for spirits" in general.

41. The date designation is actually a bit more complicated than I have indicated and invokes the *jianchu* ("establishing/removing") hemerological system; see Raz, "Creation of Tradition," 56 n.44; and for a summary explanation of the system, see Kalinowski, ed., *Divination et société dans la Chine médiévale,* 103–104.

42. *Bianzuo* 便坐. *Zuo* commonly designates an altar space, metaphorically configured as a place or seat at a banquet table, where the gods temporarily come to rest to partake of their offerings. The sense of *bian* here is that the stele is a provisional or (better) supplemental "seat" as contrasted to a more permanent shrine altar located elsewhere. See Schipper, "Une stèle taoïste des Han récemment découverte," 241 n.7.

43. This reference to the four seasons may mean not that the foods offered are seasonal but that the family makes offerings continually.

44. This passage may mean one of two things: either it describes strange sensory phenomena repeatedly observed (by family members or by an attending spirit medium) at the moment the offerings are completed, suggesting the numinosity of the recipient (thus Schipper, "Une stèle taoïste des Han récemment découverte," 241 n.9), or it describes Fei's now-retired state, no longer actively present in the world (thus Raz, "Creation of Tradition," 56). I lean toward the former interpretation. Either way, the ensuing sentence makes clear that some sort of withdrawal into inaccessibility is implied.

45. Perhaps the children of Xu Xiaochang's own family.

46. The *ci* 辭 or "lyrics" portion of a stele inscription (also known as the "hymn" [*song* 頌]) was a section in tetrasyllabic verse, often (as here) set off verbally from the prose text with

What splendor! What felicity!
The divine lord of former times: how brilliant!
Of vast renown,
He has ascended and from afar gazes upon the cosmic filaments.[47]
We sons and grandsons can merely stand here below
Looking up respectfully to you who are without hindrances.
We therefore have carved this stone
To communicate the true situation.[48]
We express the wish that you might at all times
Grant us your blessings and auspicious fortune.

Almost all stelae say something about the circumstances and sponsorship of their own making, just as many Chinese scriptures tell the stories of their own origins. This one is no exception. The sponsoring donor and implied author (or at least approver of the contents) of the inscription is named, and we learn that he, Xu Jian, is the son of Fei's patron and follower, Xu You. The whole family is hitching itself in this public pronouncement to Fei's reputation, a reputation the stone seeks to promulgate and enhance. The son as sponsor is also proclaiming his own devotion and filiality; he pronounces himself compassionate and filial, diligent and reverent, generous and pious, and has performatively demonstrated these commendable qualities by his erection of the stele we now read. The text speaks of regular familial offerings to Lord Fei (no one outside the Xu family is mentioned as participating in these), offerings that are claimed to evoke a response from their intended recipient, even if he remains obscure and largely inaccessible. The last lines of the verse lyrics make explicit the devoted family's request for blessings in return for their continued devotion to the absent-yet-present transcendent. The stele base holds three basins clearly intended to hold offering foods or lamp oil. The stele, in a neatly compact

some such phrase as "the lyrics say." According to some modern scholars, this verse portion was "the inscription's focal point, not . . . its appendage" (Brashier, "Text and Ritual in Early Chinese Stelae," 263), and it was the verses in particular that were often memorized and recited by visitors to the stele site.

47. He looks upon the "strands" or "filaments" (ji 紀) of the sky, shorthand here for certain particular constellations understood as binding the universe together; see Schafer, *Pacing the Void*, 241–242.

48. The line's meaning is rather unclear, and the situation is not helped by the fact that a graph is missing. The sense may be that the inscribers hope thereby to reach (da 達) the Lord's "feelings and understanding" (qing li 情理) so as to provoke the response described in the next line. But at this point in many inscription verses we find a statement to the effect that the stele has been erected to set forth the subject's story so that others may know of his virtue. So the line may simply be a flowery way of saying that.

fashion, serves as both inscription text and altar.[49] It is self-designated as a "provisional altar," perhaps implying that it was the conveniently accessible counterpart of a main shrine altar located elsewhere. The stone serves, as Schipper remarks, not simply as an object of memory but also as the locus of the ongoing spiritual presence (if only a periodic presence evoked by offerings) of the transcendent; it is his altar and the seat of his spirit[50]—although I would add that a stele also presumes its subject's absence: no stele would be necessary if Fei Zhi were still active in the household as he had once been. It seems likely that this altar-inscription was first erected inside the domestic compound of the Xu family and was then moved into Xu Jian's tomb upon his death, perhaps so that he could continue his devotions in the other world[51] or, more likely, as a kind of accountability report addressed by Xu Jian to his father and other ancestors in the unseen world.[52]

> The Regional Transcendent, Great Master of Five,[53] saw the barrens of the Queen Mother of the West and received [from her] a *dao* of transcendence. The disciples following the Great Master of Five were five: Tian Yu 田傴, Quan [lacuna] Zhong 全 . . . 中, Songzhi Jigong 宋直忌公, Bi Xianfeng 畢先風, and Master Xu 許先生.[54] All consumed stony fat and departed as transcendents.

The inscription closes by returning to matters of lineage. If, as seems most likely, the mysteriously titled Great Master of Five is to be understood as Fei Zhi, then we are being informed that his techniques of transcendence were directly revealed

---

49. Brashier ("Text and Ritual in Early Chinese Stelae," 269–274) argues that such was the case generally with stelae in the Eastern Han; they commonly included a hole in the front surface a certain distance down from the top—sometimes obliterating inscriptional text material—from which food offerings were suspended for the subject to whom the stele was dedicated. Stelae were not just inert texts but also integral focal points in ritual programs.

50. Schipper, "Une stele taoïste des Han récemment découverte," 239.

51. As suggested by Raz, "Creation of Tradition," 77.

52. On this function of commemorative inscriptions placed in tombs, see Schottenhammer, "Einige Überlegungen zur Entstehung von Grabinschriften." I thank Lothar von Falkenhausen for this reference

53. The wording now becomes quite ambiguous, and scholars have offered numerous hypotheses as to the identity of this 土仙者大伍公. The only thing that seems fairly certain is that this compound title must refer either to Fei Zhi or to Xu You. I believe it is Lord Fei's title in the bureaucratic hierarchy of *xian,* only now mentioned since it was bestowed on him after his ascension and would not have been used during his own lifetime (highlights of which were recounted in the body of the inscription above).

54. If we understand the Great Master of Five to be Fei Zhi, then this Master Xu must be Xu You; if the Great Master is understood as Xu You, then this Master Xu is probably Xu Jian himself. The former possibility seems to me more likely.

to him by the Queen Mother of the West in her divine precincts; whatever human teachers he may have had, he here is claimed to have enjoyed divine revelation as well. His lineage is then sketched downward in generational time from himself to five disciples, four of them otherwise unknown and one of whom is a member of the Xu family—almost certainly Xu You. All five are claimed to have become *xian* by ingesting "stony fat," the name for a class of mineral compounds mentioned in transmitted hagiographies and texts on methods.[55] We read nothing else of their exploits. Given the presence in the tomb of the skeletal remains of more than one individual, it has been speculated that the five disciples named here are the persons entombed with the inscription. But this is unknowable.

Other than the explicit internal mention by name of its sponsor, everything about the text resembles transmitted hagiographies: the organization of the narrative of the adept's exploits; the nature of those exploits (ascetic isolation, appearance at court, long-distance mastery, performance of divination on behalf of clients, refusal of ordinary economic relations); the depicted response of other people (crowds gathering, people talking, rulers sending invitations from afar, lay patronage); the construction of lineages and ascription of a following of disciples to the master. There is nothing idiosyncratic about the contents of the Fei Zhi inscription. Its 169 C.E. makers were clearly well informed of the sorts of stories told of successful adepts and the sorts of feats they were expected to perform. The only unusual—and, to us, extremely valuable—feature of the inscription is that it bears direct testimony to the linkage between an adept, his story, and the *local sponsors* of both adept and story, in this case a particular family named Xu that stood to gain status the more widely its sponsored transcendent and ancestor were recognized as *xian*. We can clearly see that in this instance it was this family that established a cult for a departed transcendent, a cult it sustained through regular offerings and through this stone proclamation, and that the transcendent in question was one to whom they claimed strong personal connections, a recent ancestor having sponsored the adept's practice and eventually followed in his footsteps to transcend in his own right.

As far as is presently known, however, the cult of Fei Zhi never spread beyond the Xu family, despite the stele's claims of Fei's widespread renown. Of the many individuals mentioned in the inscription, the only ones clearly known in received literature are two Eastern Han emperors and the ancient, legendary adept Redpine. What this perhaps suggests is a failed attempt at hagiographic persuasion. The story

---

55. For examples, see Raz, "Creation of Tradition," 74–77. Two good examples of its more luxuriant narrative possibilities may be seen in the *Traditions* hagiography of Wang Lie (*TL,* 338–341) and in several stories in which a protagonist happens upon a subterranean world in which he survives by ingesting mud-like mineral exudations, for example, *Youming lu* 63, cited in *Fayuan zhulin* 31:520c; *TPYL* 803.8a; and LX 213–214.

of Fei and Xu, admirably adapted though it was to contemporary narrative conventions and expectations surrounding the role of transcendent, seems never to have been taken up in any translocal compilation to reach wider audiences. It is possible, of course, that several or even many transmitted texts once discussed Fei and Xu, and that they have simply failed to survive down to modern times. What appears more likely is that Fei's story was never widely disseminated. After Fei's departure his story appears never to have won a wider circle of sponsors than the Xu family itself. Perhaps if his stele had been left above ground at a roadside shrine, rather than (apparently) being interred with its sponsor, it would have helped win more recognition for its subjects, a wider reputation that would have led to mentions in conversations, letters, perhaps regional histories and travel narratives, and eventual inclusion in one or more hagiographic compilations. Or perhaps the Xu family never wished to have his story spread about, though this seems very unlikely. As things stand, only since 1992 has the world become reacquainted with Lord Fei, and that in ways his story's sponsors could never have anticipated.

The second inscription is dedicated to the transcendent Tang Gongfang 唐公房.[56] This inscription, unlike Lord Fei's, has been known for many centuries and copied and discussed by Chinese scholars in transmitted texts at least since the Song (the famous Ouyang Xiu saw the stone in 1064 C.E.). It is certainly of Eastern Han date, but a more precise dating is unfortunately not yet possible.[57]

> The Lord's name was Gongfang, of Chenggu.[58] He was Thearch Yao's {descendant. Thearch Yao was sincere, reverent, able yet humble; the lord truly succeeded [10 graphs]} him. Hence he could raise up his household {achieve crossing-over, lift his home and as a transcendent [5 graphs]} depart. He soared up to the luminous brilliances, driving and riding yin and yang, flying into the limpid [heavens] and treading floating [clouds]. His allotted longevity was boundless. Although revered by kings and lords, treasured within the four seas, he would {not be moved even by a single [5 graphs]} hair. The nature of heaven and earth is what he most cherished.

---

56. Due to later avoidance of an imperial name, the *fang* of his given name is alternately written 昉. We will see other variations in his name across source texts; this is common.

57. My translation is based on the texts as reproduced in Wang Chang, comp., *Jinshi cuibian* 19:1b–2b and Chen Yuan, *Daojia jinshi lue,* 5–7. I have benefited from Raz, "Creation of Tradition," 78–96. Curly brackets { } enclose material that one or more modern scholars has suggested is missing in the lacunae. When the lacuna is longer than one graph, I supply the number of missing graphs in square brackets.

58. In the Hanzhong area. The adept in this case was thus a native of the same region in which he is now remembered and venerated.

The opening, like many biographical and hagiographical texts, establishes some of the subject's general characteristics. Among those highlighted in this case are Tang's ability to fly and ascend and his unusual longevity.

> Ancient tradition says that in the second year of Wang Mang's regency [7–8 C.E.], when the Lord was serving as commandery officer, {he was once at leisure with colleagues [4 graphs]} eating melons in the garden when there was a Perfected Person[59] nearby. None of [Tang's] companions recognized him; only the Lord presented him with fine melons and then followed him and treated him with deference and decorum.

We see here the theme of recognition: only one with the inherent makings of a transcendent can correctly discern, through visual inspection, the hidden quality of a nearby figure. The disciple-to-be follows through with appropriate deference toward this mysterious master, rather than approaching him arrogantly, thus further demonstrating his worthiness to be taught. It is also of note that Tang is here said to have been serving as a commandery officer at the time, and that a specific year is supplied for his initial meeting with his teacher.

> The Perfected Person was pleased, and consequently arranged a meeting with {the Lord} at the top of the mountain at the Xi valley entrance. There he presented the Lord with a divine medicine, saying, "After ingesting it you can travel at will[60] over thousands of miles and you will understand the speech of birds and beasts."

Two key components of any adept's reputation are the sort of method he follows to attain transcendence, and the abilities (other than long life) that accrue. In Tang's case, the vehicle of *xian*-hood is a "divine medicine" (*shenyao* 神藥)—some unspecified type of herbal or alchemical compound—and the two chief abilities conferred by this compound (and, no doubt, by its accompanying program of austerities) are flight (enabling rapid travel over long distances) and the ability to understand animals' calls. All of these are standard in the transcendent's repertoire.

> At that time the prefectural capital was at Xicheng, over seven hundred *li* from [the Lord's] home. Traveling back and forth between official audiences, within

---

59. As in the Fei Zhi inscription above, this term, *zhenren* 真人, drawn from the *Zhuangzi* (where it has quite a different meaning), denotes an accomplished transcendent.

60. Literally "move your consciousness over myriad *li*" 移意萬里, but the sense, as seen immediately below, is that Tang becomes able to travel long distances very rapidly—an ability commonly attributed to transcendents and adepts.

the blink of an eye he would arrive. All the people in the commandery were surprised by this and reported it to the prefect, who granted him an official appointment.[61]

The wondrousness of Tang's long-distance mastery draws attention. Word travels to an official, who responds by granting the adept an appointment. These are again common tropes in received hagiographies.

> [Once] a rat gnawed through the [prefect's] chariot roof. The Lord drew a jail on the ground, summoned the rat [into it] and killed it. Its belly was examined and found to contain the chariot roof. The prefect {set out} a banquet, wishing to follow the Lord and study the Dao. Gongfang did not immediately agree. The prefect angrily ordered his guards to arrest Gongfang's wife.

The plot grows more complex and suspenseful. Above it appeared that Tang and the prefect enjoyed a harmonious relationship, but now we see the trope—familiar from earlier chapters—of tension caused by an adept's refusal to transmit his esoteric methods to a pushy official. Here the official goes so far as to arrest Tang's wife, a move not only impudent but also risky. How will Tang respond?

> Gongfang quickly returned to the valley entrance and called on his master to tell him of the imminent danger. His master returned with him in order to give Gongfang and his wife an elixir to drink, saying, "You may depart." The wife loved her household and could not bear to leave it. Then the master said, "Is it that you wish your entire household to depart with you?" The wife said, "That is my wish." So they daubed the elixir on the house posts and made the live-stock and domestic animals drink it. In a moment a great wind and dark clouds appeared, gathering up Gongfang, his wife, their house and their domestic animals, all of them flying upwards and departing together.

In this case, then, the adept escapes the overweening official by means of swallowing an elixir that immediately wafts him upward. Here is narrated the crowning feat that Tang's local sponsors are proudest of.

> In the past, Qiao 喬, Song 松, Cui 崔, and Bo 白 all attained the Dao alone, but Gongfang ascended and crossed over with his entire household. Great indeed! The tradition says, "Where a worthy dwells, munificence flows for a hundred

---

61. As pointed out by Raz ("Creation of Tradition," 81 n.108), various transcriptions of the text give varying graphs here, and the more common variant, *yuli* 御吏, is problematic since *li* were functionaries appointed by local or regional magistrates, not by the court. In any case the overall sense is clear enough.

generations." He has accordingly caused Xi village to be without mosquitoes in spring and summer, free of frost in the winter. Pestilence and poisonous vermin do not linger, noxious insects are repelled, and the hundred grains can be harvested. Nowhere under heaven is there such efficacious virtue and blessing. The multitudes of transcendents are on a par with the Dao; their virtue irrigates our native soil. Those who recognize his virtue are few, and through the generations none have recorded it.

The narrative's sponsors boast of the fact that Tang did not ascend alone, nor did he merely take his wife or even, as had Liu An, his domestic animals. Tang took all these, and he also took his family's *house* into the heavens—a secondary differentiation that sets him apart from the mass of *xian* and renders him superior to four particular former transcendents of note: Wangzi Qiao, Redpine, Cui Wenzi 崔文子, and (probably) Master Whitestone 白石先生, three of whom are the subjects of received *Liexian zhuan* hagiographies and one, Whitestone, of a *Shenxian zhuan* entry.[62] Each of these former *xian* is evoked only very elliptically with one character each, a testament to how easily the writer could presume his readers would recognize the figures intended. Here it is Tang himself to whom the glory of the achievement is directed, but another storyteller with a different agenda might use this detail as an occasion to tout the benefits of the particular "divine medicine" bestowed by Tang's teacher.

Also stressed in this passage is Tang's ongoing service to the community far beyond the moment of his ascension. He still exerts a palpable if unseen influence in the region, ensuring freedom from harmful insects and vermin and from damaging weather and thus assisting the local population in earning its livelihood.

Up to this point, the inscription, like the one devoted to Fei Zhi, entirely resembles received hagiographies in its narrative organization, its religious content, and its thematic emphases. Only when the text next turns self-referentially to the circumstances of its making and to its sponsors does it diverge generically from transmitted hagiography.

I, Guo Zhi 郭芝 of Nanyang, named Gongzai, Grand Administrator of Hanzhong,[63] have cultivated my government like the north star, managing it in the

---

62. The name "Bai/Bo" in the inscription may also refer to Wei Boyang (as assumed by Schipper, "Le culte de l'immortel Tang Gongfang," 70), but the date of origin of that name is a matter of debate.

63. In modern Nanzheng district, Shaanxi Province. Hanzhong was connected with central Shu (modern Sichuan) by a famously winding north-south route through the mountains; together, the two areas were the original homeland of the Celestial Master community, and Tang's cult in the region was surely connected to this community.

manner of Zhou and Shao. Joyous at the excellence of Lord Tang's spiritual efficacy, I realized that those eminent in the Dao are renowned, and those whose virtue is distinguished are revered in temples. In order to set forth auspicious instruction, I personally offered the monies, as a leader of the group of donors, to renovate and enlarge this temple [in order to] {gather} harmony and seek blessings and spread them among the people. We inscribed this stone with glowing verses to glorify the Lord's numinous fame. The lyrics say:

> {To magnificent Lord Tang
> Whose glory reaches that of Xuanhuang roaming free in the Lacquer Garden
> Your *dao* matches that of Zhuang of Meng.}
> Consequently enjoying the divine medicine,
> You ascended floating to the clouds
> Flitting about on wings. . . .[64]

As we saw in the case of Fei, the sponsors of the stone text are named in the inscription so that they will be remembered alongside the transcendent regional patron they commemorate. As the stone "glorifies the Lord's numinous fame" (*yang jun lingyu* 揚君靈譽), it also lists the names of local worthies who, as a group, have appropriately recognized that fame and recorded its source for posterity. It announces its intention as "setting forth auspicious instruction" (*fa jiajiao* 發嘉教): the target audience, we are told, is not sufficiently aware of the Lord's virtue, and the stone seeks to remedy that.

Guo Zhi, as the "leader" (*changshuai* 倡率) of the "group of donors" (*qunyi* 群義) who contributed to the temple refurbishment and to the stele marking the occasion, enjoys pride of place on the front of the stele. But fifteen other principal donors are named on the stele's reverse side. All were officials hailing from the region where Tang had been active earlier. Nine bear the surname Zhu 祝 and were probably related by kinship. The fourth in the list, Zhu Gui 龜, is mentioned in the regional treatise *Huayangguo zhi* 華陽國志 as having been an Eastern Han appointee, and this fact, along with epigraphical analysis, is our best evidence for dating the stele to that period.[65] These are the men of means who have found it to be in their interest and that of their community to contribute funds toward the public recognition of transcendent Tang Gongfang's past achievement and his ongoing divine aid to the region. They have attached their reputations to his and have sought a place alongside him in the collective memory. They have furthermore made a

---

64. The inscription breaks off here.

65. See *Huayangguo zhi* 10C:807; and de Crespigny, *A Biographical Dictionary of Later Han to the Three Kingdoms,* 1159–1160. After having been born in Hanzhong and then studied in the capital, Zhu Gui returned to his native region and was active there from the 190s on, after having been appointed by Liu Yan (on whom see de Crespigny, ibid., 572–573).

bid to have their local *xian* acknowledged and taken up in translocal contexts by travelers, pilgrims, and text compilers.

In all of these aims they can be said to have succeeded. Unlike Fei Zhi, Tang Gongfang was rather widely mentioned in early medieval texts of several genres, attesting to the wider reputation he had won.[66] Each mention in these texts, however, was necessarily governed by its author's interests. "Tang Gongfang" comes to be a site at which various authors tell a story or relate a curious local phenomenon, their tellings framed by their respective agendas.

In the earliest of such mentions of which I am aware, Zhang Hua (d. 300 C.E.) in his *Treatise on Curiosities (Bowu zhi)* includes the following entry:

> When Tang Fang ascended to become a transcendent, his chickens and dogs went with him. There was only a rat that he didn't take with him. Out of regret, the rat empties its guts three times a month. It's called Tang's Rat.[67]

This passage occurs in the context of a still-burgeoning and once even more vast compendium of strange things from across the known world—places, peoples, customs, flora, fauna, land formations, names—a work so large and so forbiddingly full of oddities that Jin Emperor Wu reportedly asked Zhang to trim it down to a mere fraction of its original size and cut most of the disturbing anomalies.[68] What interested Zhang was not Tang's story per se but the unusual species of rat that his story was invoked to explain. But the rat's strange anatomy is inseparable from the story of Tang's ascension, since the rat's resentment at being left behind is the explanation for its anatomy.[69] Furthermore, if one's starting point was the rat, Tang's story could not be told without mentioning its most distinctive feature, the ascent of his whole household, since the rat's resentment would otherwise have no basis. As we survey the available record of Tang Gongfang's translocal reception, it becomes unclear whether Tang's story traveled widely because of interest in the rat, or whether the rat was widely talked about because it was hitched to Tang's story. But it is clear that interest in the rat helped spread and preserve the story of Tang's signature exploit. The rat's story became a vector by which Tang's story was picked up more often in translocal texts than it otherwise might have been. The rat element of the story has also undergone a strange transformation between the inscription and the *Treatise on Curiosities:*

---

66. This is not to imply, of course, that the Eastern Han stele was necessarily the sole or even the primary agent in spreading Tang's story, only that it was one known agent (with known sponsors) in a process that must remain mostly invisible to us.

67. In *Bowuzhi jiaozheng,* 125 (fragment 80), quoted in *YWLJ* 95:1659. The passage does not occur in the received versions of the text.

68. See *SW,* 127–128.

69. In traditional medical theory, resentment was associated with the gall bladder, a fact which probably bears some relation to the rat's anatomy and story.

the inscription mentions no bizarre anatomy and does not locate the rat at Tang's household. It does, however, show Tang cutting open its belly to recover the canopy top. Even in the inscription, then, the rat figures in the story because of its abdomen.

The next extant trace of Tang Gongfang's translocal reception occurs in the hagiography of Li Babai 李八百 (Li Eight Hundred) attributed to *Traditions of Divine Transcendents.*

> Li Babai was a native of Shu. No one knew his given name. Successive generations had seen him, and people of the day calculated his age to be 800, hence his sobriquet. Sometimes he secluded himself in the mountains, and sometimes he appeared in the markets.
>
> He knew that Tang Gongfang of Hanzhong had determination [to study the Way] but had not found an enlightened teacher. Li wished to teach Tang and transmit texts to him, so he first went to test him. He pretended to be a hired servant, and Tang Gongfang did not realize [who he really was]. Li hustled about his work and was diligent, quite different from other hired personnel; Tang was fond of him and wondered at him. Li then pretended to fall ill and to be near death.

After thus deploying the common tropes, first of recognition (in this case a master's recognition of the latent promise of a potential disciple), then of testing, the hagiography gives a vivid account of these tests, an account quoted in Chapter 4: Li's body develops festering sores; a doctor cannot cure him; Li requests first Tang's household maidservants, then Tang himself, and then his wife to lick the sores for him, followed by the crowning request of an enormous quantity of fine wine to bathe in—all of this simply to test Tang's character. The narrative resumes:

> Li then declared to Tang, "I am a transcendent. You possess determination, so I have tested you by these means, and you have truly proven worthy to be taught. I will now transmit to you instructions for transcending the world." He then had Tang, his wife, and the three maidservants who had licked him bathe in the wine he himself had bathed in, and they all reverted to youth, their countenances perfect and pleasing. Afterwards he transmitted a scripture on elixirs in one fascicle to Tang. Tang entered Mount Yuntai [Cloud Terrace Mountain[70]] to make the drug. When it was complete, he ingested it and departed as a transcendent.[71]

---

70. Perhaps the mountain that is meant here is the one otherwise known as Tianzhu shan (Celestial Pillar Mountain) in Cangxi district, Sichuan Province, where Zhang Ling engaged in Celestial Master practice and which is mentioned in Zhang's *Traditions* hagiography as the site of one of his trials of his disciples. (There was another Tianzhu shan in modern Anhui Province.) Three other mountains named Yuntai are located in modern Jiangsu and Anhui Provinces.

71. *TL,* 215–218, 432–433.

Ge Hong, we see,[72] does not feel bound to mention Tang's rat. He uses the case of Tang Gongfang to do three things: emphasize Li Babai's perspicacity in recognizing this householder as a promising disciple; illustrate the depth of commitment and strength of character a would-be disciple must have in order to receive a transmission of esoterica; and document the efficacy of elixir alchemy, Ge's preferred route to transcendence.[73] Nothing is said of Tang's whole household ascending with him. But there is a detail in the story that may be read as a subtle nod to that element of the body of narrative that must have been circulating by the early fourth century: Li has not only Tang but also his wife and their three maidservants bathe in the wine Li has bathed in, and "they all reverted to youth, their countenances perfect and pleasing." This reversion to youth is not celestial transcendence, but it is a striking longevity-enhancing achievement that is here credited to members of Tang's household other than Tang himself. It is as if, Tang being known primarily for having taken his household with him into the skies, Ge must mention this element. On the other hand, Ge, with his agenda of promoting alchemical elixirs as the most effective and prestigious path to *xian*-hood, clearly distinguishes between the wife and maidservants' mere "reversion to youth," induced by the wine bath, and Tang's departure into transcendence, which alone in this story is induced by a true elixir. Ge is willing to split up the household to argue the unique efficacy of elixirs (and of the scriptures that teach proper methods for making them). Ge may also have been reluctant to allow that elixirs might be used for something so base as the celestial levitation of an entire household, domestic animals and all. He does include such a substory in another hagiography, but only as an apparent addition to the narrative's end and introduced with the words, "Legend has it," which rhetorically puts some distance between the author-compiler and the content thus framed.

Chang Qu 常璩 (fl. 347 C.E.) in his *Huayangguo zhi* 華陽國志 *(Annals of the Kingdoms South of Mount Hua)* notes in passing a shrine to Tang Gongfang that was enough of an attraction in Baozhong 襃中 district, Mianyang 沔陽 commandery, to be the only feature of that place listed in this topography.[74] There was still apparently a shrine standing in the middle of the fourth century, then, at the site where Guo

---

72. If, that is, this hagiography can be safely attributed to his own compiling and editing work. The *Shenxian zhuan* material on Li and Tang is attested fairly early (see *TL*, 432–433), but here, as is the case with virtually every text from this period, it will always remain impossible to know with certainty that the original autograph text (if it even makes sense, in a manuscript culture in which authors themselves must have produced multiple versions and copies of texts over their lifetimes, to use this phrase) contained this particular entry. At best we deal in probabilities.

73. See *TL*, 30.

74. *Huayangguo zhi* 2:124. The district seat was located on the Bao River just north of where it joined the Han River, northwest of the present-day city of Hanzhong (which is also the site of the ancient Hanzhong commandery seat).

Zhi and his colleagues had sponsored work a century or two earlier. Chang does not pause to record Tang's story, but this should not surprise us since his work is quite laconic. Another early medieval topography, however, of uncertain date and authorship,[75] *Liangzhou ji* 梁州記, is more expansive:

> North of the Zhi [?] River is Zhi[?]xiang Mountain. On it is a shrine to the transcendent Tang Gongfang. There is a stele, and just north of the temple is a large hole. The stele says that this was the site of his former house; when Gong- fang lifted up his household and ascended into transcendence, it left a hole there. On the mountain there is a "guts-changing rat." Three times a month it vomits and thus changes out its guts. This is what Shu Guangwei 束廣微[76] called Tang's rat.[77]

The stele described here must have been a different one than that commissioned by Guo Zhi and colleagues. (It would not have been unusual for a shrine to have more than one stele on its grounds.) In fact, this passage probably describes a different shrine and location, though one in the same region. Through the text we glimpse a local community making the most of its association with Tang, placing a shrine at the site claimed to be his former residence that no doubt attracted pious pilgrims and curious tourists who gaped at the hole in the ground near the temple. The periodicity of the rat's odd transformation, and its linkage to the lunar cycle, suggest a kind of earthbound transcendence (or at least rejuvenation) in its own right, albeit without the finality of an elixir. The focal interest of this particular topographic text is the shrine itself, the hole near it, and especially the rat because these all constitute notable local wonders. Shrines to transcendents could be found in many places, but the hole and the strange local rat set this one apart. This text summarizes the story of Tang's ascent in one sentence, perhaps presuming its readers already know the tale; its attention is focused elsewhere. It evinces no interest whatsoever in the back- story of Tang's achievement, the trials he had to endure, nor in the specific practices, alchemical or otherwise, that enabled his ascent.

In the medium Yang Xi's Shangqing transcriptions of 364–370, collected around 500 by Tao Hongjing into *Declarations of the Perfected* (*Zhen'gao* 真誥), Tang

---

75. It probably, however, dates to no later than the early fifth century, because it (or at least a work of the same title) is twice cited in Fan Ye's *Hou Han shu*.

76. Shu Xi 晳 (ca. 264–ca. 303 C.E.) was a scholar-official famous for his broad learning. He was an acquaintance and official appointee of Zhang Hua and was involved in the editing and transcribing of the ancient texts found in the Ji tomb around 279. On Shu Xi, see *Jin shu* 51:1427–1434; and on the Ji tomb texts and Shu's work with them, see Shaughnessy, *Rewriting Early Chinese Texts,* 131–256 passim.

77. Cited in *YWLJ* 95:1658–1659.

Gongfang is, along with a great many other figures from the past, located by the Perfected in a particular station in the heavens. We learn that he holds an office overseeing records of life and death.[78] One of this text's overriding agendas is to make a hierarchy of competing religious methods, values, and exemplars by reshuffling the statuses of figures earlier claimed to have become *xian* (as well as certain of the ordinary dead); it does so, in part, by locating them in particular strata of a conveniently complex, hierarchically organized bureaucratic pantheon, and by investing this information with the status of divine revelation. Tang's sponsors might have been glad to learn that he was mentioned by the Perfected who appeared to Yang Xi and was thus recognized as holding divine office; on the other hand, they might have been chagrined that their regional patron had not climbed farther up the promotion ladder. This sort of *Zhen'gao* passage is a corrective to the hagiographies of others, a translocal (because divinely revealed) tamping down of a crowd of local figures enthusiastically boosted and anxiously inquired about by their sponsors, devotees, and relatives.

Sometime in the early fifth century, Liu Jingshu 劉敬叔, in his *Garden of Marvels* (*Yiyuan* 異苑), a large collection of anomaly accounts, included a notice on the Tang rat in a series of entries on the strange fauna of particular regions.[79]

> The Tang rat is shaped like a typical rat. It has a rather long tail and is of a greenish-black color. On the side of its belly is an appendage resembling intestines, which sometimes grows discolored and falls off. The rat is thus also called "changing-its-guts rat." Formerly the transcendent Tang Fang took his household and ascended into the heavens. His chickens and dogs all went with him. Only a rat fell back down. It did not die, but its guts now protruded three inches. It changes them every three years. It's commonly called Tang's rat. It lives in Chenggu and the Sichuan area.[80]

This is an account of anomalies; it describes things deemed strange. By the fifth century there was little that was strange, at least to a compiler of oddities, about a transcendent per se: they were a fixture of the common cultural *imaginaire*. From this text's perspective, Tang stands out among transcendents only because he "took his household," so that is the only feature mentioned. The entry quickly returns to its real subject of interest, the rat; we now get a more detailed anatomical description (along with a new schedule for the changing of its guts). But the rat's odd features cannot be accounted for without some reference to Tang's ascent. Here it is

---

78. *DZ* 1016, 13.13a4–6.
79. On this work and author, see *SW,* 78–80.
80. *Yiyuan* 3.29, cited in *TPGJ* 440:13.

an injury suffered in its fall as Tang's house rose upward, not its resentment at being left behind, that accounts for those features.

The final item in our series is Li Daoyuan's (d. 527) *Annotated Classic of Waterways,* a topographic text that generously appends both narrative and descriptive material to the old *Water Classic's* laconic listings of rivers and lakes. Li's work is invaluable for sketching some of the stories that were circulating (often on stelae) in *particular places* in the early sixth century. It is in the context of mentioning the Xu River 壻水 that the text notes the existence of a Tang Gongfang shrine near its banks.

> There is a Tang Gong shrine there. Lord Tang was styled Gongfang and was a native of Chenggu. He practiced a *dao* and became a transcendent, entering Mount Yuntai to synthesize and ingest an elixir. He ascended into the heavens in broad daylight. His cocks now crow in the heavens and his dogs bark in the clouds.[81] He left only a rat behind, due to its noxiousness. The rat was vexed at this and began spitting up its guts on the last of every month, and growing new ones. So people today call it Tang's rat.
>
> On the day Gongfang ascended and became a transcendent, his son-in-law was traveling and had not yet returned. He was unable to use the same path into the clouds that the others had. So he had to content himself with making this river his residence. It is said that there is no trouble with killing frosts, krakens, or tigers in the area. The local people credit him with this.[82] This is why [the town] is called Xu [Son-in-law] Village. This is also where the river here gets its name. The hundred surnames[83] have established a temple for him on this spot. They carved this stone and erected this stele to make manifest and spread word of these numinous wonders.[84]

Li is here, as elsewhere in his text, likely drawing on one or more stele inscriptions at the site.[85] The first paragraph compresses most elements we have seen so far—the elixir, the whole-household ascent (though this is only elliptically referred to), the rat—into one brief account. The second paragraph introduces what is to us new material on Tang's son-in-law, another figure left behind as the household ascended, who seems in his own right—perhaps between the Eastern Han and the

---

81. The same phrase is used in some accounts of Liu An, as will be seen below.

82. That is, believed that Tang's son-in-law was responsible for these blessings in their area.

83. Usually meaning "commoners," but here simply designating the local population in general.

84. *Shuijing zhu* 27:353.

85. The modern editor compares the text's wording at certain points with those of inscriptions recorded elsewhere.

early fifth century—to have become the focus of a secondary cult in the area. Just as Tang lent his name to the strange rat, his otherwise unnamed son-in-law lent his family title to the local town and even the river that runs by it. Transcendence is not claimed for him, but he has clearly acceded to the status of regional deity, credited by local people with assistance in matters of weather and harmful animals just as his transcendent father-in-law had been two or more centuries before. He may have been granted cult status because of the dangerous power of his perceived resentment at having been left behind. Li is as interested in this figure as he is in Tang, for whom a shrine still stood at or near its old site in the early sixth century.

The case of Tang Gongfang and his rat shows, then, how widely a complex of originally local narrative elements, inscribed on stone, could be taken up and refracted in translocal genres of several kinds.

Hagiographic Rehabilitation

Hagiography, which is among other things an exercise in reputation-shaping through narration, can be used to argue for a lessening of a holy person's reputation. Several transcendents whose stories Ge Hong included in his *Traditions* were, in discourses divinely vouchsafed fifty years later to Yang Xi and then collected by Tao Hongjing in *Declarations of the Perfected* around 500 C.E., argued to hold far less prestigious positions in the celestial bureaucracy than Ge's narrative had suggested and new, derogatory (though not entirely debunking) information now had the added support of the divine revelation. Hagiography could also be used to refurbish, realign, exalt, defend, upgrade, or totally remake a figure's reputation—or rather, to *argue* for these adjustments, the outcome always depending on readers' reception. No upgrade was quite so dramatic as claiming that someone who was elsewhere maintained to have died had in fact not perished but rather lived on as a transcendent. This rhetorical strategy, as we have seen, dovetailed with the lore surrounding techniques of *shijie* (escape by means of a simulated corpse) and *bingjie* (escape by feigned execution or staged violent death); in a society in which such techniques were reputed to be widely practiced, any apparent death, however seemingly final or graphic, was a candidate for reappraisal. This was especially so when the protagonist in question was said to have practiced or advocated transcendence arts. In such cases not only might an argument for transcendence carry plausibility in the eyes of some readers, there was also likely to be some pressure in that direction from caretakers of the protagonist's post mortem reputation. And so a figure reported in some quarters to have died might be argued in other texts to be living on as a *xian* in the heavens or on earth—the ultimate in hagiographic rehabilitation.

Ji Kang (223–262 C.E.), the noted poet, essayist, and zither virtuoso, was one such figure. Widely said[86] to have been imprisoned and executed in 262 C.E., he had also left behind treatises on the possibility of transcendence.[87] His reputation seems to have become heavily contested: he clearly had sponsors who wanted to see him admitted to the ranks of transcendents, but he also had detractors who wanted to keep him out. Several texts go to some lengths to point out Ji Kang's limitations as a practitioner, as does the hagiography of Wang Lie 王烈 attributed to Ge Hong's *Traditions*. In the Wang Lie story, a stony, longevity-inducing substance, then an esoteric text written in a strange script, spontaneously appear to Wang but mysteriously become unavailable when he tries to share them with Ji. Lest we miss the point, the hagiography drives it home: "Wang privately told one of his disciples that these things happened because Ji had not yet become fit to attain the Way."[88] Again, the same text's hagiography of Sun Deng 孫登 portrays that master as commenting on Ji Kang's unfitness for sustained esoteric practice—and for good measure throws in a scene in which Sun outplays Ji on the zither.[89] But a third passage in the same text—the hagiography of Ge's own father-in-law, Bao Jing—contains a passage implying that Ji, though apparently executed in 262, was still alive strumming his zither in Bao's own company long after that event.[90] The implication is that Ji's apparent execution had been an instance of "escape by weapon" and that he was still roaming the earth as a transcendent of some grade or other. The presence of divergent estimations of the same figure in a single hagiographic collection—although some or all of them were probably added to some *Traditions* copies by hands other than Ge Hong's—is testimony both to the fluidity of texts in a manuscript culture and to the literary struggle waged by many unseen parties over the reputations of former figures.[91] (It also serves to remind us of how risky it is to form conclusions about the inner mental proclivities of a particular author—Ge Hong in this case—based on a few textual passages surviving from a manuscript culture.) Clearly there were circles in which Ji Kang was regarded as a transcendent; both the positive and the negative evaluations

---

86. For example, in *Jin shu* 49. For a discussion of the historigraphic sources on him, see Holzman, *La vie et la pensée de Hi K'ang,* 12–51.

87. See Henricks, *Philosophy and Argumentation in Third-Century China,* 21–70.

88. *TL,* 339.

89. Ibid., 336; see also Campany, "Two Religious Thinkers of the Early Eastern Jin," 207–208.

90. *TL,* 295–297.

91. For two very different studies of the implications of manuscript culture for the study of premodern Chinese texts, see Tian, *Tao Yuanming and Manuscript Culture;* and Shaughnessy, *Rewriting Early Chinese Texts.*

of him in *Traditions* go to prove this.[92] Portrayals of his shortcomings as an adept would have had no point unless someone was telling stories of his success in transcendence arts—and unless someone else wanted to counter these stories.

In the case of Liu An 劉安, a prince of the Han dynasty historically recorded as having died in 122 B.C.E., we have much more explicit traces of a literary debate that raged for more than four centuries.[93] All sources agree that Liu, a grandson of the founding Han emperor and uncle of Emperor Wu, gathered masters of esoteric knowledge at his princedom in Huainan, that these scholars jointly authored the massive compendium *Huainanzi* under Liu's sponsorship, and that in 122 he was charged with treason for taking potent symbolic steps toward the proclamation of a new dynasty, to which he was moved in part by resentment over his family's treatment by the court. Sometime in the century and a half between Liu An's reported demise in 122 B.C.E. and Wang Chong's (27–97 C.E.) authoring of his *Arguments Weighed* (*Lunheng* 論衡), someone began spreading word that Liu had not in fact died, but had instead ascended into the heavens as a transcendent by means of an alchemical elixir—and that his entire household had ascended along with him.[94] We know this because it is the substance of the narrative Wang Chong summarizes in order to debunk:

Literati books say that the prince of Huainan studied *dao*s and assembled all in the realm who had a *dao*. From the worthies of the land to masters of *dao* arts, all gathered in Huainan. Whatever strange methods and anomalous arts they had, all were put forth. The prince therefore obtained *dao*s and, along with his household, ascended into the heavens. Even his livestock and domestic animals attained transcendence; his dogs and chickens were in the heavens as well and barked and crowed in the clouds. This is to say that there were some *xian* drugs left over; the dogs and chickens ate these, so they all followed the prince upward into the heavens.

---

92. For a study of other narratives concerning his relations with practitioners of transcendence arts, see Chan, "Ruan Ji's and Xi Kang's Visits to Two 'Immortals.'"

93. The best discussion in English of the historiographical (but not hagiographic) material on Liu An may be found in Loewe, *A Biographical Dictionary of the Qin, Former Han & Xin Periods,* 242–244.

94. Neither the *Shi ji* (see, for example, 118:3082) nor Ban Gu's *Han shu* (see, for example, 44:2145), compiled in the second half of the second century C.E., in their brief accounts of Liu An make any mention of his alleged personal attainment of transcendence, though both do mention his collection of masters of esoterica in Huainan, and the *Han shu* narrative mentions that the texts emanating from An's circle "spoke of arts of divine transcendence and the yellow and white" (that is, alchemy, 44:2145).

> All those who are fond of *dao*s and study transcendence say that this is so.
> It's all false.

Note Wang's penultimate comment on the ubiquity with which this story was transmitted among practitioners of *xian* arts; clearly Liu An had been appropriated by many *xian*-hood seekers as a successful exemplar. At this point in his text Wang Chong launches several arguments against the possibility of transcendence in general. The most basic is a syllogism: human beings are creatures; all creatures must die; therefore all humans must die. Another argument is taxonomic: the verbal and visual lore of transcendents pictures them as feathered, but feathers are not natural to humankind. After developing these and similar arguments, Wang returns to the case of Liu An:

> In fact, Liu An, prince of Huainan, lived during the reign of [Han] Emperor Wu. His father, Chang, had been banished to Yandao in Shu and died on reaching Yongdao. Liu An inherited the princedom and, resenting that his father had been driven to his death, harbored thoughts of rebellion; his summoning and assembling men with arts was because he wanted to launch a great affair [that is, launch a new dynasty]. Wu Pi and the others filled the palace halls and wrote treatises on *dao* arts, putting forth all sorts of deviant and strange writings. They joined together in plotting rebellion.[95] The story of the Eight Sires was intended to display their divine marvels, to make it appear as if they had obtained *dao*s, but their *dao*s in the end were not realized and proved ineffective. And so [An] plotted rebellion with Wu Pi, but the affair came to light and An committed suicide. Some say he was executed; whether he was executed or committed suicide, the reality is the same. Over the generations, people, on seeing these men's writings, deep, dark, and strange, and again upon contemplating the story of the Eight Sires, which made it seem as though they had achieved some results, came to transmit the claim that the prince of Huainan had transcended and ascended to the heavens, but this departs from the facts of the case.[96]

Wang Chong presumes his readers' familiarity with the subnarrative of the Eight Sires (*bagong* 八公); he does not even bother to summarize it, despite having told the story of Liu An's own supposed celestial ascent. He here offers a theory of the origin of the story of Liu's transcendence: the combination of the impressively abstruse content of the text now known as *Huainanzi* and the Sires' striking exploits

---

95. The text is corrupt here; I follow the suggestion of various commentators in amending it.

96. *Lunheng jiaoshi* 7:317–318, 319–320. An alternate translation may be found in Forke, *Lun-hêng,* 1:337–338.

led some to conclude that Liu An must have become a *xian* despite records to the contrary.

Moving forward another century and a half, we find Ying Shao 應劭 in his *Fengsu tongyi* 風俗通義, probably written between 194 and 206, including Liu An's story as one of the canards he must rectify in his chapter "Correcting Errors" ("Zhengshi" 正失):

> It is said by the vulgar that An, prince of Huainan, summoned several thousand masters of esoteric arts as guests; wrote the *Swan's Jewel* and *Myriad Secrets*,[97] both esoteric texts; and completed [alchemical] gold and silver in a cauldron, thus ascending to the heavens in broad daylight.

Ying Shao then quotes from Liu An's biography in the *Han shu* to the effect that when alchemical efforts at his court failed to produce an efficacious elixir, he began forging imperial seals and tallies and for this reason was publicly charged with treason, whereupon he committed suicide.

> He fell on his own sword, and his family was publicly executed. How can any of them be said to have become divine transcendents? As for the masters he was hosting, some of them probably escaped and, ashamed at how things had turned out, glossed them over with a false account (*shi zha shuo* 飾詐說) that later people picked up and spread so that it became transmitted and circulated.[98]

Just as Wang Chong had counterposed a class of written sources he distrusts—in his case "literati books" (*ru shu* 儒書)—to an authority he relies on to correct their mistakes—in his case, clear thinking about how the world works—so Ying Shao begins by citing one kind of source and then countering it with another kind he presents as more trustworthy. In Ying's case the suspect source is "a saying of the vulgar" (*su shuo* 俗說). (Perhaps we might soften it to "a common saying," but the pejorative whiff of *su*, "vulgar, common, ordinary," is unmistakable, especially in Ying's prose.) The more authoritative source applied as a corrective is Ban Gu's *History of the Han,* here treated as a sober, classic, *true* account against which common asseverations can safely be measured. In Wang Chong's case, the suspect sources cited were books, whose falsehoods could be sorted out through thinking; in Ying Shao's case, quite typically for him, the questionable source is a type of "saying"— not necessarily something strictly oral in its medium, but not necessarily something

---

97. The text has *Yuanmi* 苑秘, which makes little sense; I amend the title to fit what is given in other sources.

98. *Fengsu tongyi jiaozhu* chap. 2, 115–117.

in writing, either—and the authority is a *book* that Ying trusts and wants us to trust too. Just as Wang had his theory to account for the origin of the false narrative, Ying has his too. Wang's theory was cognitive: people not involved in the events, realizing the profundities of the writings emanating from Liu An's circle and hearing of his teacher-companions' exploits, came to credit Liu An with transcendence because this seemed a more reasonable, likely end for such a man than political execution or suicide. Ying's theory, again quite characteristically, is psychological and moral: the shame (*chi* 耻) of the whole affair led some from Liu's circle of masters to "gloss things over with a false account" that came to circulate among those far enough removed in time and space from the events that it came to seem true.

Zhang Hua (232–300 C.E.) in his late-third-century *Treatise on Curiosities* was content simply to record both sides of the still-running argument: "The Han prince of Huainan was executed for plotting rebellion. But it is also said he obtained a *dao* and ascended upward." The location of this item in Zhang's encyclopedic text is itself of interest: it heads the section titled "Disputations concerning Masters of Esoterica" ("Bian fangshi" 辨方士),[99] which is devoted to recording differences of opinion concerning particular practitioners of esoteric arts. We may infer that by the late third century Liu An's was the paramount case of a sharply disputed reputation of transcendence.

The account of Liu An attributed to Ge Hong's *Traditions,* then, was a quite self-conscious wading into a high-profile controversy of long standing. Almost certainly based on earlier sources now lost, it provides for the first time in the extant record a glimpse of the full narrative details to which the earlier, debunking passages only summarily refer.[100]

> Liu An, prince of Huainan, was a grandson of Han Emperor Gao.[101] He was
> fond of literati studies and of esoteric skills. He wrote an *Inner Book* (*Neishu*
> 内書[102]) in twenty-one chapters; he also authored "central chapters" (*zhongpian*
> 中篇) in eight sections, which spoke of matters concerning divine transcen-

---

99. *Bowu zhi jiaozheng* 64; this is item number 192 in the sequence, in chap. 5.

100. Further details are on record in a contemporaneous text, Gan Bao's *Record of an Inquest into the Spirit-Realm (Soushen ji),* in which item 1:15 records a song Liu An is reported to have sung on meeting the Sires.

101. That is, Gao zu or "the Exalted Progenitor," the founder of the Han dynasty, Liu Bang (reigned 202–195 B.C.E.).

102. This is the work now known as *Huainanzi,* which still exists in twenty-one chapters (one important recension is preserved in the Ming Daoist canon as *DZ* 1184); *Inner Book* was its original name because it formed the esoteric part of a trilogy of collections of essays. For more on this designation and its history, see Roth, *Textual History,* 12, 16, 20, 23. Scholars agree that Liu An did not independently write this and the other treatises listed here; rather, these works were written at his court by masters he had assembled.

dents and the "yellow and white"[103] and were titled *The Swan's Jewel (Hongbao* 鴻寶). And he wrote the *Myriad Ends (Wanbi* 萬畢) in three fascicles, which discussed ways of transformation.[104]

There were Eight Sires[105] who went to call on him. The gatekeeper, acting on his own initiative, harried them with questions, saying, "The prince's foremost desire is to obtain ways of extending one's years, forestalling the time [of one's death], [getting] long life, and non-aging. His next desire is to obtain great scholars who are broadly learned and can enter into the subtle meanings [of texts]. And his last desire is to obtain brave, stalwart warriors with the strength to lift cauldrons and the ferocity to scare off tigers. Now you gentlemen are already decrepit. Obviously you possess neither the arts with which to forestall your decline nor the [natural] strength of a [Meng] Ben or a [Xia] Yu.[106] How could you penetrate [matters such as those discussed in] the *Three Tombs (Sanfen), Five Exemplars (Wudian), Eight Cords (Basu),* or *Nine Hills (Jiuqiu),* or reach matters of the utmost depth and remoteness, or exhaust hidden principles and natures? And since you fall short in these areas, I dare not proceed further."

The Sires laughed and replied: "We have heard that the prince honors the worthy and is fond of scholars, treating them with indefatigable courtesy, so that even those with only a single talent are unfailingly brought in. The ancients esteemed the nine times nine [types of] study and supported even those [whose only talent was] to mimic birdcalls and dogbarks. Their earnestness was such that they desired to buy mere horses' bones so as to collect a Qiji and serve a Master Guo as their teacher so as to assemble a crowd of erudites. Although we are decrepit and do not match what the prince is seeking, we still wish to be allowed to see him just once. Even if we bring him no benefit, we will not, on the other hand, cost him any loss. And why should we be disliked on account of our old age? It must be that the prince declares anyone who is young to be in possession of a way and anyone whose hair has turned white to be a common person. But we fear that that is not what is known as 'turning over a stone to find jade' or 'reaching into a grotto to find a pearl.' If he is treating old men such as we as of no account, then let us now become young."

---

103. That is, matters of gold and silver, or alchemy.

104. See *TL,* 233–234 and 442–447, for comments on these titles, which need not detain us here.

105. A passage in Ge's *Inner Chapters (NP* 11:208) may reflect a later development of these figures. It names "eight transcendent sires" (*xianren bagong* 仙人八公), describing their regimens and resulting esoteric skills. The skills do not match up closely with the ones described here.

106. Meng Ben and Xia Yu are two heroes of Warring States times whose names became synonymous with bravery. The several other historical allusions and mentions of obscure texts below are explained in the annotations in *TL;* I omit them here.

As soon as they had spoken these words, the Eight Sires transformed into youths of fifteen with elaborately coiffed black hair and skin the color of peach blossoms. At this, the gatekeeper was shocked and ran to inform the prince. Upon hearing the news, the prince immediately rushed out to greet them, not even stopping to put on his shoes. Together they climbed the Longing for Transcendence Tower, where [the prince] spread out brocade canopies and ivory mats, lit hundred-harmonies incense, brought out stools of gold and jade, and comported himself as a disciple. Facing north,[107] he folded his hands and said, "Despite my only average talent, I have loved the Dao and its Power since my youth. But I am reined and fettered by the affairs of this world. Mired among the common run of humanity, I am unable to leave behind my ties, shoulder a satchel, and dwell in mountains and forests. Nevertheless, morning and night I have hungered and thirsted after divine illumination and the cleansing of my defilements. My dedication has been shallow, my ambition unfulfilled, and [my goals lie] as distant as the Milky Way. I did not expect to receive such great favor as this descent and visit from you lords of the Dao. It must be due to [what is written in] the register of my allotted lifespan that I am being thus promoted. Confronted by both joy and fear, I do not know what to do; I only beg you lords of the Dao to take pity on me and teach me, that I might, like a caterpillar who borrows a swan's wings, depart from earth and fly up to heaven!"

At this, the Eight Sires changed back into old men and declared to the prince: "Although our knowledge, too, is shallow, we are each equipped with what we have previously studied. Knowing that you love the Dao, we have come to attend you, but we do not yet know which [of our arts] interests you. One of us can sit and summon wind and rain, stand and call up clouds and fog, draw on the ground to form rivers, and pile up soil to form mountains. One of us can topple mountains, plug up springs, tame tigers and leopards, summon dragons and krakens, and dispatch spirits and ghosts. One of us can divide himself into multiple bodies, alter his countenance, appear and disappear at will, conceal the six [types of] troops, and bring on darkness in broad daylight. One of us can ride in emptiness, pace the void, cross over the ocean waves, enter and exit where there is no open space, and go a thousand *li* in a single breath. One of us can enter fire without being burned, enter water without getting wet, take knife blows without being cut, get shot at without being pierced, not feel cold in the depths of summer and not sweat in the height of summer. One of us can transform himself in a myriad ways, become whatever he pleases, turn into a bird, beast, plant, or tree in an instant, move all manner of creatures and

---

107. To face north was to assume the lower position in a hierarchy of social and religious authority.

land formations at will, and transport palaces and houses. One of us can quell fires, rescue others from danger, avoid all manner of calamities, extend his years, and lengthen his lifespan [to reach] long life. And one of us can decoct clay to form gold, distill lead to form mercury, refine the eight minerals, fly aloft with the 'flowing pearl,'[108] ride dragons hitched to cloud[-carriages], and drift and wander about in the [Heaven of] Grand Purity. [Which arts you study] depends entirely on your desire."

From this point on, An paid obeisance to the Eight Sires day and night, personally serving them liquor and fruit. Before [studying] each art, he asked for a demonstration of it; all of them—the transformations, the winds, rains, clouds, and fogs—proved effective. So he came to receive from the Sires a scripture on elixirs,[109] [one on] thirty-six esoteric methods involving "liquid silver," and others.

[Later,] when Liu An was falsely accused by the Gentleman of the Interior Lei Bei of plotting rebellion, he ascended into heaven with the Eight Sires. Imprints were made in the mountain stone on which they [last] stepped, and today the tracks of humans and of horses are still visible there.

Legend has it that, as An was in the process of departing as a transcendent, there was a bit of his medicinal compound left over in a basin in the court. His chickens and dogs pecked at or licked out the basin and they all flew upwards as well.[110]

This account is careful to defend Liu An against the charge of treason; it mentions in passing that the accusation was false but also slyly uses it as the narrative turn that triggers Liu's group ascension into the heavens. It certainly credits Liu with celestial transcendence, but mostly it focuses on the Eight Sires (who here ascend with Liu) and on Liu's deferential, self-deprecating response to their arrival at his gate—a response that modeled the way in which practitioners of esoterica hoped to be welcomed by high officials. It includes, seemingly as a nod to the most widely known element of Liu's story, the ascent of his domestic animals in his wake. This detail is certainly comedic, but in this context it also constitutes an argument for the power of elixirs: they are so effective that they can convey even dogs and chickens to transcendence.

So much for the counter-narrative offered in *Traditions* to earlier debunkings of Liu An's claimed *xian*-hood. Ge Hong also recorded counter-narratives to this counter-narrative. The reader will recall Ge's *Inner Chapters* account of one Xiang

---

108. Denoting some sort of alchemical product; see the annotation in *TL*, 237, for details.
109. Or perhaps "a scripture on cinnabar."
110. *TL*, 233–240, 442–447.

Mandu, who told colorful tales of his celestial adventures in quest of transcendence and whom Ge considered a charlatan.[111] Among the details Xiang is said to have recounted we find this one:

> In former times when Liu An, prince of Huainan, ascended to the heavens for an audience with the Thearch on High, he sat spread-legged, spoke loudly, and referred to himself as "I, the single man." For this he was assigned to guard the celestial latrine for three years.[112]

Although Ge Hong dismisses Xiang's entire narration as so much nonsense, for us this detail is a valuable instance of recorded oral counter-narrative, surprisingly complex for being so brief.[113] On the one hand, it grants that Liu An ascended into the heavens, to this extent agreeing with the side that favored transcendence in the long-running debate (though whether the story is attributing full-blown transcendence to Liu, or only a temporary ascent, is unclear). But on the other hand it irreverently charges Liu with a grave lapse of manners. This portrayal echoes the old charges of treason and undermines the hagiographic insistence on his deference toward the Sires in its clever suggestion that he never shed his overweening, presumptuous attitude, even in the heavens. The form of self-reference here attributed to the prince—"I, the single man"—was reserved for rulers; it was not a prerogative that Liu An had legitimately enjoyed on earth and was certainly not one he should have presumed in heaven before the celestial Thearch. His other behaviors are likewise laughably inappropriate: he speaks too loudly, and his spread-legged seated posture, literally "like a winnowing basket," was used to ward off demons; by Han times it was understood as a gesture of contempt and was thus expressly prohibited by the rules of gentlemanly etiquette given in the *Book of Rites*.[114] The courteous prince of the *Traditions* account, whose one overriding characteristic is appropriate deference to his spiritual betters, is here deftly refigured not only as boorish but, worse, as arrogant and presumptuous: he carries his overreaching tendencies up to heaven with him and pays a stiff price there as here.

In the *Traditions* hagiography we saw this detail in the celestial ascent scene: "Imprints were made in the mountain stone on which they [last] stepped, and today the tracks of humans and of horses are still visible there." The passage reminds us that the reputations of *xian,* the cycles of stories of their exploits, were anchored

---

111. Discussed in Chapter 5.

112. *NP* 20:350.

113. One detects a bit of class warfare, with the haughty prince being taken down several notches, but without information on Xiang Mandu's social background it is impossible to do more than speculate on this aspect of the narrative.

114. See Harper, "A Chinese Demonography of the Third Century B.C.," 483–485.

to particular sites on the landscape; sometimes, as here, they were literally embedded or inscribed in the ground. This passing mention in the *Traditions* almost certainly indicates that a cult site dedicated to Liu An and the Eight Sires had already been established in the Huainan area by Ge Hong's day. In Li Daoyuan's *Annotated Classic of Waterways* we have valuable eyewitness testimony to the existence of this site at the end of the fifth century. After remarking that "Ge Hong realized that [Liu An] had attained the Dao, and he included the matter in his *Master Who Embraces the Unhewn* and *Traditions of Divine Transcendents,*" Li Daoyuan describes his visit to the temple to Liu An on Eight Sires Mountain in or near Shouchun 壽春 district:

> I climbed to the top of the mountain. I heard nothing of the tracks of men and horses, and only the temple [and its] image were still extant. In the temple was drawn an image of An and the Eight Sires. They were shown seated casually under a canopy, all dressed in beautiful gowns and feathered cloaks. Their mats, bottles, and pillows were all like ordinary ones. In front of the temple is a stele that was erected in the tenth year of the *yongming* reign period of the Qi dynasty [late 492 or early 493 C.E.]. The mountain has hidden chambers and stone wells.... Climbing the northern peak, you see the *dao* chamber of [the prince of] Huainan and, near it, the Eight Sires' stone well.[115]

In modern Fengtai district, Anhui Province, there is an Eight Sires Mountain, presumably the one Ge's account mentions and Li tells of having climbed. I have not yet ventured there to see whether a temple to Liu An still stands, but I suspect it does.

Hagiographic Co-Optation

Hagiographic refashioning of reputations could be extreme. Nowhere is this seen more clearly than in the outright stealing of figures from other traditions to be remade, in some busy workshop of textual production, into advocates for transcendence arts or even transcendents themselves.

Outright stealing occurs in the treatment of the Han courtier and author Dong Zhongshu 董仲舒 (who probably died between 119 and 114 B.C.E.) in the *Traditions of Divine Transcendents* hagiography of Li Shaojun.[116] The hagiography itself aptly summarizes Dong's stance on the pursuit of transcendence as recorded in histories:

---

115. *Shuijing zhu* 32:407. Compare the citation of this passage in *TPYL* 43:6b.

116. The best recent summary in English of Dong's official biographies may be found in Loewe, *A Biographical Dictionary of the Qin, Former Han & Xin Periods,* 70–73; for an excellent study of his political and cosmological thought, see Queen, *From Chronicle to Canon.*

He had studied the Five Classics extensively but had never attained an under-standing of *dao* arts. He often scoffed at people of the world for ingesting drugs and practicing *dao*s. He presented memorials to Emperor Wu arguing that human life was limited by an allotted lifespan and that aging was a naturally given process, such that it could not be lengthened by *dao* arts. He maintained that even if there were apparent exceptions to this rule, they were due to natural endowment, not to arts.[117]

This recorded stance, however, along with Dong's attendance at the court of an emperor famous for his interest in esoteric arts, only made him a tempting target for advocates of the quest for *xian*-hood. The hagiography tells of how Dong's "close friend" Li Shaojun had made a medicine from a secret recipe for Dong before departing from court for good. Later, when Dong was gravely ill, he remembered this medicine.

He tried taking less than half a dose: his body grew light and strong, and his ill-ness was suddenly healed. Then he took a full dose: his breath and strength were as they had been when he was young. Only now did he believe that there was a way of long life and deathlessness. He quit his official post and traveled in search of a master of a *dao* whom he could ask about the method [for making the drug he had taken]. He never succeeded in grasping all of it; he only managed to prevent his hair from going white and to stay very healthy. Only when he was more than eighty years old did he finally die. Before he died, he told his son, Daosheng, "When I was still young, I obtained Li Shaojun's esoteric medicine. At first I didn't believe in it; after using it, I regained strength, but then I was never able to grasp [the method for making] it. I will carry my regret over this with me to the Yellow Springs [that is, to the realm of the dead]. You must go and search out a master of esoterica, someone who can explain this method. If you persist in taking this medicine, you will certainly transcend the world."[118]

There is, of course, the faintest of possibilities that the story describes a real change of heart on Dong's part; we will never know for sure. But it looks as if some clever story-makers managed not only to turn the narrative tables on a famous scholar-courtier who was on record as having argued against the possibility of *xian*-hood, but also to get their story taken up into Ge Hong's *Traditions,* thus winning for it the patronage and textual sponsorship, as it were, of a highly suc-cessful and long-transmitted compilation that we know to have been copied and

117. See *TL,* 224.
118. Ibid., 224–225.

chanted throughout the Tang and into the Song, not to mention the fact that we are still reading and discussing it today. The shapers of this counter-narrative of Dong Zhongshu surely never imagined it would be so successful.

I know of no hagiographic co-optation, however, bolder than that of Kong Anguo 孔安國.[119] Han and early medieval readers would have recognized this name as that of a direct descendant of Confucius who, during the reign of Han Emperor Wu (note again this association), held various court and regional appointments and allegedly discovered an "old text" version of chapters of the *Book of Documents* embedded in the walls of his illustrious ancestor's family home.[120] His family pedigree as well as his association with "old text" ideology put him at the farthest possible remove from both the quest for transcendence and the cluster of cosmological and physiological assumptions that made it thinkable. Yet there he is, in passages attributed to Ge Hong's *Traditions,* the hero of a hagiography crediting him with transcendence:

Kong Anguo was a native of Lu.[121] He habitually circulated *qi* and ingested lead and cinnabar.[122] He reached 300 years of age and had the appearance of a boy. He secluded himself in Mount Qian,[123] [but] he had hundreds of disciples as followers. Each time he abstained from grains and entered his chamber, he would reemerge after a year and a half even younger-looking than before. During the times when he was not within his chamber, he ate and drank normally and was in this respect no different than ordinary people.

As a person, Anguo was very serious. He guarded the essentials of his Way with unusual care and was unwilling to transmit them lightly. He examined for five or six years the character of those who served him and only then made a transmission to them. There was a certain Chen Bo 陳伯, a native of Anle,[124] who sought to serve him. Anguo took him on as a disciple, and he stayed for three years. Anguo then knew Bo was trustworthy, so he told him: "When I was young, I worked even harder in search of arts of the Dao, and there was no place I did not go. But I was unable to obtain a divine elixir or any method for ascending to heaven by means of the eight minerals; I only received methods

119. Almost as bold is the transformation of the Warring States figure of Mozi into a transcendent; see ibid., 329–330.

120. See Loewe, *A Biographical Dictionary of the Qin, Former Han & Xin Periods,* 206–207; on the "old/new texts" controversy, see Nylan, "The *Chin wen/Ku wen* Controversy in Han Times."

121. An area in what is now southern Shandong Province, and the ancient home of Confucius, as any contemporary reader would have known.

122. Or "an elixir made from lead."

123. In modern Qianshan district, Anhui Province.

124. That is, of Anle district, situated in modern Shunyi district, Hebei Province.

for attaining earthbound transcendence that would allow one to postpone one's death. But then I began to serve a fisherman by the sea. This fisherman was the minister of the ancient kingdom of Yue, Fan Li 范蠡,[125] who had changed his names and remained in reclusion to escape perilous times. He took pity on me for my determination and transmitted to me secret macrobiotic methods by which one is able to transcend the world. It was by them that Da Wu, Si Cheng, Zi Qi, Jiang Bo, and Tu Shan[126] managed to revert to youthful appearance after reaching 1,000 years in age. Since the time when I received this Way, I have been ingesting its drugs for over 300 years. I transmitted just one of the methods to Cui Zhongqing 崔仲卿[127] when he was 84 years old, and he has been taking the product for 33 years now. If you examine his skin and build, you will see that his breath and strength are extremely healthy, his hair has not gone white, his teeth are all intact and firm. You should go and serve him." So Chen Bo did so. He received his methods, and he, too, transcended the world and did not grow old.

There was also the wife of a certain Zhang He 張合. At the age of 50, she ingested [the elixir] and reverted to the appearance of someone in her early twenties. The whole district wondered at this. At the age of 86, she gave birth to a son.

Anguo also taught several other people; they all lived 400 years. Afterward he entered the mountains and departed.[128]

Thus reads one of the most bizarre hagiographies attributed to *Traditions*. It is bizarre not for the sort of story it tells, which is utterly typical, but because of its subject. I am aware of no subsequent counter-narratives, but it is certain that some readers would have been shocked, others bemused, others simply amused at what is asserted here: Confucius' direct descendant numbered among *xian* of old! As if anticipating this reaction, the text furnishes certain details that might serve to explain why Kong Anguo had such an utterly different reputation in the more mainstream historical

---

125. The minister Fan Li is attested in several ancient texts, receives a hagiography in *Traditions of Exemplary Transcendents,* the content of which is partially reflected in our text (Kaltenmark, *Le Lie-sien tchouan,* 102–104), and figures in a few early medieval accounts of anomalies (see *SW,* 198). An ancient text of uncertain date and seemingly alchemical content, the *Fan zi Jiran,* was ascribed to him; fragments survive, one of them (cited in *TPYL* 812:7a) describing the transformation of black lead filings into "yellow cinnabar" and its successive transformation into "watery powder."

126. The text is here difficult to interpret. These figures, about whom nothing is known, may have been legendary Zhou officials, thus contemporaries of Fan Li.

127. Of whom nothing further is known, except that Ge Hong mentions in passing having seen books by a man apparently named Cui Zhong (*NP* 15.272), who may be the same person.

128. *TL,* 311–312, omitting the last line, which is obviously a much later addition to the text.

accounts. His extreme secrecy, his utmost caution in transmitting secret methods only to choice disciples, and the statement that "during the times when he was not within his chamber, he ate and drank normally and was in this respect no different from ordinary people" all conspire to offer the puzzled or skeptical reader an implied theory of why Kong has heretofore been known only as a Han official and old-text-discoverer: he kept his secrets very well indeed, leading a double—and very long—life.

This extraordinary co-optation may not have originated with Ge Hong; I suspect he was here, as in many other cases, drawing on already current traditions. In his *Inner Chapters,* Ge cites a work titled simply *Esoterica* (*Miji* 秘記) that is attributed to Kong Anguo. The cited passage concerns Zhang Liang 張良 (d. 187 B.C.E.), a figure known in the histories and other texts as an advocate of Laozian values at the early Han court. It maintains that Zhang was in fact a student of the ancient Sire Yellowstone (Huangshi gong 黃石公) and his teachers the Four Elders (Sihao 四皓[129])—all of whom are here credited with having been transcendents themselves. Zhang had, thanks to methods received from them, achieved transcendence despite popular opinion that he died.[130]

The implicit if unsubtle agenda, both of the hagiography and of the attribution of the *Esoterica* story to Kong Anguo, is to win legitimacy in readers' eyes for the transcendence quest. Even Kong, the argument runs, a direct descendant of Confucius himself (a descent line with maximal cultural capital attached to it), wrote about matters of esoteric practice and attained *xian*-hood. If he did this, yet did it in secret so that historians and court chroniclers had no knowledge of it, perhaps many others around you are doing so as well. And if many others, past and present—even Confucius' descendants—were in quest of transcendence and seeking out its arts and texts, perhaps the reader should do so as well.

There were practitioners, and there were accounts of practitioners. Whether or not the practitioners attained their goals of bodily deathlessness and celestial appointment (or, it may be, ongoing life here on earth), some of them, at least,

---

129. On them, see ibid., 307 n.67.

130. *NP* 5:113. An old man who associates himself with the "yellow stone" at Mount Jicheng, and who bestows an esoteric military manual on Zhang Liang, appears in *Han shu* 40.2024. Sire Yellowstone receives a biography in Huangfu Mi's *Traditions of Eminent Masters* (*Gaoshi zhuan* 高士傳 2:12a–13a), and military manuals (perhaps including methods for summoning spirit-troops) were attributed to him (see *Sui shu,* "Jingji zhi," 1013, for several titles). Two versions of a "silk text" attributed to him also are preserved in the Daoist canon (*DZ* 1178, 1179); both have Song commentaries and consist of mostly moral and political instruction for rulers, and the preface to the latter version says the text was found during the Jin disorder in Zhang Liang's tomb. The entry on *DZ* 1179 in Schipper and Verellen, eds., *The Taoist Canon,* 64–65, holds open the possibility that this text really does derive from Zhang Liang of the Han.

attained the sort of immortality bestowed by collective memory, in that we still read and discuss their stories today. These stories were shaped and transmitted by many parties with many concerns. Adepts themselves had a role in such narration, as we saw in Chapter 5, but the story-making by no means stopped there. It was a continuous process of contestation. Many sorts of persuasive work were done by many parties through the vehicle of *xian* stories, some more successfully than others. A family might in effect nominate a practitioner it sponsored for inclusion in translocal arrays of *xian,* hoping thus to enhance its own prestige; the nomination might or might not be ratified by collectors of *xian* accounts. Figures on record as having died could be brought back to life in narrative. Individuals who had argued against the possibility of transcendence could be turned into its advocates. From the obscure but productive mills of collective memory and its narrations, even a descendant of Confucius—revered font of a tradition inimical to almost every aspect of the quest for transcendence—could emerge as a successful *xian.* Of this making of stories, counter-stories, and counter-counter-stories there was, and is, no end.

Epilogue

IN LATE CLASSICAL and early medieval China, individuals became transcendents not solely by their own efforts but by those of many other people as well. They came to be recognized as transcendents in the course of their multifaceted interactions with others, and, as a result of people's responses to them, during and after their active presence in communities. Their reputations were formed by social and conversational processes that occurred mostly outside the texts that survive for us to read today. But these are processes to which our texts bear considerable witness, if we read them with the right questions in mind; also, they are processes in which our texts themselves participated, along with many others now lost. Although there was no official body or formal procedure governing these social, verbal, and textual processes of recognition—unlike the canonization process developed by the Roman Catholic church in medieval and modern times—they were no less decisive for being decentralized and informal. Transcendence, like any other designation of the achievement of holiness or spiritual virtuosity in any religious or cultural tradition, was socially constituted. Each chapter of this book has taken up a facet of these complex social processes.

As I was writing this book, I was fortunate enough to be invited to present my work-in-progress to several academic audiences. More than once someone asked a version of the following question, here phrased as bluntly as possible: Many practitioners of transcendence arts, I seemed to be saying, were faking it. My talk of performance, of playing the role of transcendent-to-be before audiences of other people, my emphasis on the reception by others of the adepts' performances as a key determinant of their success in playing the role, all seemed to add up to an imputation of insincerity. Was it not possible that some adepts, at least, really believed that their arts would result in long life and ascent into the celestial hierarchy and that many among their audience and clientele similarly believed in the reality of their achievements and goals?

My answer was always a version of the following. First, as indicated at several points throughout this book, the discernment of this or that *particular* adept's sincerity or depth of conviction, from our historical distance and from the sorts of evidence that survive, is simply impossible. Second, there was certainly a climate of widespread belief in the possibility of transcendence by means of various arts, in certain specific notions and images of transcendence, and in the success of particular adepts in having achieved this state. It was this general (which is not at all to say universally shared) climate of belief, and the shared imaginaire that gave it coherence and structure, that made all particular cases possible. Third, my framing things in terms of performance, role, and reception is not meant to imply disbelief on the part of the historical actors studied here. To say that transcendence-seekers *performed the role* of transcendence-seeker in society is not at all to say, or even imply, that they *just* played a role in whose ontological underpinnings and cosmo-theological goals they lacked any conviction. It is surely the dramaturgical analogy itself that encourages this misunderstanding: the theatrical audience knows that the actor is not really the character he plays on the stage; he is "just performing." A skilled actor can make his audience forget, for a time, that they are seeing a play, but at curtain call the audience is reminded of the "just-pretend" aspect of what they have just witnessed. My analogy, in this sense, is flawed. Practitioners of transcendence arts—at least the sincere ones—aimed to *become* the sorts of beings their arts were designed to create. They were engaged in gradual processes of profound, momentous self-transformation, and their reception by audiences (at least nonskeptical audiences) was premised on an understanding of this fact. They were not temporarily and self-consciously *just pretending* to be seekers of transcendence.

But I also want to insist that the dyads of belief/nonbelief, sincerity/fraudulence, or being/pretending, are much too simple to fit the empirical, psychological, human facts here. A glance at one example from anthropological literature will help to clarify this. Such reports are useful because they document eyewitness observations of situations seen in the round, in which many persons, with their multiple perspectives, participated; they are thus less limited in scope than most historical documents, each of which has its own point of view to advance. Claude Lévi-Strauss, in his essay "The Sorcerer and His Magic," summarizes two stories, each drawn from earlier published anthropological reports, of sorcerers or shamans at work in their social environments. The stories emphasize the key role of audiences' responses and expectations as well as the complexity and mutability of the adept's own state of mind concerning the abilities he is credited with having. For brevity's sake, I will focus on just one story, first related by M. C. Stevenson based on fieldwork among the Zuni people of New Mexico.

A girl suffers a nervous seizure after an adolescent boy had grabbed her by the hands. The boy is accused of sorcery and subjected to a judicial procedure. At first he denies having any knowledge of occult power, but he sees that this defense will not work, and since sorcery is punishable by death, he changes his tactics. He improvises a story of how he had been initiated, saying he had received two substances from his teachers, one of which drove girls mad while the other cured them. Ordered to produce the medicines, he goes home under guard and returns with two roots, which he uses in a complex ritual; he simulates a trance after taking one of the drugs, then pretends to return to normal after taking the other. He administers the remedy to the afflicted girl and declares her cured. During a break in the proceedings, he escapes, but is recaptured and put back on trial, this time by the girl's own family. They reject his first story, so he invents a new one, saying his relatives were all sorcerers and had given him the ability to change shapes and kill human victims by shooting cactus needles into them—abilities, he claimed, which are due to the powers of certain plumes. The judges demand that he produce his plumes as proof. After many excuses and attempts to forestall the process, he finds, after several hours of taking apart the walls of his home where he had claimed the fictive source of his powers was hidden, an old plume in the plaster. He presents it as evidence; he is made to explain how it is used. He is then dragged into the plaza and made to repeat his entire story, on which he elaborates further. He finishes by lamenting the loss of his special powers. Reassured, his accusers free him.[1]

Lévi-Strauss astutely comments:

By his confession, the defendant is transformed into a witness for the prosecution, with the participation (and even the complicity) of the judges. Through the defendant, witchcraft and the ideas associated with it cease to exist as a diffuse complex of poorly formulated sentiments and representations and become embodied in real experience. The defendant, who serves as a witness, gives the group the satisfaction of truth, which is infinitely greater and richer than the satisfaction of justice that would have been achieved by his execution. And finally, by his ingenious defense which makes his hearers progressively aware of the vitality offered by his corroboration of their system . . . , the youth, who at first was a threat to the physical security of the group, became the guardian of its spiritual coherence.

But is his defense merely ingenious? Everything leads us to believe that after groping for a subterfuge, the defendant participates with sincerity and—the word is not too strong—fervor in the drama enacted between him and his judges. He is

---

1. Lévi-Strauss, *Structural Anthropology*, 172–173. My thanks to Bob Hymes for reminding me of this essay.

proclaimed a sorcerer; since sorcerers do exist, he might as well be one. And how would he know beforehand the signs which might reveal his calling to him? Perhaps the signs are there, present in this ordeal and in the convulsions of the little girl brought before the court. For the boy, too, the coherence of the system and the role assigned to him in preserving it are values no less essential than the personal security which he risks in the venture. Thus we see him, with a mixture of cunning and good faith, progressively construct the impersonation which is thrust upon him—chiefly by drawing on his knowledge and his memories, improvising somewhat, but above all living his role and seeking, through his manipulations and the ritual he builds from bits and pieces, the experience of a calling which is, at least theoretically, open to all. At the end of the adventure, what remains of his earlier hoaxes? To what extent has the hero become a dupe of his own impersonation? What is more, has he not truly become a sorcerer? We are told that in his final confession, "The longer the boy talked the more absorbed he became in his subject. . . . At times his face became radiant with satisfaction at his power over his listeners." The girl recovers after he performs his curing ritual. The boy's experiences during the extraordinary ordeal become elaborated and structured. Little more is needed than for the innocent boy finally to confess to the possession of supernatural powers that are already shared by the group.[2]

We see here a *type* of process of finding one's way into a role about which one is ambivalent, a type of process that is, I suspect, not at all uncommon in many societies, whether the role in question is that of sorcerer, magician, wonder-worker, healer, preacher, or teacher. It is clear that in this case at least three things in the world *really change* as a result of this remarkable process. First, a boy comes to be newly seen by others as a sorcerer; second, a girl believed to be under the grip of sorcery, exhibiting disturbing symptoms, recovers; and third, a community's loosely organized beliefs about sorcery are clarified and reaffirmed by a detailed public examination of a single instance of its workings. But it seems a fourth thing also changes, namely, the boy's notion of himself, his sense of his role among others, his identity. Initially accused of having acted from a role he does not actually inhabit (or, perhaps better, a role he does not yet think of himself as inhabiting), he proceeds, in effect, by resorting to generally available knowledge about how sorcery works, to talk and act his way into that very role in order to save his life. Whether we measure by his own attitude and deportment or by the effects of his activities on others and their reception of him, he has, by the end of the process, indeed *become a sorcerer.* Yet—here is, for me, the crux of the matter—at no point in the process would we want to say that the dyads "sincere/faking it" or "believes/does

---

2. Ibid., 173–175.

not believe" are anywhere close to adequate in describing the complexity of the boy's actual, shifting states of mind.

Surely something similar was often the case among our seekers of transcendence, even if the extant documents about them, with their constraints of genre and point of view, mostly deny us any such candid, up-close look at how they thought of themselves moment by moment.

Another question I was often asked, in contexts ranging from invited lectures to classroom work, boils down to this. What have been passed in review here are merely some stories (and their associated ideas and assumptions) from the past. Is it not possible to know *what really happened?* The answer I have given to this question remains the same today.

I could well wish for the sort of informant Michel de Montaigne described in his essay "Of Cannibals," written between 1578 and 1580:

> I had with me for a long time a man who had lived for ten or twelve years in that other world [Brazil] which has been discovered in our century....This man I had was a simple, crude fellow—a character fit to bear true witness; for clever people observe more things and more curiously, but they interpret them; and to lend weight and conviction to their interpretation, they cannot help altering history a little. They never show you things as they are [*ils ne vous representent jamais les choses pures*], but bend and disguise them according to the way they have seen them; and to give credence to their judgment and attract you to it, they are prone to add something to their matter, to stretch it out and amplify it. We need a man either very honest, or so simple that he has not the stuff to build up false inventions and give them plausibility; and wedded to no theory. Such was my man; and besides this, he at various times brought sailors and merchants, whom he had known on that trip, to see me. So I content myself with his information.[3]

When studying phenomena as far removed from us as the quest for transcendence in early medieval China, what a luxury it would be to have at our disposal this sort of neutral witness, an informant who told of what simply *was,* not of what was *seen* from some limited point of view, and who in doing so added nothing, no invention or amplification, one who, further, had nothing at stake—no theory, no interest—in his telling and its reception by us listeners. But, of course, the very idea of such a witness is sheer fantasy. Even the most self-consciously and scrupulously objective historical accounts bend events in the telling of them, if there is even any

---

3. Frame, tr., *The Complete Essays of Montaigne,* 150–152. For a reflection on the passage in its Renaissance context, see Greenblatt, *Marvelous Possessions,* 146–151.

such thing as an "event" apart from some embedding chain of narrative. The vast preponderance of evidence we have about the quest for transcendence is textual evidence, much of it narrative in genre, and narratives and other texts by definition "never show you things as they are but bend and disguise them according to the way they"—their narrators—"have seen them."[4] The real questions, then, are ones such as these: Who were the narrators or text-makers, the subjects, the listeners, and the readers? What sorts of stories did the narrators tell, and how did they function to invest their subjects (and sometimes their tellers) with the sort of authoritative persona that would be recognized by others as an authentic transcendence-seeker? What were the interests and aims at stake in these exchanges? What larger ideas and assumptions made such texts sensible, plausible, and possible? What other sorts of activities surrounded these story-telling, story-receiving, text-fashioning activities? How did audiences respond and relate to practitioners of esoteric arts? These are the sorts of questions I have attempted to answer in this book. They, too, are questions about *what really happened,* in that they are about the real activities of many people and the traces of those activities that remain for us to study.

To become a successful *xian* required not only the pursuit of esoteric disciplines. One also had to be deemed by others to have transcended. This process of deeming—of the reception and perception of adepts by communities of others, conditioned only partially by whatever the adept himself said or did—is attested, by texts both sympathetic and hostile, to have centrally involved the fashioning and exchange of narrative and other texts by many parties. The stories of how adepts became *xian,* and the recording and transmission of these stories, were essential to the self-presentation of adepts and to the responses of others. When we consider the essential role of stories and other texts in the fashioning of the adepts' social identities and in their reception and remembrance by audiences, no easy dichotomy can be drawn between story or text and practice, between what happened and the story of what happened or texts prescribing what should happen, that would allow us to keep the practices and events while discarding the stories and texts about

---

4. Abraham Lincoln, the most important figure in his country and time, died in a small room crowded with people in an era of mass media, but accounts published immediately and slightly later do not agree on the solemn words pronounced by his secretary of war, Edwin Stanton, on this momentous occasion. Furthermore, he was shot in a theater full of people, but no one could agree later on just what the murderer, John Wilkes Booth, shouted, or exactly when he shouted it—not even Booth himself; see Gopnik, "Angels and Ages"; and compare Singer, "The Castaways," for a case in which even participants in an event later give accounts that disagree on important details and in which media reports tweak the details this way and that in line with their interests. The moral: *all* stories are interested; none are pure (which is not to say that all are untrue). This makes knowing *what really happened* a difficult business indeed, at least in any way of "knowing" that would satisfy the curiosity that drives the question.

them. Events and practices, the experiences of adepts, their modes of self-presentation, and their reception by clients, came already textually shaped and collectively structured, life and art imitating each other in a continual feedback loop.

I am reminded of Clifford Geertz's "Indian story . . . about an Englishman who, having been told that the world rested on a platform which rested on the back of an elephant which rested in turn on the back of a turtle, asked . . . what did the turtle rest on? Another turtle. And that turtle? 'Ah, Sahib, after that it is turtles all the way down.'"[5] In trying to understand the quest for transcendence, however deep we dig, what we find, along with methods and ideas, is mostly texts, in varying versions and of varying uses—texts all the way down. But they sustained a world.

---

5. Geertz, *The Interpretation of Cultures,* 28–29.

Bibliography

Abbreviations and Works Cited by Acronym

CEA	*Cahiers d'Extrême-Asie*
DKW	*Dai kanwa jiten* 大漢和辭典. Comp. Morohashi Tetsuji. 13 vols. Tokyo: Taishūkan shoten, 1957–1960.
DZ	See Schipper and Verellen, eds., *The Taoist Canon*, in Secondary Sources
HJAS	*Harvard Journal of Asiatic Studies*
HR	*History of Religions*
HY	*Harvard-Yenching Sinological Index Series*
JAOS	*Journal of the American Oriental Society*
JCR	*Journal of Chinese Religions*
LX	Lu Xun 魯迅, ed., *Gu xiaoshuo gouchen* 古小說鉤沈. Beijing: Renmin wenxue chubanshe, 1954.
NP	*Baopuzi neipian jiaoshi* 抱朴子內篇校釋 by Ge Hong 葛洪. Ed. Wang Ming 王明. Beijing: Zhonghua shuju, 1985.
SW	See Campany, *Strange Writing*, in Secondary Sources
T	*Taishō shinshū daizōkyō* 大正新修大藏經. Ed. Takakusa Junjirō and Watanabe Kaikyoku. Tokyo: Daizōkyōkai, 1924–1935. Texts are cited by the number assigned them in this edition.
TL	See Campany, *To Live as Long as Heaven and Earth,* in Secondary Sources
TP	*T'oung Pao*
TPGJ	*Taiping guangji* 太平廣記. Comp. Li Fang 李昉 et al. 4 vols. Shanghai: Shanghai guji chubanshe, 1990.
TPYL	*Taiping yulan* 太平御覽. Comp. Li Fang 李昉 et al. Facsimile rpt. of Shangwu yinshuguan 1935 printing from a Song copy. 4 vols. Beijing: Zhonghua shuju, 1992.
TR	*Taoist Resources*
YJQQ	*Yunji qiqian.* DZ 1032 (see numbered entry in Primary Sources by Category)
YWLJ	*Yiwen leiju* 藝文類聚. Comp. Ouyang Xun et al. Modern recension by Wang Shaoying. 2 vols. continuously paginated. Beijing: Zhonghua shuju, 1965.

Primary Sources, by Category

PRIMARY SOURCES IN THE DAOIST CANON, CITED BY NUMBER ASSIGNED IN *DZ*

185   *Chisongzi zhongjie jing* 赤松子中誡經
283   *Huangdi longshou jing* 黃帝龍首經
284   *Huangdi jinkui yuheng jing* 黃帝金匱玉衡經
285   *Huangdi shou sanzi xuannü jing* 黃帝授三子玄女經
292   *Han Wudi neizhuan* 漢武帝內傳
293   *Han Wudi waizhuan* 漢武帝外傳
294   *Liexian zhuan* 列仙傳
388   *Taishang lingbao wufu xu* 太上靈寶五符序
598   *Shizhou ji* 十洲記
682   *Daode zhenjing zhu* 道德真經註
786   *Taishang laojun jinglü* 太上老君經律
818   *Taiqing daoyin yangsheng jing* 太清導引養生經
881   *Taiqing shibi ji* 太清石壁記
883   *Taiqing jing tianshi koujue* 太清經天師口訣
885   *Huangdi jiuding shendan jingjue* 黃帝九鼎神丹經訣
1016 *Zhen'gao* 真誥
1018 *Huangdi neijing suwen buzhu shiwen* 黃帝內經素問補註釋文
1020 *Huangdi suwen lingshu jizhu* 黃帝素問靈書集註
1032 *Yunji qiqian* 雲笈七籤
1168 *Taishang laojun zhongjing* 太上老君中經
1178 *Huangshi gong sushu* 黃石公素書
1179 *Huangshi gong sushu* 黃石公素書
1184 *Huainan honglie jie* 淮南鴻烈解 (also cited in another edition as *Huainanzi*; see below)
1437 *Taishang laojun kaitian jing* 太上老君開天經

PRIMARY SOURCES CITED BY TITLE
Bowu zhi 博物志 by Zhang Hua 張華
      Bowu zhi jiaozheng 博物志校証. Ed. Fan Ning 范寧. Beijing: Zhonghua shuju, 1980.
Chuci jizhu 楚辭集註. N.p.: Saoye shanfang, n.d.
Daode jing 道德經
      Lao-tzu Te-tao ching: A New Translation Based on the Recently Discovered Ma-wang-tui Texts. Tr. with intro. and commentary by Robert G. Henricks. New York: Ballantine Books, 1989.
Fa yan 法言 by Yang Xiong 揚雄. Zhuzi jicheng ed.
Fayuan zhulin 法苑珠林 by Daoshi 道世. T 2122
Fengsu tongyi 風俗通義 by Ying Shao 應劭
      Fengsu tongyi jiaozhu 風俗通義校注. Ed. Wang Liqi 王利器. 2 vols. continuously paginated. Beijing: Zhonghua shuju, 1981.

Gaoshi zhuan 高士傳 by Huangfu Mi 皇甫謐
  Gujin yishi 古今遺史 ed. Shanghai: Commercial Press, 1937.
Gaoseng zhuan 高僧傳 by Huijiao 慧皎. T 2059.
Han Feizi jijie 韓非子集解. Sibu kanyao ed., 1896. Rpt. Taibei: Shijie shuju, 1974.
Han shu 漢書. Zhonghua shuju ed.
Han Wudi gushi 漢武帝故事. LX ed.
Hou Han shu 後漢書. Zhonghua shuju ed.
Huainanzi 淮南子. Zhuzi jicheng ed.
Huayangguo zhi 華陽國志 by Chang Qu 常璩
  Huayangguo zhi jiaozhu 華陽國志校注. Ed. Liu Lin 劉琳. Chengdu: Bashu shu-
  she, 1984.
Jin shu 晉書. Zhonghua shuju ed.
Liezi jishi 列子集釋. Ed. Yang Bojun 楊伯峻. Beijing: Zhonghua shuju, 1979.
Liji zhengyi 裡記正義. Shisanjing zhushu ed. Shanghai: Shanghai guji chubanshe, 1990.
Lunheng 論衡 by Wang Chong 王充
  Lunheng jiaoshi 論衡校釋. Ed. Huang Hui 黃暉. 4 vols. continuously paginated.
  Beijing: Zhonghua shuju, 1990.
Mencius
  Mencius. Tr. with intro. by D. C. Lau. Harmondsworth: Penguin, 1970.
Mingxiang ji 冥祥記. LX ed.
Mozi jijie 墨子集解. Ed. Zhang Dunyi 張純一. Chengdu: Chengdu guji shudian, 1988.
Shi ji 史記. Zhonghua shuju ed.
Shijing 詩經. Cited in edition *Shijing jizhuan* 詩經集傳, ed. Zhu Xi 朱熹. Shanghai:
  Shanghai guji chubanshe, 1987.
Shishuo xinyu 世說新語. Ed. Yang Jialuo. Facsimile rpt. of a Song ed. with annotations
  by Liu Jun. Taipei: Shijie shuju, 1982.
Shiyi ji 拾遺記 by Wang Jia 王嘉. *Zengding Han Wei congshu* edition.
Shuijing zhu 水經注. By Li Daoyuan 酈道元. Ed. Dai Zhen 戴震. Taibei: Shijie shuju,
  1988.
Shuyi ji 述異記 by Ren Fang 任昉. *Zengding Han Wei congshu* ed. Wang Mo 王謨 comp.
  N.p., n.d.
Shuyi ji 述異記 by Zu Chongzhi 祖沖之. LX ed.
Soushen houji 搜神後記 attributed to Tao Qian 陶潛
  Ed. Wang Shaoying. *Gu xiaoshuo congkan* series. Beijing: Zhonghua shuju, 1981.
Soushen ji 搜神記 by Gan Bao 干寶
  Xinjiao Soushen ji. Ed. Yang Jialuo. Taibei: Shijie shuju, 1982.
Sui shu 隋書. Zhonghua shuju ed.
Taipingjing hejiao 太平經合校. Ed. Wang Ming 王明. Beijing: Zhonghua shuju, 1960.
Xinyu 新語 by Lu Jia 陸賈. *Zhuzi jicheng* ed.
Yiyuan 異苑 by Liu Jingshu 劉敬叔. Baibu congshu jicheng ed. Ed. Yan Yiping 嚴一萍.
  N.p.: Yiwen yinshuguan, n.d.
Youming lu 幽明錄. LX ed.
Zhuangzi 莊子. HY ed.

SECONDARY SOURCES

Andersen, Poul. "Talking to the Gods: Visionary Divination in Early Taoism (The San-huang Tradition)." *Taoist Resources* 5.1 (1994): 1–24.

Atkinson, J. Maxwell, and John Heritage, eds. *Structures of Social Action: Studies in Conversation Analysis.* Cambridge: Cambridge University Press, 1984.

Austin, J. L. *How to Do Things with Words.* Oxford: Clarendon, 1962.

Balazs, Etienne. *Chinese Civilization and Bureaucracy.* Ed. Arthur F. Wright. Tr. H. M. Wright. New Haven: Yale University Press, 1964.

Bauman, Richard. *Story, Performance, and Event.* Cambridge: Cambridge University Press, 1986.

Baxandall, Michael. *Patterns of Intention: On the Historical Explanation of Pictures.* New Haven, CT: Yale University Press, 1985.

Bellman, Beryl Larry. *The Language of Secrecy: Symbols and Metaphors in Poro Ritual.* New Brunswick, NJ: Rutgers University Press, 1984.

Benn, James A. *Burning for the Buddha: Self-Immolation in Chinese Buddhism.* Honolulu: University of Hawai'i Press, 2007.

Berkowitz, Alan. *Patterns of Disengagement: The Practice and Portrayal of Reclusion in Early Medieval China.* Stanford: Stanford University Press, 2000.

Berlinerblau, Jacques. "Max Weber's Useful Ambiguities and the Problem of Defining 'Popular Religion.'" *Journal of the American Academy of Religion* 69 (2001): 605–626.

Birrell, Anne. *Chinese Mythology: An Introduction.* Baltimore: Johns Hopkins University Press, 1993.

Bodde, Derk. *Festivals in Classical China.* Princeton, NJ: Princeton University Press, 1975.

Bohannan, Paul. *How Culture Works.* New York: Free Press, 1995.

Bokenkamp, Stephen R. *Ancestors and Anxiety: Daoism and the Birth of Rebirth in China.* Berkeley: University of California Press, 2007.

———. *Early Daoist Scriptures.* With a contribution by Peter Nickerson. Berkeley: University of California Press, 1997.

———. "The Peach Flower Font and the Grotto Passage." *JAOS* 106 (1986): 65–77.

———. "Simple Twists of Fate." In *The Magnitude of Ming: Heaven's Command and Life's Lot,* ed. Christopher Lupke, 151–168. Honolulu: University of Hawai'i Press, 2004.

Bourdieu, Pierre. *Language and Symbolic Power.* Ed. John B. Thompson. Tr. Gino Raymond and Matthew Adamson. Cambridge, MA: Harvard University Press, 1991.

Boyd, David C. "Transcendents in Transition: The Origins and Development of *Xian* 僊 in Ancient China." M.A. thesis, University of Colorado, 2005.

Brashier, K. E. "Longevity like Metal and Stone: The Role of the Mirror in Han Burials." *TP* 81 (1995): 201–229.

———. "Text and Ritual in Early Chinese Stelae." In *Text and Ritual in Early China,* ed. Martin Kern, 249–284. Seattle: University of Washington Press, 2005.

Brown, Miranda. *The Politics of Mourning in Early China.* Albany: State University of New York Press, 2007.

Brown, Peter. *The Cult of the Saints: Its Rise and Function in Latin Christianity.* Chicago, IL: University of Chicago Press, 1981.

————. "Enjoying the Saints in Late Antiquity." *Early Medieval Europe* 9 (2000): 1–24.

————. "The Rise and Function of the Holy Man in Late Antiquity." *Journal of Roman Studies* 61 (1971): 80–101.

————. "The Rise and Function of the Holy Man in Late Antiquity, 1971–1997." *Journal of Early Christian Studies* 6 (1998): 353–376.

————. "The Saint as Exemplar in Late Antiquity." In *Saints and Virtues,* ed. John Stratton, 3–14. Berkeley: University of California Press, 1987.

Bruner, Jerome. *Actual Minds, Possible Worlds.* Cambridge, MA: Harvard University Press, 1986.

————. "The Narrative Construction of Reality." *Critical Inquiry* 18 (1991): 1–21.

Bujard, Marianne. "Le culte de Wangzi Qiao ou la longue carrière d'un immortel." *Études chinoises* 19 (2000): 115–158.

————. *Le sacrifice au ciel dans la Chine ancienne: Théorie et pratique sous les Han occidentaux.* Paris: École Française d'Extrême-Orient, 2000.

Bulling, A. *The Decorations of Mirrors of the Han Dynasty: A Chronology.* Artibus Asiae Supplement 20, 1960.

Bumbacher, Stephan P. "The Fragments of the *Daoxue zhuan:* Critical Edition, Translation and Analysis of a Medieval Collection of Daoist Biographies." Inaugural-Dissertation, Universität Heidelberg, 1995.

Burke, Peter. *The Art of Conversation.* Ithaca, NY: Cornell University Press, 1993.

————. *History and Social Theory.* Ithaca, NY: Cornell University Press, 1993.

Cahill, Suzanne E. *Transcendence and Divine Passion: The Queen Mother of the West in Medieval China.* Stanford, CA: Stanford University Press, 1993.

Cammann, Schuyler. "The 'TLV' Pattern on Cosmic Mirrors in the Han Dynasty." *JAOS* 68 (1948): 159–167.

Campany, Robert Ford. "Buddhist Revelation and Taoist Translation in Early Medieval China." *TR* 4.1 (1993): 1–29.

————. "The Earliest Tales of the Bodhisattva Guanshiyin." In *Religions of China in Practice,* ed. Donald S. Lopez, Jr., 82–96. Princeton, NJ: Princeton University Press, 1996.

————. "Eating Better than Gods and Ancestors." In *Of Tripod and Palate: Food, Politics, and Religion in Traditional China,* ed. Roel Sterckx, 96–122. London: Palgrave, 2005.

————. "Ghosts Matter: The Culture of Ghosts in Six Dynasties *Zhiguai.*" *Chinese Literature: Essays, Articles, Reviews* 13 (1991): 15–34.

————. "Living off the Books: Fifty Ways to Dodge *Ming* 命 in Early Medieval China." In *The Magnitude of Ming: Heaven's Command and Life's Lot,* ed. Christopher Lupke, 129–150. Honolulu: University of Hawai'i Press, 2005.

————. "Long-Distance Specialists in Early Medieval China." In *Journeys West and East,* ed. Eric Ziolkowski, 109–124. Wilmington: University of Delaware Press, 2005.

————. "The Meanings of Cuisines of Transcendence in Late Classical and Early Medieval China." *TP* 91 (2005): 126–182.

———. "Narrative in the Self-Presentation of Transcendence-Seekers." In *Literature and Interpretation in Early Medieval China,* ed. Alan K. L. Chan and Y. K. Lo. Albany: State University of New York Press, forthcoming.

———. "Notes on the Devotional Uses and Symbolic Functions of Sutra Texts as Depicted in Early Chinese Buddhist Miracle Tales and Hagiographies." *Journal of the International Association of Buddhist Studies* 14.1 (1991): 2872.

———. "On the Very Idea of Religions (in the Modern West and in Early Medieval China)." *HR* 42 (2003): 287–319.

———. "The Real Presence." *HR* 32.3 (1993): 233–272.

———. "Secrecy and Display in the Quest for Transcendence in China, ca. 220 B.C.E.–350 C.E." *HR* 45 (2006): 291–336.

———. *Strange Writing: Anomaly Accounts in Early Medieval China.* Albany: State University of New York Press, 1996.

———. *To Live as Long as Heaven and Earth: A Translation and Study of Ge Hong's Traditions of Divine Transcendents.* Berkeley: University of California Press, 2002.

———. "Two Religious Thinkers of the Early Eastern Jin: Gan Bao 干寶 and Ge Hong 葛洪 in Multiple Contexts." *Asia Major* 3rd ser. 18 (2005): 175–224.

Carr, David. "Narrative and the Real World: An Argument for Continuity." *History and Theory* 25 (1986): 117–131.

———. *Time, Narrative, and History.* Bloomington: Indiana University Press, 1986.

Carrithers, Michael. *The Forest Monks of Sri Lanka: An Anthropological and Historical Study.* Oxford: Oxford University Press, 1983.

———. *Why Humans Have Cultures: Explaining Anthropology and Social Diversity.* Oxford: Oxford University Press, 1992.

Castelli, Elizabeth A. *Martyrdom and Memory: Early Christian Culture Making.* New York: Columbia University Press, 2004.

Cedzich, Angelika. "Corpse Deliverance, Substitute Bodies, Name Change, and Feigned Death: Aspects of Metamorphosis and Immortality in Early Medieval China." *JCR* 29 (2001): 1–68.

Chan, Tim Wai-Keung. "Ruan Ji's and Xi Kang's Visits to Two 'Immortals.'" *Monumenta Serica* 44 (1996): 141–165.

Chang, K. C. "Ancient China." In *Food and Chinese Culture: Anthropological and Historical Perspectives,* ed. K. C. Chang, 23–52. New Haven, CT: Yale University Press, 1977.

Chard, Robert L. "The Imperial Household Cults." In *State and Court Ritual in China,* ed. Joseph P. McDermott, 237–266. Cambridge: Cambridge University Press, 1999.

———. "The Stove God and the Overseer of Fate." In *Proceedings of the International Conference on Popular Beliefs and Chinese Culture,* Center for Chinese Studies Research Series, no. 4, 2:655–682. Taipei: Center for Chinese Studies, 1994.

Chatman, Seymour. *Story and Discourse: Narrative Structure in Fiction and Film.* Ithaca, NY: Cornell University Press, 1978.

Che, Philippe. *La voie des divins immortels: Les chapitres discursifs du Baopuzi neipian par Ge Hong.* Paris: Gallimard, 1999.

Ch'en, Kenneth K. S. "Inscribed Stelae during the Wei, Chin, and Nan-ch'ao." In *Studia Asiatica: Essays in Asian Studies in Felicitation of Professor Ch'en Shou-yi,* ed. Laurence G. Thompson, 75–84. San Francisco: Chinese Materials Center, 1975.

Chen Yuan 陳垣. *Daojia jinshi lue* 道家金石略. Beijing: Wenwu chubanshe, 1988.

Chittick, Andrew. "The Development of Local Writing in Early Medieval China." *Early Medieval China* 9 (2003): 35–70.

Christian, William A., Jr. *Local Religion in Sixteenth-Century Spain.* Princeton, NJ: Princeton University Press, 1981.

Clark, Elizabeth A. "Holy Women, Holy Words: Early Christian Women, Social History, and the 'Linguistic Turn.'" *Journal of Early Christian Studies* 6 (1998): 413–430.

Cole, Alan. "Simplicity for the Sophisticated: Rereading the *Daode jing* for the Polemics of Ease and Innocence." *HR* 46 (2006): 1–49.

Collins, Randall. *Interaction Ritual Chains.* Princeton, NJ: Princeton University Press. 2004.

Collins, Steven. *Nirvana and Other Buddhist Felicities.* Cambridge: Cambridge University Press, 1998.

Confino, Alon. "Collective Memory and Cultural History: Problems of Method." *American Historical Review* 102 (1997): 1386–1403.

Connerton, Paul. *How Societies Remember.* Cambridge: Cambridge University Press, 1989.

Cook, Constance A., and John S. Major, eds. *Defining Chu: Image and Reality in Ancient China.* Honolulu: University of Hawai'i Press, 1999.

Cornell, Vincent J. *Realm of the Saint: Power and Authority in Moroccan Sufism.* Austin: University of Texas Press, 1998.

Crapanzano, Vincent. "'Self'-Centering Narratives." In *Natural Histories of Discourse,* ed. Michael Silverstein and Greg Urban, 106–127. Chicago, IL: University of Chicago Press, 1996.

Cronon, William. "A Place for Stories: Nature, History, and Narrative." *Journal of American History* 78 (1992): 1347–1376.

Crump, J. I. *Chan-kuo Ts'e.* 2nd ed. Ann Arbor: Center for Chinese Studies, University of Michigan, 1996.

Csikszentmihalyi, Mark. "Han Cosmology and Mantic Practices." In *Daoism Handbook,* ed. Livia Kohn, 53–73. Leiden: E. J. Brill, 2000.

———. *Material Virtue: Ethics and the Body in Early China.* Leiden: E. J. Brill, 2004.

———. "Reimagining the Yellow Emperor's Four Faces." In *Text and Ritual in Early China,* ed. Martin Kern, 226–248. Seattle: University of Washington Press, 2005.

Cutter, Robert Joe. "Cao Zhi's (192-232) Symposium Poems." *Chinese Literature: Essays, Articles, Reviews* 6 (1984): 1-32.

Davis, Natalie Zemon. *Fiction in the Archives: Pardon Tales and Their Tellers in Sixteenth-Century France.* Cambridge: Cambridge University Press, 1987.

Davis, Richard H. *Lives of Indian Images.* Princeton, NJ: Princeton University Press, 1997.

De Crespigny, Rafe. *A Biographical Dictionary of Later Han to the Three Kingdoms (23–220 A.D.).* Leiden: E. J. Brill, 2007.

Delehaye, Hippolyte. *The Legends of the Saints: An Introduction to Hagiography.* Tr. V. M. Crawford. 1907. Rpt. South Bend, IN: University of Notre Dame Press, 1961.

Delooz, Pierre. *Sociologie et canonisations.* The Hague: Martinus Nijhoff, 1969.

Demiéville, Paul. 1986. "Philosophy and Religion from Han to Sui." In *The Cambridge History of China.* Vol. 1, *The Ch'in and Han Empires, 221 B.C.–A.D. 220,* ed. Denis Twitchett and Michael Loewe, 808–872. Cambridge: Cambridge University Press, 1986.

DeWoskin, Kenneth J. *Doctors, Diviners, and Magicians of Ancient China: Biographies of "Fang-shih."* New York: Columbia University Press, 1983.

———. "The Six Dynasties *Chih-kuai* and the Birth of Fiction." In *Chinese Narrative: Critical and Theoretical Essays,* ed. A. H. Plaks, 21–52. Princeton, NJ: Princeton University Press, 1977.

———. "A Source Guide to the Lives and Techniques of Han and Six Dynasties *Fang-shih.*" *JCR* 9 (1981): 79–105.

———, and J. I. Crump, Jr. *In Search of the Supernatural: The Written Record.* Stanford, CA: Stanford University Press, 1996.

Dickie, Matthew W. *Magic and Magicians in the Greco-Roman World.* London: Routledge, 2001.

Diény, Jean-Pierre. *Les poèmes de Cao Cao.* Paris: Collège de France, Institut des Hautes Études Chinoises, 2000.

Dudbridge, Glen. *Religious Experience and Lay Society in T'ang China: A Reading of Tai Fu's "Kuang-i chi."* Cambridge: Cambridge University Press, 1995.

Durrant, Stephen W. *The Cloudy Mirror: Tension and Conflict in the Writings of Sima Qian.* Albany: State University of New York Press, 1995.

Ebersole, Gary L. *Captured by Texts: Puritan to Postmodern Images of Indian Captivity.* Charlottesville: University of Virginia Press, 1995.

Ebrey, Patricia. "Later Han Stone Inscriptions." *HJAS* 40 (1980): 325–353.

Edwards, E. D. "Principles of Whistling—Hsiao Chih—Anonymous." *Bulletin of the School of Oriental and African Studies* 20 (1957): 217–229.

Emmerich, Reinhard. "Bemerkungen zu Huang und Lao in der frühen Han-Zeit: Erkenntnisse aus *Shiji* und *Hanshu.*" *Monumenta Serica* 43 (1995): 53–140.

Erickson, Susan N. "Money Trees of the Eastern Han Dynasty." *Bulletin of the Museum of Far Eastern Antiquities* 66 (1994): 6–115.

Faraone, Christopher A., and Dirk Obbink, eds. *Magika Hiera: Ancient Greek Magic and Religion.* Oxford: Oxford University Press, 1991.

Fentress, James, and Chris Wickham. *Social Memory: New Perspectives on the Past.* Oxford: Blackwell, 1992.

Finsterbusch, Kate. *Verzeichnis und Motivindex der Han-Darstellungen.* 2 vols. Wiesbaden: Otto Harrassowitz, 1971.

Flood, Gavin. *The Ascetic Self: Subjectivity, Memory and Tradition.* Cambridge: Cambridge University Press, 2004.

Forke, Alfred. *Lun-hêng.* 2 vols. Rpt of 1907–1911 ed. New York: Paragon Book Gallery, 1962.

Foucault, Michel. *The Archaeology of Knowledge.* Tr. A. M. S. Smith. New York: Pantheon, 1972.

Frame, Donald M., tr. and ed. *The Complete Essays of Montaigne.* Stanford, CA: Stanford University Press, 1965.

Frank, Georgia. *The Memory of the Eyes: Pilgrims to Living Saints in Christian Late Antiquity.* Berkeley: University of California Press, 2000.

Frankel, Hans H. "Fifteen Poems by Ts'ao Chih: An Attempt at a New Approach." *JAOS* 84 (1964):1–14.

————. *The Flowering Plum and the Palace Lady: Interpretations of Chinese Poetry.* New Haven, CT: Yale University Press, 1976.

Frazer, James G. *The Golden Bough: A Study in Magic and Religion.* 2nd [abridged] ed. New York: Macmillan, 1951.

Gallagher, Catherine, and Stephen Greenblatt. *Practicing New Historicism.* Chicago, IL: University of Chicago Press, 2000.

Geertz, Clifford. *The Interpretation of Cultures.* New York: Basic Books, 1973.

Gelber, Hester Goodenough. "A Theater of Virtue: The Exemplary World of St. Francis of Assisi." In *Saints and Virtues,* ed. John Stratton Hawley, 15–35. Berkeley: University of California Press, 1987.

Gellner, Ernest. "Political and Religious Organization of the Berbers of the Central High Atlas." In *Arabs and Berbers: From Tribe to Nation in North Africa,* ed. Ernest Gellner and Charles Michaud, 59–66. London: Duckworth, 1973.

————. *Plow, Sword, and Book: The Structure of Human History.* Chicago, IL: University of Chicago Press, 1992.

Gleason, Maud. 1998. "Visiting and News: Gossip and Reputation-Management in the Desert." *Journal of Early Christian Studies* 6 (1998): 501–521.

Godlove, Terry. "In What Sense Are Religions Conceptual Frameworks?" *Journal of the American Academy of Religion* 52 (1983): 289–305.

Goffman, Erving. *Frame Analysis: An Essay on the Organization of Experience.* 1974. Rpt. Boston: Northeastern University, 1986.

————. *Interaction Ritual: Essays on Face-to-Face Behavior.* New York: Anchor, 1967.

————. *The Presentation of Self in Everyday Life.* New York: Anchor, 1959.

Golomb, Louis. *An Anthropology of Curing in Multiethnic Thailand.* Urbana: University of Illinois Press, 1985.

Goodman, Howard L. *Ts'ao P'i Transcendent: The Political Culture of Dynasty-Founding in China at the End of the Han.* Seattle: Scripta Serica, 1998.

Gopnik, Adam. "Angels and Ages: Lincoln's Language and Its Legacy." *The New Yorker,* May 28, 2007, 30–37.

Graf, Fritz. "Prayer in Magic and Religious Ritual." In *Magika Hiera: Ancient Greek Magic and Religion,* ed. Christopher A. Faraone and Dirk Obblink, 188–213. Oxford: Oxford University Press, 1991.

Graham, A. C. *The Book of Lieh-tzu: A Classic of the Tao.* New York: Columbia University Press, 1990.

————. *Chuang-tzu: The Inner Chapters.* London: HarperCollins, 1981.

————. *Studies of Chinese Philosophy and Philosophical Literature*. Singapore: Institute of East Asian Philosophies, 1986.

Greenblatt, Stephen. *Hamlet in Purgatory*. Princeton, NJ: Princeton University Press, 2001.

————. *Learning to Curse: Essays in Early Modern Culture*. 2nd ed. New York: Routledge, 2007.

————. *Marvelous Possessions: The Wonder of the New World*. Chicago, IL: University of Chicago Press, 1991.

————. *Renaissance Self-Fashioning: From More to Shakespeare*. Chicago, IL: University of Chicago Press, 1983.

————. "The Touch of the Real." In *The Fate of "Culture": Geertz and Beyond,* ed. Sherry B. Ortner, 14–29. Berkeley: University of California Press, 1999.

Gusfield, Joseph R. "The Bridge over Separated Lands: Kenneth Burke's Significance for the Study of Social Action." In *The Legacy of Kenneth Burke,* ed. Herbert W. Simons and Trever Melia, 28–54. Madison: University of Wisconsin Press, 1989.

Halbwachs, Maurice. *On Collective Memory*. Ed. and tr. Lewis A. Coser. Chicago, IL: University of Chicago Press, 1992.

Hanks, William F. "Exorcism and the Description of Participant Roles." In *Natural Histories of Discourse,* ed. Michael Silverstein and Greg Urban, 160–200. Chicago, IL: University of Chicago Press 1006.

Harper, Donald. "A Chinese Demonography of the Third Century B.C." *HJAS* 45 (1985): 459–498.

————. *Early Chinese Medical Literature*. London: Kegan Paul, 1998.

————. "Resurrection in Warring States Popular Religion." *TR* 5.2 (1994): 13–29.

————. "Warring States Natural Philosophy and Occult Thought." In *The Cambridge History of Ancient China*. Vol. 1, *From the Origins of Civilization to 221 B.C.,* ed. Michael Loewe and Edward L. Shaughnessy, 813–884. Cambridge: Cambridge University Press, 1999.

————. "Warring States, Qin, and Han Manuscripts Related to Natural Philosophy and the Occult." In *New Sources of Early Chinese History: An Introduction to the Reading of Inscriptions and Manuscripts,* ed. Edward L. Shaughnessy, 223–252. Berkeley: Society for the Study of Early China and Institute of East Asian Studies, University of California, 1997.

Hartman, Charles. "Stomping Songs: Word and Image." *Chinese Literature: Essays, Articles, Reviews* 17 (1995): 1–49.

Hawkes, David. "Ch'u tz'u." In *Early Chinese Texts: A Bibliographical Guide,* ed. Michael Loewe, 48–55. Berkeley: Society for the Study of Early China and the Institute of East Asian Studies, University of California, 1993.

Hawley, John Stratton, ed. *Saints and Virtues*. Berkeley, University of California Press, 1987.

Hayashi Minao 林 已奈夫. "Chūgoku kodai no sennin no zuzō ni tsuite" 中国古代の仙人の図像について. *Kōkogaku zasshi* 87 (2003): 193–206.

Heffernan, Thomas J. *Sacred Biography: Saints and Their Biographers in the Middle Ages*. New York: Oxford University Press, 1988.

Hendrischke, Barbara. "Early Daoist Movements." In *Daoism Handbook,* ed. Livia Kohn, 134–164. Leiden: E. J. Brill, 2000.

———. *The Scripture on Great Peace: The* Taiping jing *and the Beginnings of Daoism.* Berkeley: University of California Press, 2006.

———, and Benjamin Penny. "*The 180 Precepts Spoken by Lord Lao:* A Translation and Textual Study." *TR* 6.2 (1996): 17–29.

Henricks, Robert G. *Philosophy and Argumentation in Third-Century China: The Essays of Hsi K'ang.* Princeton, NJ: Princeton University Press, 1983.

Henry, Eric. "The Motif of Recognition in Early China." *HJAS* 47 (1987): 5–30.

Hightower, James R. "Allusion in the Poetry of T'ao Ch'ien." *HJAS* 31 (1971): 5–27.

Ho Peng Yoke, Goh Thean Chye, and David Parker. "Po Chü-i's Poems on Immortality." *HJAS* 34 (1974): 163–186.

Hobsbawm, Eric, and Terence Ranger, eds. *The Invention of Tradition.* Cambridge: Cambridge University Press, 1983.

Holzman, Donald. *Immortals, Festivals and Poetry in Medieval China: Studies in Social and Intellectual History.* Aldershot: Ashgate, 1998.

———. "Ts'ao Chih and the Immortals." *Asia Major* 3rd ser. 1.1 (1988): 15–57.

———. *La vie et la pensée de Hi K'ang (223–262 ap. J.-C.).* Leiden: E. J. Brill, 1957.

Hucker, Charles O. *A Dictionary of Official Titles in Imperial China.* Stanford, CA: Stanford University Press, 1985.

Huntington, Rania. "Crossing Boundaries: Transcendents and Aesthetics in the Six Dynasties." In *Chinese Aesthetics: The Ordering of Literature, the Arts, and the Universe in the Six Dynasties,* ed. Zong-qi Cai, 191–221. Honolulu: University of Hawai'i Press, 2004.

Hymes, Robert. *Way and Byway: Taoism, Local Religion, and Models of Divinity in Sung and Modern China.* Berkeley: University of California Press, 2002.

Iser, Wolfgang. *The Act of Reading: A Theory of Aesthetic Response.* Baltimore: Johns Hopkins University Press, 1978.

Johnson, David. 1980. "The Wu Zixu *Pien-wen* and Its Sources." *HJAS* 40 (1980): 93–156, 465–505.

Jordan, David K., and Daniel L. Overmyer. *The Flying Phoenix: Aspects of Chinese Sectarianism in Taiwan.* Princeton, NJ: Princeton University Press, 1986.

Juliano, Annette. *Teng-hsien: An Important Six Dynasties Tomb.* Artibus Asiae Supplement 37, 1980.

Kalinowski, Marc, ed. *Divination et société dans la Chine médiévale.* Paris: Bibliothèque nationale de France, 2003.

Kaltenmark, Maxime. *Lao Tzu and Taoism.* Tr. from *Lao tseu et le taoïsme* [1965] by Roger Greaves. Stanford: Stanford University Press, 1969.

———. *Le Lie-sien tchouan: Biographies légendaires des immortels taoïstes de l'antiquité.* Peking: Université de Paris, Centre d'Études sinologiques de Pékin, 1953.

Kao, Karl S.Y. *Classical Chinese Tales of the Supernatural and the Fantastic: Selections from the Third to the Tenth Century.* Bloomington: Indiana University Press, 1985.

Kern, Martin. *The Stele Inscriptions of Ch'in Shih-huang: Text and Ritual in Early Chinese Imperial Representation.* New Haven, CT: American Oriental Society, 2000.

Kieckhefer, Richard, and George D. Bond, eds. *Sainthood: Its Manifestations in World Religions.* Berkeley: University of California Press, 1988.

Kieschnick, John. *The Eminent Monk: Buddhist Ideals in Medieval Chinese Hagiography.* Honolulu: University of Hawai'i Press, 1997.

Kirkland, Russell. "The Making of an Immortal: The Exaltation of Ho Chih-chang." *Numen* 38 (1991): 214–230.

Kleeman, Terry F. "Licentious Cults and Bloody Victuals: Sacrifice, Reciprocity, and Violence in Traditional China." *Asia Major* 3rd series 7 (1994): 185–211.

———. 1994. "Mountain Deities in China: The Domestication of the Mountain God and the Subjugation of the Margins." *JAOS* 114 (1994): 226–238.

Knechtges, David R. "Fa yen." In *Early Chinese Texts: A Bibliographical Guide,* ed. Michael Loewe, 100–110. Berkeley: Society for the Study of Early China and the Institute of East Asian Studies, University of California, 1993.

———. *Wen xuan, or Selections of Refined Literature.* Vol. 3, *Rhapsodies on Natural Phenomena, Birds and Animals, Aspirations and Feelings, Sorrowful Laments, Literature, Music, and Passions.* Princeton, NJ: Princeton University Press, 1996.

Knoblock, John. *Xunzi: A Translation and Study of the Complete Works.* 3 vols. Stanford: Stanford University Press, 1988–1994.

———, and Jeffrey Riegel. *The Annals of Lü Buwei.* Stanford, CA: Stanford University Press, 2000.

Kohn, Livia, ed. *Daoism Handbook.* Leiden: E. J. Brill, 2000.

———. *Early Chinese Mysticism: Philosophy and Soteriology in the Taoist Tradition.* Princeton, NJ: Princeton University Press, 1992.

———. *Laughing at the Tao: Debates among Buddhists and Taoists in Medieval China.* Princeton, NJ: Princeton University Press, 1995.

———. *Monastic Life in Medieval Daoism: A Cross-Cultural Perspective.* Honolulu: University of Hawai'i Press, 2003.

Kovacs, Maureen. *The Epic of Gilgamesh.* Stanford, CA: Stanford University Press, 1989.

Kroll, Paul W. "An Early Poem of Mystical Excursion." In *Religions of China in Practice,* ed. Donald S. Lopez, Jr., 156–165. Princeton, NJ: Princeton University Press, 1996.

Kwong, Yim-tze. "Naturalness and Authenticity: The Poetry of Tao Qian." *Chinese Literature: Essays, Articles, Reviews* 11 (1989): 35–77.

LaFleur, William R. "Buddhism in a Fail-Safe Mode: Examining 'Medieval' Japan." *HR* 43 (2004): 224–232.

Lau, D. C. *Lao Tzu Tao Tê Ching.* Harmondsworth: Penguin, 1963.

Le Blanc, Charles. "A Re-Examination of the Myth of Huang-ti." *JCR* 13–14 (1986): 45–63.

Legge, James. *The Li Ki.* 2 vols. 2nd ed. Oxford: Oxford University Press, 1926.

Le Goff, Jacques. *The Birth of Purgatory.* Tr. Arthur Goldhammer. Chicago, IL: University of Chicago Press, 1984.

Lévi, Jean. "L'abstinence des céréales chez les taoïstes." *Études chinoises* 1 (1983): 3–47.

———. "The Body: The Daoists' Coat of Arms." In *Fragments for a History of the Human Body,* ed. Michel Feher, 1:105–126. New York: Zone, 1989.

———. "Les fonctionnaires et le divin: Luttes de pouvoirs entre divinités et administrateurs dans les contes des Six Dynasties et des Tang." *CEA* 2 (1986): 81–110.

Lévi-Strauss, Claude. *Structural Anthropology*. New York: Basic Books, 1963.

———. *Totemism*. Tr. Rodney Needham. Boston: Beacon Press, 1971.

Lewis, Mark E. *The Early Chinese Empires: Qin and Han*. Cambridge, MA: Harvard University Press, 2007.

———. "The *Feng* and *Shan* Sacrifices of Emperor Wu of the Han." In *State and Court Ritual in China,* ed. Joseph P. McDermott, 50–80. Cambridge: Cambridge University Press, 1999.

———. *Sanctioned Violence in Early China*. Albany: State University of New York Press, 1990.

———. *Writing and Authority in Early China*. Albany: State University of New York Press, 1999.

Li Gang 李剛. "Cao Cao yu daojiao" 曹操與道教. *Shijie zongjiao yanjiu* 世界宗教研究, 4 (2001): 51–61.

Li Hui-Lin. *Nan-fang ts'ao-mu chuang: A Fourth Century Flora of Southeast Asia*. Hong Kong: Chinese University Press, 1979.

Li Ling 李零. *Zhongguo fangshu kao* 中國方術考. 2nd ed. Beijing: Dongfang chubanshe, 2000.

———. *Zhongguo fangshu xukao* 中國方術續考. Beijing: Dongfang chubanshe, 2000.

Lim, Lucy et al. *Stories from China's Past: Han Dynasty Pictorial Tomb Reliefs and Archaeological Objects from Sichuan Province, PRC*. San Francisco: Chinese Culture Foundations of San Francisco, 1987.

Lincoln, Bruce. *Myth, Cosmos, and Society: Indo-European Themes of Creation and Destruction*. Cambridge, MA: Harvard University Press, 1986.

———. *Theorizing Myth: Narrative, Ideology, and Scholarship*. Chicago, IL: University of Chicago Press, 1999.

Lindstrom, Lamont. *Knowledge and Power in a South Pacific Society*. Washington, D.C.: The Smithsonian Institute, 1990.

Lippiello, Tiziana. *Auspicious Omens and Miracles in Ancient China: Han, Three Kingdoms and Six Dynasties*. Sankt Augustin: Steyler Verlag, 2001.

Little, Stephen. "Daoist Art." In *Daoism Handbook,* ed. Livia Kohn, 709–746. Leiden: E. J. Brill, 2000.

———, ed., with Shawn Eichman. *Taoism and the Arts of China*. Chicago, IL: Art Institute of Chicago, 2000.

Liu Shufen. "Jiankang and the Commercial Empire of the Southern Dynasties: Change and Continuity in Medieval Chinese Economic History." In *Culture and Power in the Reconstitution of the Chinese Realm, 200–600,* ed. S. Pearce, A. Spiro, and P. Ebrey, 35–52. Cambridge, MA: Harvard University Press, 2001.

Loewe, Michael. *A Biographical Dictionary of the Qin, Former Han & Xin Periods (221 BC–AD 24)*. Leiden: E. J. Brill, 2000.

———, ed. *Early Chinese Texts: A Bibliographical Guide*. Berkeley: Society for the Study of Early China and the Institute of East Asian Studies, University of California, 1993.

———. "Hsin yü." In *Early Chinese Texts: A Bibliographical Guide,* ed. Michael Loewe, 171–177. Berkeley: Society for the Study of Early China and the Institute of East Asian Studies, University of California, 1993.

———. "K'uang Heng and the Reform of Religious Practices (31 B.C.)." *Asia Major* 2nd series 17 (1971): 1–27.

———. "The Religious and Intellectual Background." In *The Cambridge History of China.* Vol. 1, *The Ch'in and Han Empires, 221 B.C.–A.D. 220,* ed. Denis Twitchett and Michael Loewe, 649–725. Cambridge: Cambridge University Press, 1986.

———. *Ways to Paradise.* London: Allen & Unwin, 1979.

———, and Edward L. Shaughnessy, eds. *The Cambridge History of Ancient China: From the Origins of Civilization to 221 B.C.* Cambridge: Cambridge University Press, 1999.

Lopez, Donald S., Jr., ed. *Religions of China in Practice.* Princeton, NJ: Princeton University Press, 1996.

Lu Qinli 逯欽立, ed. *Xian Qin Han Wei Jin Nanbeichao shi* 先秦漢魏晉南北朝詩. Beijing: Zhonghua shuju, 1983.

Lu Xun 魯迅. *Gu xiaoshuo gouchen* 古小說鉤沈. Beijing: Renmin wenxue chubanshe, 1954.

———. *Zhongguo xiaoshuo shilue* 中國小說史略. Beijing: Beixin shuju, 1926.

Machor, James L., and Philip Goldstein, eds. *Reception Study: From Literary Theory to Cultural Studies.* New York: Routledge, 2001.

Mair, Victor. *Mei Cheng's "Seven Stimuli" and Wang Bor's "Pavilion of King Terng": Chinese Poems for Princes.* Lewiston: Edwin Mellen Press, 1988.

Major, John S. *Heaven and Earth in Early Han Thought: Chapters Three, Four, and Five of the "Huainanzi."* Albany: State University of New York Press, 1993.

Martin, Dale B. *Inventing Superstition: From the Hippocratics to the Christians.* Cambridge, MA: Harvard University Press, 2004.

Martin, Wallace. *Recent Theories of Narrative.* Ithaca, NY: Cornell University Press, 1986.

Maspero, Henri. *Taoism and Chinese Religion.* Tr. F. A. Kierman, Jr. Amherst: University of Massachusetts Press, 1981.

Mather, Richard B. *Shih-shuo Hsin-yü: A New Account of Tales of the World.* Minneapolis: University of Minnesota Press, 1976.

Mattingly, Cheryl. *Healing Dramas and Clinical Plots: The Narrative Structure of Experience.* Cambridge: Cambridge University Press, 1998.

Mauss, Marcel. *A General Theory of Magic.* Tr. Robert Brain. New York: Norton, 1972 [1902–1903].

McDermott, Joseph P., ed. *State and Court Ritual in China.* Cambridge: Cambridge University Press, 1999.

McRae, John R. *Seeing through Zen: Encounter, Transformation, and Genealogy in Chinese Chan Buddhism.* Berkeley: University of California Press, 2003.

Metcalf, Peter, and Richard Huntington. *Celebrations of Death: The Anthropology of Mortuary Ritual.* 2nd ed. Cambridge: Cambridge University Press, 1991.

Miller, Patricia Cox. *Dreams in Late Antiquity: Studies in the Imagination of a Culture.* Princeton, NJ: Princeton University Press, 1994.

Miller, Roy Andrew. "Shih ming." In *Early Chinese Texts: A Bibliographical Guide,* ed. Michael Loewe, 424–428. Berkeley: Society for the Study of Early China and the Institute of East Asian Studies, University of California, 1993.

Mink, Louis O. *Historical Understanding.* Ithaca, NY: Cornell University Press, 1987.

———. "History and Fiction as Modes of Comprehension." *New Literary History* 1 (1970): 541–558.

———. "Narrative Form as a Cognitive Instrument." In *The Writing of History,* ed. R. H. Canary and H. Kozicki. Madison: University of Wisconsin Press, 1978.

Mitchell, W. J. T., ed. *On Narrative.* Chicago, IL: University of Chicago Press, 1981.

Miyakawa Hisayuki. "Local Cults around Mount Lu at the Time of Sun En's Rebellion." In *Facets of Taoism: Essays in Chinese Religion,* ed. Holmes Welch and Anna Seidel, 83–102. New Haven, CT: Yale University Press, 1979.

———. *Rikuchō shūkyō shi.* 2nd ed. Tokyo: Kokusho kankōkai, 1974.

———. *Rikuchōshi kenkyū: Shūkyōhen.* Kyoto: Heirakuji shoten, 1964.

Mixian Dahuting Han mu. Beijing: Wenwu chubanshe, 1993.

Nanyang Handai huaxiang zhuan. Beijing: Wenwu chubanshe, 1990.

Nattier, Jan. *A Few Good Men: The Bodhisattva Path according to The Inquiry of Ugra (Ugrapariprcchā).* Honolulu: University of Hawai'i Press, 2003.

Needham, Joseph, et al. *Science and Civilisation in China.* Vol. 2, *History of Scientific Thought.* Cambridge: Cambridge University Press, 1956.

———. *Science and Civilisation in China.* Vol. 3, *Mathematics and the Sciences of the Heavens and the Earth.* Cambridge: Cambridge University Press, 1959.

———. *Science and Civilisation in China.* Vol. 5, *Chemistry and Chemical Technology.* Pt. 2, *Spagyrical Discovery and Invention: Magisteries of Gold and Immortality.* Cambridge: Cambridge University Press, 1974.

———. *Science and Civilisation in China.* Vol. 5, *Chemistry and Chemical Technology.* Pt. 3, *Spagyrical Discovery and Invention: Historical Survey, from Cinnabar Elixirs to Synthetic Insulin.* Cambridge: Cambridge University Press, 1976.

Ngo, Van Xuyet. *Divination, magie et politique dans la Chine ancienne.* Paris: Presses Universitaires de France, 1976.

Nickerson, Peter. "Shamans, Demons, Diviners and Taoists: Conflict and Assimilation in Medieval Chinese Ritual Practice (c. A.D. 100–1000)." *TR* 5.1 (1994): 41–66.

Nienhauser, William H., Jr., ed. *The Grand Scribe's Records.* Vol. 1, *The Basic Annals of Pre-Han China by Ssu-ma Ch'ien.* Bloomington: Indiana University Press, 1994.

———, ed. *The Grand Scribe's Records.* Vol. 2, *The Basic Annals of Han China by Ssu-ma Ch'ien.* Bloomington: Indiana University Press, 2002.

———. "The Origins of Chinese Fiction." *Monumenta Serica* 38 (1988–1989): 191–219.

Noble, Thomas F. X., and Thomas Head, eds. *Soldiers of Christ: Saints and Saints' Lives from Late Antiquity and the Early Middle Ages.* University Park: Pennsylvania State University Press, 1995.

Nylan, Michael. *The Canon of Supreme Mystery: A Translation with Commentary of the T'ai Hsüan Ching.* Albany: State University of New York Press, 1993.

———. "The *Chin wen/Ku wen* Controversy in Han Times." *TP* 80 (1994): 83–145.

Ochs, Elinor, and Lisa Capps. *Living Narrative: Creating Lives in Everyday Storytelling.* Cambridge, MA: Harvard University Press, 2001.

Ōfuchi Ninji 大淵忍爾. *Shoki no dōkyō* 初期の道教. Tokyo: Sōbunsha, 1991.

Ohnuki-Tierney, Emiko, ed. *Culture through Time: Anthropological Approaches.* Stanford, CA: Stanford University Press, 1990.

Olick, Jeffrey, and Joyce Robbins. "Social Memory Studies: From 'Collective Memory' to the Historical Sociology of Mnemonic Practices." *Annual Review of Sociology* 24 (1998): 105–140.

Ortner, Sherry B., ed. *The Fate of "Culture": Geertz and Beyond.* Berkeley: University of California Press, 1999.

———. "Patterns of History: Cultural Schemas in the Foundings of Sherpa Religious Institutions." In *Culture through Time: Anthropological Approaches,* ed. Emiko Ohnuki-Tierney, 57–93. Stanford, CA: Stanford University Press, 1990.

———. "Thick Resistance: Death and the Cultural Construction of Agency in Himalayan Mountaineering." In *The Fate of "Culture": Geertz and Beyond,* ed. Sherry Ortner, 136–163. Berkeley: University of California Press, 1999.

Pankenier, David W. "The Cosmo-Political Background of Heaven's Mandate." *Early China* 20 (1995): 121–176.

Penny, Benjamin. "Immortality and Transcendence." In *Daoism Handbook,* ed. Livia Kohn, 109–133. Leiden: E. J. Brill, 2000.

Pokinghorne, Donald E. *Narrative Knowing and the Human Sciences.* Albany: State University of New York Press, 1988.

Poo, Mu-chou. "The Images of Immortals and Eminent Monks: Religious Mentality in Early Medieval China." *Numen* 42 (1995): 172–196.

———. *In Search of Personal Welfare: A View of Ancient Chinese Religion.* Albany: State University of New York Press, 1998.

Porter, Bill. *Road to Heaven: Encounters with Chinese Hermits.* New York: Mercury House, 1993.

Pregadio, Fabrizio. "The Book of the Nine Elixirs and its Tradition." In *Chūgoku kodai kagaku shiron,* vol. 2, ed. Yamada Keiji and Tanaka Tan, 543–639. Kyoto: Kyoto daigaku jinbun kagaku kenkyūjo, 1991.

———. *Great Clarity: Daoism and Alchemy in Early Medieval China.* Stanford, CA: Stanford University Press, 2006.

Puett, Michael J. *The Ambivalence of Creation: Debates Concerning Innovation and Artifice in Early China.* Stanford, CA: Stanford University Press, 2001.

———. "Nature and Artifice: Debates in Late Warring States China concerning the Creation of Culture." *HJAS* 57 (1997): 471–518.

———. "Sages, Ministers, and Rebels: Narratives from Early China concerning the Initial Creation of the State." *HJAS* 58 (1998): 425–479.

———. *To Become a God: Cosmology, Sacrifice, and Self-Divinization in Early China.* Cambridge, MA: Harvard University Press, 2002.

———. "Violent Misreadings: The Hermeneutics of Cosmology in the *Huainanzi*," *Bulletin of the Museum of Far Eastern Antiquities* 72 (2000): 29–47.

Qing Xitai 卿希泰. *Zhongguo daojiao shi* 中國道教史.Vol. 1. Chengdu: Sichuan renmin chubanshe, 1988.

Queen, Sarah A. *From Chronicle to Canon: The Hermeneutics of the "Spring and Autumn," According to Tung Chung-shu*. Cambridge: Cambridge University Press, 1996.

Raphals, Lisa. *Knowing Words: Wisdom and Cunning in the Classical Traditions of China and Greece*. Ithaca, NY: Cornell University Press, 1992.

Raz, Gil. "Creation of Tradition: The Five Talismans of the Numinous Treasure and the Formation of Early Daoism." Ph.D. dissertation, Indiana University, 2004.

Reader, Ian, and George J. Tanabe, Jr. *Practically Religious: Worldly Benefits and the Common Religion of Japan*. Honolulu: University of Hawai'i Press, 1998.

Ren Jiyu 任繼愈, ed. *Zhongguo daojiao shi* 中國道教史. Shanghai: Shanghai renmin chubanshe, 1990.

Rickett, W. Allyn. *Guanzi: Political, Economic, and Philosophical Essays from Early China*. Vol. 2, *Chapters XII, 35–XXIV, 86*. Princeton, NJ: Princeton University Press, 1998.

———. "Kuan tzu." In *Early Chinese Texts: A Bibliographical Guide*, ed. Michael Loewe, 244–251. Berkeley: Society for the Study of Early China and the Institute of East Asian Studies, University of California, 1993.

Ricoeur, Paul. *Time and Narrative*. 3 vols. Vols. 1–2 tr. K. McLaughlin and D. Pellauer; vol. 3 tr. K. Blamey and D. Pellauer. Chicago, IL: University of Chicago Press, 1984–1987.

Riegel, Jeffrey. "Do Not Serve the Dead as You Serve the Living: The *Lüshi chunqiu* Treatises on Moderation in Burial." *Early China* 20 (1995): 301–330.

———. "Kou-mang and Ju-shou." *CEA* 5 (1989–1990): 55–83.

Robinet, Isabelle. *La révélation du Shangqing dans l'histoire du taoïsme*. 2 vols. Paris: École française d'Extrême-Orient, 1984.

———. *Taoism: Growth of a Religion*. Tr. Phyllis Brooks. Stanford, CA: Stanford University Press, 1997.

———. "The Taoist Immortal: Jesters of Light and Shadow, Heaven and Earth." *JCR* 13–14 (1986): 87–105.

Roth, Harold D. *Original Tao: Inward Training and the Foundations of Taoist Mysticism*. New York: Columbia University Press, 1999.

———. *The Textual History of the Huai-nan Tzu*. Ann Arbor: Association for Asian Studies Monograph Series, 1992.

———. "The Yellow Emperor's Guru: A Narrative Analysis from *Chuang Tzu* 11." *TR* 7.1 (1997): 43–60.

Rushton, Peter. "An Interpretation of Hsi K'ang's Eighteen Poems Presented to Hsi Hsi on His Entry into the Army." *JAOS* 99 (1979): 175–190.

Ryckmans, P. "A New Interpretation of the Term *Lieh-chuan* as Used in the *Shih-chi*." *Papers on Far Eastern History* 5 (1972): 135–147.

Ryle, Gilbert. "'Thinking and Reflecting' and 'The Thinking of Thoughts': What Is 'le Penseur' Doing?" In *Collected Papers*, vol. 2 of *Collected Essays, 1929–1968*, 465–496. London: Hutchinson, 1971.

Sahlins, Marshall. *Apologies to Thucydides: Understanding History as Culture and Vice Versa.* Chicago, IL: University of Chicago Press, 2004.

Sailey, Jay. *The Master Who Embraces Simplicity: A Study of the Philosopher Ko Hung, A.D. 283–323.* San Francisco: Chinese Materials Center, 1978.

Saussy, Haun. *The Problem of a Chinese Aesthetic.* Stanford, CA: Stanford University Press, 1993.

Schafer, Edward H. "The Grand Aurora." *Chinese Science* 6 (1983): 21–32.

———. *Mirages on the Sea of Time: The Taoist Poetry of Ts'ao T'ang.* Berkeley: University of California Press, 1985.

———. *Pacing the Void: T'ang Approaches to the Stars.* Berkeley: University of California Press, 1977.

———. "The Scripture of the Opening of Heaven by the Most High Lord Lao." *TR* 7.2 (1997): 1–20.

———. "The Transcendent Vitamin: Efflorescence of *Lang-kan.*" *Chinese Science* 13 (1978): 27–38.

Schechner, Richard. *Performance Theory.* Rev. ed. New York: Routledge. 2003.

Schipper, Kristofer M. "Le calendrier de jade: Note sur le Laozi zhongjing." *Nachrichten der Gesellschaft für Natur- und Völkerkunde Ostasiens* 125 (1979): 75–80.

———. *Le corps taoïste: Corps physique, corps social.* Paris: Fayard, 1982.

———. "Le culte de l'immortel Tang Gongfang." In *Cultes populaires et sociétés asiatiques: Appareils culturels et appareils de pouvoir,* ed. Alain Forest et al., 59–72. Paris: Éditions l'Harmattan, 1991.

———. *L'empereur Wou des Han dans la légende taoïste: Han Wou-ti nei-tchouan.* Paris: École française d'Extrême-Orient, 1965.

———. "The Inner World of the *Lao-tzu chung-ching.*" In *Time and Space in Chinese Culture,* ed. Chun-chieh Huang and Erik Zürcher, 114–131. Leiden: E. J. Brill, 1995.

———. "Purity and Strangers: Shifting Boundaries in Medieval Taoism." *TP* 80 (1994): 61–81.

———. "Une stèle taoïste des Han orientaux récemment découverte." In *En suivant la voie royale: Mélanges offerts en homage à Léon Vandermeersch,* ed. Jacques Gernet and Marc Kalinowski, with collaboration by Jean-Pierre Diény, 239–247. Paris: École française d'Extrême-Orient, 1997.

———. "Taoism: The Story of the Way." In *Taoism and the Arts of China,* ed. Stephen Little, 33–55. Chicago, IL: Art Institute of Chicago, 2000.

———. *The Taoist Body.* Tr. Karen C. Duval. Berkeley: University of California Press, 1993.

———, and Franciscus Verellen, eds. *The Taoist Canon: A Historical Companion to the Dao-zang.* Chicago, IL: University of Chicago Press, 2004. When referring to works in the Ming-era Daoist canon *(Zhengtong daozang),* I cite them by the abbreviation *DZ,* followed by the number assigned to them in this work (and then, when citing particular passages, by chapter and page number, the letters a and b indicating recto and verso sides of folio pages). When referring to this work's entries on canonical texts, I cite them in the usual manner in which monographs are cited, by author, title of work, and page numbers.

Schopen, Gregory. *Buddhist Monks and Business Matters: Still More Papers on Monastic Buddhism in India.* Honolulu: University of Hawai'i Press, 2004.

Schottenhammer, Angela. "Einige Überlegungen zur Entstehung von Grabinschriften." In *Auf den Spuren des Jenseits: Chinesische Grabkultur in den Facetten von Wirklichkeit, Geschichte und Totenkult,* ed. Angela Schottenhammer, 21–59. Frankfurt am Main: Peter Lang, 2003.

Searle, John. *Speech Acts: An Essay in the Philosophy of Language.* Cambridge: Cambridge University Press, 1969.

Seidel, Anna. "Imperial Treasures and Taoist Sacraments: Taoist Roots in the Apocrypha." In *Tantric and Taoist Studies in Honour of R. A. Stein,* ed. Michel Strickmann, 291–371. Brussells: Institut Belge des Hautes Études Chinoises, 1983.

Shaughnessy, Edward L., ed. *New Sources of Early Chinese History: An Introduction to the Reading of Inscriptions and Manuscripts.* Berkeley: Society for the Study of Early China and Institute of East Asian Studies, University of California, 1997.

———. *Rewriting Early Chinese Texts.* Albany: State University of New York Press, 2006.

Shaw, Teresa M. "*Askesis* and the Appearance of Holiness." *Journal of Early Christian Studies* 6 (1998): 485–499.

Shinohara Koichi. "Two Sources of Chinese Buddhist Biographies: Stupa Inscriptions and Miracle Stories." In *Monks and Magicians: Religious Biographies in Asia,* ed. Phyllis Granoff, 119–228. Oakville, Ontario: Mosaic Press, 1988.

Shryock, J. K., tr. *The Study of Human Abilities: The "Jen wu chih" of Liu Shao.* Ann Arbor: University Microfilms, 1937.

Sichuan Handai shique. Beijing: Wenwu chubanshe, 1992.

Silverstein, Michael, and Greg Urban, eds. *Natural Histories of Discourse.* Chicago, IL: University of Chicago Press, 1996.

Simmel, Georg. 1906. "The Sociology of Secrecy and of Secret Societies." *American Journal of Sociology* 11 (1906): 441–498.

Singer, Mark. "The Castaways: A Pacific Odyssey." *The New Yorker,* February 19 and 26, 2007, 137–151.

Sivin, Nathan. "Huang ti nei ching." In *Early Chinese Texts: A Bibliographical Guide,* ed. Michael Loewe, 196–215. Berkeley: Society for the Study of Early China and the Institute of East Asian Studies, University of California, 1993.

Smith, Barbara Herrnstein. "Narrative Versions, Narrative Theories." *Critical Inquiry* 7 (1980): 213–236.

———. *On the Margins of Discourse: The Relation of Literature to Language.* Chicago, IL: University of Chicago Press, 1978.

Smith, Jonathan Z. *Drudgery Divine: On the Comparison of Early Christianities and the Religions of Late Antiquity*. Chicago, IL: University of Chicago Press, 1990.

———. "What a Difference a Difference Makes." In *"To See Ourselves as Others See Us": Christians, Jews, "Others" in Late Antiquity,* ed. Jacob Neusner and Ernest S. Frerichs, 3–48. Chico: Scholars Press, 1985.

Smith, Thomas E. "Ritual and the Shaping of Narrative: The Legend of the Han Emperor Wu." Ph.D. diss., University of Michigan, 1992.

Sofukawa Hiroshi 曾布川 寬. "Kandai gazōseki ni okeru shōsenzu no keifu 漢代畫像石における昇仙圖の系譜." *Tōhō gakuhō* 65 (1993): 23–222.

———. "Konron-san to shōsenzu 崑崙山と昇仙圖." *Tōhō gakuhō* 51 (1979): 83–185.

Sperber, Dan. *Explaining Culture: A Naturalistic Approach*. Oxford: Basil Blackwell, 1996.

Spiro, Audrey. *Contemplating the Ancients: Aesthetic and Social Issues in Early Chinese Portraiture*. Berkeley: University of California Press, 1990.

———. "How Light and Airy: Upward Mobility in the Realm of Immortals." *TR* 2.2 (1990): 43–69.

Staiger, Janet. *Interpreting Films: Studies in the Historical Reception of American Cinema*. Princeton, NJ: Princeton University Press, 1992.

———. *Perverse Spectators: The Practices of Film Reception*. New York: New York University Press, 2000.

Stein, Rolf A. "Religious Taoism and Popular Religion from the Second to the Seventh Centuries." In *Facets of Taoism: Essays in Chinese Religion,* ed. Holmes Welch and Anna Seidel, 53–82. New Haven, CT: Yale University Press, 1979.

Strenski, Ivan, ed. *Malinowski and the Work of Myth*. Princeton, NJ: Princeton University Press, 1992.

Strickmann, Michel. *Chinese Magical Medicine*. Ed. Bernard Faure. Stanford, CA: Stanford University Press, 2002.

———. "The Mao Shan Revelations: Taoism and the Aristocracy." *TP* 63 (1977): 1–64.

———. "Saintly Fools and Taoist Masters (Holy Fools)." *Asia Major* 3rd series 7.1 (1994): 35–57.

Styers, Randall. *Making Magic: Religion, Magic, and Science in the Modern World*. Oxford: Oxford University Press, 2003

Sukhu, Gopal. "Monkeys, Shamans, Emperors, and Poets: The *Chuci* and Images of Chu during the Han Dynasty." In *Defining Chu: Image and Reality in Ancient China,* ed. Constance A. Cook and John S. Major, 145–166. Honolulu: University of Hawai'i Press, 1999.

Sullivan, Lawrence E. "Sound and Senses: Toward a Hermeneutics of Performance." *HR* 26 (1986): 1–33.

Swidler, Ann. *Talk of Love: How Culture Matters*. Chicago, IL: University of Chicago Press, 2001.

Tambiah, Stanley J. *The Buddhist Saints of the Forest and the Cult of Amulets*. Cambridge: Cambridge University Press, 1984.

Teiser, Stephen F. *The Ghost Festival in Medieval China*. Princeton, NJ: Princeton University Press, 1988.

————. "'Having Once Died and Returned to Life': Representations of Hell in Medieval China." *HJAS* 48 (1988): 433–464.

Tian, Xiaofei. *Tao Yuanming and Manuscript Culture: The Record of a Dusty Table*. Seattle: University of Washington Press, 2005.

Tiryakian, Edward A., ed. *On the Margin of the Visible: Sociology, the Esoteric, and the Occult*. New York: John Wiley & Sons, 1974.

————. "Toward the Sociology of Esoteric Culture." *American Journal of Sociology* 78 (1972): 491–512.

Todorov, Tzvetan. *The Fantastic: A Structural Approach to a Literary Genre*. Tr. R. Howard. Ithaca, NY: Cornell University Press, 1975.

Tsien, T. *Written on Bamboo and Silk: The Beginnings of Chinese Books and Inscriptions*. Chicago, IL: University of Chicago Press, 1962.

Turner, Edith. *Experiencing Ritual: A New Interpretation of African Healing*. Philadelphia: University of Pennsylvania Press, 1992.

Turner, Victor. *The Drums of Affliction: A Study of Religious Processes among the Ndembu of Zambia*. Ithaca, NY: Cornell University Press, 1981. Originally published in 1968 by Oxford University Press.

————. *From Ritual to Theatre: The Human Seriousness of Play*. New York: PAJ Publications, 1982.

————. *On the Edge of the Bush: Anthropology as Experience*. Ed. Edith L. B. Turner. Tucson: University of Arizona Press, 1985.

————. "Social Dramas and Stories about Them." In *On Narrative*, ed. W. J. T. Mitchell, 137–164. Chicago, IL: University of Chicago Press, 1981.

Twitchett, Denis. *The Writing of Official History under the T'ang*. Cambridge: Cambridge University Press, 1992.

————, and Michael Loewe, eds. *The Cambridge History of China*. Vol. 1, *The Ch'in and Han Empires, 221 B.C.–A.D. 220*. Cambridge: Cambridge University Press, 1986.

Urban, Hugh B. "Elitism and Esotericism: Strategies of Secrecy and Power in South Indian Tantra and French Freemasonry." *Numen* 44 (1997): 1–38.

————. "The Torment of Secrecy: Ethical and Epistemological Problems in the Study of Esoteric Traditions." *HR* 37 (1998): 209–248.

Valantasis, Richard. "Constructions of Power in Asceticism." *Journal of the American Academy of Religion* 63 (1995): 775–821.

Van Dam, Raymond. *Saints and Their Miracles in Late Antique Gaul*. Princeton. NJ: Princeton University Press, 1993.

Van Gulik, Robert. *The Lore of the Chinese Lute: An Essay in Ch'in Ideology*. Tokyo: Sophia University Press, 1940.

Van Zoeren, Steven. *Poetry and Personality: Reading, Exegesis, and Hermeneutics in Traditional China*. Stanford, CA: Stanford University Press, 1991.

Vervoorn, Aat. *Men of the Cliffs and Caves: The Development of the Chinese Eremetic Tradition to the End of the Han Dynasty.* Hong Kong: Chinese University Press, 1990.

Von Falkenhausen, Lothar. "Sources of Taoism: Reflections on Archaeological Indicators of Religious Change in Eastern Zhou China." *TR* 5.2 (1994): 1–12.

Waley, Arthur. *The Book of Songs.* Rev. ed. London: George Allen & Unwin, 1960.

Wang Chang 王昶. *Jinshi cuibian* 金石萃編. Rpt. ed. 5 vols. Beijing: Xinhua shudian, 1985 [1805].

Wang Yucheng 王育成. "Dong Han daojiao diyi keshi Fei Zhi bei yanjiu 東漢道教第一刻石肥致碑研究." *Daojiaoxue tansuo* 到教學探索 10 (1997):14–28.

Watson, Burton, tr. *Records of the Grand Historian: Han Dynasty II.* Rev. ed. New York: Columbia University Press, 1993.

Weber, Max. *The Protestant Ethic and the Spirit of Capitalism.* New York: Scribners, 1958.

Weinstein, Donald, and Rudolph M. Bell. *Saints and Society: The Two Worlds of Western Christendom, 1000–1700.* Chicago, IL: University of Chicago Press, 1982.

Welch, Holmes. *Taoism: The Parting of the Way.* Rev. ed. Boston: Beacon, 1965.

Welch, Holmes, and Anna Seidel, eds. *Facets of Taoism: Essays in Chinese Religion.* New Haven, CT: Yale University Press, 1979.

Wertsch, James V. *Voices of Collective Remembering.* Cambridge: Cambridge University Press, 2002.

Westbrook, Francis A. "Landscape Transformation in the Poetry of Hsieh Ling-yün." *JAOS* 100 (1980): 237–254.

White, Hayden. *The Content of the Form.* Baltimore: Johns Hopkins University Press, 1987.

———. *Tropics of Discourse: Essays in Cultural Criticism.* Baltimore: Johns Hopkins University Press, 1978.

———. "The Value of Narrativity in the Representation of Reality." In *On Narrative,* ed. W. J. T. Mitchell, 1–24. Chicago, IL: University of Chicago Press, 1981.

Wile, Douglas. *Art of the Bedchamber: The Chinese Sexual Yoga Classics, Including Women's Solo Meditation Texts.* Albany: State University of New York Press, 1992.

Wilson, Thomas A. "Sacrifice and the Imperial Cult of Confucius." *HR* 41 (2002): 251–287.

Wimbush, Vincent L., and Richard Valantasis, eds. 2002. *Asceticism.* 2nd ed. New York: Oxford University Press, 2002.

Wong, Dorothy C. *Chinese Steles: Pre-Buddhist and Buddhist Use of a Symbolic Form.* Honolulu: University of Hawai'i Press, 2004.

Wright, Arthur F. *Studies in Chinese Buddhism.* Ed. Robert M. Somers. New Haven, CT: Yale University Press, 1990.

Wu Hung. *The Wu Liang Shrine: The Ideology of Early Chinese Pictorial Art.* Stanford, CA: Stanford University Press, 1989.

Wyatt, F. "The Narrative in Psychoanalysis: Psychoanalytic Notes of Storytelling, Listening, and Interpreting." In *Narrative Psychology: The Storied Nature of Human Conduct,* ed. T. Sarbin, 193–210. New York: Praeger, 1986.

Yang, Lien-sheng. "An Additional Note on the Ancient Game *Liu-po.*" *HJAS* 15 (1952): 124–139.

———. "A Note on the So-Called TLV Mirrors and the Game *Liu-po* 六博." *HJAS* 9 (1947): 202–206.

Yates, Robin D. S. 1995. *Five Lost Classics: Tao, Huanglao, and Yin-Yang in Han China.* New York: Ballantine Books, 1997.

———. "State Control of Bureaucrats under the Qin: Techniques and Procedures." *Early China* 20 (1995): 331–366.

Yoshikawa Tadao 吉川忠夫. "Seishitsu kō 靜室考." *Tōhō gaku* 59 (1987): 125–162.

Yu, Anthony C. *State and Religion in China: Historical and Textual Perspectives.* Chicago, IL: Open Court, 2005.

Yü, Ying-shih. "Han Foreign Relations." In *The Cambridge History of China.* Vol. 1, *The Ch'in and Han Empires, 221 B.C.–A.D. 220,* ed. Denis Twitchett and Michael Loewe, 377–462. Cambridge: Cambridge University Press, 1986.

———. "Life and Immortality in the Mind of Han China." *HJAS* 25 (1964–1965): 80–122.

Zhao Chao. "Stone Inscriptions of the Wei-Jin Nanbeichao Period." *Early Medieval China* 1 (1994): 84–96.

Index

accounts of anomalies, 7, 241; as earliest Chinese "fiction," 9

adepts: bodies of, as ascetically enhanced, 47–50; relations of, with communities, 151–185; relations of, with rulers and officials, 86

agriculture: adepts' withdrawal from cycles of, 199–200; myth of origins of, 64–65; political and symbolic centrality of, 68–70

allotted lifespan *(ming)*, 46, 194; healing and, 162; as prerequisite for receiving esoterica, 100, 105; system of, 174–175

altars: for offerings to *xian,* 228, 230; for transmission of scriptures, 97. See also *sheji*

ancestors: care of, xiv, 218–220; cult of, and the quest for transcendence, 86, 186–190; imperial, 199; temple to royal or imperial, 69

animals, adepts' mastery of, 54, 233, 250

Annotated Classic on Waterways (Shuijing zhu), 7, 183, 224, 242, 253

An Qi, 118, 123, 182, 204

apocrypha. *See* weft texts

Arguments Weighed (Lunheng), 7, 136, 245

ascetic disciplines: as deployments of taxonomies, 44; social nature of, 23–24

audiences: differential responses by, 142; drawn by adepts' presence and actions, 153; expectations of, 25, 260; of inscriptions, 223–224; of performance of ascetic disciplines and selves, 23,

31; responding to adepts' verbal self-presentation, 130–150, 260–263; role of, in social networks centering on adepts, 6, 25, 109, 153–154; as shaping the hagiographic process, 16, 21, 264

Austin, J. L., 30

avoiding grains, 47, 51, 63; attributed to Buddhist monks, 59; extrinsic meanings of, 62–87, 200; as feature in repertoire of transcendents, 62–87

Ban Gu, 201, 245n94, 247

banished transcendents, 102, 136–137, 141, 180n92

Bao Jing, 147, 244

Baopuzi. See Master Who Embraces Simplicity

Baxandall, Michael, 216, 217

Bell, Rudolph, 14–15

Berkowitz, Alan, 119

birds, adepts as similar to, 49, 52, 124

bodilessness, ideology of, 48, 74

body, of adept: as visible sign of ascetic achievement, 132, 145, 149, 157

Bo He, 96, 180n92

bones, as seat of allotted lifespan, 103, 198

Book of Change (Yijing), 140

Book of Documents (Shujing), 255

Book of Odes (Shijing), 63–64, 90

Book of Rites (Liji), 62–63, 65–66, 68, 70, 252

Bo Shanfu, 197

Box-carrying Master (Fuju xiansheng), 172–173

"Inner Training," 66–67
inscriptions: as artifacts of collective
    memory, 223; as historical sources,
    8, 14, 177; placed at shrines, 221;
    rhetorical aspects of, 222–243; as
    sources of transmitted hagiographies,
    224; vocalization of, 223
interest, as governing exchange of stories,
    10, 16, 17, 263–264
isolation, as trait attributed to transcendence
    seekers, 51–54, 151–154, 186

Jiao Xian, 108, 110–112
Jie Xiang, 112–113, 170, 226
Ji Han, 139, 140
Ji Kang, 139, 147, 244–245
Jin Emperor Wu, 237

karma, 189
Kern, Martin, 200
Kong Anguo, 100, 255–257
Kong Yuanfang, 95, 101, 191
Kou Xian, 125
Kuan Shu, 118

Laozi, as cosmic deity, 50n31, 135
Laozi zhongjing, 94
lay patrons: of adepts, 175–181, 227–228;
    as participants in social networks, 6
Le Goff, Jacques, 21
Lévi, Jean, 132
Lévi-Strauss, Claude, 85, 120n89, 260–263
Li A, 155
Liangzhou ji, 240
Li Babai, 13, 104, 155, 238–239
Li Changzai, 162, 192, 194–196
Li Daoyuan, 7, 224, 242, 253
life, and narrative, 8–22
Li Gen, 144
Li Kuan, 155–158
Li Nan, 196
Lincoln, Bruce, 42, 63
lineages, 151; narrative constructions of,
    134, 150, 227
Ling Shouguang, 1, 175–176
Li Shaojun, 117–121, 127, 145, 147, 163,
    221, 253–255

Li Shaoweng, 121, 123, 126
literature, and religious life, 9, 13
Liu An, 99, 115, 137, 190, 235, 245–253
Liu Bang, 248n101
Liu Biao, 212
liubo (sixes), 141
Liu Gang, 198
Liu Gen, 132, 159, 218–220
Liu Jingshu, 241
Liu Ping, 166
Liu Xiang, 7, 99
Li Yiqi, 164, 190
Loewe, Michael, 199
long-distance specialists, adepts as, 135,
    164–165, 226
Lu, Master, 124
Luan Ba, 112, 165, 166–168
Luan Da, 121, 123, 210
Lü Gong, 196
Lu Jia, 186
Lu Nüsheng, 191
Luofeng, 188
lute, 142n29

Mahāyāna sutras, 140n25
Maid Ma, 102
Malinowski, Bronislaw, 138
Mao Ying, 165, 189–190
markets, adepts sell goods in, 107, 158, 160,
    171
marvels, display of, 112, 115
Marx, Karl, 26
masters of esoterica (fangshi), 47, 89;
    appearing at court, 118–125; as
    self-occluding, 106–108
Master Who Embraces Simplicity (Baopuzi),
    7, 78, 79, 83, 96, 99, 105, 157; title of,
    107
Mattingly, Cheryl, 12
Mauss, Marcel, xvn7, 16n49, 24n73,
    128n109
Mawangdui manuscripts, 72, 73–75, 85, 91
McRae, John, 14n45
meaning, as created by reception, 26
meat, as sacrificial offering, 68–69
mediators, adepts as, 119, 121–125,
    128–129, 150, 171, 207

About the Author

Robert Ford Campany is professor of religion and East Asian languages and cultures at the University of Southern California. He is the author of *To Live as Long as Heaven and Earth: A Translation and Study of Ge Hong's Traditions of Divine Transcendents* (University of California Press, 2002), *Strange Writing: Anomaly Accounts in Early Medieval China* (State University of New York Press, 1996), and numerous articles on religious life and thought in early medieval China and on methods for the study of religion.

Production Notes for Campany / Making Transcendents

Jacket design by Santos Barbasa, Jr.

Text design by University of Hawai'i Press production staff
with text in Bembo and display in ATRotis Semiserif

Text composition by Lucille C. Aono

Printing and binding by The Maple-Vail Book Manufacturing
Group